W9-BCW-263

A12900 267781

67287

PN
1995
.9
.C55
M38
1979

MAST
The comic mind.

Illinois Central College
Learning Resources Center

The Comic Mind

THE
COMIC
MIND

Comedy and the Movies

Second Edition

GERALD MAST

The University of Chicago Press
CHICAGO AND LONDON

The University of Chicago Press, Chicago 60637
The University of Chicago Press, Ltd., London

86 85 84 83 82 81 80 79   54321

Library of Congress Cataloging in Publication Data

Mast, Gerald, 1940–
    The comic mind.

    Bibliography: p.
    Includes index.
    1.   Comedy films—History and criticism.
I.   Title.
PN1995.9.C55M38   1978   791.43′02907   78-68546
ISBN 0–226–50976–1
ISBN 0–226–50978–8 pbk.

Acknowledgments

I would like to thank all those who helped this book to be and those who helped it to be what it is. First, there are those who gave their wise and generous advice that I might not always have been wise or gracious enough to accept. To Joe Adamson, Diane Giddis, and Burnell Sitterly my thanks for working their ways through the heavy manuscript—and more than once at that. To Leo Braudy, Marshall Cohen, Herman G. Weinberg, and Joel Zuker my thanks for contributing their expertise and insight to those chapters in which their knowledge and experience far exceed mine.

Then there are those film archives which, over the last three years, have made it possible for me to see (or see again) all the films discussed in this book. Not only can seeing films be terribly expensive; it is often impossible to see certain films at all. To Charles Silver and the Museum of Modern Art, Patrick Sheehan and the motion picture collection of the Library of Congress, James Card and the George Eastman House, Jeremy Boulton and the British Film Institute, my thanks for their care, attention, and courteous service. Without people and collections of this kind, film research would be impossible.

I would also like to thank several commercial film companies who graciously lent me prints of films that could not be seen in any archive. To Adam Reilly of Contemporary Films–McGraw-Hill, Walter J. Dauler of Audio-Brandon, and Murray Glass of the Em Gee Film Library, my thanks for caring about the study of film. To Mary Corliss of the Museum of Modern Art and Paula Klaw of *Movie Star News*, my thanks for helping me gather the book's stills. To Bill Reiter, my thanks for making frame blow-ups of films when the stills were not sufficient.

Finally, my thanks to the Research Foundation of the City University of New York, which provided the funds that helped make the costly business of film research possible.

Contents

Introduction   ix

I

ASSUMPTIONS, DEFINITIONS, AND CATEGORIES

CHAPTER 1. *Comic Structures*   3
CHAPTER 2. *Comic Thought*   14
CHAPTER 3. *Comic Films—Categories and Definitions*   20

II

PRIMITIVES

CHAPTER 4. *Jests, Tricks, and the First Comic Personalities* 31
CHAPTER 5. *Mack Sennett*   43

III

CHAPLIN AND KEATON

CHAPTER 6. *Chaplin: From Keystone to Mutual*   61
CHAPTER 7. *Chaplin: First Nationals and Silent Features*   85

CHAPTER 8. *Chaplin: Sound Films*   105
CHAPTER 9. *Keaton*   125

IV

OTHER SILENT CLOWNS

CHAPTER 10. *Harold Lloyd*   149
CHAPTER 11. *Harry Langdon*   165
CHAPTER 12. *More Fun Shops*   179

V

SOUND COMEDY

CHAPTER 13. *Sound and Structure*   199
CHAPTER 14. *Ernst Lubitsch and René Clair*   206
CHAPTER 15. *Jean Renoir*   232
CHAPTER 16. *The Dialogue Tradition*   249
CHAPTER 17. *The Clown Tradition*   280
CHAPTER 18. *The Ironic Tradition*   320

The Case for Comedy   338

Notes   343

Selective Bibliography   346

APPENDIX A. *Distributors of Comic Films*   349

APPENDIX B. *Photo Credits*   351

Index   353

Introduction

It is a cliché that clowns cry; it has rarely been admitted that they might also think. This book examines a specific breed of clown—the one who translated comedy into cinematic terms—and tries both to establish that he did think and to indicate how.

Surprisingly little attention has been paid to the intellectual complexity of comic films. Surprising for two reasons. First, the historical argument can probably be made that comic films have also been the best films. Such a position seems irrefutable for the silent period. The greatest non-comic silent films inevitably require some kind of apology (*Intolerance*—the imbalanced structure and overstated moralizing; *Potemkin*—the over-idealization of the sailors and people of Odessa; *The Last Laugh*—the artificial happy ending; *The Passion of Joan of Arc*—the intrusive and disruptive titles; etc.). The greatest silent comedies require few excuses or qualifications. Second, literary critics have observed that the twentieth century is (literarily, of course) a comic century, that our greatest novelists and playwrights are comedians (Shaw, Joyce, Beckett, Brecht, Ionesco, Saul Bellow, Joseph Heller, Kingsley Amis, Anthony Burgess, Philip Roth, and so on), and that the comic, ironic reaction of twentieth-century literature is an understandably human, reasonable, and healthy response to the devastating chaos of twentieth-century life, politics, morality, and science.

There has been little attempt to draw comic films into this mainstream of twentieth-century artistic thought. For example, in Wylie Sypher's essay, "The Meanings of Comedy,"[1] he refers to such comic works and workers as Giacometti's sculpture, Picasso's "Guernica," Kafka's K., Dostoyevsky, Kierkegaard, and Nietzsche, without including a single reference to a film performer or director. Elder Olson's *The Theory of Comedy*[2] includes two casual references to films (one to Harpo Marx, the other to W. C. Fields), without including the specific titles of the films—and this from a scholar who is meticulous about including the title of every medieval aesthetic tract or lost New Comedy to which he refers!

This exclusion of film comedy by literary critics is rather ironic, for the writers they study are often highly indebted to comic films. The very serio-comic basis of much modern literature is a product of the writer's experience at his local movie house. The bowler hats and the comic business with them in *Waiting for Godot* are obviously related to the costumes and business of Chaplin and of Laurel and Hardy. But Samuel Beckett's roots in the cinema go even deeper. In *Murphy*, for example, he refers to a dream as parallel to "a piece of biograph." And in *Watt* he refers to a healthy tree as a "hardy laurel" (a truly Laurel and Hardyish pun too!). Beckett's mentor, James Joyce, managed the first nickelodeon in Dublin and remained a film addict for as long as he could see them. Without Chaplin there would never have been a Brecht—or not the same Brecht. And so forth.

Certainly not all comic films are part of this twentieth-century serio-comic tradition. And so this book is evaluative, not just descriptive. It begins with the intention of revealing serious thought in the comic film form. And it assumes that the best comedies (even the funniest comedies) are those which achieve something that is more than simply funny. But a specific discussion of comic films cannot proceed until after such an abstract statement—and my understanding of it—has been carefully examined. That examination—and the definition of some key terms—is the business of the first section.

The Comic Mind

I

ASSUMPTIONS, DEFINITIONS, AND CATEGORIES

CHAPTER 1

Comic Structures

I DO not intend to enter the swamp of abstract debate on the nature of comedy and the comic, for that is a quicksand out of which many never climb. The problem—briefly—with discussions of the nature of comedy is that no single definition adequately includes every work traditionally recognized as comic and excludes every work traditionally recognized as non-comic. If comedy's aim is to reform individual transgressions of acceptable social behavior, then how is one to include Aristophanes or Chaplin, who ridicule the accepted social order and acceptable social behavior? If comedy's aim is moral improvement, a very sugar-coated pill, then how does one include *Twelfth Night* or Terence? If comedy treats only of light, unimportant matters, then how does one include Ionesco, who depicts man's bestial drive either to destroy his fellows or to join the rest of the herd, or *Doctor Strangelove*, which depicts the cataclysmic end of the human race? If comedy excludes pathos and emotional empathy, then why are *City Lights* and *The Merchant of Venice* and *Emma* comic?

Theories that comedy originates in the mythic cycles of birth, death, and rebirth fail to explain how comedy survived the death of those myths, except by postulating that the myths still live dormant in the human psyche—an interesting but not demonstrable assertion. Theories that comedy pertains to manners rather than ethics and to social questions rather than moral questions of good and evil are contradicted by comic works that pertain to matters of life and death, good and evil.

For a clear idea of the deficiencies of theories about comedy, one need read only the first section of any work on the subject, in which the author inevitably disposes of other theories before he goes on to write what will become fodder for the next theorist's section one. Even Henri Bergson, as useful a comic theorist as ever wrote, reveals uncomfortable lapses. In his identification of comedy and the mechanical (a comic line, action, plot, or character reduces some human process to a mechanical one), Bergson has unquestionably illuminated a valid and functional principle of comedy—particularly in a mechanical medium like the movies. But Bergson's insistence on the social utility of laughter as a means of correcting that mechanical behavior does not conform to experience. That is not the reason I laugh at Chaplin or Keaton—to urge them to correct their behavior. Although both clowns turn themselves and their cinematic worlds into kinds of machines and mechanical processes, there is nothing morally reprehensible about their doing so. Further, Bergson insists on denying emotion a place in his comic universe. Of course, his subject is *not* comedy (his title is "Laughter"). But his refusal to show how "laughter" and "comedy" interrelate dooms him to fail at explaining the comic mysteries of a Chaplin or a Shakespeare, whose comedy includes much that is not laughable.

On the other hand, it is impossible to talk about film comedy without some definitions. For example, is John Ford to be one of the comic directors that this book on comedy will discuss? A simple answer is that John Ford is not a comic director. Though Ford uses some comic touches and characters, his overall aim (in most of his major films) is not comic.* This answer is as unsatisfactory as it is simple. While it is seemingly impossible to apply a single theory to all comic works, perhaps one can compile a list of characteristics that seem to be true for all comic films.

Comic Plots

There are eight comic film plots, eight basic structures by which film comedies have organized their human material. The film shares six of the eight with both the drama and the novel, one of the eight with only the novel, and one seems completely indigenous to the cinema.

1. The first is the familiar plot of New Comedy—the young lovers finally wed despite the obstacles (either within themselves or external) to their union. Boy meets girl; boy loses girl; boy gets girl. Many twists and surprises have been injected into this structure—in fact, it was full of twists and surprises in its infancy with Plautus and Terence. Shakespeare used trans-sexual twists in *Twelfth Night* and *As You Like It*; in *A Midsummer Night's Dream* he twists the romantic platitude that beauty is in the eye of the beholder; in *Much Ado About Nothing* the twist is the irony that the boy and girl do not know they are the boy and girl. Shaw reversed the

* I am excluding, of course, *The Quiet Man*. By major Ford films I mean the literary adaptations of 1935–41 and the Westerns.

active and passive sexes of New Comedy in *Man and Superman*. Ionesco burlesqued boy-gets-girl in *Jack, or The Submission*. This plot, with or without unexpected wrinkles, serves as the structural model for such films as *Bringing Up Baby* (the girl is the aggressive kook), *The Marriage Circle, Adam's Rib*, and *The Awful Truth* (boy and girl happen to be husband and wife), *It Happened One Night, Trouble in Paradise, Seven Chances, The Graduate* ("the other woman" is the girl's mother), and many, many more.

Merely concluding the action with a marriage (or an implied union of the romantic couple) is not sufficient for creating a comic plot. Many non-comic films end that way—*The Birth of a Nation, Stagecoach, The 39 Steps, Way Down East, Spellbound*. But in such films the final romantic union is parenthetic to the central action—the overcoming of a series of dangerous, murderous problems. After successfully combating terrible foes, the protagonist earns both life and love as his rewards. This is the typical plot of melodrama (in more dignified terms, "action" or "adventure" films). The adventure plot is a contemporary, totally secularized descendant of the medieval romance, and such films might be truly labeled "romances." In the comic plot, however, the amorous conclusion grows directly and exclusively from amorous complications.

The next three comic plots are all distillations of elements that were combined in Aristophanic Old Comedy.

2. The film's structure can be an intentional parody or burlesque of some other film or genre of films. Aristophanes parodied Euripides; Shakespeare parodied both classical heroism and courtly romance in *Troilus and Cressida*; Fielding began by parodying Richardson in *Joseph Andrews* and heroic tragedy in *The Tragedy of Tragedies* and *The Covent Garden Tragedy*; Ionesco parodies the well-made *boulevard* play in *The Bald Soprano*. In films there were specific parodies of silent hits—*The Iron Nag, The Halfback of Notre Dame*. Mack Sennett parodied melodrama and Griffith's last-minute rescues in *Barney Oldfield's Race for Life* and *Teddy at the Throttle*.

Parody plots flourished in the days of the one- and two-reelers. Feature-length parodies have been rarer. Keaton's *The Three Ages* is a parody of *Intolerance*, and his *Our Hospitality* parodies both the stories of the Hatfield-McCoy feuds and Griffith's last-minute rescue from the murderous falls in *Way Down East*. Many Abbott and Costello films parodied serious horror films. Woody Allen's *Take the Money and Run* is a series of parodies of film genres and styles; his *Bananas*, a series of parodies of specific films. The parodic plot is deliberately contrived and artificial; it is not an "imitation of a human action" but an imitation of an imitation. Perhaps, for this reason, it is best suited to the short form.

3. The *reductio ad absurdum* is a third kind of comic plot. A simple human mistake or social question is magnified, reducing the action to

chaos and the social question to absurdity. The typical progression of such a plot—rhythmically—is from one to infinity. Perfect for revealing the ridiculousness of social or human attitudes, such a plot frequently serves a didactic function. After all, reduction to the absurd is a form of argument. Aristophanes used it by taking a proposition (if you want peace, if you want a utopian community, if you want to speculate abstractly) and then reducing the proposition to nonsense—thereby implying some more sensible alternative.

But the *reductio ad absurdum* need not serve didactic purposes exclusively. Feydeau typically takes a small human trait—jealousy, extreme moral fastidiousness—and multiplies it to infinity. Ionesco combines the farcical and intellectual potential of the *reductio ad absurdum* in plays such as *The Lesson*—which reduces the process of education to the absurd —and *The New Tenant*—which reduces man's dependence on material objects to the absurd.

In films, too, the *reductio ad absurdum* has served as the basis for both pure farce and bitter intellectual argument. The Laurel and Hardy two-reelers are the perfect example of the *reductio ad absurdum* as pure fun— a single mistake in the opening minutes leads inexorably to final chaos. However, some of the most haunting and bitter film comedies are those which take some intellectual position and reduce it to horrifying nonsense. The reason both *Monsieur Verdoux* and *Doctor Strangelove* are comedies *structurally* (they are comedies for other reasons, too), despite their emphasis on deaths and horrors, is that they share this common comic shape. *Verdoux* reduces to the absurd the proposition that murder serves socially useful and emotionally necessary purposes; *Strangelove* deflates the proposition that man needs atomic weapons and military minds to preserve the human race. There is also an implied reduction to the absurd in Renoir's *The Rules of the Game*, although that is not its primary structural principle. Renoir's film is built on the proposition that good form is more important than sincere expressions of feeling. He reduces the proposition to death.

4. The structural principle of this Renoir film is more leisurely, analytical, and discursive than the taut, unidirectional, rhythmically accelerating *reductio ad absurdum*. This structure might be described as an investigation of the workings of a particular society, comparing the responses of one social group or class with those of another, contrasting people's different responses to the same stimuli and similar responses to different stimuli. Such plots are usually multileveled, containing two, three, or even more parallel lines of action. The most obvious examples of such plots are Shakespeare's comedies in which love (*A Midsummer Night's Dream*), deceptive appearances (*Much Ado About Nothing*), or the interrelation of human conduct and social environment (*As You Like It*) is examined from several social and human perspectives. Many Restoration comedies

(Congreve's *Love for Love*, Wycherley's *The Country Wife*) and their descendants (Sheridan's *The Rivals*) are constructed on similar principles. In films, this multilevel social analysis serves as the basis of many Renoir films (*Boudu sauvé des eaux*, *The Rules of the Game*, *The Golden Coach*), of Clair's *À Nous la liberté*, Carné's *Bizarre, Bizarre*, and Chaplin's *The Great Dictator*. In films there is something very French about this structure.

5. The fifth comic-film structure is familiar in narrative fiction but very uncommon on the stage. It is unified by the central figure of the film's action. The film follows him around, examining his responses and reactions to various situations. This is the familiar journey of the picaresque hero— Don Quixote, Huck Finn, Augie March—whose function is to bounce off the people and events around him, often, in the process, revealing the superiority of his comic bouncing to the social and human walls he hits.

This form is probably less suited to the stage simply because its sprawling structure requires a series of imaginative encounters for the *picaro* that could not be effectively depicted on a stage, given the theater's boundaries of time and space. But the film, completely free from such tyrannies (one of the points at which the film is closer to narrative fiction than to the drama), can give the *picaro* as interesting and believable a series of opponents as any novelist. The most outstanding film *picaro* is, of course, Chaplin. Significantly, he begins to use the picaresque structure as he begins to mature with the Essanay films of 1915 (very few of his Keystones use it) and keeps it until *Modern Times* (1936), after which he drops it (for aesthetic reasons that will become clear). The other major film *picaro* is Jacques Tati. But few of Chaplin's silent rivals ever used the loose, personality-centered structure: Langdon (traces of the picaresque only in *Tramp, Tramp, Tramp* and *The Strong Man*), Keaton (perhaps in a few two-reelers but not in the features), Lloyd (never the *picaro*; always up to his neck in a very clear, goal-oriented plot). The picaresque structure also shapes such bitter comedies as *Nights of Cabiria* and *A Clockwork Orange*.

6. The next comic-film plot is one that would seem to have no analogue in any other fictional form. The structure might best be described with a musical term—"riffing." But it could as easily be called "goofing," or "miscellaneous bits," or "improvised and anomalous gaggery." This was the structure of most of Chaplin's Keystones, simply because it was one of the two major Sennett structures (parody was the other). The Sennett riffing films take some initial situation—perhaps a place (a beach, a lake, a field), an event (auto races, a dance contest, a circus), an object (Tin Lizzies), an animal (lion), and then run off a series of gags that revolve around this central situation. The only sources of such a film's unity (other than the place, event, thing, or animal) are the performers' tendency to reappear from gag to gag and the film's unceasing rhythmic motion. Pace and

motion become unifying principles in themselves. Perhaps the riffing film has no literary analogue because no other form (dance and music would be the closest) is so dependent on pace, motion, and physical energy. The outstanding examples of more recent riffing films are the two Richard Lester–Beatles pictures, A *Hard Day's Night* and *Help*, Louis Malle's *Zazie dans le métro*, and the Woody Allen comedies, which riff with a fairly anomalous collection of parodies and jokes.

Each of these six plots usually produces a comedy, though there are obvious exceptions. *King Lear* uses the multi-plot structure (4) for tragic ends, and many Elizabethan and Jacobean plays (*Doctor Faustus*, *The Changeling*, Beaumont and Fletcher's) interweave multiple lines of action for non-comic effects. In films, *Children of Paradise*, *Ship of Fools*, and *The Magnificent Ambersons* might be described as non-comic films with multilevel structures. And the amorous plot of boy-eventually-gets-girl (1) can serve as the basis of weepy melodramas as well as comedies. The difference between Lubitsch's *The Merry Widow* (1934) and von Stroheim's (1925) is the difference between a comic and non-comic use of the same structural pattern.

Finally, there are two other plots that have been used as frequently for non-comic ends as comic ones.

7. One is the kind that is also typical of melodramatic (or adventure or "romance") films. The central character either chooses to perform or is forced to accept a difficult task, often risking his life in the process. The plot then traces his successful accomplishment of the task, often with his winning the battle, the girl, and the pot of gold at the end of the rainbow. Non-comic versions of this plot include *My Darling Clementine*, *North by Northwest*, *Rio Bravo*, *Tol'able David*, *The Maltese Falcon*, *The Thief of Bagdad* (1924), and thousands of other films—many of which contain comic elements and touches. Comic versions of the plot include *The General*, *The Navigator* (indeed, most of Keaton), *The Kid Brother*, *The Mollycoddle*, *The Lavender Hill Mob*, and many others. The difference between a comic and non-comic use of the plot depends entirely on whether the film creates a comic "climate" in the interest of arousing laughter or a non-comic one in the interest of arousing suspense, excitement, and expectation.

8. The same distinction holds true for the final plot form of comic films—the story of the central figure who eventually discovers an error he has been committing in the course of his life. This is, of course, the plot of *Oedipus Rex*, *Macbeth*, *Othello*, and any prototypic Aristotelian-Sophoclean tragedy. But it is also the plot of *Tartuffe*, *The Plain Dealer*, and *Major Barbara*. In films, the plot serves comically in *Mr. Smith Goes to Washington*, *The Freshman*, *Sullivan's Travels*, *Hail the Conquering Hero* (indeed, much of Sturges), *The Apartment* (and much of Wilder), and many others. The comic versions of the plot take place in a comic climate,

which is a function of who makes the discovery, what the discovery is, and what the consequences of the discovery are.

Comic Climate

This term condenses the notion that an artist builds signs into a work to let us know that he considers it a comedy and wishes us to take it as such. Once again, it is functional to sidestep theory on the premise that we pretty much know what *a* comedy is even if we do not know what Comedy is. What are the signs by which we recognize that we are in the presence of a comic work?

Here Elder Olson's concept of "worthlessness" is useful. A worthless action is one that we do not take seriously, that we consider trivial and unimportant rather than a matter of extreme importance, of life and death.* Now, if comedy does indeed depict matters of life and death, then the reason such depiction remains comic is because it *has not been handled as if it were* a matter of life and death. This device will, at some point, lead the audience to reflect that it has been lulled into taking the supremely serious as trivial—a reflection that is precisely the aim of much contemporary comedy. But whether a comedy asks for such reflection or not, the comic craftsman plants a series of signs that lets us know the action is taking place in a comic world, that it will be "fun" (even if at some moments it will not be), that we are to enjoy and not to worry.

1. When the film begins, perhaps even before it, the filmmaker transmits cues to our responses. The first might be the title. It is not worth making too much of titles, and obviously titles such as *The General, Modern Times*, and *The Marriage Circle* do not tell us a lot—although Bergson notes that most comedies bear generic titles (*The Alchemist*) rather than specific names (*Macbeth*). But titles such as *Much Ado About Nothing, Super-Hooper-Dyne Lizzies, Three's a Crowd, Sullivan's Travels*, and *Doctor Strangelove: or How I Learned to Stop Worrying and Love the Bomb* tell us a good deal about what to expect from what follows.

2. The characters of the film rather quickly tell us if the climate is comic. If a familiar comedian plays the central role, we can be *almost* certain that the climate is comic (unless the filmmaker deliberately plays on our assumptions). Keaton's presence makes *The General* take place in a comic world—despite the fact that the film is full of adventure, suspense, war, and death. When Chaplin dropped the picaresque journey for other plot structures, he still used our expectations about Charlie to tell us in

---

* Olson *op. cit.*, 35–44, defines comedy as "the imitation of a worthless action . . . effecting a *katastasis* of concern through the absurd." The other key term, "*katastasis*," will receive discussion here shortly.

what light to view the action. He first appears in *Monsieur Verdoux* trimming flowers, showing great concern for a tiny caterpillar, his familiar mustache turned up in an insane, amputated version of Dali's. Meanwhile the remains of his last wife are going up in smoke (literally) in an incinerator in the rearground of the frame. Chaplin's comically finicky character informs us how to view the grisly activities in his incinerator. His familiar comic *persona* influences every reaction we have to the film, much as the sight of Will Kemp or Robert Armin must have done for audiences in the Theater or the Globe.*

One-dimensional characters who represent comic types, either physically or psychologically, also line up our responses in the intended direction. Because of the pervasiveness of these types, critics have consistently identified comic character with "the base," "the lowly," "the mechanical," or "the ridiculous." But such identifications are not necessarily valid. Such terms fail to fit any of the great comic film *personae*. Many comic films deliberately use inelastic, mechanical types in the minor roles and perfectly supple, non-stereotypic human beings in the major ones—just as Shakespeare did in his comedies.

3. The subject matter of the film's story might also inform us of a comic climate. Subjects such as trying to invent doughnuts without holes or participating in a cross-country walking race are necessarily comic. But if the subject matter is not intrinsically trivial, a comedy reduces important subject matter to trivia. In *Doctor Strangelove* a serious subject, the destruction of the human race, is treated as if it were no more important than inventing hole-free doughnuts. And in *Bananas*, a political assassination (a topic horrifyingly fresh in the American memory) is staged as if it were a televised sporting contest.

4. The dialogue can let us know the climate is comic—because it either is funny or is delivered in a funny, incongruous, mechanical, or some other unnatural way. The opening sequence of Preston Sturges' *Sullivan's Travels* is a breathless series of one-line jokes in which a studio chief and a young, idealistic director debate the validity of making films with a social message. The comic dialogue of this opening scene is essential to the effect of the rest of the film, which gets precariously close to the edge of bathos in its later sequences (indeed it may fall over that edge despite the opening jokes). The suave dialogue between Herbert Marshall and the waiter taking his order for supper in *Trouble in Paradise* informs us that the action and world to follow are comic, as do the subjects and manner of Cary Grant's breathlessly rapid discussion with his former wife in the opening scene of *His Girl Friday*.

5. Any hint of artistic self-consciousness—that the filmmaker knows he

---

* In *King Lear* Shakespeare toyed with his audience's expectations as much as Chaplin did in *Verdoux* or *Limelight* by casting the clown, Armin, as a very wise, philosophical fool.

is making a film—can wrench us out of the illusion of the film and let us know that the action is not to be taken seriously. Such self-consciousness can assert itself in moments of burlesque or parody of topical issues or figures, parodies of other films or film styles, in gimmicky cinematic tricks, or in any other device that reminds the audience it is watching something artificial, "worthless." *Singin' in the Rain* self-consciously parodies the story of a star's meteoric rise from obscurity to fame and fortune; *Trouble in Paradise* parodies picture-postcard romance by juxtaposing a garbage collector and a shot of romantic Venice; *Doctor Strangelove* begins with a parody of a love scene as two planes enjoy sexual intercourse to the violinic strains of "Try a Little Tenderness." One trend in recent films is to add self-conscious, intrusive manipulation of cinematic elements to non-comic films as well. Such films, while proclaiming the film event as "not real," attempt to create an intense kinetic metaphor for the feeling of an event rather than comic detachment.

6. The examples above reveal that the motion picture can use distinctly cinematic tools to create its comic or non-comic climate. What the director shoots, how he shoots and edits it, and how he underscores the pictures for the ear establish the way an audience responds. A piece of comic business at the beginning of a film can color our responses for the next two hours—or until the film informs us to alter them.* Chaplin and Lubitsch are two masters at creating hilariously informative business for the beginnings of their films. In *The Gold Rush* Charlie enters the screen world unknowingly pursued by a bear; in *City Lights* he is grandiosely unveiled as he sleeps on the statue of Civic Virtue and Justice. Whatever else such shots mean in the films—and they mean plenty—they are hilariously funny surprises. Lubitsch's *So This Is Paris* begins as an apparent parody of a Valentino sheik-type movie, only to surprise us by revealing an ordinary domestic couple practicing a dance routine. *The Merry Widow* captures a gaudy military parade as Maurice Chevalier sings "Girls, Girls, Girls." Then two oxen walk ploddingly down the street in the opposite direction, disrupting the order and precision of the singer and the marching band. The apparent "seriousness" of this display of European pageantry has been permanently and effectively ruptured. The manipulation of physical business, so important to an art that depends on the visual and, hence, physical, provides one of the important clues about a film's emotional climate.

So does the director's handling of camera angle, editing, lighting, and sound. Are the shots close or distant? Does he shoot from below, from above, or at eye level? Is the lighting bright and even, or somberly tonal? Is the editing invisible or obtrusive, rapid or languid with dissolves? Is the

---

* Although the comic climate persists throughout a comic film, I have been concentrating on how we feel that climate at a film's beginning. Establishing the comic climate is, in effect, an element of exposition.

sound track cheery, tense, contrapuntal, silent? There are no formulas as to what techniques and methods will or won't inevitably produce comic effects, but that the union and combination of lighting, camera angle, decor, editing rhythm, music, etc. do shape the way we respond is undeniable.

In the film medium the handling of physical action, the photographing of images, the styles of camera, editing, and sound are far more important than Aristotle accorded "melody" and "spectacle" in the drama. Whereas Aristotle relegated these two concrete physical assaults of the drama to the two least important aesthetic places, the motion picture, given its greater physical freedom, is far more dependent on them. The handling of image and sound becomes literally, a part of a film's "diction"—its method of "saying" what it has to "say." The common view that there is a grammar and rhetoric of film underscores the fact that cinematic technique is a kind of language. Whereas imagery in a literary form transmits itself verbally, imagery in the films is explicitly visual. Just as jokes, puns, wit, or comic imagery shape our reaction to a comic novel or play, a film's cinematic "diction" shapes our awareness that the action takes place in a comic or non-comic world.

A comic film, then, is either (a) one with a comic plot and comic climate or (b) one with a not necessarily comic plot but a pervasive enough comic climate so that the overall effect is comic. For example, the reason von Stroheim's *Merry Widow* is melodrama while Lubitsch's *Merry Widow* is comedy is that Lubitsch has created a comic climate for his film by almost all available means. Von Stroheim's subject matter is gloomy and brutal (duels, deaths, and semi-rapes); his characters are often vicious and perverted; and his manipulation of cinematic devices—camera angle, rhythms of cutting, lighting—is quiet and gloomily tonal. Lubitsch, using the same basic story and characters with the same names, fleshes out the structure with frivolous incidents; and he uses song, farcical minor characters, clever physical business, and self-conscious games with the camera and sound track.

An even more revealing (and more complicated) contrast is that between a comic film such as *The General* and a non-comic one such as *The 39 Steps*. Both use the same plot (the series of dangerous obstacles), the same motivation (both protagonists must overcome obstacles to survive), the same conclusion (both men succeed and win the lady fair). Both films are journeys. Both turn upon accidents and ironies.

But *The 39 Steps* is a heroic action performed by a non-heroic character; *The General* is a heroic action performed by a comic character. *The General* establishes a comic climate early and maintains it throughout the film. Gags define Buster Keaton's character as comic before he ever begins his adventure in search of a locomotive; *The General* introduces slapstick gags even at the most perilous moments. While *The 39 Steps* has wonderful comic moments—the feuding man and woman handcuffed together in a double bed; the man delivering a rousing impromptu political speech although ignorant of the views of the expected speaker—these moments of themselves do not, and are not intended to, create a comic climate.

CHAPTER 2

Comic Thought

—

THE difference between the function of the comedy in *The 39 Steps* and in *The General* is crucial to a definition of the comic film. In the former, comic moments work to make a potentially unbelieving audience *accept as credible* a farfetched heroic tale. Comic touches are used similarly in other Hitchcock films and in such exciting, heroic movies as *Stagecoach* and *The Big Sleep*. In these films we are asked to accept the action as "true," as "fact," to enter into the emotions of the characters and experience their adventures as ours. The heroic "romance" seeks to convince us that the represented action is humanly probable and, consequently, important, of value, "worthwhile."

The function of comedy in *The General* is exactly the opposite: to make the audience accept a potentially exciting, heroic adventure as not strictly credible, as not real, as "worthless." The comic climate subverts our belief in what we see. This reduction of probability is at the heart of film comedy. One kind of film comedy deliberately flaunts its impossibility (*The Gold Rush*, most of Mack Sennett, *À Nous la liberté*, *Boudu sauvé des eaux*, *La Ronde*), exuberantly reducing reality (or elevating it!) to the "worthless." These films are sequences of events that could never possibly happen; in fact, the artist wishes us to take them as such. A second kind of comedy uses events that could indeed occur in reality (*Bringing Up Baby*, *College*, *The Palm Beach Story*, *The Rules of the Game*), but even this kind often deliberately introduces coincidences, plot twists, and individual pieces of business that rupture human probability. The two kinds of comedy can be seen in clear oppositions: Old and New Comedy, Shakespearean comedy and Jonsonian comedy, *Waiting for Godot* and *The Importance of Being Earnest*, *Rhinoceros* and *The Caretaker*. The former of each of the pairs might be thought of as a metaphoric representation of an impossible action; the latter as a literal imitation of a possible (but not necessarily plausible) action.

That we do not believe in comedy's reality, that we consciously recognize the imitation as imitation, produces an intellectual-emotional distance from the work that is the essential comic response. It is this attitude that Olson calls "katastasis"—a relaxed, unconcerned detachment.

Banishing emotion (sentiment and suspense) from comedy is an extreme oversimplification—as Shakespeare and Chaplin, among others, show. Both artists inject pathos into their comedy at crucial moments. But even when Charlie gets sad (and we feel sad with him), we still remain in the region of the comic. First, the comic climate of the work assures us that we will not feel sad for long. Second, Chaplin will deliberately slam the audience (and Charlie) with a joke out of their sadness and back into their roles as detached, laughing observers. Shakespeare similarly alternates sentiment and farce to maintain the essential comic distance.

This detachment, which artists as diverse as Ben Jonson, Shaw, Brecht, Ionesco, Chaplin, and Renoir have consistently traded upon, allows our intellect to roam over comedy's events and characters, enabling us to make connections, see parallels, become aware of ironies, perceive contradictions, consequences, causes and effects. This may very well sound like a restatement of Brecht's *Verfremdungseffekt*, and indeed it is. Brecht's theory of "Epic Theatre" is essentially a comic theory: make the audience aware of stage artifice; reveal the workings of lights and sets; turn the humans into puppets on stilts; use mechanical gimmicks such as slides, placards, and follow-spots. The baring of theatrical artifice stimulates reflection by reducing illusion. Although Brecht thought that our reflection would probe the political and social causes of the events depicted on stage, that reflection might just as well probe the artist's emphasis on the artificial. Nevertheless, a kind of reflection it is.*

One way that film comedies communicate serious thought about human values is to stimulate audience reflection on the ironies, ambiguities, and inconsistencies presented in the comedy. This kind of stimulation is the intention of most comedies that depict an impossible action that must be taken as a metaphoric representation of human action rather than a literal one. *Boudu sauvé des eaux* urges on us the contradiction between the bookseller's humanistic clichés and the way he actually lives. *Modern Times* ironically calls attention to the different ways people feed and are fed upon: Charlie fed by machine in the factory; Charlie feeding lunch to his co-worker who has, himself, been accidentally fed into a machine; Charlie stealing a huge meal so he can return to a comfortable prison cell; Charlie and the Gamin eating in the department store where he is night

---

* It is worth noting that many so-called Brechtian films—for example, Godard's—are much less "Brechtian" than Chaplin's comedies.

watchman; Charlie as a waiter trying to deliver a roast duckling to a hungry customer in a crowded restaurant. *Doctor Strangelove* notes such ironies as nations using "doomsday machines" to preserve the human race; our nation's dependence on a "reformed" Nazi scientist; pilots working feverishly to repair a damaged bomb door so they can destroy not only themselves but the entire human race; lines like, "You can't fight . . . in the War Room," when the Russian ambassador tussles with Pentagon personnel; the Russian's insistence on taking photographs of "secret" military maps just before the earth is about to evaporate.

This style of comedy—dark irony; metaphoric, almost allegorical examinations of human and social values; outrageously outlandish or horrifying events presented with the most good-humored matter-of-factness—is the particular gift of our own century. Although death and comedy are traditionally mutually exclusive (for the horror or sadness of a human death usually violates comic detachment), these grimly comic films treat death as a bitter or foolish joke, thereby reducing death (that supremely important fact of human existence) to the merely "worthless." They are similar in spirit to Kafka, Beckett, Brecht, Ionesco, Flannery O'Connor, Faulkner's *As I Lay Dying,* Ford's *The Good Soldier,* Heller's *Catch-22,* and other literary manipulations of comic grimness.

Yet another irony about this kind of comedy so dependent on irony is that although the intentions of such a work are clearly intellectual—to stimulate reflection, to ask the audience to perceive ironies—the works never tell the viewer precisely what to think, reflect about, or perceive. The viewer is free to roam over the work's details, picking out the important ones for himself, then doing his own addition. The artist, of course, if he has built his structure and patterns properly, has subtly guaranteed the sum.

A second way that film comedies communicate ideas is with a more traditional, familiar method. The film's action, dialogue, or both can explicitly describe or even promote certain values. A classical example of such a comedy is Jonson's *Alchemist,* whose action depicts how easily the greedy get gulled and then introduces an authorial spokesman (Lovewit) to state the case plainly. The same is true of Ibsen's *Wild Duck,* that foreshadowing of our century's deadly comedy, which dramatizes the danger of destroying functional illusions and includes an authorial spokesman (Dr. Relling) to tell us precisely the same thing.

Preston Sturges' *Sullivan's Travels* is a series of adventures aimed to show us that (*a*) wealthy, sophisticated moviemakers are incapable of telling stories about unhappy, starving people, and (*b*) even if they could, such a film would serve no useful purpose since the unhappy, starving people would rather laugh their troubles away than see accurate depictions of their own misery. In support of the action, Sullivan directly states what he has learned as a result of his travels. Frank Capra's *Mr. Deeds Goes to*

Town contrasts the human, folksy, sensitive ways of the rural Mr. Deeds with the sophisticated, snobbish, money-hungry, callous ways of big-city people. The action concludes with an almost-peroration, a courtroom climax in which Deeds (seconded by the impartial judge) directly states the superiority of his values. Whereas the audience must infer the moral values of the ironic comedy, this second kind of comedy directly hands the audience every intellectual morsel it is expected to swallow, usually by making each incident in the plot revolve about the central moral issue and often by including some spokesman to provide a summation.

A third way that film comedies communicate serious ideas is also a descendant of older forms. Even the most lighthearted, escapist piece of fun inevitably implies serious values. The audience, however, might fully understand the comedy without examining any of its values; and the artist (or artisan) might not care whether anyone can find a serious implication in it, might not even know what values he used to build it. Whereas the first kind of comedy allows the audience to infer values (but insists that they do so) and the second kind tells the audience its values, this third kind only implies values, and it may make no difference to the comic effect whether the audience sees those implications or not. For example, it is perhaps possible to enjoy *As You Like It* greatly without speculating that two brothers are doing nasty things to two other brothers, that a clown and a shepherd debate amusingly about appropriate behavior in the court and in the forest, that the characters include a literary, pastoral shepherd and a real shepherd, that all the trouble occurs in court and all the solutions in a mythical forest, that a misanthropic gentleman doubts the value of any human action. Though one might find the play amusing without considering the implications of such facts, its structure and intentions cannot be understood without doing so.

But then, *As You Like It* is Shakespeare. What about brainless television comedies, Broadway comedies, and Hollywood comedies which imply serious values and moral assumptions even if their creators wouldn't recognize an "idea" if they stepped in it? It is impossible to construct an "imitation of a human action" without implying the moral values on which that action is based. The reason that so many popular works do not raise speculation is that the creator has purposely used the most commonly accepted formulas and clichés of morality, so as not to cause speculation, but to drown such speculation in pleasantries.

Finding the moral values of a work in which they are only implied and might not even ask to be inferred is a tricky business for the critic. Such exercises lead to political interpretations of the "Little Orphan Annie" comic strip; to productions of Shakespeare's comedies that present the director's view of the "spirit of the play's implications" rather than the apparent spirit of the text; to ingenious interpretations in which the critic seems to put his own values above the author's. In film criticism, some of the most comic results (and the laughs are unintentional) come from critical evaluations of "pure" comedies such as Mack Sennett's, the Marx Brothers', or Laurel and Hardy's.

Raymond Durgnat, for example, parallels a Laurel and Hardy short, *The Music Box*, in which the two clowns must haul a heavy piano up an immense, steep, narrow flight of steps, to the Sisyphus myth.[1] One might just as well liken the task to Christ's carrying the cross up Calvary, or to Capitalism's oppression of the Worker's Spirit. One can find such interpretations interesting, but it is impossible to agree or disagree with them because their assertions are not based on evidence in the film. Durgnat also calls *The Music Box* "a study in absurdity that one has not the slightest hesitation in ranging alongside the few best examples of the theatre of the absurd."[2] His "one" would indeed be a single opinion in search of a second (*The Music Box* alongside *Waiting for Godot?*).

Durgnat, in the attempt to make his subject seem significant, has been guilty of overstating the case for comedy—or for that comedy. There are many serious implications in *The Music Box*—the psychological relationship of the two clowns as they grow more and more frustrated; the attitude of the film toward the nurse, the cop, the "professor," and toward material objects of any kind. On the other hand, a very early Chaplin film for Essanay, *Work*, begins with a sequence in which Charlie hauls an immense wagon all through town and up a steep hill; he stands in the place usually reserved for a horse or mule; the owner of the wagon sits inside it, cracking his whip—Charlie must transport the boss as well as the goods in the boss' wagon. Chaplin photographs the scene in an extreme long shot, making little Charlie and the large wagon two black silhouettes against the sky, emphasizing the steep incline of the hill. Now this must surely be interpreted as a visual translation of the class system—Capital and Labor, Master and Slave, the man with the wealth and power, the man with nothing but the guts to pull that wagon. One could even begin to make parallels with Pozzo and Lucky of *Waiting for Godot*. For reasons in the films themselves, one is on safer ground with Chaplin than with Laurel and Hardy.

To recapitulate, comic films, because of their "worthlessness" and often deliberately flaunted incredibility, detach the emotion of the spectator from the illusion of the work, leaving the intellect free to perceive the issues of the work. The spectator perceives those issues either by (1) inferring them from the intentional ironies and incongruities of the film; (2) seeing and perhaps hearing those issues specifically represented; or (3) inferring them from unstated but implied values on which the characters and events of the film are based. This last method requires a special effort on the part of the critic, because such a comic film is often not conscious of its serious values and seeks only to produce laughter and pleasure. Such an admission might well contradict the premise of comedy's appeal to intellect unless I postulate (as many theorists have) that laughter is itself a physical-emotional response produced by intellectual recognition. The intellectual basis of comedy's emotional effect (laughter) is precisely what gives it its power as an intellectual tool.

CHAPTER 3

Comic Films— Categories and Definitions

———

I T should now be clear that this book is not a study of comic performers but of comic films, not of the jester who performs the gags (although he may be such) but of the master of the revels who constructs the gags and fits them into a pattern. This is not a history of film comedy or comedians but a historical survey of the most significant minds that have worked with the comic-film form. The study will predictably neglect those comic performers who exerted little control over the antics they performed and no control over the way those antics were shot, edited, and scored. Further, the book's focus is not only how and why these comic minds were funny, but what they had to "say" and how (or if) they were successful at "saying" it.

Inevitably, the comic film "says" something about the relation of man to society. The comedy either (*a*) upholds the values and assumptions of society, urging the comic character to reform his ways and conform to the societal expectations; or (*b*) maintains that the antisocial behavior of the comic character is superior to society's norms. The former function of comedy underlies most pre-twentieth-century theory (and practice). Jonson, for example, presented characters of "humours," whose overzealous preoccupation with a single need or desire was an offense against both nature and society. Jonson's plays and prologues urge the offender to purge the "humour" and return to balance. Bergson similarly finds laughter a social cure (even the metaphor parallels Jonson's) for the disease of "mechanical inelasticity"; when the comic figure fails to exhibit the elasticity that social life demands, our laughter serves to turn the human machine back into malleable flesh and soul.

Underlying such a definition of comedy is an assumption about the relationship between nature and society. Although Jonson and other Renaissance thinkers may have been engaged in a "nature-nurture controversy," Jonson seems to avoid the dilemma by implying that the demands of society and of nature are allied, that it is inherent in *human* nature to live socially (hence his use of animal names for antisocial behavior in *Volpone*). Bergson similarly equates social behavior and natural behavior, as opposed to antisocial behavior and unnatural ("mechanical") behavior.

Modern thought, however, makes very different assumptions; rather than allying nature and society, the twentieth-century thinker sees the two as antithetical. The hero of modern comedy is the natural rebel who, intentionally or unconsciously, exposes the shams of society: Shaw's Dick Dudgeon and Saint Joan, Ionesco's Berenger, Brecht's Azdak, Heller's Yossarian, Mann's Felix Krull. In such comic works, the central figure's errors in society's eyes are his virtues in the eyes of his creator. Even antiheroism is a virtue in a world in which heroism either does not exist or has no value. In Bergsonian terms, one might say that in modern comedy, society and its representatives have become encrusted with the mechanical, rather than the comic protagonist with a comic flaw. Only he, because of that "flaw," is elastic enough to expose society's petrifaction.

In this same tradition, the most thoughtful film comedies are iconoclastic. The movies are, after all, a twentieth-century medium. The greatest comedies throw a custard pie (sometimes literally) in the face of social forms and assumptions. The greatest film comedians are antisocial, but in this antagonism they reveal a higher morality. Ironically, these iconoclastic comedies are products of a commercial system that depended on the support of mass audiences composed of anything but iconoclasts. Perhaps the enjoyable silliness of a comedy muted the underlying attack; perhaps comic iconoclasm provided the audience with a useful emotional release, an opportunity to indulge their own antisocial urges without damaging the social fabric; perhaps the iconoclast was free to speak against social and moral values because he used the entertaining comic form—a traditional privilege of comedians since Aristophanes.*

Many other film comedies—often very entertaining ones—do not confront the mores of the status quo. Some avoid any appearance of a social

* Chaplin's iconoclasm eventually caught up with him. As it became more overt, the public became increasingly hostile.

or moral issue by basing the action and the characters' motivations on literary formulas and moral platitudes: rich people are invariably unhappy; man must work to be happy; self-indulgence is necessarily self-abuse; fate inevitably rewards the virtuous and punishes the vicious. Such comedies cannot be said to contain "thinking" at all, since their value systems defy serious reflection and since an audience accepts such systems (if at all) solely because they are the hackneyed descendants of so many other books, plays, films, and political speeches.* Other comedies tackle moral and social issues without overturning the prevailing order by making error and evil the result of a single human's warping or perverting of that order (Frank Capra is the master of this method). But the comedies that look best today are those which challenge society's ability to make human experience meaningful. That also implies something about today.

One distinction, then, among "serious" comedies is whether they are iconoclastic or apologetic. Another is whether the film transmits its values exclusively by comic devices or by serious sections interspersed with comic ones. Frank Capra and Preston Sturges frequently split their films into comic and serious servings, the success of the film varying inversely with the quantity of serious footage. Mr. Deeds Goes to Town seems less labored than Mr. Smith Goes to Washington because Mr. Deeds contains few purely serious passages, whereas Mr. Smith abounds with loving shots of Washington's buildings and monuments and culminates in jingoistic speeches inside the Lincoln Memorial and Senate chamber. Mr. Deeds generates its ideas through comedy—comic dialogue, characters, business, human interaction—whereas Mr. Smith provides serious ideas and comedy. Chaplin's Monsieur Verdoux is a schizophrenic mixture of 14 comic reels and two sermonizing ones.

Chaplin's great gift was his ability to convey moral attitudes without moralizing. A one-second piece of comic business could reveal a whole philosophy of human experience, as, for example, in The Pilgrim. Because Charlie is an escaped convict, he takes refuge by impersonating a parson. Called on by villagers to deliver the Sunday sermon, Charlie walks to the pulpit. He leans on the rostrum and then, instinctively, lifts his right foot to set it on a bar railing (which, of course, isn't there). The gesture of lifting his foot and then jerkily trying to find a railing to support it economically suggests the similarities and differences between churches and taverns, and the nature of human instinct, which, regardless of disguise, reacts to new situations in terms of familiar ones. Because Chaplin was so brilliant at creating seriousness through comedy, the final reels of Monsieur Verdoux are a startling departure from his artistic objectivity—though not enough of one to nullify the brilliance of the first 14.

* Films using such platitudes often earn the hoots and howls of a later audience that no longer accepts the same clichés. Given enough of these, the film transcends the realm of platitude into the stratosphere of camp.

The greatest film comedies communicate serious values through the comedy itself; they do not serve a comic *digestif* between the serious courses. Indeed, a comedy that sermonizes at us might well be more banal, less complex, less serious than a totally wacky film that goes about its silly business without a conscious idea in its head (or its characters' mouths). The lunacy might contain a very complex underlying view of human experience, whereas any ideology that can be summed up neatly in a piece of explicit, terse movie dialogue is going to "say" less than it says.

As a result, the most effective film comedies—as well as the most thought-provoking ones—are mimetic rather than didactic, descriptive rather than prescriptive. They present a picture of a particular social or human condition without tacking on a simplistic moral solution to the comic problems, and without telling the viewer to apply the solution to his own life. The human problems depicted in *Modern Times, The Rules of the Game, Trouble in Paradise, The General, The Italian Straw Hat, Mr. Hulot's Holiday,* and *Smiles of a Summer Night* do not admit easy solutions. Often when the comic filmmaker does provide one—the utopian idyll at the end of *À Nous la liberté,* the reformation of all the crooks and the eradication of poverty at the end of *Easy Street*—it deliberately shows the ridiculousness of expecting easy solutions.

Not only does the effective comic film present its serious values through the means of comedy itself, but its comic and serious matter are inseparable. Indeed, the film's view of human experience is a function of its comic technique, and its comic technique is a function of its view of human experience. Keaton and Chaplin films "say" different things about human experience because Keaton and Chaplin have different comic styles, find different things funny, use different comic principles. And they are different as comics because they have different views of human experience. When we add cinematic style—angles and distances of shots, lighting, pace and style of cutting, principles of combining sound and image—as a function of comic style (and vice versa), we get the three mutually dependent elements that form the compound of the greatest comic films. Cinematic style is a function of comic style is a function of philosophic vision is a function of cinematic style and so forth around the perfect and unbreakable circle.

Silence and Sound

The great silent comedies revolve about the body and the personality of its owner; the great sound comedies revolve about structure and style— what happens, how it happens, and the way those happenings are depicted. Film comedy, as well as film art in general, was born from delight in physical movement. The essence of early filmmaking was to take some object (animate or inanimate) and simply watch it move. The essential comic object was the human body, and its most interesting movements were running, jumping, riding, colliding, falling, staggering, leaping, twirling, and flying. The early comic filmmakers soon learned that to make better comic films, they needed better comic bodies that could do interesting and surprising tricks. They needed athletes, not wits; men who could turn in the air and take a fall, not turn a phrase. The university for such athletes was not the legitimate stage but vaudeville, burlesque, the music hall, and the circus. Many of the great film clowns later paid fond tribute to their alma maters (Chaplin's *The Property Man, A Night in the Show, Limelight*; Arbuckle's *Backstage*; Keaton's *The Playhouse*).

In the vaudeville house the film clowns learned valuable physical lessons that they never forgot—even after the greatest ones had added a head to the body. Chaplin's most famous routine with the Karno Pantomime Troupe was his impersonation of a comic drunk. That drunk act recurs throughout Chaplin's 50-year career in films. In *The Rounders* (1914) he sways, slides, and staggers while linked to Fatty Arbuckle (and Chaplin is drunk in over a dozen other Keystones). In *A Night Out* (1915) he re-creates the Arbuckle routines with Ben Turpin. In *One A.M.* (1916) he plays the routine alone—except for a house full of objects. And so on, until he staggers into a fancy nightclub in *City Lights* (1931) with his millionaire friend and, 20 years later, enters his boarding house drunk in the opening scene of *Limelight*. The solidity of Chaplin's schooling shows in the eternal usefulness of his basic routines.

The silent clown began with magnificent physical control. Although he usually tried to look funny, it was what he could do with his body that really counted. Ben Turpin's crossed eyes were his trademark, but Turpin could take tremendous falls, turn his legs into rubber bands, or, conversely, stiffen his frame into an unbendable plank. Although Arbuckle was famous for being Fatty, no fat man could move so fast or fall so hard as Arbuckle. This physical control explains why many sound comedies that try to evoke the Sennett spirit fail. They may use Sennett's undercranked camera; they may manipulate pace and nonsense and non sequitur; they may conjure up chase after chase after chase. But they (Kramer's *It's a Mad, Mad, Mad, Mad World*, for example) must depend on funny-looking comic personalities rather than human pretzels, balls, and rubber bands.

The sound comedy is far more literary. Given the opportunity to use the essential tool of literature, words, as an intrinsic part of the film's conception, the filmmaker did not hesitate to do so. In silent films, the use of words in titles was intrusive, a deliberate interruption of the cinematic medium and a substitution of the literary one. We stop looking and start reading. But the sound film provided the means to watch the action and listen to the words at the same time. Whereas the silent performer was a physical being—and only through the physical an intellectual one—the sound performer was both physical and intellectual at once.

Another difference is that because he could talk, the sound performer was more like an ordinary human being in society than a specially gifted comic-athlete-dancer-gymnast-clown. Further, the visual interest in sound films was not the physical motion of the performer but the visual juxtaposition of the people with their social and physical milieu. Images and imagery replaced movement. All such shifts were in what can be termed a "literary" direction, making the film far more like a play or novel. And as in the play or novel, the underlying unity of such comedies was provided by structure—what the characters did, what happened to them as a result, contrasts between the characters, conflict between the characters and the social milieu, stylistic contrasts, oppositions, parallels, and balances. This style of comedy reached its full development in France in the 1930s, but it is also the comedy of Lubitsch, Capra, Ophuls, late Chaplin, Hawks' comedies, Bergman's, Kubrick's *Doctor Strangelove*, and many others.

Early American sound comedy was not so quick as the French to desert the old silent forms. The great American clowns of the 1930s and their films—W. C. Fields, Mae West, the Marx Brothers—were curious hybrids of silent and sound principles. Theirs are comic films of personality (like the silents) in which the central clown primarily uses his mouth rather than his body (like the talkies). The Marx Brothers and Mae West came to Hollywood from Broadway, and Fields, great vaudeville buffoon and juggler that he was, became more celebrated in films for his misanthropic, under-the-breath mutterings than for his deftness at juggling cigar boxes, pool cues, croquet mallets, whisky bottles, or whatever came to hand. Perhaps the reason the "American Comedy," the comedy of personality, died is that as a style of physical comedy its natural medium is silence. The first decade of sound was close enough to the silent era so that the American physical comedy of personality retained much of its vitality.

But if silent comedy was dominated by physical personalities and sound comedies by more complex structures and careful manipulations of style, there are unique and revealing exceptions to this rule. Lubitsch and Clair made structural, stylistic comedies in the 1920s. It was therefore no accident that they made the best early sound comedies in the 1930s. Tati and Chaplin made comedies of physical personality in the sound years. But Chaplin's one structural comedy of the 1920s—*A Woman of Paris*—sorely misses the vital presence of his personality. And after making two comedies of personality in the 1930s without synchronized sound, Chaplin, beginning with *The Great Dictator*, built his dialogue comedies on structure and style—even when his personality also dominated them. Indeed, Chaplin's refusal to use synchronized dialogue in his first two sound films was a realization of the antithesis of the comedy of physical personality and the structural demands of a comedy that uses words to communicate the characters' feelings and thoughts.

The Art That Conceals Art

Finally, a word must be said about one of the most difficult aesthetic questions about comedy, a question so closely related to personal taste and audience psychology that aestheticians usually avoid it altogether. When is a film (or gag, or line, or character) that is intended to be funny truly funny? What is the difference between meaning to be funny and *being* funny?

Imprecise as it may be, the only answer seems to be this: A film (or gag, or line, or character) is truly funny when the audience is not conscious that it intends to be funny. As soon as one becomes aware of artifice and fakery (not the kind that often functions as an integral part of the comic climate), comedy disintegrates into banal and obnoxious posturing. Although intellectual detachment is crucially related to the experience of successful comedy, when the detachment becomes so great that the mind is no longer amused and engaged but notes the gap between intention and accomplishment, conception and execution, the comedy fails to amuse and entertain.

Perhaps the only term for describing the successful marriage between comic intention and execution is one of the key concepts of the Renaissance—*sprezzatura*. *Sprezzatura* might be defined as the art that conceals art, the supremely artificial that strikes us as supremely natural. The great comedy endows the most contrived and artificial situations (comedy has always been dependent on artifice) with the impression of spontaneity. Although the events and characters of a comedy might seem improbable in relation to reality (as developed in Chapter 2), they must seem probable, lifelike, and "real" in relation to one another.

To get an idea of this *sprezzatura* at work in a comic film, one need only recall some of the supreme moments of comic films—Chaplin's fantasy ballet with the globe in *The Great Dictator*, Keaton's montage sequence in *Sherlock Jr.*, the dinner table sequence in *Bringing Up Baby*, Tati's tennis game in *Mr. Hulot's Holiday*, the raucously farcical and complicated evening party in *The Rules of the Game*—all of which are totally unnatural and contrived, yet feel spontaneous and alive. Or rather, they feel that way for those who find them funny. Conversely, those who do not find Jerry Lewis or Danny Kaye or Red Skelton funny (and I am one of those) are really saying that their attempts to be funny are obvious and hence do not succeed at making comic life out of contrived business.

As with any other matter of artistic creation, there are no specific rules or formulas for converting comic contrivance into comic life, for endowing a comedy with *sprezzatura*. In general, the impression of *sprezzatura* is a matter of rhythm and emphasis—when to cut and when not to cut, what to emphasize and what to gloss over. And the comic develops this perfect rhythm and emphasis in the handling of all those comic elements discussed in Chapter 1: when to use the close-up to reveal a human reaction or concrete detail, when to stay farther away to allow the viewer to infer it; how long to remain with that close-up; what kinds of business are genuinely funny, what angle and distance illuminate that humor; when to cut quickly away from a facial reaction, a piece of business or a line and when to prolong the shot.

Failures to produce comic life in a film, to create *sprezzatura*, are inevitably failures of rhythm and emphasis—usually failures of overstated emphasis and underpaced rhythm, which produce effects commonly known as "heavy-handed," "overdone," and "doing too much." Understatement seems to be the key to comic-film success. In a form in which intelligence plays such an important role, it is a mistake to insult the audience's intelligence.

This study, then, examines comedies that seem to be not only serious but also successfully funny. Only by being successfully funny can a comic work capture human experience. And only by capturing human experience can a comic work be serious.

II

—

PRIMITIVES

II

PRIMITIVES

CHAPTER 4

Jests, Tricks, and the First Comic Personalities

I N the beginning was the jest. In 1895, while the Lumière brothers were carrying about their new Cinématographe to photograph such factual subjects as workers leaving the Lumière factory, a train arriving in a station, a baby eating its dinner, and a wall being demolished, they also used it to film a fictional piece of clowning. Even this film, *L'Arroseur arrosée*, was not the first comic motion picture. Thomas Edison's earliest known film on celluloid, *Fred Ott's Sneeze* of 1889, was a medium close-up of Edison's comical worker sneezing at and for the camera. But *Fred Ott's Sneeze* was a piece of comic business, not a comic action.

The French title of *L'Arroseur arrosée* is itself a comic tongue-twister, a linguistic play on repetition and noun used as verb. Like any linguistic gag, it is untranslatable. The closest English equivalents would be "the gardener gardened," "the sprinkler sprinkled," "the waterer watered." Such a title indicates that the essence of the action is surprise and reversal. A gardener goes about his business of watering plants with a hose. A boy sneaks up behind him, steps on the hose, and the water ceases to flow. The gardener stares at the hose to find the source of the trouble, the boy removes his foot, and the gardener receives a faceful of water. The gardener then discovers the source of the prank, chases the boy, catches him, spanks him, and the film ends.

It is not worth trying to turn this little film into a miniature *chef d'oeuvre* of the comic intellect. But the extreme simplicity of the compound makes it very easy to analyze its chemistry. The elements of the film are four: (1) a comic protagonist wants to perform a task; (2) a comic antagonist interferes with that performance; (3) a comic object begins as a tool and ends as a weapon; (4) the protagonist makes a comic discovery of the problem and takes action on the basis of that discovery. Each of these elements exists in a very simple, uncomplicated form in the film. The protagonist's task is an ordinary domestic one that he either desires to perform or has been hired to perform (we do not know who owns the garden that he waters). The antagonist's motivation is pure mischievousness. The comic object—the hose—is a familiar domestic one. The discovery fulfills itself in purely physical and psychologically obvious terms—tit for tat. We know nothing about the personalities of the characters, except as they relate to the jest. Is the boy always mischievous? Has the gardener a quality that makes people want to trick him? Have the characters any relationship other than as butt and trickster? In fact, we have no sense of the two figures as characters at all. The film's single long shot reveals only the different shapes and sizes—not faces, eyes, smiles, or any other personal, distinguishing traits.

As simple as this initial film jest was, it contained elements that could be combined and expanded into much more complex films. The protagonist: Who is he? What does he want to accomplish? What is at stake? Why? The antagonist: What is the basis of his antagonism? What does that antagonism imply? How does he go about it? The comic object: How familiar is it? What is its usual function? How many are there? What metamorphoses does it undergo? To what unfamiliar uses is it put? The comic discovery: How does it come about? What does it in turn produce? What would happen without it?

The sophistication of this apparently artless Lumière jest becomes clear when compared to the physical-prank films that Edison was making at about the same time. *Fun in a Chinese Laundry* (c. 1896) is merely an extension of *Fred Ott's Sneeze*—a piece of comic business, not a comic action. A policeman chases a man (presumably Chinese) around a set painted with the words "Chinese Laundry." The two men run about, perform gymnastic tricks above and around the painted set, run in and out of doors, leap, twirl, chase, and dash. It is a film of motion, not action. Other Edison films show that his director, probably Edward Kuhn, had been watching Lumière. In *A Wringing Good Joke* (c. 1896), a mischievous boy puts a wet washcloth on the face of a man sleeping in a laundry. The startled man wakes up; his chair falls over and spills a nearby bucket of water all over him. In *Washday Troubles* (c. 1898), yet another mischievous boy upsets a tub of soapy water, soaking the woman who has been trying to do her laundry.

The longevity of these 30-second films that build (feebly) to a single jest is amazing. A 1902 Biograph comedy, *The School Master's Surprise*, shows two mischievous boys pouring flour into a kerosene lantern; the schoolmaster enters, takes the chimney off the lantern, and gets a face full of powder. *Finis*. And this was the same year as Méliès' *A Trip to the Moon* and several years later than the imaginative films of James Williamson and G. A. Smith in England. Two other 1902 Biographs are a bit more complex psychologically, but are equally dependent on a single jest. In *She Meets with Wife's Approval*, the boss' wife visits the office to inspect his new typist, who appears to be sufficiently ugly. After the wife leaves, the typist removes her ugliness disguise and kisses the boss. In *Shut Up* a drunken man arrives home to a stream of abuse from his awakened wife. He shuts her up—literally—by folding her away in her Murphy bed.

As late as 1905 Biograph was still peddling one-joke pranks. In *The Adjustable Bed*, a man and woman sit on the arms of a reclining chair. The chair collapses; both figures fall to the floor; the gentleman then assists the lady to her feet and kisses her. The end. Such comedies represented no refinement or improvement over the comic elements of *L'Arroseur arrosée* of ten years before. The human motivation is just as formulaic; the personal individuation is no more detailed; the comic objects are a bit more surprising, but as simple.

Even those American comedies which claimed to be built around a central personality were no more than a combination of jest and motion. There were several early comedy series in the first five years of this century—Alphonse and Gaston, Foxy Grandpa, Uncle Josh, Buster Brown. Although these films used a consistent central figure, he remained a distant personage rather than a distinct personality. In *Foxy Grandpa Tells the Boys a Funny Story* (1902), an old man in country clothes (presumably Foxy) does about 30 seconds of distant miming and making faces while two boys laugh. In *Foxy Grandpa Shows the Boys a Trick or Two with the Tramp* (also 1902), Foxy accosts a tramp sleeping on a bench, fights him, and drives him offscreen. The title is almost longer than the film (it is certainly more interesting).

Uncle Josh at the Moving Picture Show (again 1902) is much more imaginative (Edwin S. Porter directed it), but it also fails to develop any Uncle Josh. A man—another country-rube type—sits in a movie theater. He sees a film of a "Parisian Dancer" and starts dancing and gyrating. He sees a roaring train (actually Edison's *Black Diamond Express* of 1896) and ducks with fear. He sees a filmed "Country Couple"—two pugnacious fellow rubes—and wants to fight them. Eventually Uncle Josh pulls down the screen, tussles with a stagehand, and the film ends. The motif of the country yokel who does not understand the principle of a moving picture would become the basis of many later films and film sequences—Sennett's *Mabel's Dramatic Career* and the hilarious movie sequence of Godard's *Les Carabiniers* among them. But this early treatment, despite its imaginative use of split screen, is extremely crude, simply because as a character Uncle Josh, who performs the antics, does not exist. He could as easily be called Foxy Grandpa, Simple Simon, or John Q. Rube. His only recognizable human traits are the clichés of country stupidity and orneriness.

The underlying moral attitude of these early jests (admittedly rather fuzzy) reflected the attitudes of the primarily male and proletarian audiences for whom the first films were made. The moral targets of these films were the people who did not go to see them—country folk who lacked city sophistication (movies were then a city pleasure); moralistic ladies and womanish men who tried to stop real men from drinking, smoking, gambling, swearing, fighting, and going to the movies; high-toned society snobs whose pleasures consisted of boring books, balls, and musicales. And mixed with all these targets was plenty of masculine knockabout—fighting, kicking, running, jumping. Despite the crudeness of these films and their lack of consciousness about such implications, the American comic film would be built on this contempt for affectation and pretension—a tradition that stretches from Foxy Grandpa and *Shut Up* through John Bunny, Sennett, Chaplin, Laurel and Hardy, the Marx Brothers, W. C. Fields, Jerry Lewis, and Woody Allen.

The Comic Magician

The first comic director who achieved some measure of imaginative mastery over his craft shared the same contempt for pretension—George Méliès. Although Méliès is more famed for his tricks and fantasy, those tricks, and his manipulation of them, were essentially comic devices for comic effects. Méliès' fancy, elaborate productions—*A Trip to the Moon*, *The Palace of the Arabian Nights*, *Conquest of the Pole*—are the ones most often anthologized for viewing today. Even these have wonderful comic touches that burlesque professors, scientists, doctors, anyone who claims "to know." But many of Méliès' less elaborate films clearly reveal that his effects flow from the same source as the comic jests and physical pranks.

Méliès' films consistently manipulate two principal effects—comic physical motion and surprising appearances, disappearances, and conversions. Most of the Méliès films employ a troupe of acrobats who leap, tumble, twirl, twist, jump, and cavort in a variety of guises—devils, elves, gremlins, moon creatures. Although the guises and costumes change, the little quirky, jerky acrobatics of these limber gremlins do not. Their active, unnatural, jumpy contortions ("the body encrusted with the mechanical") give the same pleasure as the movement in the little prank films and, especially, Edison's *Fun in a Chinese Laundry*. Both *The Enchanted Well* (1903) and *The Cook in Trouble* (1904) depend almost exclusively on tumbling. In both films, a rejected gypsy casts a spell on the central object (a well in the former, a stove in the latter).* After receiving the spell, the cursed object emits a host of devils, and the rest of the film merely chronicles the St. Vitus activities of devils tumbling out of the well and around the stage, or out of the stove and around the stage. And with Méliès it was always a stage. The bouncy moon creatures in the justifiably more famous *Trip to the Moon* provide the same pleasures.

But even Méliès' camera tricks were also a kind of cinematic jest and prank. The primary comic deficiency of the earliest jest films was their failure to create any specific character to perform the jest; the interrelation of character and gag that was to become the foundation of every great comic film had hardly been imagined by 1905. Méliès' films did not at all depend on character. If motion pictures provided only distant physical fun, then Méliès could develop a second way for the cinema to provide such fun. His camera tricks were merely another kind of physical movement. Something appearing out of nothing is a kind of movement, as is nothing appearing in place of something, a man appearing in place of a dog, and so on. Méliès' tricks provided *motion in time*, as well as the motion in space of the jests and pranks.

Méliès' films were also another kind of jest or prank. In them, the prank is not perpetrated by a mischievous boy but by the mischievous filmmaker. Méliès becomes the prankster and the audience the butt of his pranks, but so delighted a butt that we also applaud and enjoy the incongruous surprises. This invisible prankster (who often made himself visible by playing the central role) was perhaps the one "character" that the Méliès films successfully created. That prankster-magician's clever intelligence was perhaps the most human, personal element to be seen (or not seen) in a film before Griffith.

Méliès was the first filmmaker who deliberately pushed himself into the illusion of the film. He was conscious of making films and informing his audience that it was watching a film. Whereas a Lumière or Edison or Biograph jest tried to convince the audience that it was watching reality, Méliès let everyone know he was watching artifice and fiction. The roles that Méliès played in his films—magician, leader of an expedition, chief wizard—were often parallel to his offscreen function as the film's chief

---

* This rejected-gypsy motif is probably the most common plot device in the first 15 years of cinema history. One wonders what the movies would have done without those spiteful gypsies.

mind and wizard. This self-consciousness, which deliberately flaunted the artificiality of the motion picture, foreshadowed the cinematic machinations of such filmmakers as Mack Sennett, Ernst Lubitsch, René Clair, Richard Lester, and Woody Allen, who similarly cast their own "minds" and imaginations as intrusive characters in their films.

The Adventures of Max

Max Linder was the first internationally famous comic-film star. He was also the first comic performer and director to succeed at combining character and jest. Beyond these two certainties, Linder's importance, influence, and accomplishments are matters of debate. French film critics chauvinistically laud the little clown as a major figure of the silent film and a primary influence on Chaplin and the direction of film comedy. American critics and historians usually overlook him altogether.* The truth about Linder's contribution probably lies somewhere between the two extremes.

The critic has several problems in evaluating Linder's work. First, few of his 350-plus films survive today, especially in America. Second, Linder's career divides neatly into two halves—he made short films in France from 1905 to 1915 and longer ones in America from 1917 to 1922. Those critics who argue for Linder's influence use the French shorts as their evidence; those who argue for Linder's comic ingenuity rely on the American films. This disunity and disruption in the Linder film career is at the heart of the critical problem.

The early Linder shorts suffer from the same cinematic distance and inarticulateness of most pre-Griffith films; Linder did not master the cinematic language until he came to America, where the mastery had already been achieved for him. This sudden inheritance of an already codified cinematic style led to a highly impersonal lack of style in Linder's late films, whereas his early films, as clumsy as they might have been, had a crude personal style, even if it was not always effective. Linder's bad luck in not being able to mature simultaneously as a comic and a director points to Chaplin's extraordinary good luck in being able to mature as a comic performer while and where the cinema matured as a medium.

Linder's comic *persona* has been frequently compared with Chaplin's. Chaplin himself acknowledged Linder's influence, calling him both his "professor" and "master." But Max is worlds distant from Charlie. Whereas Charlie plays the figure who aspires to respectability, Max *is*

---

* For example, his name appears only once in Lewis Jacobs' *Rise of the American Film*, once in Rotha-Griffith's *Film Til Now*, and only three times in Terry Ramsaye's mammoth *A Million and One Nights*, which is almost exclusively devoted to the pre-1920 American cinema.

respectable. Whereas Charlie's costume reveals pretensions to the dandy (bowler and cane) that are contradicted by the reality of ill-fitting trousers, vest, and shoes, Max is a genuine and convincing dandy. His clothes— typically a tailcoat, carnation in the buttonhole, white gloves, elegant cane, top hat, starched white shirt, clean collar, crisp tie—fit him perfectly, both physically and temperamentally. Add to the tidy, fashionable clothing Max's strong, handsome features, his perfectly brushed and trimmed mustache, and his controlled, self-assured carriage, and the result is a proper, elegant gentleman who is completely at ease with his surroundings and his fellow beings, who all share the same social assumptions.

Any great American comic who began with this premise would develop comic gags that worked with the self-satisfied character in a single way— every gag would aim at unmasking the artful masquerade. The Max exterior would be proved a lie, and some more responsive way of comporting oneself would be substituted. That is not Linder's method. He essentially disregards everything he has built into the character to plunge himself into some problem or task that *any* kind of character might face in the same way. After establishing this *grand bourgeois* (Max is far too careful and immaculate to be *petit*), Linder turns him into an anonymous John Q. Public. He is Anyman, not Everyman.

Linder's comic problems and solutions are in no way a function of the Max character: He tries to ice-skate, take care of himself after his wife leaves him, act in amateur theatricals, ski, box, smoke a cigar, paint, dance, fight a duel, drive a taxi, speak English, and so on. The most common titles of the Linder shorts were either a declarative sentence (Max *does* something) or a simple conjunction (Max *and* something). For example, *Max Plays at Drama, Max fait du ski, Max pratique tous les sports, Max and the Quinquina, Max Virtuoso, Max et les crêpes*. There is a subject and either a verb or an object. The relation between the two grammatical terms is never any closer in the film than it is in the title.

In *Les Débuts d'un patineur* (1905)—one of the earliest extant Linder films—Max goes ice-skating. He puts on a pair of skates and then trips, slips, slides, falls. The whole reel chronicles his clumsy, frantic attempts to skate. But those efforts could have been performed by any character; the film is really an extension of the short physical jests, relying on movement, physical surprise, and comic pain for its effect. Although one critic sees the film as an influence on the skating sequences in Chaplin's *The Rink* and *Modern Times*,[1] Max's gag of the clumsy man who can't skate is a rather common and predictable comic situation. In Chaplin's skating sequences, the tramp reverses the expectation and skates brilliantly; his agility and gracefulness on skates, not a clichéd clumsiness, generate the comedy and meaning.

In *Max and the Quinquina* (1911), Max takes some medicine to perk him up, and it instead sends him on a drunken spree. The film then contains some very funny gags—insults to other men, mistaken identities, drunken tangles with people, taxis, and clothing that parallel similar troubles in the later Chaplin-Arbuckle *The Rounders* or the Lloyd *High and Dizzy*. But the effect of these comic difficulties is curiously impersonal; Max staggers from gag to gag without concern for characterization, consistency, or climax.

In *Max Plays at Drama* (c. 1912) Max longs to demonstrate that he is a great tragedian. Once again the film contains some funny moments—a delightful parody of classical French tragedy in which two women fight a duel over the love of Max; the seventeenth-century figures use the telephone, and Max has trouble with a wig that keeps flopping in his face and a sword that won't flop out of his scabbard. This flair for parody and anachronism would culminate in Linder's later feature, *The Three Must-Get-Theres*. But, again, in this film Max remains a figure, not a person; a performer of gags, not a human being who gets into comic trouble.

The real basis of the early Max films is an extension (not a complication) of the first Lumière jest. Linder strings together a series of jests, unified solely by the figure performing them, without attempting to develop either that figure or a dynamically unified structure. The same is true of Linder's best film, *Seven Years Bad Luck* (1921), a feature with a tremendous number of brilliantly comic, imaginative sequences that are unrelated to each other. The surface plot of the film is that Max breaks a mirror, thereby bringing seven years bad luck down upon his head. The real structure of the film, however, is a series of Max's adventures and misadventures, without causality or motivation to link them.

The first hilarious sequence of the film is a drunken Max's return to his house after a stag party that has celebrated his impending marriage. Max mistakes his closet for the window and vice versa; he then fastidiously hangs up his clothes by throwing them out the window and gets a breath of air by throwing open the closet door. The sequence is a rather bald copy of Chaplin's 1915 Essanay, *A Night Out*, but is funny nonetheless.

The second memorable sequence of the film—perhaps its most inventive one—hinges on the fact that Max's servants have broken his full-length dressing mirror. Attempting to cover their mistake, one of the servants tries to convince Max that the mirror still exists by perfectly duplicating Max's morning shave. This scene, a precursor of the famed mirror scene in *Duck Soup*, is enacted with the greatest physical precision and timing (precision is Linder's greatest comic gift).* Linder closes the mirror sequence brilliantly. Max has discovered the servants' duplicity and is now aware that the mirror is merely air. But the servants have called a glazier to replace the mirror without Max's knowledge. Max strides back into the

* Georges Méliès also made an ingenious film with a vanishing mirror—*The Adventures of M. Le Baron*—that foreshadows both Linder and the Marx Brothers. But of course "mirror gags" were also a staple of the music-hall and variety theater.

room, laughs at his reflection in the glass, which he assumes is a fake, and then tosses a shoe at it. The mirror smashes before his eyes; the gag has come full circle.

Next Max goes to see his fiancée, Betty. Being warned by a fortune-teller that he will die from the bite of a mad dog (don't ask why), Max is afraid of his sweetheart's petite poodle. He resolves his fears by dumping the pathetic poodle in a vase of flowers. After a preliminary quarrel over this pup with Betty, he returns to her house to apologize. But while waiting for his sweetheart, he slips a jazzy record on the phonograph and then uncontrollably starts bouncing, playing the piano, twirling on the piano bench, toe tapping, knee slapping, and dancing with the chambermaid. Betty, appalled at this jivey display, throws Max out of her house and heart forever.

So Max sets off to the country to forget. After being robbed of his money, Max gets stuck—literally—on the daughter of the railroad station master when his hands become coated with the paste for freight labels and stick to the girl's dress. When the station master comes in, Max, in his fright, rips off the poor girl's dress and then flees from the scene.

In the film's epilogue, "Seven Years Later," Max and his wife (either Betty or the station master's daughter; the lack of close-up or individuating detail makes her identity unclear) stroll down the street followed by seven little children all dressed like Max (one for each year of bad luck—and a pretty irrelevant sight gag) and a dozen little puppies (indicating that Betty is probably the bride). Is that why Max was to beware of a dog's bite? The irrelevance of this ending—marrying either woman would be equally probable or improbable—the fact that the ending has more to do with the film's title than its action, is a sign that the film is interested in a gag, not a story to contain the gags or a character to perform them.

Similarly, the sequence in which Max dances with the maid is delightfully visual, rhythmic, bouncy, clever. But the device that triggers the scene is totally improbable and irrelevant. Would a man who has come to apologize to the woman he loves play a record and start jiving around her home in such a reckless, thoughtless manner? Does he love her or not? Does it make a difference? Linder liked the comic idea of the sequence and did not care if it grew out of the action, the situation, or the people surrounding it. The film's structure and comic interests are contradictory. Although the film masquerades as a human, boy-girl story, it is really a riffing film of gags—without the necessary riffing rhythm and accumulation.

The same is true of *The Three Must-Get-Theres* (1922), a delightful parody of the Fairbanks swashbuckling films that were so popular at the time. There are very clever things in the film: a parody of a farewell scene in which a mule and a cow who are lovers must bid each other a tearful adieu; a series of anti-heroic burlesques of romantic conventions in Max's duels, love affairs, and equestrian exploits (his horse is a mule, and he rides it backward); a series of surprising anachronisms (the queen signals her distress by using the telephone and typing a letter; her ladies-in-waiting play the saxophone and trombone). But the result is no funnier and no more significant than Chaplin's burlesque on *Carmen*—Linder's obvious model—of seven years earlier.

Ingenuity, comic imagination, and an abundance of gags mark the late Linder films. The early Linder films, despite their cinematic crudeness and lack of personal detail, established a film face and figure that were recognized world wide. Linder's career between 1910 and 1915 earned him millions of fans and francs; his great international fame led Essanay to import him from France after Chaplin left them for Mutual. But because he never integrated character, structure, vision, gag, and cinematic style, Max Linder today remains a historical film figure of some interest who exerted *some* influence on the future direction of film comedy.* Linder's career and life ended tragically when, after three years of failure and frustration, he and his wife committed double suicide in 1925. Ironically, the films themselves never reflect the introspection, the neurosis, the shadows that lurked beneath the comic surface and emerged only with his death.

A Funny Bunny

John Bunny was the first star of American comic films. Bunny, who was born in England, rose to success in American minstrel shows, in vaudeville, and on the legitimate stage. In 1910 he left the stage, where he was making $150 a week, to work for Vitagraph for $40.[2] Between 1910 and 1915 Bunny made some 150 films, almost all of which have been lost. In his five-year career—the same five years as Linder's greatest period of success—Bunny became the second most popular American film personality (right behind "Broncho Billy"). Although he never matched Max's international fame and fabulous salary, Bunny was far more popular than Max in America; although he was never the imaginative creator and innovator that Linder was, Bunny had a much stronger sense of who and what he was. If Linder's career has attracted the zealous overstatement of his supporters, Bunny's career has received only silence and neglect. And yet Bunny was a very funny man, and both the style and values in his comedy foreshadow the later work of the Marx Brothers, W. C. Fields, and Jackie Gleason.

* It is very difficult to make a strong case for Linder's influence. How can one say he influenced Chaplin's drunken routines, for example, when such routines were standard vaudeville acts and when Chaplin himself had been doing a drunk act on the stage for years before he did it in films?

If there was ever an appropriate name for a personality, Bunny had it. John Bunny was a ponderous, rabbity fat man who could look both jolly and dour. He played a character who could tell funny stories and perform amusing physical antics, who liked to drink, gamble, swear, and flirt. His fat, bulbous body implied years of overindulgence, of too much food and booze. His chubby face was both sweet and sour, kindly and gruff, a cross between a porker and a porcupine.

The standard method of the Bunny Vitagraph comedies was to saddle the amoral fat man with some very heavy domestic freight. The sensualist suffered an obligatory domestication, and the source of his domesticity was his wife, usually portrayed by Flora Finch. Flora was a tall, skinny, pointy-featured crow. (Her birdlike name was as appropriate as her husband's animal label.) Flora's tight-lipped, hard-staring acerbity played in comic counterpoint to Bunny's joviality. Flora was moralistic and mean, a waspish (both wasp and WASP) harpy whose life's work was to make Bunny toe the Protestant-ethic line. The consistent contrast of Bunny's style and values with Flora's gave the Vitagraphs their humor, charm, and moral attitudes.

In *A Cure for Pokeritis* (1912), Bunny drinks and plays poker. His wife, Flora, wants to stop such sinning. Bunny pretends to go to lodge meetings, but Flora sends her cousin Freddie—who teaches Bible classes—to spy on him. When Flora finds out that the "meetings" are merely camouflage for poker playing, Flora, Freddie, and the rest of the Bible class masquerade as policemen; they stage a mock raid of the poker party and terrify the husbands into submission. Beneath the domestic comedy the film is anti-moralist and anti-feminist. It favors the free, easy, and masculine—poker games rather than Bible classes, men who act like men rather than women, and women who act like governesses. As such, the values of the film are clear outgrowths of the masculine, proletarian jests that dominated the first decade of American comedy.

Those values can also be seen in *John Bunny Dips into Society* (c. 1912), which contrasts the working-class clothes and attitudes of Bunny with those of the society swells who find him amusing. And *Stenographer Wanted* (1912) is a complication of the earlier jest *She Meets with Wife's Approval*. Bunny and his business partner need a new secretary, and they intend to base their choice on the physical attributes rather than the secretarial competence of the candidates. After the two men scrutinize the qualifications of both blondes and brunettes, their wives enter to do their own scrutinizing. Their immediate choice is Flora Finch, the tall, skinny prune who is so ugly that she makes her two bosses faint. The wives drag their husbands by the hair—literally—and force them to hire Flora. In the film's final scene Flora sits typing like a demon. Bunny casts a glance at her spectacular ugliness and decides he needs a drink.

The John Bunny comedies contrast the man of nature with the stringent

rules of a moralistic society. Their comedy stems from the conflict between the funny fatso and the sentimental sermonizers who refuse to let
him be. Although Bunny always loses the battle, his comical being reveals
the superiority of his natural ways to the refinements of women and the
womanish. These early comedies were the first full statements of the
dominant motif in American comedy—the ridiculing of social, moral, and
intellectual pretension. This ridicule would later show itself in Sennett's
attitude toward cops and society people; in Chaplin's treatment of preachers, politicians, and social workers; in W. C. Fields' insistence that he
liked his children fried; and in Groucho's goosing—both figurative and
literal—of Margaret Dumont. The domestic life shared by Bunny and
Flora predates the wife and family that W. C. Fields is saddled with in
It's a Gift, The Pharmacist, and *The Bank Dick.* Although both fat men
adopt the outward forms of bourgeois, moralistic propriety to appease their
shrill spouses, neither ever surrenders his opinion of such stagnant propriety. Those opinions betray themselves through the amazed glints in
Bunny's eyes and the misanthropic mumblings beneath Fields' breath.

CHAPTER 5

Mack Sennett

———○

THE Mack Sennett Keystone Comedies were the culmination of 15 years of comic primitivism—the characterless jest and the excitement of motion raised to the nth power. The Sennett comedies paid little regard to internal psychology, human motivation, or personal emotion. Characters behaved as they did for the same simple and formulaic reasons that mischievous boys perpetrated their mischief in *L'Arroseur arrosée*, *Washday Troubles*, and *The School Master's Surprise*. Like Méliès, Sennett relied on the acrobatics of human beings and the mechanical surprises of the motion-picture camera. Like Edison's *Chinese Laundry* and Zecca's films at Pathé, Sennett relied on the chase—people running after people, things, animals; things and/or animals running after people. To these effects of movement Sennett added tremendous energy, a breathtaking pace, a reveling in the incongruous and the non sequitur, and a taste for burlesquing people, social custom, intellectual pretension, and the conventions of other films.

Although critics usually treat Mack Sennett's films as a single, unchanging product, there is no such thing as *a* Mack Sennett comedy. Sennett's almost 30-year career went through at least five clear stages. He personified the growing separation of director and producer in this century's second decade. Early in his career he directed his films personally. As he became more and more successful, the distance between him and the films that bore his name as producer became wider and wider. By the end of his career Sennett was more a film executive than creator; although his presence influenced these later films, they really bore the personal stamp of their younger, more nimble writers, directors, and stars.

1. *The Biograph Period* (1908–12). Sennett went to work at Biograph

in 1908 as actor, handyman, and "gofer." Although he steadily learned a lot about making films from acting in them, he learned very little about acting. Sennett was a hammy, overdemonstrative performer, both for Griffith and in his own films. He constantly tried to demonstrate how funny he was, and constantly failed. But Sennett tagged along behind Griffith on the "Old Man's" long walks, picking up whatever bits of technique and information he could. By 1909 Sennett was writing scripts for Griffith. By 1911 he had begun directing comedies for Biograph under Griffith's supervision. And by 1912 he was responsible for most of Biograph's comic product.

2. *The Keystone Period* (1912–15). This is the most exciting and important Sennett era—the period often taken as representative of Sennett's work as a whole. Sennett himself directed many of these films and kept close watch over the others. The Keystone corps included those he had brought with him from Biograph—Ford Sterling, Mabel Normand, Fred Mace, Del Henderson, Henry "Pathé" Lehrman—as well as such newcomers as Roscoe Arbuckle, Hank Mann, Slim Summerville, Tom and Edgar Kennedy, Chester Conklin, and, of course, Charles Chaplin.

The Keystone years blazed with furious, improvisational comic activity; it was an atmosphere highly creative for gag writers, comic performers, and new directors, a frantic mixture of funny business and businesslike fun. Chaplin's year at Keystone is often treated as his year of penal servitude, in which he suffered the torments of Sennett's speed and mechanization. But the freedom of the Keystone era, the fact that performers worked very fast but also made many films, allowed Chaplin to experiment with the medium and absorb many valuable lessons from the sheer quantity of activity. The exciting ingenuity of Chaplin's year at Keystone was a sign of the health of the whole organism.

3. *The Triangle-Paramount–First National Periods* (1915–22). Mack Sennett was swept up in two motion-picture trends, both deadly to the free spirit of the Keystones but temporarily healthy for his bankbook. As other small-time film producers began to turn into moguls, Sennett decided to attempt the same metamorphosis. First, his studio got larger, his payroll longer, his production companies more numerous. From one reel a week (1,000 feet) that cost less than $1,000 to shoot in 1912, Sennett production jumped to two two-reel comedies a week (4,000 feet) that cost a total of about $50,000 in 1916.[1]

Second, the Sennett studio changed not only in the quantity but in the quality of the films it produced. The films became steadily more expensive, more high-toned, more "tasteful." They lost the ramshackle, improvisatory feeling of the early Keystones and substituted fancy scripts, sets, costumes, and title cards (with fancy puns on them). The rough and tumble of the Keystones began to disappear, to be replaced by more complicated and coherent stories, more attention to human motivation, more gentility and "class." Ironically, Sennett never became an Ince or Goldwyn or Zukor, because a comic film still played a secondary role on the exhibitor's bill in support of the full-length features that the moguls offered.

4. *The Pathé Period* (1923–29). These Sennett films were really the products of their individual stars, who maintained their own teams of writers, directors, and production crews—primarily Ben Turpin, Harry Langdon, and Billy Bevan. In the Bevan films, however, there was a rebirth of the old Sennett insanity. Because Bevan was never so strong a personality as Turpin or Langdon, he became the perfect center for irrational jests-in-motion that depended on Tin Lizzies, lions, elephants, dogs, airplanes, chimpanzees, and the like rather than on people. Many of the Bevan films of the 1920s are closer in spirit to the romps of ten years earlier than to the intervening aspiration toward gentility and polish.

5. *The Paramount–Educational Sound Period* (1929–34). Although Sennett takes credit for discovering and developing the cinematic potential of both Bing Crosby and W. C. Fields,[2] his contribution to the early years of sound seems quite minor. Perhaps Sennett was incapable of integrating his comic ideas with the new sound techniques; perhaps the Sennett ideas of comedy could no longer exist in a world of noises; or perhaps Sennett ran out of ideas altogether. Whatever the precise explanation, Sennett went into involuntary retirement in 1935 when the old Zukor-Paramount organization collapsed.

What did Mack Sennett really know about comedy? He certainly knew about making money and furthering his own ambitions. He knew about rhythm and pace and the impact of burlesque yocks and knocks. (He first appeared on stage in burlesque as, literally, a horse's ass.) Were the great Keystones a product of the Sennett imagination or a fortuitous combination of energetic, creative people working together in an exhilarating artistic climate at an exhilarating time in an exhilarating new art form? The question is unanswerable.

Biograph Days

D. W. Griffith directed comedies as a necessary part of the yearly Biograph product. Sennett claimed that Griffith cared very little about comedy, and the artistic carelessness of many of the Griffith Biograph comedies supports the claim. As late as 1911, two years after Griffith had begun developing the "grammar and rhetoric" of film construction, his comedies were often static, inert, indoors, with obviously painted sets, theatrical staging, and none of his famous cutting whatever. In *After the Ball* (1911), for example, one shot equaled one scene; there was no cutting within a scene at all. Although Griffith's domestic, urban comedies at Biograph were indeed clumsy and careless, he did devote great care to the rural, folksy comedies such as *All on Account of the Milk* (1909), *Examination Day at School* (1910), and *A Country Cupid* (1911). Griffith's feeling for the gently comic ways of rural life would, of course, dominate such later features as *True Heart Susie* and *Way Down East*.

Griffith's clumsy domestic comedies are an interesting transition between the proletarian-masculine jests of the early twentieth century and the more specific contempt for moralizing and pretension of the John Bunny and Mack Sennett comedies. In *His Wife's Mother* (1909), Griffith depicts a husband's problems with his nagging mother-in-law. In order to dispose of this gorgon who won't let him smoke a cigar, drink wine with dinner, or fondle the maid who serves it, the clever husband dreams up a sneaky plan. He flirts with his mother-in-law, driving his wife to insane fits of jealousy. The angry wife then tosses her own mother out of the house.

In *Mr. Jones Has a Card Party* (1909)—one of the "Mr. Jones" series starring John Compson—the wives do not approve of their husbands' card playing and hard drinking. The hubbies disguise their activities by reading temperance tracts, but Mrs. Jones finds the booze hidden in her house and Mr. Jones catches hell. In *After the Ball* (1911), an angry wife waits up for her night-owl husband (played by Sennett), who has been out drinking and dancing. She greets him with a rolling pin.

Sennett shared Griffith's attitudes toward moralistic dispensers of "social uplift." Whatever critics may say about Griffith's sentimental Victorianism, there was a certain kind of moralistic cant that made his skin creep, and both he and Sennett treated the purveyors of such cant as either hypocrites or buffoons. Sennett's Biograph comedy *The Furs* (1912) shows the same masculine attitude toward mothers-in-law as Griffith's *His Wife's Mother*. His first Biograph comedy, *Comrades* (1911), contains the same motif as Griffith's early comedy *The Clubman and the Tramp* (1908), both of which provide a tramp the opportunity to mingle with society snobs and enjoy the food, furniture, and comforts of a real house. Many of Sennett's 1911 Biograph comedies are indistinguishable from Griffith's, both in technique and in attitude.

By 1912 some of the Sennett Biographs had become more distinctive. First, many of them were outdoor rather than indoor films. (Many of the Griffith Biographs look stagey because they were indeed shot indoors on a stage. The best Griffith comedies at Biograph—the rural ones—were so because they were outdoor films.) The outdoors provided Sennett not only visual freedom but the freedom to move. And movement was still the heart of a movie. People could run around outdoors, and the camera could follow them.

One of the camera's favorite runners in these 1912 Sennett Biographs was Mabel Normand. Mabel's spunky personality and limber body became the focus of some of the best Sennett Biographs. In *The Brave Hunter,* Mack is terrified of a bear he meets in the woods. (Already Sennett is employing two of his famous devices—the ferocious beast and the chase.) Mabel, however, calmly walks up to the bear and then rides it, strolls with it, and makes it perform tricks. In *Tomboy Bessie,* Mabel plays a rough-and-tumble tomboy, and the camera records her antics: she rides a bicycle sitting on the handlebars, robs a chicken coop, uses a slingshot. The mischievous brat of *L'Arroseur arrosée* has been reincarnated in female form; and Sennett caps her mischief with a frantic chase. The leap from these Biographs to the early Keystones is very short indeed.

Sennett had even begun to indulge his taste for parody at Biograph. One of his most ironic early parodies is *Help! Help!* (1912), a delicious mockery of the last-minute rescue that his boss had developed so excitingly at Biograph. The irony of *Help! Help!* is that it is a specific parody of Griffith's *Lonely Villa* (1909), for which Sennett himself had written the script. In *Help! Help!* a husband leaves his wife (Mabel) at home and goes to work. His wife thinks she sees a burglar prowling around and telephones her husband to come save her. He drives home furiously to the rescue and arrives in the nick of time. The film is a carbon copy of the plot of *Lonely Villa,* including the telephone device. The only difference is the spoof of the rescue process itself. Rather than showing the furious pace of the husband's returning home (as Griffith did), intensified by the master's rhythmic cutting, Sennett shows all the problems that can beset a man racing to the rescue. His car stalls. Then starts. Then stalls again. He jumps into a wagon. The mule refuses to move. He runs across a field. A farmer chases him with a shotgun. Sennett depicts the difficulties and indignities of a "race for life." He would ring other changes on it in later films such as *Barney Oldfield's Race for Life* and *Teddy at the Throttle.* Sennett's parody showed how close the suspenseful, exciting, last-minute rescue is to the comic chase. Scramble the editing rhythms, distort the difficulties, alter the personalities, expand the sense of time ridiculously— and tense melodrama dissolves in laughter.

Krazy Keystones

As Sennett liked to tell the story, he conned a couple of fly-by-night bookies to cancel his $240 pony tab and set up an ignorant, know-nothing yokel in the picture business. Sennett never let fact get in the way of a good story.* The two supposedly fly-by-night bookies, Kessel and Bauman, had not taken a bet for four years and were doing very nicely in the picture business as owners of the Bison Company, producing the early pictures of a rather accomplished director named Thomas Ince.[3] The know-nothing yokel they hired, Mack Sennett, had as much experience in the picture business as anybody (four years) and had directed perhaps two dozen films that were almost as good as Griffith's (which means almost as good as anybody's). Sennett even claims that his Biographs made more money than Griffith's.[4] Although Sennett would like us to believe that the founding of Keystone was a cockamamie accident that just happened to turn out well, the union of Kessel, Bauman, and Sennett was a shrewd business proposition that was carefully supported by both dollars and sense.

Another of Sennett's yarns that is more colorful than true is his version of the shooting of the first Keystone in California. According to Sennett, no sooner had his tiny company stepped off the train in Los Angeles than they saw a parade of Shriners marching down the street. He told Mabel to take a doll, pretend it was her illegitimate and abandoned child, and accost the parading Shriners with her tale of woe. Then Ford Sterling, the alleged father of the brat, would interrupt Mabel's plea to the Shriners and try to pick fights with some of the most belligerent and defensive paraders. Sennett claimed that his first Keystone was thus shot within a half hour of their arrival in California. Unfortunately for Sennett's story, no such Keystone exists or was ever released. The first Keystones were *Cohen Collects a Debt*, one of Sennett's many comedies built on social and racial stereotypes, and *The Water Nymph*, a story of love and flirtation at the seaside.[5]

Although Sennett's story was apocryphal, it does point to an essential feature of the early Keystones—and the particular flavor of the Keystones that gave them their excitement and charm. Many early Sennett comedies were shot off the cuff. Something was inevitably happening within 30 miles of the Sennett studios—the draining of the Silver Lake reservoir, another company shooting an epic movie, auto races, a dance contest, a rainstorm. Sennett packed his cameras, crew, and players off to the scene of the activity, shot some footage with his central players in the frame, and then returned to the studio to shoot the interlinking story. Such improvisatory filming not only provided the Sennett company with spectacular events that cost nothing (one of his boasts), but gave the Sennett production the feeling of spontaneity and freshness. It also guaranteed that much of the

---

* Sennett is not a very trustworthy historian—he takes credit for discovering Buster Keaton (who never worked for him); he lengthily describes Mabel Normand and Chaplin working together while studying French so they could converse with Max Linder on his trip to America (Charlie and Mabel worked together in 1914, but Linder did not first come across until 1916); etc.

film would take place outdoors, and, as in the Biograph days, the outdoors gave Sennett's people and objects the freedom to move.

Chaplin's first effective screen performance (his second film for Sennett), *Kid Auto Races at Venice* (1913), was such an improvisatory film built around an afternoon of actual auto races. In this delightfully ironic film about the cinema itself, the camera plays an important role. A camera crew pretends to shoot documentary footage of the races. Charlie, wearing his tramp apparel for the first time, pretends he doesn't know what a camera is or what the camera crew is doing. He repeatedly stands in front of the lens, blocking the camera's view, enraging the director, Henry Lehrman, who tries repeatedly to boot the tramp out of the frame—without success. Further ironies about this little film about filmmaking are that it really mirrors Chaplin's first observation of a crew shooting a film in England (when a bystander blocked the lens and caused a near riot), that Chaplin knew very little about filmmaking, and that Chaplin and Lehrman did not get along.

Improvisation was also the basis of *A Muddy Romance* (1913, also known as *Muddled in Mud*), a love triangle built around the draining of the Silver Lake reservoir; *The Water Nymph* (1912), a love triangle built around swimming at Santa Monica beach; and *Tango Tangles* (1914), a love triangle built around a tango contest in an actual dance hall.

This last film, the only one that combined all four of Keystone's greatest comics—Chaplin, Normand, Arbuckle, and Sterling—reveals another of Sennett's qualities, pure looniness. The action of the film is essentially dancing and fighting. Charlie plays a drunk who dances with Mabel; Sterling fights with Arbuckle over Mabel and then with Charlie. Between the comic duels there is a lot of slipping and sliding across the rosined dance floor. But the wackiest moments in the film are the sequences that were shot inside the Sennett studio, intended to match the shots that had been filmed on location at the real *bal masqué*. A quick glance at the dancers, Sennett's extras, in this studio footage reveals the oddest assortment of couples in the most bizarre masquerade costumes, wearing the silliest expressions, dancing with partners who are horrendously mismatched in size, shape, type, and sex (for example, a convict dances with his jailer). These dancers, who are supposed to match the real dancers in the real dance hall, are incapable of matching any real human beings in any real place. Such Sennett touches can be called mad, or surreal, or absurd, or just silly. Whatever they are called, they show that the Keystone world had very little to do with reality, except as a distorted and speeded-up reflection of it.

The essence of the Keystones was movement—not thought, emotion, desire, need, or human reaction. The essential Keystone actions were dash, crash, smash, and splash. Figures ran after things they wanted, ran away from things they wanted to avoid, ran over mountains, over dangerous ledges, fields, beaches. If they didn't run, they rode—in cars, in boats, on animals, on bikes. And they kept running from the start of the film until they smashed into something that stopped them, fell into something that soaked them, or simply fainted from exhaustion.

By using human beings as projectiles and missiles, Sennett effected the conversion of people into "Bergsonian" things. The Sennett figures are not mortal beings of flesh and spirit but mechanical toys of steel and bolts. No human body could possibly bear the physical torture of the Keystone world. And yet we have absolutely no fear for the health and safety of the Keystone clowns (this despite the fact that four people once died filming a Keystone stunt!) because we don't think of the Sennett people as human bodies but as machines—which might break but can always be fixed or replaced. The earlier film jests similarly divested their characters of human personality, but they made the mistake of trying to pretend the figures were human beings. Sennett put puppets into a puppet world.

He endowed this world with comic life by making it a completely enclosed universe with its own laws of nature, bearing little relationship to the real world of nature or actual human life. This separate, "unnatural" universe also produced the detachment that comedy requires, for the audience perceives that mortality and injury are absent from such a world and that bullets, knives, collisions, and falls can neither hurt nor kill.

This reduction of people to puppets seems to contradict Sennett's own opinion that he was indeed interested in developing "character" and the fact that so many of the Keystone clowns seemed to be "characters." But a closer look at Sennett's notion of character and the particular talent of the Sennett clowns reveals that they were physical types, not three-dimensional beings; externalized personages with funny costumes and makeup, not internalized hearts, brains, and souls. The acting style in the Keystones—demonstrative, excessive, ridiculous burlesques of human attitudes and emotions—further reduced men and women to dolls and dummies.*

Mabel Normand—as pretty, cute, and pert as she was—was a pretty-girl *type* with a spry and limber body. Although in later comedies such as *Mickey* and *Molly O* she showed more subtlety and personality, she was never any more striking than in *The Water Nymph*, her first Keystone, in which she displayed her shapely body in a bathing suit and then demonstrated its finesse by performing magnificent high dives into the Pacific. Ford Sterling was most famous for his "Dutch makeup"—super-dark eyebrows and tiny goatee—for his position as Chief of the Keystone Police Force, for his rubber-bandy legs, and for his acrobatic twirls, rather than for any quality of mind. Arbuckle was the cherubic, placid young fat man

---

* Donald McCaffrey in *Four Great Comedians* (London and New York, 1968, pp. 8–24) maintains that the acting in Sennett films was poor. On the contrary, it was extremely appropriate for the films' styles, attitudes, and views of human emotions.

who was so quick on his feet he could outrace a matador. (He once did, in Tijuana.) Mack Swain was the older, gruffer fat man—hairbrush mustache; darkened, world-weary eye sockets; a touch of vanity in the spit curl over his forehead, trying to disguise the reality of his balding head. Chester Conklin had his walrus mustache and beady eyes; Slim Summerville was a tall, elastic pretzel; Phyllis Allen was sour-pussed, tight-lipped, and dumpy. And so forth through the whole rogue's gallery of sizes, shapes, and anatomical specialties. Chaplin's problem at Keystone was partially that Sennett merely wanted a scrappy runt *type* whereas Chaplin wanted to create a human being who was a scrappy runt as well as a lot of other things. Keystone clowns were bodies, not brains.

One consequence of the Sennett mechanical world is the importance of objects in it. If human beings are really mechanical toys, then they are close cousins to other toys that were never alive. If Sennett turns the living being into the inanimate object, he conversely translates the inanimate object into the living being. The Keystones use two kinds of objects: mechanical objects that move—because motion is the essence of the films; and simple objects that cause pain—although puppets cannot really feel pain. In the first category, there are Lizzies (which race backward and forward, fly in the air, fall to pieces, somersault, topple, tumble, and twirl), rollercoaster cars, speedboats, rowboats, bicycles, airplanes. In the second, there are pistols, rocks, bricks, buckets of water, sticks, boots (good for kicking others in the pants), and, of course, custard pies (good for "schlupping" others in the face).* Such objects were clear descendants of that first hose in *L'Arroseur arrosée*.

The interrelationship between man and machine in the Keystone world is such that the Keystone Kops, themselves incompetent toy soldiers, depended on machines (autos, boats, paddy wagons) with precisely the same inefficiencies. This was yet another way in which Sennett differed from Chaplin. Where Sennett used objects that were consistently frenetic, destructive, and violent, Chaplin started to develop objects (the cane, the bowler hat, anything else he touched) that led a more subtle and supple life.

Another consequence of the Sennett premise is that the camera and the filmmaking process itself play a central role in creating his mad, mechanical, frantically paced world. Long shots, far shots, and extreme far shots dominate the Keystones. These shots both diminish the closeness and presence of the players and increase the effects of shapes in motion. There are certainly medium shots and close-ups in the Keystones, but not many,

---

* Custard pies for the movies were really made of blackberries—which showed up better on screen. These pies were specially baked for throwing, carefully weighted to permit the maximum accuracy and range. Mabel Normand improvisationally hit Arbuckle in the face with the first flying pastry in *A Noise from the Deep* (1913). Although Sennett said that Ben Turpin was the recipient, Ben did not work for Sennett until 1916 (see Lahue and Brewer, *op. cit.*, p. 42).

and Sennett's breakneck pace strips them of the impact of Griffith's careful and tender shots of hands and faces.

Tricks with camera speed, with pace and rhythm further diminish the impression of reality and increase the sense of a surreal netherworld. People cannot move in reality the way they move in Keystones; machines on our planet cannot do what machines do in Keystone comedies. Sennett's tricks with pace included undercranking as well as editing out every third or fourth frame. Others were shooting scenes backward and then inverting the strip in the final editing (those trains that appear to race along at eighty miles an hour and then stop instantaneously before demolishing a lady or a Lizzie) and undercranking so severely that slow-moving automobiles appeared to be careening and colliding at 60 miles an hour.

Behind all the camera trickery was not only the striving to get laughs with impossible, irrational surprises, but also the filmmaker's deliberate acknowledgment that his work of artifice was highly artificial. Like Méliès' Star Films, Sennett's Keystones played jokes on its audience while, at the same time, allowing the audience to participate in them. One of the great moments of *The Knockout* (1914) is Fatty Arbuckle's undressing for a prizefight. He starts to remove his trousers, only to notice that the peeking camera is revealing his entire body to the snooping audience. Arbuckle motions the camera to raise itself, to show some propriety by photographing him above the waist exclusively. As Arbuckle gestures, the camera slowly tilts up, removing all of those vast expanses below the belt from view. (Arbuckle used the same bit in one of his later Comique comedies.) The camera and the filmmaker are visible players in the Keystone world. This jocular admission of artifice contributes to the spirit and fun of the Sennett romps.

A final consequence of the Sennett premise is that there is an apparent structure of his films and a real one. There are three apparent Sennett structures—"riffing," "spoofing," and "peppering." The first two have already been defined; "peppering" is a sort of Sennett hybrid of the two. Many Keystones take a completely straight plot (love triangle; country boy has troubles in the city; country girl has troubles in the city) and then pepper it up with irrelevant gags. The effect of this spicing is partly to burlesque the serious versions of this plot and partly to throw in as many amusing, nonsensical bits as possible. But beneath all three of these apparent structures, the Keystones generally move in one direction—toward greater and greater insanity, movement, and chaos. Bergson describes this movement metaphorically as a snowball rolling down a mountain, gathering greater momentum and bulk as it descends. Similarly, the Sennett structure begins with a few characters who make a few mistakes and ends with a whole mess of characters in a whole mess of mess. The chase (or "rally" as Sennett called it) is the perfect climax for the Keystones' momentum.

What are the Keystones about? What do they say? Sennett liked to

The first comic jest—the Lumières' *L'Arroseur arrosée*.

Edwin S. Porter's *Uncle Josh at the Moving Picture Show*—a distant Uncle Josh shares the frame with a movie screen.

Georges Méliès' *The Cook in Trouble*—comic acrobats.

Mack Sennett's *Lizzies of the Field*—the triumph of the comic machine.

The first comic stars. Max Linder on skates in *Les Débuts d'un patineur*; John Bunny and his acerbic wife, Flora Finch, in *Bunny Attempts Suicide*.

The Sennett acting "method"—Sennett, Ford Sterling, and Mabel Normand parody melodrama in *Barney Oldfield's Race for Life*.

Sennett parody—Ben Turpin as von Stroheim in *Three Foolish Weeks*.

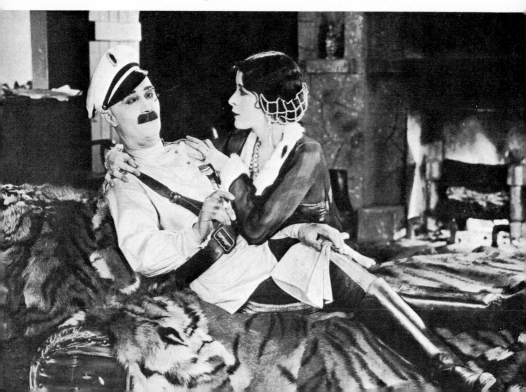

Sennett stars. Fatty Arbuckle as "Miss Fatty." Billy Bevan is *Caught in the Kitchen* (with Natalie Joyce).

Chaplin's first two films for Keystone. The music-hall costume in *Making a Living* and the tramp in *Kid Auto Races at Venice*.

Chaplin discoveries. Bringing the inanimate to life in *Mabel's Married Life*; taking to the road in *The Tramp*.

Charlie as *poseur* in the *haut monde* in *The Adventurer*.

Charlie and Edna as poor and hungry outsiders facing Eric Campbell in *The Immigrant*.

think that his films "whaled the daylights out of Authority and Pretension with a bed slat." He describes his youthful impressions of burlesque and the funny people who worked and played there:

Their approach to life was earthy and understandable. They whaled the daylights out of pretension. They made fun of themselves and the human race. They reduced convention, dogma, stuffed shirts and Authority to nonsense, and then blossomed into pandemonium. . . . I thought all this was delightful. I especially enjoyed the reduction of Authority to absurdity, the notion that sex could be funny, and the bold insults that were hurled at Pretension.[6]

Durgnat waxes more philosophical about Sennett's implications:

Much of Sennett's comedy is about the shock of speed, its insult to man. . . . Sennett's films register not only the shock of speed but the spreading concept of man as an impersonal object existing only to work rapidly, rhythmically, repetitively.[7]

Such philosophical speculations tickled Sennett, who whaled intellectual critics with his own verbal bed slats. One of his favorite "Pretentious" critical terms was "cineplastic," and he ridiculed those writers who likened his romps to ballet. He had never seen a ballet.

The most strikingly serious element of the Keystone capers is that they do not contain a single serious element. They are devoid of genuine human emotion. All emotions in the films—love, jealousy, lust, anger, greed, vengefulness—are strictly literary conventions. Given that the films' plots are merely apparent structures, collections of literary formulas and clichés to hang the gags on, it follows that their human motivation and consequences are equally conventional and irrelevant. The films do not depend on psychology or credible motivation.

There is not a single serious social issue in the films. Social groups are reduced to comic stereotypes: Jews (the "Cohen" series); blacks (the lazy, superstitious variety with titles like *Rastus and the Game Cock*); Germans (characters named Meyer and Schultz whose lives seemed to revolve around Limburger cheese). Even Sennett's cops, his prime example of a sally against Authority, are silly and lovable as well as incompetent and frantic. The difference between Chaplin's cops—who represent awesome propriety, the social Establishment, and the laws of those who can afford to make them—and Sennett's goofy klutzes is the difference between a man with a social conscience and a man without one.

Sennett's films are blissfully devoid of conscience as well as intellectual self-consciousness. The Keystones make fun of things without turning the fun into something that can also bite. Compared with even the early Chaplin Essanays, the Sennett romps are toothless. Chaplin's bite (as well as his bark) was something Sennett could never understand. Throughout Sennett's autobiography, a grudging respect for Chaplin's comedic genius veils the clear opinion that Chaplin was a nasty, ungrateful, pretentious bigmouth. The remarkable thing about the Keystones is that they reduce potentially important social and human issues to totally nonsensical hysteria. They lack two of today's dominant social attitudes—self-consciousness about who might be insulted and guilt for all the suffering that has been inflicted on the downtrodden by Society and History. The Keystones are outrageously, refreshingly impolite. There is something healthy about a film with racial jokes that could make even members of the "insulted" race laugh.

The Keystones were magnificent in this brash and honest refusal to take anything seriously. They were an exuberant, vital reaction to the seriousness of the "genteel tradition" that was then only beginning to invade the movies. Life existed so that Sennett and company could make a joke of it. There are many worse attitudes a man could take toward life.

After the Ball

The Sennett spirit did not die immediately with the merger of Keystone and Triangle in the fall of 1915; there were still delicious pieces of lunacy in the Triangle period. No greater piece of cinematic madness exists than *The Surf Girl* (1916);[8] there were still parodies of other film styles—*His Bitter Pill* (1915), *Teddy at the Throttle* (1917). Steady Keystone staples such as the "Ambrose and Walrus" series (Mack Swain and Chester Conklin) and the "Mabel and Fatty" series continued in the Triangles, but the rough, lunatic edge of these Keystone originals had been buffed. Mabel and Fatty became a more polished, domesticated couple in the Triangles; gone was the makeshift fun of *That Little Band of Gold, Mabel and Fatty's Simple Life, Cast Adrift—and How, Mabel and Fatty's Married Life,* or *Miss Fatty's Seaside Lovers.** The parodies of other films (for example, *Teddy at the Throttle* compared to *Barney Oldfield's Race for Life*) were still violently funny, but were more dependent on production values (rainstorms, crowd scenes, complicated plots) than the Keystone parodies that could make a film with four principals, six cops, a train, and an automobile.

The direction of Sennett's ambitions had been indicated by his biggest Keystone project, *Tillie's Punctured Romance,* a six-reel comic feature that brought together all the talent on the Sennett lot—and then some. In 1914, the year that the feature film really seized control of the American film industry, Sennett decided that his comedies might be expanded into

---

* Arbuckle was a great drag performer who slipped into a dress in at least half of his own Comique comedies. The fat, smooth-faced, kewpie-doll comedian was a delight in a dress, especially when he added his fat agility at mimicking a lady's mincing, flirtatious flutterings. These drag appearances also take on an interesting historical irony in the light of the sexual scandal that Arbuckle generated in 1921.

features too. To sell the big film, Sennett convinced the stage star Marie Dressler to make her first picture. She had earlier given the young iron-worker an introduction to David Belasco; now Sennett was in a position to repay the favor. To Dressler's physical talents and stage reputation Sennett added most of the clowns in his stable—Chaplin as her co-star, Normand as "the other woman," Mack Swain, Hank Mann, Al St. John, Chester Conklin, Phyllis Allen, Minta Durfee, and the Keystone Kops in lesser roles. Sennett underscored the importance of the project by directing the film personally.

The plot of *Tillie's Punctured Romance* was an adaptation of Dressler's most recent stage success, *Tillie's Nightmare*. It was a conventional tale of a country gal who gets swindled by a sharpie from the big city. The sharpie (Chaplin) is about to drop her when Tillie inherits a pile of money from a rich uncle presumed dead in a mountain-climbing accident. Charlie and Tillie move into a posh house, pretend to be swells, give large parties, dance the tango, and do all the other naughty things that rich city folk were wont to do in the early movies. Meanwhile, Charlie and his real love, Mabel, are trying to bilk bulky Tillie of her inherited riches. Their under-handed schemes explode, however, when Charlie is exposed and Tillie's rich uncle turns up alive. After a chase (of course), poor Tillie is finally hoisted out of the Pacific Ocean—a sadder, wiser, and wetter girl.

As in most of the Keystones, the plot simply supplies the pretext for a series of gags, mounting in rhythm and intensity, culminating in a rally. *Tillie's Punctured Romance* is one of Sennett's "peppered" films. Tillie's drunken dances—both alone and with tiny Charlie—are far more im-portant to the film than the plotty attempts to swindle her out of some cash. The "serious" motifs of the film are examples of the typical Key-stone method of reducing all potentially serious material to predictable literary clichés. The film includes an obvious contrast of simple, unaffected country ways (personified by the rowdy blimp, Dressler) and deceitful, affected city ways (personified by the jaunty shrimp, Chaplin). The film refuses to take this contrast seriously—as those ridiculous personifications show. Sennett borrowed this formulaic theme from other films of the same time, perhaps from Griffith himself.

Yet *Tillie's Punctured Romance* points unmistakably toward a later Sennett feature, *Mickey* (1916–18), which takes the city-country contrast quite seriously. In the later six-reel film, Mabel Normand personifies the natural, free, charming, tomboyish country girl (so believable as to fit the Marsh-Gish-Pickford mold perfectly). The film's treatment of the hoity-toity rich is also far more human and credible, and, as a result, far less ridiculous and funny in *Mickey* than it is in *Tillie's Punctured Romance*.

Keystone-Triangles such as *The Danger Girl* (1916), one of Gloria Swanson's first major roles, similarly tried to depict the *haut monde* in humanly credible terms rather than with lunacy, demonstrating that it is both funnier and wiser to see a cliché treated as a laughable cliché than to see it passed off as reality. The plot of this film is so complicated (a switcheroo story of two couples who get intertwined and wind up with different partners) that it is almost impossible to follow. Mabel and Fatty in *He Did and He Didn't* (1916) are so spiffed up (Fatty even wears a tuxedo) that they are almost unrecognizable as the two loons who hoofed it in earlier films. In *The Clever Dummy* (1916), Turpin's first major role for Sennett, the camera carefully and slowly records not fast-moving, chaotic antics, but Turpin masquerading as a dummy. Human motivation, rigid plotting, a realistically slow pace, and predictable fictional logic replaced non sequitur, frenzy, irrationality, and breathlessness.

This story of degeneration is not without its happy reversal. The reversal centers about two of Sennett's stars of the 1920s—Ben Turpin and Billy Bevan. To Turpin went the Keystone flair for parody; to Bevan went the Keystone mania for irrational motion. Turpin, whose skinny, agile body, high forehead, and wildly crossed eyes made him one of the silliest-looking clowns in film history, was the perfect embodiment of Sennett's anti-romanticism and anti-heroism. Cross-eyed Ben invariably and ironically played the romantic cliché of a movie hero in two-reel parodies of specific hit films and stars. He parodied Valentino, von Stroheim, William S. Hart, Douglas Fairbanks—any other striking, captivating film idol—simply by wearing a ridiculously gaudy romantic costume and by staring at (but obviously not seeing) the camera. And Turpin's stories also parodied the most popular genres—Wild West, Far North, desert sheik, European chic. Turpin's crossed eyes shot satiric, deflating darts into the gaudy hot-air-filled balloons that Hollywood passed off as art on its tinsel-blinded public.

Billy Bevan is not so familiar to audiences today as Ben Turpin, simply because Bevan lacked Turpin's dominant physical and facial trademarks.* Bevan's distinguishing marks were his huge walrus mustache and his big mouth (in both size and sound). The character he developed was a brash, vulgar, overactive "middle American"; his clothes were too loud, his jokes too cruel and crude, his body too flabby, his efforts to be seductive and charming too obvious. He was always too much (and, hence, not enough). In *The Beach Club* (1928) he wears tasteless plaids, works too hard to impress the bathing beauties, takes merciless advantage of a man too fat to fight him, cheats on his bar bill, and dreams up the most obnoxious practical jokes.

But other Bevan films use his personal traits less and emphasize instead his funny face and body as passive responders to the chaos that surrounds him. Bevan gets tangled with the world—lions, Lizzies, cops, air-

---

* Bevan is so unfamiliar that Raymond Durgnat incorrectly identifies him as Chester Conklin in *The Crazy Mirror*. Bevan resembled Conklin but was a much bigger man.

planes, elephants, vacuum cleaners, a spiteful oyster—all of which go mad and hurl him about until they decide to eject him. The premise of the Bevan films is the same as *Love, Speed, and Thrills* or *Barney Oldfield* or *The Surf Girl*—motion, frenzy, and the multiplication of absurdity.

The Bevan films concoct some of Sennett's greatest visual gags. The films still maintain some feeling of improvisation, but to shoot their fantastical physical delights took more planning on the drawing board, money to execute, and obvious camera tricks. In *Lizzies of the Field* (1924), autos fly through the air, crash into each other, carom in impossible patterns, extend themselves in space, scoop up passersby, and collapse in heaps of rubble—all the while appearing to travel at 100 miles per hour. In *Super-Hooper-Dyne Lizzies* (1924), autos react wildly when manipulated by remote control, dashing across the screen and around the town in impossible visual patterns. Another of the highlights of this film is Billy's pushing a long line of Lizzies (thinking he is only pushing his own car) all over town in interesting lines, wiggles, and circles.

In *Circus Today* (1924), a mammoth three-vehicle chase ensues—but what vehicles! Billy dashes off with a chariotload of lions; his boss follows him in a second circus chariot; and both of them are pursued by a galloping elephant which has wedged his jumbo body into a circus tent. In *Wandering Willie* (1924), Billy is outwitted by a viciously snapping oyster in his bowl of oyster stew.

These Bevan-Sennett films once more turn people (and animals) into frantic toy machines—zipping, colliding, and crashing up, down, and across the screen in incredible patterns at incredible speeds. Any queries about logical, consistent human motivation are buried under an avalanche of anomalous gags. In the final sequence of *Circus Today*, the one following that three-vehicle chase, lions run loose, freed from their cage when Billy's chariot overturns. One of the lions powders Madeleine Hurlock's back, using his bushy tail as a powder puff. Another chases after Billy and Andy Clyde, trapping them in a tiny cabin. Unfortunately, the little cabin has itself been accidentally carried thousands of feet into the air by an ascending balloon. If Billy stays in the cabin, he faces the lion; if he steps out of the cabin, he faces a 5,000-foot drop to the earth below. The dilemma resolves itself when the cabin crashes to earth; both men and the lion sit dazedly on the ground; the lion has a black eye, and little animated stars twirl around his head. Once again, the Sennett film simply ends with exhaustion—theirs and ours.

That is how Sennett solved an "impossible" dilemma—by following what would seem to be a climactically zany, anomalous chase with even more zany, anomalous gags. And that is what Sennett films do when they really work. No other filmmaker duplicated this delight in illogic and pace in such swift and surprising movement that no one notices (or cares) that he has been sucked into a process that intentionally makes no human sense whatever. Speed and movement create a separate and self-contained universe that makes perfectly good sense when judged exclusively in terms of its own laws.

III

—

CHAPLIN
AND
KEATON

CHAPTER 6

Chaplin: From Keystone to Mutual

——

THE movement of the human body in the crudest early jests and chases evolved into the complex and chaotic physical activities and patterns of the Keystones. Film comedy then turned in a different direction. Rather than exhibiting a mere physical object—a body—Charles Chaplin and Buster Keaton revealed a soul, a mind, and a brain within the body. To be sure, their bodies actually depicted their brains, but the gyrations and contortions of those superb bodies implied and created much beneath the surface of the physical.

It is difficult to compare Chaplin's and Keaton's gifts. Chaplin's fertile period lasted 38 years (some say even longer); Keaton's lasted about ten. Chaplin's art depended upon a minute perfection and precision; Keaton's relied on speed and a tumult of imaginative, farfetched ideas. Although Chaplin the director was more an intellect than Keaton the director, Charlie the character was less an intellect than Buster the character. Although women were important metaphorically in Chaplin films, sexual attraction and masculine virility were far more dominant in Keaton's pictures. The Chaplin films were smaller—centering on small facial gestures and objects; the Keaton films were larger—centering on human figures against a vast physical environment and huge, complicated objects. The Chaplin films moved slowly and quietly; the Keaton films with great pace and vigor. And yet Charlie was the character who laughed, smiled, and cried, whereas Buster was the one who rarely moved a facial muscle.

Chaplin's career is astonishing in that he could make so many films of such consistent thematic content and high quality over such a long period of time; Keaton's career is astonishing in that he could make so many films of such consistency and energy in such a short time. The two artists, the two screen characters, and the two film careers reveal opposite achievements of the very best that is possible in motion pictures.

The Chaplin Career and Chaplin Clichés

Charles Chaplin is the greatest film artist in motion-picture history. He is to the movies what Shakespeare is to the drama. And, like Shakespeare, he is so because he has both something interesting inside his head and the technical skill to take what is inside and turn it into something objective and visible that is powerful, stimulating, haunting, and moving. Whereas Shakespeare's tools were dramatic structure and the English language, Chaplin's were his hypnotic performances themselves and his cinematic ability to capture and communicate those performances.

Chaplin was born on April 16, 1889. Both his parents were music-hall performers. His father drank; his mother suffered from ill health. By the time he was ten, Chaplin had experienced a broken home, the death of his father, the insanity of his mother, almost two years in an orphanage for the poor, and several months of bumming around the London streets homeless, hungry, and penniless. He had also worked on the stage, where, from the time he was ten, his career was steady and distinguished. The gifted and famous child performer eventually became a headliner in England's leading music-hall company, the Fred Karno Pantomime Troupe. He toured America several times with the Karno company, and on one of the tours he received an offer to work for Mack Sennett.*

Chaplin went to work for Sennett in December of 1913 at $150 a week. In a little over a year he made 35 Keystones varying in length from a half reel to six reels, about two-thirds of which he directed himself. He then made 14 films for Essanay in 12 months (1915–16), plus parts of several other films that Essanay later edited and compiled. At Essanay he enjoyed a measure of directorial and authorial freedom, plus the tidy salary of $1,250 a week. Next he made 12 films for Mutual in 18 months (1916–17), on which he enjoyed even more artistic freedom, and for

* Credit for discovering Chaplin has been claimed by Sennett himself, by Mabel Normand, and by Kessel and Bauman. Contrary to apocryphal stories, Chaplin's vaudeville fame was international (see Huff, *Charlie Chaplin*); he was not some little nobody whom a film producer happened to discover. He was acknowledged in both England and America as being at the top of his profession.

which he received $670,000. Then he made eight films for First National in the next five years (1918–22), several of them exceeding the two-reel length of most of his previous films, for which he received a million-dollar contract plus plenty of bonuses and percentages of the profits. And finally, he made eight feature films for United Artists, a company he helped to found, over the next 30 years (1923–52), all of which made money. (Even *Monsieur Verdoux* broke even; its worldwide earnings overcame its failure in the United States.)

In 1952 Chaplin took a vacation to Europe; he refused to return to the United States. The precise reasons for this refusal are unclear. Chaplin claims that the State Department refused him readmission on moral grounds and that the Internal Revenue Service demanded excessive tax money, violating an agreement he had earlier made with them. Contributing to his decision was public hostility against Chaplin for never having become a United States citizen, for his scandalous "love affairs," and for his "pinkish" leanings. Since 1952 Chaplin has made two uneven films in Europe, *A King in New York* and *A Countess from Hong Kong*. He has lived in Switzerland since 1953, not visiting the United States until 1972, when he received a triumphant welcome from the American press and a special Oscar (his only one) from the Motion Picture Academy, two groups that had contributed to Chaplin's banishment (either overtly or tacitly) 20 years earlier.

These are the sketchy dates and figures. Within these outlines lies the most remarkable career in the history of films—the accomplishments of an artist who did not make a single unremarkable film from 1917 to 1952. Just as the wonder of Shakespeare is that he wrote not only *Hamlet* but also *A Midsummer Night's Dream* and *Othello* and *As You Like It* and *Antony and Cleopatra* (and the "ands" go on), the wonder of Chaplin is that he made so many brilliant works and that the totality of his creations is even more overpowering than the near perfection of any one.

Before 1950, rhapsodies to Chaplin's art were quite common—by such respectable voices as Alexander Woollcott, Gilbert Seldes, George Bernard Shaw, and James Agee. Between 1950 and 1970, however, a leveling and debunking tone became the fashion of those who found great flaws in Chaplin's work and argued that other film comedians—both ancient and modern —were just as good in different ways. This shift in attitude has several possible causes.

(1) The flaws (and there are flaws of overstatement and oversentimentality) in Chaplin's later work led some critics to see the same ones throughout the Chaplin canon and to let them overwhelm the virtues. (2) The misanthropy and unpleasantness of Chaplin's ideas both on the screen and in print led some critics to prefer more wholesome, optimistic, cheerful comics. (3) The fact that most of the Chaplin films had been

out of circulation for so long perhaps took some of the wonder out of the critics' memories of Chaplin films. A whole generation of critics had never seen much Chaplin. (4) The status of film criticism in the 1970s is simply different from what it was in the previous 50 years. Film devotees once had to grind their axes in support of the artistic and intellectual equality of the motion picture. Chaplin was the most suitable material for axe-grinding because his films were obviously as complex and intelligent as other "great art." Today, with the artistic potential of films universally accepted in cultural circles, critics can trim the giants and grind their axes in favor of such competent technicians as Allan Dwan, Roger Corman, and George Cukor, pushing the mountains into the valleys. It is worth clearing away a few of these critical cobwebs—the clichés that have been passed from critic to critic about Chaplin's aims and art.

There is the view that Chaplin was a very funny man without a real idea in his head. According to such writers (Keaton and Sennett implied the same opinion), Chaplin was a comic genius who should have kept his mouth shut. Pointing to Chaplin's lack of formal education, they find his toying with Nietzsche and Marx and Schopenhauer a pretentious game. In fact, Chaplin often had trouble when he opened his mouth—both on and off the screen. Words were not his medium. But that he had complex ideas about human conduct and social organizations and that he could express them brilliantly are undeniable. His means of expression were his face, his hands, his body—and the eye that recorded them. I have already described one of Chaplin's "ideas" about human instinct in *The Pilgrim*. There are thousands of these in the canon.

To cite just one other example: In *City Lights*, Charlie, wearing tails, is driving along in a Rolls Royce. (Both suit and car are gifts from a drunken millionaire.) Charlie spots a man smoking a cigar. He follows him patiently down the street in the Rolls until the smoker drops that cigar butt. Charlie then stops the Rolls, leaps out toward the cigar, and force-fully pushes away an old tramp who had himself bent over to pick up the butt. After picking up the bit of cigar, Charlie sticks it into his mouth, leaps back into "his" Rolls, and drives off smoking. The bum stands and stares in stunned disbelief. The contrast of wealth and poverty, apparent riches with actual need, in this little piece of business cannot be reduced to a simple sentence or two. This is not just a funny gag but a glimpse of a way of life. Chaplin's ideas reveal themselves not merely in bits of this kind but in the premise and structure of each mature film, which show a real intellect at work.

Structure, the second flaw that critics see in Chaplin's works, is really one of his greatest strengths.[1] Chaplin's films have been attacked for their weak structures, their weak stories. Before a critic makes such an accusation, he ought to ascertain if the work is supposed to tell a story. One could easily attack *Remembrance of Things Past, Ulysses*, and *Waiting for Godot* on the same grounds.* Chaplin's structures are not stories but thematic investigations—putting the wandering *pícaro*, the homeless tramp (or some variation of him) in juxtaposition with a particular social and moral environment. The film's structure is based on this juxtaposition. This structure, which Chaplin really did not fix upon until the Mutual period, dominates every film he made thereafter. Before accusing Chaplin of weak plot-making, the critic ought to think about the reason for Chaplin's generic film titles—*The Gold Rush, Modern Times, The Pilgrim*, and so on. The films are not structured around stories—what happens to the characters—but around an investigation of the theme implied by the title. And this includes even those films (such as *Verdoux* and *Shoulder Arms*) which do not appear to have generic titles. "Good" structure is not a fixed quality but a function of the whole work's intentions. As such, Chaplin's film structures are as "good" as anybody's and better than most.

A similar kind of Chaplin criticism accuses him of being "bad" cinematically. According to such a view, Chaplin didn't understand composition, editing, lighting, and sound; many of his best bits would be as good on the stage as on a screen. Once again, such a position assumes that "good" cinematic technique is fixed rather than a function of the particular work. It also ignores the greater intimacy of the film medium—and intimacy is at the heart of Chaplin's cinematic method. The intimate relationship of spectator and performer in the cinema—the subtle delicacy of Chaplin's gesture and expression—could not possibly exist on the legitimate or music-hall stage. Further, the view of Chaplin as an incompetent technician does not square with the facts of Chaplin's films. For those who think he could not manage a camera, I suggest they look again at the composition of the "house of mirrors" scene in *The Circus*, the restaurant scene where Charlie tries to serve a duckling in *Modern Times*, and the flower-shop scene where Verdoux makes love by telephone in *Monsieur Verdoux* —to give just three examples. In each of these scenes the camera has found precisely the right angle to communicate the pictorial, intellectual, and emotional values of the shot.

In the mirror scene we see Chaplin's figure multiplied a hundred times so that it is impossible to distinguish the reflections from the man. That perfection is not an accident. In the waiter scene, Chaplin, shooting downward from a high angle, reveals Charlie, holding a tray aloft, swamped by a floor full of dancers. They push the little waiter (and that seemingly floating tray) all over the dance floor, like waves pushing a bit of driftwood. In the *Verdoux* scene, as Charlie in the center of the frame spews romantic lies over the telephone to Madame Grosnay (whom he is planning to murder),

* In fact, critics did attack all three works on precisely those irrelevant grounds.

the flower girl in the foreground listens and is bathed with tears from the "most beautiful speech she ever heard." The tension in this shot between foreground and rearground perfectly mirrors its content, which is a tension between the apparent sentiments and the real ones.

Although Chaplin prefers the fixed composition of a passive camera, he does know how to use a moving camera on the rare occasion when he wants that sort of effect. For example, in *Modern Times* the moving camera rides on a truck as Charlie marches behind it waving a red flag that dropped off the truck. Then a leftist political parade turns a corner to march behind Charlie without his knowing it. The moving camera technique is the perfect means of comically depicting how an innocent pedestrian can be mistaken for a political agitator. Chaplin's sense of composition allows him to find exactly the right spot for filming a scene so that it remains perpetually interesting regardless of its length.

This brings us to Chaplin's "poor editing." It is true that Chaplin edits very sparingly; he allows scenes to play themselves out for minutes without a cut. But this is extremely effective editing for Chaplin because the scenes remain hypnotic regardless of their length. Cutting is not capricious or mechanical; one only cuts to reveal something that the previous shot did not. Cutting can, however, become intrusive and destroy the magic. That is the primary reason for Chaplin's editing restraint. The lack of cutting increases the intimacy of the Chaplin business and *persona*. His leisurely cutting is the ally *in time* of his intimate composition *in space*.

A second reason for Chaplin's unobtrusive cutting is that we must believe absolutely in his body's ability to perform the feats it does. Part of the magic of the Chaplin world is that it uses no cinematic tricks: it is physical perfection without trick. Editing (as Bazin noted) instantly produces the suspicion of trickery. Chaplin's refusal to edit very long scenes is a sign of both his artistic intuition and his assurance. Who else could let a scene go on so long?

Yet other Chaplin scenes—for example, Hynkel's dance with the globe-balloon in *The Great Dictator*—use many cuts and yet give the impression that the scene is a single long take. Chaplin's cutting is fluidly unobtrusive (the hypnotic travels of the balloon mask every cut), so as never to divert the spectator from the human and comic business. Chaplin's editing is exactly right for Chaplin.

Similarly, those who think Chaplin never learned to use light ought to look at the opening night sequences of *A Woman of Paris*, the New Year's Eve sequences of *The Gold Rush*, and the audition sequence of *Limelight* —again to name just three—for their evocative contrasts of light and darkness. Those who think his avoidance of sound stemmed from fear and clumsiness ought to think a bit more about the opening nonsense speech of *City Lights* (or the whistle sequence of the same film), the stomach gurgling in *Modern Times*, Martha Raye's offscreen laughter in *Verdoux* (which instantly reveals that the loud, vulgar broad is nearby), or the differences between the sequences with a natural sound track, with music, and with silence in *Limelight*.

Indeed, it is even tempting to see Chaplin's most acknowledged technical sloppiness—his lack of concern for atmosphere and décor—as a virtue. When Chaplin constructed and decorated the worlds of *City Lights*, *Modern Times*, *Great Dictator*, *Verdoux*, and *Limelight*, he merely re-dressed the same sets with decorative trimming, transporting the same architectural edifice from Tomania to Paris to London with the aid of a new window frame, awning, or coat of paint. One becomes as familiar with the Chaplin streets that recur in every film as with one's own neighborhood. But again Chaplin seems to perceive that elaborate and careful décor—usually a cinematic virtue—can be a great fault if it diverts the viewer's attention from the film's central human and comic matters.

There has never been a better film technician than Chaplin because Chaplin's technique was perfectly suited to communicate what he wanted. And that is as good as technique can ever be.

Chaplin was a meticulous craftsman. No one ever took longer to make a film: hundreds of takes on short scenes; dozens of retakes if the scenes were not right; shooting ratios of 100 to 1; months and months of editing and reediting.* How do these critics suppose Chaplin spent that time? Chaplin's films reflect his craftsmanship in their costs. The short Mutual two-reelers cost almost $100,000 each (just a bit less than *The Birth of a Nation!*).[2] The First Nationals cost almost as much as Keaton's features (and they were much shorter and much less spectacular); *The Kid* cost more than *The General!* The money that Chaplin spent on his films did not show in the usual way that money shows in a film. As opposed to the costumes, extras, and ornate sets in a De Mille or Griffith extravaganza, the money went into the quality of the filmed material, not its quantities. He invested the money in time, not space. And that kind of expensive perfection does indeed show in the films.

A final criticism of Chaplin is that he reached brilliant perfection in the Mutuals and then got longer, duller, more banal, less unified, less funny, more saccharine in the later films. There is a kind of truth in the claim. The most effective Mutuals—*One A.M.*, *The Pawnshop*, *The Rink*, *Easy Street*, *The Immigrant*, and *The Adventurer*—are flawless gems of comic business in a compact structure. And several of the other Mutuals are not far behind them. But the longer features, despite occasional lapses into sentimentality, slow pacing, or overstated moralizing, are far more impressive expressions of the human spirit. They are flawed, but they work with more complex emotional and intellectual material. And they generally suc-

---

* A shooting ratio is the amount of footage shot as opposed to the amount of footage in the final print. Most Hollywood films have shooting ratios of between 5 and 10 to 1.

ceed magnificently despite the lapses. To prefer the perfection of the Mutuals is to prefer the perfection of *The Comedy of Errors* to the difficulties and flaws of *As You Like It, Henry IV, Hamlet, Antony and Cleopatra,* and *The Tempest.*

Lessons at Keystone

When Chaplin arrived at Keystone in 1913, he knew little about making films. He was puzzled with the way scenes were shot out of sequence; he could not understand how to relate to a nonexistent being who would be added in some later shot; he, in effect, was ignorant of the role of editing in building a film story. In his first few months he received a crash course in the evolution of film technique from Edison to Griffith—by working on a set, of course. Less than a year after he started working in films, Chaplin would conceive and direct some of the best films that Keystone produced: *The Rounders, The New Janitor,* and *Dough and Dynamite.*

For most historians, one important lesson that Chaplin learned at Keystone was his gradual discovery and development of the tramp costume. In his first film, *Making a Living,* he sported a corny English music-hall get-up, complete with monocle and walrus mustache. For his second, *Kid Auto Races at Venice,* he decided to try a huge pair of Fatty Arbuckle's pants, Ford Sterling's immense shoes (left shoe on right foot, and vice versa), as well as a tight-fitting jacket, a derby that was too small for him (borrowed from Minta Durfee's father), a toothbrush mustache trimmed down from one of Mack Swain's, and a cane (perhaps an idea borrowed from Max Linder). Although Chaplin assembled this costume for his second film, he did not wear it consistently in the Keystones. For example, he was much more dapper and polished in one of his later Keystones, *Tillie's Punctured Romance.* Further, although Chaplin discovered the components of the tramp costume at Keystone, he discovered all the components of the tramp character not there but at Essanay. The side of the tramp that emerged at Keystone was the tough, violent, scrappy, almost sadistic one, not the little man's recognition of a very clear code of human morality.

The most significant lesson that Chaplin learned at Keystone (other than the way to shoot and assemble a film) was to become the cornerstone of his technique from *His Favorite Pastime* (1914) to *Limelight* (1952). Chaplin learned how to relate to objects and how to make objects relate to him. He learned how to talk to objects, and in return he taught them how to talk back to him. This was probably a technique that Chaplin brought with him from the stage, but the greater intimacy of the motion picture—even given Sennett's insistence on banishing intimacy from the

Keystone lot—allowed Chaplin's relationship to things to become more intimate. Charlie could communicate the interrelationship of man and much smaller things, and he could communicate it in a much smaller way.

Chaplin's first film—*Making a Living*—is so poorly acted and so unfunny primarily because Chaplin has nothing to play off and against. He simply stands around fuming, and stomping, and fussing; like so many Sennett characters, he demonstrates abstract clichés of passions. He has nothing concrete to manipulate. His one great moment is with an object—a slipping cuff. But his second film, *Kid Auto Races*, gives him something more concrete—a prop camera—and he uses the little box for all it is worth. Chaplin's first half-dozen films—through *Tango Tangles*—are primarily knockabout farces. His best moments in them use the concrete—a flight of steps, a banister, a slippery floor, another human body. In several of these early films he plays a drunk, his old Karno routine, which gives him a further method of responding to any object that he comes across, runs against, or falls beside.

But his seventh film, *His Favorite Pastime*, contains one piece of business that is a bit different. Charlie plays a drunk again. His "favorite pastime" is drinking, and he attempts to enter his favorite place—a saloon—to do some. He meets the swinging saloon door. He pushes it, and it returns to boff him in the face. He kicks it, and it boots him back. He puts up his dukes and starts to spar with it; it gets in all the good punches. Charlie gives up and crawls under it. The saloon door is the ancestor of every inanimate thing that Charlie later succeeded in bringing to life; he turns a piece of wood into a living opponent. He succeeds in treating one kind of object as if it were a different kind of being. Although historians usually refer to this technique as Chaplin's "transposition of objects," "metamorphosis" would be a much more accurate term, for the object is not instantaneously transposed into something else but undergoes the complete transformation process before our eyes.

The effects of this metamorphosed door were so successful and felicitous that Sennett shortly after allowed Chaplin to build a whole film—*Mabel's Married Life*—around a weighted boxing dummy that whips Charlie in pugilistic combat. The elemental door also comes back to life later as a Murphy bed in *One A.M.* (it duels with Charlie; he gives up and sleeps in the bathtub), as an assembly line in *Modern Times* (he tries to play according to its rules but gives up and goes berserk, dancing and splattering oil all over the factory), and in countless other guises.

The personality, the vitality of other objects in the Keystones also show Chaplin's imagination and growing sureness of comic technique. In *Gentlemen of Nerve*, he flirts with Mabel Normand at the auto races by snatching a bottle of soda and then playing with both it and its straw in the most pixyish, flirtatious ways. In *Getting Acquainted* he again flirts with Mabel, on a park bench, by lifting up her skirt with his cane. He then looks surprisedly at the cane and spanks it, as if the cane and not his arm were the offender.

Perhaps Chaplin's best Keystone with objects is *Dough and Dynamite,* one of his most famous. The film is a typically Sennettesque bit of riffing in a bakery. Its primary action is dough-slinging between Charlie and Chester Conklin, who spend most of the film bashing each other with dough, pies, bread, and sacks of flour. The chaos ends in a mammoth explosion as some striking bakers sneak a stick of dynamite into a loaf of bread. Despite the purely Sennett premise of the film, it is dominated by the Chaplin style of paying close attention to what he can do with a bit of inanimate matter. Before the film has finished, Chaplin has used the dough as boxing gloves, bracelets, quicksand, a mallet, a slingshot, a discus, a chair, and something to occupy his roaming hands while flirting with a pretty girl.

In this film Chaplin also creates one of his classic bits. Holding aloft a whole tray of bread loaves, he runs, dances, twirls, pirouettes, and somersaults without spilling a single loaf. Then, when he stoops down casually to pick one loaf off the floor, the whole tray of loaves slips and falls. Charlie does the supremely difficult balancing act with great ease; it is the simple, ordinary task that boggles him. This balancing act would be reincarnated over and over again in the later Chaplin films—as late as *Verdoux* when he tumbles with a teacup in his hand without spilling a drop.

There are glimmers of other elements of Chaplin's mature technique in the Keystones. Several of the films contain veiled social implications. Chaplin's masculine disdain for the moral constraints of married life shows in the way he reacts to wife and baby in *His Trysting Places* and the way the drunken Charlie and Fatty react to their severe and snippy wives in *The Rounders.* Such marital tensions are, of course, outgrowths of themes that had been conventional since the earliest American jests and the Griffith-Sennett Biographs. The typical Chaplin contrast between rich and poor can be seen in *Caught in a Cabaret,* in which Charlie, a waiter, poses as O. T. Axle, Ambassador for Grease. However, Charlie's adventures as poseur in this early film are far less funny and far less pointed than in later films with the same motif—*The Count, The Rink, The Idle Class,* and *City Lights.*

Another important Chaplin motif—Charlie's ability to experience human happiness vicariously but not directly—also pops up in one of the Keystones. In *Twenty Minutes of Love,* Charlie observes two lovers kissing on a park bench while he sits on the branch of a tree. Carried away by this passion, Chaplin begins to hug and embrace the tree trunk. A tree is his only lover (and again wood becomes human).

Finally, a sense of who the tramp is and how respectable society sees him begins to emerge in the Keystones. In *The New Janitor,* an apparently respectable employee is an embezzler who robs the company safe. This

Chaplin theme—that an apparently honest member of the Establishment uses that appearance as a disguise—recurs in *The Floorwalker, The Fireman, The Pawnshop,* and several other later films. But further, when the boss walks into the office and sees the janitor, Charlie, holding the respected employee at bay with a pistol, his immediate conclusion is that Charlie is the culprit who has robbed him. The pretty secretary, who has seen the whole robbery, must explain that the scruffy Charlie is hero, not villain.

Charlie's method of saving the secretary from the thief is also only a step away from Chaplin's mature style and theme. When he sees the thief threatening her with a pistol, he immediately and instinctively bashes the gun out of the thief's hand with the door of the office safe. Throughout the film, Charlie's strategies based on immediate, instinctive responses are consistently more effective than his more leisurely, planned methods of attack. Even in this early film Chaplin seems to perceive that Charlie's greatest ally is surprise that stems from a quick flash of instinctive inspiration. Give the bigger, tougher foe time to think, and little Charlie is lost.

A further indication of the later Chaplin in the film is that, although the building has an elevator, Charlie, a mere laborer, must trudge up the stairs whenever he wants to get to an upper story from his basement closet. This allows him some funny business with climbing stairs, as well as social comment on who rides and who walks.

There are other pieces of business in the Keystones that are pure Chaplin. One subtle comic bit that Sennett would never have taken the time to shoot is in *Caught in the Rain*, the first film that Chaplin directed by himself. Mack Swain and his wife argue violently in their hotel room. A chambermaid knocks at the door and enters. Instantaneously, Mack and his wife stop shouting and start smiling at each other, sweetly and silently. As soon as the maid leaves, they begin screaming at each other again. This bit brilliantly sums up the difference between real feelings and external appearances, the respectable class and the serving class, the fervor of rhetoric and the tepidness of a passion that can be quickly turned on and off.

On the other hand, the famed Chaplin "tramp" figure, the sentimental, warmhearted Everyman, does not yet exist in the Keystones—except for his wiry toughness. This toughness would always underlie the more ethereal emotions that the tramp suggested. Toughness allowed the little guy to survive; if Charlie couldn't boot an assailant in the pants, he was lost. In the Keystones, however, he doesn't do much else than boot people in the pants—assailants and neutrals alike. In *The Property Man*, one of Chaplin's memories of music-hall days, he plays a scrappy stagehand who boots, smashes, rips, and wrecks everything. The cruelest of his antics is to make a helpless, broken, feeble old man do all the heavy labor while Charlie sits around idly puffing on a pipe, occasionally booting and slapping the octogenarian for good measure. Charlie's only reason for torturing the old man is simply that comic torture was a staple of the Sennett product.

Chaplin's cinematic methods in the Sennett era were also indistinguishable from those of the boss. His camera still works far from the figures, emphasizing shapes rather than faces. In many of the films, we feel we'd like to see something more closely, but Chaplin never permits this kind of view. Not until the middle of the Essanay period does he discover the desirable intimacy of middle-distance and close-up shooting.

Growth at Essanay (1915–16)

At Essanay Chaplin discovered who the little tramp figure was and how he related to the world of respectability and propriety that both surrounded and excluded him. To the tramp's pluck and toughness developed at Keystone, Chaplin added a greater sensitivity to those beings—usually personified by a woman, Edna Purviance—who deserved his sympathy. The tramp's enemies took more specific form. No longer were they any human being that he could kick with his oversized shoe; they became representatives of antagonistic social and moral forces. Whereas Charlie would make unpragmatic self-sacrifices for those troubled beings who deserved his help, he turned his runty defiance on those who tried to squash him. Such a personality necessarily led to social implications. Charlie's tramp character, plucky, human, sensitive, warm, alternately generous and tough, down and out in society's eyes, was in sharp contrast to the mean, ornery, often dishonest, usually ungrateful, smug, and insensitive bullies who persecuted him and who, in society's eyes (i.e., their own), were very much up and in.

Chaplin learned other things at Essanay as well, most of them radiating from the pivotal discovery of the tramp's essence. He began to see that his tramp was doomed to fail at obtaining earthly rewards. Success was snatched from his hands; he either lost something he had temporarily won, or awoke to discover that his triumph was a dream. Chaplin also began to set his films in situations with decidedly social overtones—doing a job, working in a bank, interrelating with the police. His films gradually left Sennett's miscellaneous locales (parks, beaches, movie studios) and began to center around the human necessities for survival—food, shelter, and love. Into his Essanays Chaplin began to interject a subtle and understated irony, a trait that was to become increasingly pronounced as his career matured. He began to use the dominant visual metaphor of his many films—the flower—a perfect, beautiful, yet terribly fragile link between man and nature. And he began to move the camera closer to the players, steadily finding more revealing positions and approaches to illuminate both comedy and emotion.

But Chaplin did not learn these lessons all at once. Many of his Essanay films are closer in spirit to the Keystones than to the later films. His first five films at Essanay were very much in the Keystone pattern—except that they were all two reels long (only four of the Keystones that Chaplin directed were two-reelers) and invested more time in Chaplin's relationship to situations and objects. *His New Job*, the first Essanay, takes the same setting as his Keystone *The Masquerader*,[3] and follows Charlie's disruptive antics in a movie studio. There is wonderful parody of grandiose costume epics: Charlie looks ridiculous in his oversized Cossack costume; he flicks his cigarette ashes with his huge scimitar; when he stoops to kiss the leading lady's hem, he pulls off her train. Like Sennett, Chaplin builds the film to chaos and then simply stops it. *A Night Out*, the second Essanay, is a repeat of *The Rounders*, with Turpin substituting for Arbuckle. Its second reel duplicates the motif of *Caught in the Rain*. (A man's wife mistakenly gets into Charlie's bedroom.) And the film has a typically Sennett ending—Chaplin doused in a bathtub. The next three Essanays also are Sennett progeny: *The Champion* (a boxing setting parallel to *The Knockout*); *In the Park* (flirting, cops, and thieving in a park, parallel to *Twenty Minutes of Love, His Trysting Places*, and *Getting Acquainted*); and *The Jitney Elopement* (Charlie posing as a count as in *Caught in a Cabaret*, followed by a wild, Sennett-style Lizzie chase).

But Chaplin's sixth Essanay film of 1915, *The Tramp*, struck a different chord. From that film on, the Chaplin film and the Charlie tramp acquired a clear individuality. Even his lighter, spoofy, purely funny films would have a greater richness and texture. *The Tramp* begins with a great gag as well as an important piece of psychological and social definition. (That combination of laugh plus implication is the essence of the mature Chaplin.) Charlie, the tramp, walks along a dusty rural road. A large automobile roars past, knocking him down and splattering him with dust. Charlie not only must walk rather than ride, but must suffer the carelessness and contempt of those who can afford an automobile. But he picks himself up, whisks himself off, and continues on his journey—dirtied but undaunted.

Shortly afterward, Charlie performs the first genuine moral act in his films. Edna has been robbed by other tramps (theoretically Charlie's comrades). Charlie, touched by Edna's tears, retrieves the money from his own kind and gives it back to Edna. His act is unselfish and contrary to his own interest, yet he performs it. But Chaplin's comic sense and knowledge of the tramp character is so great by this point that he does not simply leave the act of generosity there. After Charlie hands Edna the wad of bills, he slyly remembers to take back a few for himself (an act duplicated in *The Immigrant* and modified in *City Lights*). The act of self-sacrifice is the essential act of human compassion for Chaplin—the act that separates the selfless tramp from the other brutally selfish beings in his world. In the later feature films Chaplin would equate self-sacrifice with love and then assert that such love was the only means of making life possible or livable.

Later in the film Charlie performs a second act of self-sacrifice. He has gone to work for Edna and her father on their farm. Those crooked tramps want to rob Charlie's new protector. Although Charlie plays along with them, he informs the farmer of their designs, and the two unite to repulse the invaders. In the scuffle Charlie receives a painful bullet wound in the leg. And this event in *The Tramp* sets another kind of pattern: the act of self-sacrifice inevitably causes Charlie pain (either physical, psychological, or both).

But the sacrifice is still valuable to him—despite the pain. Edna nurses him back to health, and Charlie falls in love with her gentleness—the first sincere, tender emotion in a Chaplin film. But Edna's rich, handsome boyfriend comes to see her from the city, and Charlie realizes that Edna is not for the likes of him. He takes to the road again—alone. We see his sad, lonely figure, shuffling slowly down the road away from the camera. Suddenly he stops, begins to pick up his heels in a snappy, march-time tempo, and then continues jauntily down the road—diminished but not defeated. The film has come full circle; the final scene is a mirror image of the first one with the automobile. And in that unity of beginning and ending, the film shows an unmistakable structural pattern. Things in this film happen twice—two setbacks, two sacrifices, two acts of loyalty, two experiences of pain.

The Tramp's structure is a tremendous advance over Sennett's chaos building to collapse. It moves in a circle—from the road to the road, from rebuff to rebuff. Each of its parts carefully turns the circle. And this circular journey is, paradoxically, a kind of progress, for in the course of it Charlie learns about human experience and asserts his relation to it. The cinematic technique of *The Tramp* is also much surer, effectively controlling the different potentials of long shot, medium shot, and close-up. The contrast between Chaplin's handling of composition in this film and the clumsy staginess in the one that preceded it—*The Jitney Elopement*—is astounding.

Chaplin's next important Essanay,* *Work*, is not so unified as *The Tramp*. Its brilliant first half dissolves in a climactic sequence of gooey paste-slinging, reminiscent of the earlier *Dough and Dynamite*. *Work* begins with Charlie as the beast of burden, toting the heavy cart that carries his master and their gear through the city and up an immense hill. Sig-

---

* Excluding the one-reel, Sennettesque *By the Sea*.

nificantly, little Charlie is the only one who does any work in the film. The boss (Charles Insley) rides in the cart. He also sits lazily around the house while Charlie blunderingly tries to hang the wallpaper. The boss is greeted cheerfully by a farmhand, who does not even notice Charlie exists. When Charlie and the boss arrive at the lady's house, she too greets the boss, but after taking one look at Charlie she quickly locks all her valuables in the safe. The social and human commentary of this opening sequence is, again, at once sharply pointed and comically unobtrusive. The boss, a huge brute of a fellow, is far better equipped than Charlie to do physical work, but Charlie, because of his social powerlessness, is the one who must do the work. The boss, because he owns things, is treated as a human being; Charlie, because he owns nothing, is treated as a beast or a criminal, if anyone bothers to treat him at all.

The second section of the film—Charlie's botch of the paper-hanging—contains one gem of a bit that is pure Chaplin. In the rich lady's house Charlie notices a plaster statuette of a woman. He tips his hat to her. What else do you do to a lady? He eyes her; she is "artistically" bare. So he takes a lampshade and delicately hangs it over her bottom half. Charlie stares at this now proper plaster lady. Then he pushes the lampshade, and we suddenly see it turn into a hula skirt; the plaster figurine, as if by magic, dances the hula (better yet, the "hootchy kootchy"). Then Charlie's curiosity gets the best of him; he lifts the lampshade-skirt, which he himself added, to peek at the lady-figurine's forbidden parts. In this action Chaplin endows an inanimate object with life; he magically raises the dead and converts the corpse into the most wayward of women; and he confers sex appeal on the sexless. There is magic in this metamorphosis, indeed.

After his next Essanay, *A Woman* (a more Sennettesque film built around Charlie masquerading in drag), Chaplin made *The Bank*, another step toward maturity. The plot is very close to that of *The New Janitor*: Charlie is an incompetent office worker who saves the pretty girl from danger and the company from robbers. But there are significant differences in this later film. First, the company is no longer a miscellaneous office, but a bank, that center of commerce and of class differentiations. And Chaplin does not keep those serious overtones a secret. The film begins with another brilliant bit that combines comic surprise and serious implication. Charlie strides into the bank, walks authoritatively toward the huge vault, impressively begins twirling the dials (checking his cuffs where he has written the combination), opens the heavy door, steps into the financial cavern, and returns with his mop and pail.

A second change from *The New Janitor* is that after Charlie has performed his feats of heroism he awakes from a dream to discover himself kissing his smelly mop (another Chaplin circle, from mop to mop), not Edna's lovely face. Edna has rejected him; his heroism is pure illusion. He still holds the flower that he intended to give to Edna but she rejected. As in *The Tramp*, Charlie fails to attain his desires; his only recourse is to dream.

Third, the flower metaphor plays its first full role in *The Bank*. For Chaplin, flowers become surrogates for the real human beauty he wants to possess; he can at least hold a flower, if not the lady for whom it is intended. In addition, flowers, like dreams, fade and wither. Earlier Essanays had toyed with the flower motif. As Turpin drags Charlie along in *A Night Out*, the drunken tramp casually picks a flower. Working on the farm in *The Tramp*, Charlie picks a flower for Edna. But the flower in *The Bank* is less casual, more central to the emotional texture of the whole film than in the earlier Essanays. Flowers would remain in Chaplin films until their ultimate ironic incarnation in *Monsieur Verdoux*, a man who carefully cultivates flowers and just as carefully murders women, who sends flowers to ladies so that he can subsequently marry and murder them.

Shanghaied, Chaplin's next film, is a slighter mixture of gags ashore and aboard ship. *A Night in the Show*, another slight comedy, is, however, a delightful recollection of Chaplin's years in the music hall. It is a film version of the Karno feature that led to Chaplin's movie career—*A Night in an English Music Hall*. Yet an additional delight of the film is that Charlie plays two roles in it—Mr. Pest (the fashionable theatergoer) and Mr. Rowdy (the troublemaker in the gallery)—a double role he would repeat in *The Idle Class* and *The Great Dictator*. And in *Limelight*, Chaplin would return more poignantly and nostalgically to this music-hall world.

Carmen (or *Chaplin's Burlesque on Carmen*) was his next Essanay release. Despite its greater length (padded to four reels by Essanay), the film is merely a parodic, mock-heroic, anti-romantic look backward at Sennett and Chaplin's *His New Job*. Chaplin plays Don José (here called Darn Hosiery) and looks ridiculous in his fancy dragoon costume. Symptomatic of the spirit of the film is a scene in a café where Charlie watches Escamillo eat dinner. Escamillo soaks up the gravy on his plate with his bread; he works so thoroughly that Charlie picks up the plate and uses it as a mirror. In another hilarious scene, Charlie murders a rival in a duel (with a soft, squishy sword, no less). Suddenly remorse and horror flash across Charlie's face. "What have I done?" asks Charlie with great pathos. Then he tenderly begins to stroke the slain opponent's corpse. His strokes turn into harder squeezes. Suddenly he is kneading the muscles, giving the corpse a massage. The bit is pure Chaplin in the smoothness of the metamorphosis from one kind of action (stroking) to another (massaging) with no perceptible gaps between them, and also in the way he creates a moment of pathos and then lets the air out of it with a joke.

The ending of the film is another superb example of the same technique. Carmen rejects Charlie. His eyes (in a very effective close-up) fill with tears. With the greatest sorrow he draws his knife and stabs her. She dies slowly; he kisses her tenderly. He then stabs himself and dies, slowly. The pathos and seriousness of the death scene are almost believable (more believable than the serious De Mille version of the same film, I would imagine). Escamillo enters, sees them, and recoils with horror. Charlie's foot then rises and boots Escamillo in the face. Snap goes the pathos.

Police, the last of the Essanays, is perhaps the best. It certainly points the way most clearly toward later Chaplin films. The new ingredient of *Police* is a bitter, almost misanthropic irony; it is the first in a line of films that includes *Easy Street, Sunnyside, The Pilgrim, Modern Times,* and *Monsieur Verdoux.* They might be called Chaplin's mordant strain, and the wonder is that he can make such basically cynical, unpleasant material into something so funny and exciting. *Police* is built around the moralistic line, "Let me help you go straight." By the end of the film, Charlie learns that whenever he hears these words, he'd better watch out. The representatives of "straightness" in the film are hypocrites or idiots. Better to be bent like Charlie.

At the film's opening Charlie is a criminal, just emerging from prison. A preacher-looking man with a Bible comes up and urges him to go straight. He urges him so well that Charlie cries, so well that Charlie doesn't feel the preacher stealing his release money, so well that Charlie refuses to pick a very tempting, easy-to-steal watch from a drunk man's pocket. Charlie leaves the watch alone only to discover that the preacher has himself stolen it as well as his own money. Charlie later gives this hypocrite a boot in the pants.

Rejecting the urge to go straight, Charlie joins forces with another crook, and they set about trying to rob Edna's house. Edna calls the cops, but those pillars of "straightness" are totally untouched by her need. They take their sweet, bureaucratic time answering her call for distress. When Edna appeals to Charlie, however, he, a crook, responds compassionately to her entreaties. He helps her against his own colleague (just as he did in *The Tramp*). Charlie is more responsive to human need than the men of law who have been created and hired to serve that need.

In this film Chaplin treats police specifically for the first time. Like those of the thieving preacher in the first sequence of the film, the actions of the police contradict the uniforms they wear. Consistently in the later Chaplin films these men of law are very good at terrifying the little tramp with their awesome authority and totally incompetent at helping people who really need help. They pick on the tramp because he is an easy target. When the tramp himself needs help (in *A Dog's Life,* in *The Kid*), they are useless.

At the end of the film, Edna returns Charlie's kindness by lying for him to the police—after they finally arrive. She claims that Charlie is her husband. But she makes the fateful plea to Charlie—"Let me help you go straight." Charlie, no romantic stars in his eyes at this point, leaves the house and returns to the open road. In the final shot of the film, Charlie is walking away from the camera down the road again. But rather than walking with sadness or remorse, as at the end of *The Tramp*, he walks spiritedly and stretches his arms upward in the free air. Better free on the road than "straight." Then a cop begins to pursue him; Charlie must pick up the pace and take to his heels. The free road has its drawbacks, too.* This inevitable and irreconcilable conflict between freedom and rootlessness would become the primary source of ambivalence in the mature Chaplin films.

Mutual Maturity (1916-17)

Chaplin's period with Mutual was more a summing up than a moving forward. Chaplin primarily manipulated gags, situations, and events that he had used earlier—improved by his increased knowledge of timing and pacing, his greater awareness of how far and how long a gag could be stretched, his wiser sureness of who his tramp figure was and what kinds of business he ought to handle, his tighter and smoother control of cinematic technique, and his stronger and more unified film structures. Many of the old motifs return in the Mutuals: accomplishing a heroic task (by unheroic means)—*The Floorwalker, The Fireman, The Pawnshop;* fighting with a co-worker—*The Rink, The Pawnshop;* exposing a crooked employee for stealing from his own business—*The Floorwalker, The Fireman;* posing as a man of wealth and position—*The Rink, The Count;* helping Edna in distress—*The Fireman, The Vagabond, The Immigrant, The Adventurer;* causing chaos in a movie studio—*Behind the Screen;* having troubles with the law—*The Floorwalker, The Adventurer;* performing his drunken specialty act—*One A.M., The Cure.* As always Chaplin makes these familiar situations and gags seem fresh by creating a unique new context for them.

The outstanding element of the Mutuals is the essential Chaplin skill that he had begun to master in the Keystones and here brings to complete perfection—the delineation of character, emotion, and thought through Charlie's relation to tangible, physical objects. In the typical Chaplin manner, the objects he uses are rather small things that can be grasped,

* The editing of *Police* (as with *Carmen*) was tampered with after Chaplin left Essanay. There are several versions of its continuity. The one I have accepted seems most in keeping with the terms, ideas, and unity of the piece.

twisted, thrown, lifted, or folded. Chaplin's manipulatory skills reach their highest expression in two Mutuals—*The Pawnshop* and *One A.M.*—which are perhaps the two best films with and about objects ever made.

The Pawnshop features such lively inanimate things as a ladder, which Charlie uses for trapping his rival and later straddles in a dangerous balancing act; doughnuts that are so hard they break plates; cups and saucers which Charlie runs through a washing-machine wringer; and pawnshop globes which Charlie uses as balls and weapons. But the ultimate object in *The Pawnshop* is a little alarm clock that a man brings in to pawn. Charlie examines it as if it were a medical patient; a priceless jewel; a can of tuna; a plank of wood; a tooth with a cavity.

One A.M., after a short introductory scene with a taxi driver, contains no other human except Charlie—and a house full of objects. Although these objects are not human, they do become living beings. Charlie plays with and against a goldfish bowl, a circular table, a bottle of seltzer, a cigarette, matches, a tiger rug, a flight of stairs, a coat rack, a strip of carpet, a huge grandfather clock. *One A.M.* climaxes with a five-minute duel between Charlie and a Murphy bed; the bed is one of the few inanimate objects in film history that could have been nominated as best supporting actor.

There are plenty of new gags and motifs that Chaplin sprinkles through the Mutuals, many of which would become standard pieces in his gag repertoire. In *The Floorwalker*, he uses his first modern machine, an escalator, which causes him severe troubles every time he tries to ride it. He inevitably tries to run up the down escalator and vice versa. *Modern Times* would be his ultimate extension of this escalator, full of machines that theoretically should serve man, but instead seem to operate according to their own laws, enslaving man rather than freeing him. In *The Rink*, Chaplin first appears on roller skates—an act he would duplicate in *Modern Times*. Chaplin on skates was like the Greek tragedian in buskins; the skates ennobled him, increased his stature, magnified his grace. In *The Fireman*, Charlie has learned how to evoke sympathy from a girl after he has done her the kindness of saving her life. When Edna's interest in him begins to fade, he does a mock swoon and feigns painful injury. In both *The Pawnshop* and *The Adventurer*, he similarly feigns injury to evoke Edna's softer instincts.

Several of the Mutuals also introduce realistic, physically unpleasant details that would seem to have no place in broad comedy. In *The Vagabond*, Charlie searches through Edna's hair and finds a flea. In *The Cure*, he clumsily spills a cup of water and then embarrassedly pretends that the puddle is the product of a toy dog standing nearby. In *Easy Street*, a baby's formula spills out of its bottle on Charlie's pants; Charlie, however, fears that another kind of liquid has been visited upon him. Such reminders of man's physical, animal existence, which many critics found offensive, would return later in the fake-bottomed chair that Charlie constructs for the wetting baby in *The Kid*, the gurgling-stomach scene in *Modern Times*, and the baby who wets Hynkel's hand in *The Great Dictator*.

In the Mutuals, Chaplin also perfected his formula for integrating sentimental material and comedy. The method derived from the *Burlesque on Carmen*; Chaplin merely applied that method to material that was not inherently silly. He took a moment of pathos, let it be felt, and then suddenly popped the emotional balloon with a stinging, surprising joke. In *The Pawnshop*, his boss fires him for incompetence and impertinence. Charlie begs for his job. He sorrowfully pantomimes his hunger, then each of his starving children. His boss finally relents. Charlie joyfully jumps on his boss and briefly rides him like a pony—immediately after which he cuffs his rival with a belt in the face. The ride and the belt undercut the sorrowful mime.

Later in *The Pawnshop*, a broke, broken, down-and-out old actor comes into the shop and tells Charlie his tale of woe. Tears well up in Charlie's eyes. He begins to sob. He sobs so hard that he spits the crumbs of Edna's doughnut all over the counter. Then, touched to the quick, he gives the old guy a ten-dollar bill. The "bum" adds the bill to a huge wad of others in his pocket and gives Charlie five dollars in change. Bam!

In *The Immigrant*, Charlie sits at a restaurant table gazing rapturously into Edna's face. His gaze is so intent that to maintain it he puts his chin in his hand and unthinkingly dunks his elbow in a bowl of beans. The beans squelch the rapture.

The Vagabond, one of the early Mutuals, is a significant departure from the earlier films in that Chaplin not only integrates pathos but builds the plot so that it culminates in pathos—as *The Kid* and *City Lights* would do later. Chaplin plays a street musician (the begging street musicians return in *Limelight*) who takes to the country and saves a gypsy girl (Edna) from a monster of a father. Edna and Charlie band together to live as tramp-gypsies. But a rich city painter sees Edna and, attracted to her beauty, paints her picture. She too is smitten with his respectable good looks. When a wealthy patroness of the arts sees this painting and recognizes her long-lost daughter (stolen away by gypsies—there's that motif again), she goes with the painter to retrieve her girl in an automobile. After a sad farewell to Charlie, Edna climbs into the posh car; she is lured by the painter's attractive face and the implied riches of her life to come. But as she sits in the big car, she realizes that it is Charlie she really loves and that life with him is really important. She orders the car to return to the tramp, and the film ends with a happy reunion.

During the scene in which Edna leaves him and until she returns, Charlie's face is a poignant mask of sorrow. He tries to kick up his heels unconcernedly as he did at the end of *The Tramp*, but the energy just won't come. His resiliency has actually worn thin and almost out. He slumps slowly against the gypsy caravan where they had been so happy together. Chaplin does not interrupt this sadness with a joke. It remains until Edna returns.

The Vagabond also shows a similarity to some of Chaplin's later works in his attempts to integrate plotty, melodramatic material with human comedy—not always with believable results here or elsewhere. The recognition scene in *The Vagabond* is a standard device of melodrama and sentimental comedy. It is so unprepared for in this little two-reeler that the film's ending seems terribly rushed and contrived. There are too much plot and too many twists in too little time. Chaplin had not yet worked out a film structure to allow and prepare for the kind of melodrama that would be much more carefully developed in *The Kid* and *A Woman of Paris*.

The Vagabond is one of the weakest of the Mutuals structurally. Many of the Mutuals build a solider structure by exploring a social or financial institution, culminating when Charlie ironically saves the institution from disaster (*The Floorwalker, The Fireman, The Pawnshop, Behind the Screen*). The structure of *One A.M.*, despite the appearance that Charlie merely "goofs" with objects, is based on Charlie's attempts to enter his house, get upstairs, and go to bed. *The Cure* follows the progression (or regression) of an alcoholic sanitarium to drunken frenzy. The three strongest films of the Mutual group structurally—*The Immigrant, The Adventurer,* and *Easy Street*—are probably the best of the 12 films.

The Immigrant comically examines the problems of coming to this country from Europe. The first section chronicles problems on the boat—cardsharps, thieves, bad food, seasickness—all handled hilariously. The second section chronicles problems once the immigrant arrives—no job, no money, no dinner, no family life. Again, serious meaning is implicit in a hilarious dining sequence in which Charlie desperately searches for a coin to pay for his and Edna's dinner. He has seen how the huge waiter (Eric Campbell) mercilessly beats those customers who are only a dime short.

Within the film's structure, there are marvelously observant details. For example, when the immigrants first see the Statue of Liberty, a title-card announces, "The land of liberty." Then uniformed immigration officials rope all the foreigners together like cattle, checking the little name and number tags that have been pinned on them. People have been reduced to inanimate quantities; liberty has been reduced to bondage.

Two other ironic touches in *The Immigrant* comment upon etiquette. In the first, Charlie does not know that he is expected to remove his hat in a restaurant, and the waiter keeps batting it off his head. It is highly ironic that this brutish, sadistic waiter should be concerned with such social niceties. In the second, Charlie and a rich benefactor stage an

obligatory fight over who is going to pay the check—even though Charlie
hasn't a dime to his name. A final irony of the film is the device that saves
Charlie and Edna from the waiter's thrashing. A wealthy painter (Henry
Bergman) wants to use Charlie and Edna as models—they are so "picturesque." What is picturesque to an aesthete is a life-and-death matter to
an immigrant.

The Adventurer is one of Chaplin's circular plots; it begins and ends
with Chaplin fleeing from the police. Between his two flights he wanders
briefly into the haut monde (parallel to The Tramp, with a rich, urban
house substituted for a farm). In The Tramp, however, the farmer and his
daughter appreciate Charlie's aid; in The Adventurer, the rich man (Eric
Campbell again) is ungrateful to Charlie for saving his life—so ungrateful,
in fact, that he personally betrays Charlie to the police.

One of the crucial elements of the Mutuals was obviously the presence
of Eric Campbell. He plays in every Mutual except, of course, One A.M.
If Edna stands on one allegorical side of Charlie—sweet, gentle, alluring,
loving, lovable—then Eric stands on the other—glowering, menacing,
spiteful, vicious, hating, hateful. Campbell is a physical foil to Chaplin
as well as a mental one—a tall, fat, powerful, mean bull. Campbell's type
is an outgrowth of a Sennett tradition, a Mack Swain or Fatty Arbuckle.
But Chaplin adds an important social and emotional dimension to this
physically "heavy" type. Campbell is almost always a member of a higher
class than Charlie; he is Charlie's employer, his foreman, or a gentleman of wealth and leisure. Given his social position, he can get away with
illegal, immoral, and unkind acts, while Charlie inevitably is punished for
them. Eric Campbell is at the same time a comic physical foil and a clear
representative of hypocritical social and moral values. He stands for everything that hates Charlie and that Charlie hates (and tries to trick, kick, or
dodge) in return.*

The greatest of the Mutuals is Easy Street. Its combination of comic
business, intellectual irony, structural soundness, and social implication
was not equaled by any other in the group. Structurally the film is another
of Chaplin's circles. It begins with a scene in the Hope Mission; Charlie,
asleep on a stoop, awakens to the sound of angelic singing and enters the
mission. The film also ends in the mission, now called the "New Hope
Mission" because a former den of thieves has been reconverted into a much
glossier house of worship. Between the two mission sequences little Charlie
has gone out into the world of slums, poverty, and crime, routed the foes
of goodness, and then led them all to realize the joys of religious worship
that so uplifted and ennobled him.

* Campbell did not make any films with Chaplin after 1917. Just as he was preparing to make films on his own, he died in an automobile accident in December of
1917.

This sounds like a very strange Chaplin plot. Chaplin is not one to promote beatific ideals and moral uplift; the notion of him as social savior (wearing a police uniform, no less) is ludicrous. Such apparent departures from the Chaplin norm merely indicate that *Easy Street*, like *Police* before it, is delicately ironic. There is a tension between what the film says on the surface and what Chaplin would have us read into it. That tension is summarized by the name Chaplin gives to the mission—"Hope." The film is full of hope, unfortunately contradicted by social and human realities. The primary opposition that underlines every event and conflict in the film is between the way we would like the world to be and the way it is. And the result of Chaplin's hilarious contrast is the bitter, pessimistic position that the hope and the reality are permanently irreconcilable.

Even the film's title is ironic. Easy Street is a vile, inhuman, brutal slum. The police are powerless to protect the people from the bullies (Eric Campbell, of course); Charlie becomes a policeman because all the other cops have been maimed. After Charlie coyly, comically subdues the monster Eric by gassing him with a street (gas) lamp, everyone on the street stands in awe of him, the bully-beater. He struts about as they recoil in terror.

The film's conclusion is equally ironic. Edna has been kidnapped from her mission by the thugs; Charlie too has been trapped in their hideout. He mistakenly sits on a syringe full of dope, gets tremendously hopped up, and demolishes the foes of goodness in stoned frenzy. That dope should be a device to help a cop beat up a group of crooks is more than a touch ironic. That an enslaving opiate of the slums should be a tool for social utility is completely consistent with the caustic tone of the whole film. With such a detail Chaplin shows how he can turn the sordid into comedy (which he also did in *Sunnyside, The Gold Rush, Modern Times, The Great Dictator*, and *Monsieur Verdoux*), how unashamed he is to include unpleasant realistic details in his comedies (such as fleas and urine), and how acutely aware he is of genuine social problems such as drug addiction in the slums.

At the end of *Easy Street* all the residents march meekly and joyfully into the New Hope Mission (formerly the place where Charlie got his shot of dope) for the Sunday sermon. Even Eric Campbell smiles pleasantly and tips his new hat politely to his neighbors. This ending is very closely related to the ones in which Charlie awakes from a dream to discover that his heroism is an illusion. In *Easy Street*, the dreamer does not awake; he passes the dream off to us as reality, all the while letting us know that the solution is less believable than any dream. *Easy Street* solves the social problems it presents with a deliberate, Pollyannaish hoax; the implication is that fake solutions are the only kind to be found. The parallels between such a premise and that of Brecht (especially in *The*

Threepenny Opera and *The Good Woman of Setzuan*) are very striking, and as Chaplin's career matured he would continue to be very "Brechtian" (or, rather, Brecht would be very "Chaplinesque"). These parallels between Chaplin and Brecht continue throughout Chaplin's career, and they reveal Chaplin's mature style of irony as well as the human sources of Brecht's inspiration.

CHAPTER 7

Chaplin: First Nationals and Silent Features

─

THE groundwork for Chaplin's mature films had been laid in his years of one- and two-reelers. Many of the later films return to themes, locations, and situations that Chaplin first developed in short films; many of the gags are identical to earlier ones. And yet the wonder of these repetitions is that, as with the motifs that recur in the Mutuals, they seem fresh, completely integrated into and shaped by the context of the new material. When Charlie and the millionaire drunkenly cause chaos in a nightclub (*City Lights*), Chaplin repeats the situation, indeed many of the gags, from such films as *The Rounders* and *A Night Out*, both of which contain café sequences. But in the feature film, the gags are modified by the specific circumstances that have brought Charlie and his companion together. First, the partner is a millionaire—not just a drinking chum, like Fatty or Turpin. Second, the millionaire is treating the pauper, Charlie, to a special night of fun on the town that only millionaires can afford. Third, Charlie has just convinced the millionaire not to commit suicide. They are on the town rather than in the river. These three social and moral circumstances make their drunken business more than a series of funny café-drunk gags.

Similarly, Charlie gliding magnificently on roller skates in *Modern Times* mechanically repeats his elegant, graceful skating routines from *The Rink*. But in *Modern Times* Charlie does his skating in a department store, a place that exchanges goods for money; he has just gotten a night-watchman's job so that he and the Gamin (Paulette Goddard) can afford to eat; they have borrowed the skates from the toy department, thereby converting a commercial product into an expression of human joy and grace; and Charlie, despite his magnificent control on skates, is in great danger and does not know it: the protective railing has been removed from the edge of the floor; Charlie can easily skate over the edge to his death, yet he blithely skates on, blindfolded. This final circumstance lifts the sequence out of the mere physical exhilaration and hypnotic motion of the skating in *The Rink* and suggests a metaphor that uniquely applies to the tramp character Charlie has created. Even when Charlie seems to be in complete control, he is merely one step from disaster. Ironically, he loses his control only when he discovers his danger.

As a final example of an old bit in new clothes, there is the crushing opening scene of *Limelight*. Chaplin makes his appearance in the film drunk, as he made his appearance in many a film. He then executes some typical drunken business with a flight of steps and a key that won't slip into the lock. But the difference in *Limelight* is that Chaplin is not the youthful, elastic, jaunty Charlie. He is an old man; his hair is gray; his face is wrinkled; his shoulders are hunched; his "comic" movements seem pathetically feeble and broken. Further, we hear the sound of real traffic on the street as Chaplin does his "act." This is not an imaginary, balletic, comic-film world; this is a drunk in reality. The familiar funny business has turned sour from its context.

Further, our feelings about this opening drunk scene continue to affect our responses to the sequence that follows. Once Chaplin gets inside the house, he smells something bad. His first impulse is to sniff his cheap cigar and then to check the bottoms of his shoes for what he might have stepped in (that kind of Chaplin detail again). Then he snaps out of his drunken lethargy, pulls himself together, and races upstairs to burst open the door of a person trying to commit suicide. The conversion from drunkenness to alertness in the opening minutes of *Limelight* is a metaphor for the whole film.

First National (1918–22)

The eight films Chaplin made for First National form a group unified in theme, situation, and emphasis. Their first characteristic is Chaplin's firm consciousness (even self-consciousness) of Charlie's identity. It is no longer accident or intuition that makes Charlie a social outsider, a little guy who is extremely resilient and tough, an asocial clown who survives because of his brilliant instincts—for the good and beautiful as well as the dangerous. That Chaplin was conscious of this *persona* shows in the first of the First Nationals, *A Dog's Life*, in which Chaplin creates another living being—the mongrel, Scraps—whose personality, virtues, and problems exactly parallel Charlie's; and in the last of the First Nationals, *The Pilgrim*, in which Charlie chooses as the topic of his sermon the story of David and Goliath—for Charlie, like David, is a little guy who comes through. And it shows in the other First Nationals in Chaplin's choices of people to play with and against (for example, little Jackie Coogan in *The Kid* is another version of Charlie himself—small but tough, alternately sweet and strong) and in his choices of situations and problems for Charlie to face.

All of the First Nationals, with the exception of the first, put Charlie in a social situation where you would not expect to find him. In a sense, they all follow the lead of *Easy Street*. In what unlikely circumstances would you expect to find Charlie a cop? When there were no remaining legitimate cops and when being a cop was dangerous, worthless, and unprofitable. In the First Nationals, Charlie finds himself in seven unlikely situations: (1) as soldier (*Shoulder Arms*), for military regimentation and the martial life are not for the likes of pragmatic tramps who fight only when trouble finds them; (2) as embodiment of rural Americana (*Sunnyside*), for the city-dwelling tramp is no "Man with the Hoe"; (3) as family man (*A Day's Pleasure*), for where would an asocial tramp get a family? (4) as father (*The Kid*), for how can an unmarried free spirit acquire a son? (5) as rich socialite (*The Idle Class*), for where would Charlie get the money and social influence? (6) as working man (*Pay Day*), for Charlie wouldn't want and couldn't keep a steady job; (7) and finally—indeed ultimately—as preacher (*The Pilgrim*), for Charlie seems even less suited to a clergyman's habit than to a policeman's uniform. By dropping Charlie into each of these anomalous environments, Chaplin develops the contrast between the tramp, whose character and instincts are by now familiar, and the foreign surroundings. The films ironically juxtapose the expectations of each of these respectable social roles with the human, instinctive responses of the disrespectful, unrespectable tramp.

The dominant conflict of the First Nationals is between instinct and masquerade, nature and artifice, essence and form. If Charlie wears a series of unlikely guises, his solid instinct gives him his identity and helps him pull through every strange scrape. The first film of the group, *A Dog's Life*, is consistent with the other seven, for although Charlie wears no disguise in the film, it begins the study of the power of instinct. Charlie parallels his own existence to that of a dog, whose sense of survival—eating, shelter, self-defense, preservation of freedom—is entirely instinctual. Charlie's clever instincts also keep him alive in *Shoulder Arms* and even allow him to perform heroic acts. In the dream sequence of *The Kid*, Charlie wears a pair of angel's wings; but the wings don't feel natural. Charlie instinctively scratches these itchy additions.

In *The Pilgrim*, instinct predominates. When Charlie, an escaped criminal, buys a train ticket, he instinctively puts his hands on the bars of the wicket. After buying the ticket, he instinctively begins to crawl underneath the train until a porter tells him that his ticket entitles him to ride inside on a seat. Upon arriving in Devil's Gulch, he instinctively fears the sheriff, despite the lawman's warm greeting. When preaching his sermon, he instinctively feels himself, at appropriate moments, in a courtroom, a barroom, and a theater. After delivering his sermon, complete with an instinctively theatrical flourish of an ending, Charlie's instinct tells him it is time for his exit. Then when one of the young parishioners applauds, Charlie instinctively returns to the pulpit for his bow.

A *Dog's Life* (1918) begins with Charlie asleep (as in *Easy Street*, *Sunnyside*, and *City Lights*). The film then sets up a tension between the blissful state of sleep and the instinct that awakens Charlie. In *A Dog's Life*, that instinct is hunger; Charlie sniffs the aroma of a nearby frankfurter. But as he helps himself to a peddler's hot dog, a cop spies him and Charlie must postpone eating to dodge this figure of authority. Charlie eventually loses his morning meal in the clever, acrobatic process of losing the cop. Chaplin then cuts to a shot of a little mongrel, Scraps, who is also asleep. Scraps is also hungry. Scraps soon has trouble with the same cop. The opening sequence of the film securely establishes the parallels between Charlie and Scraps (her name implies both scrappiness and the necessity of surviving on the leavings of others); both mongrels, Charlie and Scraps, seem easy targets for the bigger breeds.

The opening section culminates in two parallel scenes, tied together by Chaplin's cross-cutting (seven years before Eisenstein's *Strike*). Charlie, trying desperately to get a job, is outshoved and outraced by bigger, faster rivals in the rush to the window where the jobs are handed out; by the time he gets there, all the jobs are gone. He can't even be "legitimate" when he wants to be. Similarly, Scraps, minding her own business, gets into a fight with a group of larger, meaner dogs which pick on her. Charlie rushes into the fray, scoops Scraps up, and the two of them remain comrades for the rest of the film.

Together Charlie and Scraps do a lot better than either did alone. As partners, they succeed in robbing the owner of a food stall by tricky and diversionary activities. Scraps soon discovers in Charlie's hovel a money-filled wallet previously buried by two crooks. Ironically, the awesome cop was unsuccessful at stopping the two thugs from mugging a rich drunk; he is successful only at stopping Charlie from eating a single frankfurter.

Charlie and Scraps return to one of their hangouts, a dance hall and café, where they suddenly receive decent treatment—now that they have money. But the two thugs are also there, and they recognize their missing wallet. The film climaxes in some very clever and comic struggles for that money-filled wallet. Charlie eventually wins the wallet and marries the equally unfortunate Edna, who had worked in the dance hall but was fired when she refused to do more than sing for its lewd customers. The prostitution of woman, an increasingly prominent Chaplin theme, is a metaphoric corollary of the film's frantic (and comic) struggle for money and survival. Edna is a third "mongrel," at the mercy of the big, rich, and tough.

After Charlie and Edna marry, they buy a farm. In the final sequence of the film, Edna does her kitchen chores, Scraps lies in the crib nursing a litter of pups (Scraps' sex has been rather uncertain up to this point), and Charlie, wearing overalls and a straw hat, works a-planting in the fields, sticking his finger in the soil. This ending is a bit too happy, too pat, too contrivedly sweet (like that of *Easy Street*). Charlie looks terribly out of his element in the fields. His finger does not look as if it belongs in that alien soil; he looks more like a reluctant swimmer testing the temperature of ice-cold water. Although the ending of A *Dog's Life* does not push the ironies and incongruities of its facile happiness, Chaplin does seem to be pointing the way toward *Sunnyside*, which begins with rural Pollyanna and then makes us choke on it.

Between Charlie's two dips into country life came *Shoulder Arms* (1918). In this film, considered one of Chaplin's best, he started with a subject that America took very seriously and turned it into comedy. *Shoulder Arms* did with World War I what *The Great Dictator* would do with World War II. With *Shoulder Arms* Chaplin seemed to assert fully and for the first time that anything human was laughable and anything laughable was human—a position that he never deserted even when the American people did.

In the first sequence of *Shoulder Arms*, Charlie plays a new recruit, trying to absorb the basic training that every inductee receives. But Charlie is utterly incapable of following the commands to march, turn, go forward, go back, shoulder arms, stand at attention, and all the rest, not simply because he is a dumb klutz (unlike, say, Abbott and Costello or Martin and Lewis later on), but because he is not the kind of being who can follow commands. He is incapable of living in a regimented, perfectly ordered, mechanical world. The soldier is asked to perform like a machine, and Charlie, the natural man, is the opposite of a machine. His failure at drilling recurs ten years later in *The Circus* when Charlie fails at the standard circus-clown acts but is brilliant at his own improvisations. Charlie is bad at all standard routines; he is adept only at accomplishing a task in his own personal, unexpected way.

This characteristic proves to be to his advantage in the later sections of

Shoulder Arms. In the trenches Charlie does quite well; he uses the enemy's bullets to open his wine bottle and light his cigarettes. He even performs a heroic mission by disguising himself as a tree—another transposition of man into object. He is so good at improvising that he caps his heroism by capturing the Kaiser personally. But in this film Charlie's success once again proves to be chimera. He awakens in training camp to discover that all his exploits have evaporated into the mist of dreams.

Shoulder Arms is remarkable in its range of emotions, from the broadest, most farcical parody to moments of genuine sadness and melancholy. The film contains a parody of the Sergeant York incident (Charlie captures 13 Germans; he claims he surrounded them) and a parody of the stereotypic vicious "Hun"—modeled specifically either on von Stroheim's characterizations or on reigning clichés. From such nonsense the film leaps to a scene in which Charlie receives no mail and must experience tender human companionship vicariously by reading (and reacting to) the letter of another soldier, over his shoulder.

Yet Chaplin does not linger on the pathos for long. Immediately after the poignant letter scene Charlie does indeed get a parcel from home. Unfortunately, it contains not a message of love but a hunk of Limburger cheese (one of the comic objects that appear again and again in silent films and seem since to have disappeared from the earth). The cheese smells so bad that Charlie must put on his gas mask to eat it (ironic transposition of military object into domestic tool). But then Charlie gives up and hurls the hunk of cheese over the trench; it clonks the German general, a three-foot dwarf, on the head. Charlie as soldier does better with butter than with guns.

Sunnyside (1919) plays on a single, more ironic, more bitter string than *Shoulder Arms*. But what it loses in diversity it gains in concentrated irony and unified point of view. Although the film is generally considered one of Chaplin's minor works, it is one of the most subtle and biting of his films. Its title, like that of *Easy Street*, is ironic; *Sunnyside* is not so sunny. In his investigation of the rural American ideal, Chaplin indicts the pastoral society for its hypocrisy, its money grubbing, its inhumanity, its worship of forms rather than essences. The film opens with a shot of a cross on a rural church; *Sunnyside*'s next image is of the inevitable wall sampler reading "Love Thy Neighbor." It is Sunday, the day of rest, and so Charlie is asleep. His boss, however, the owner of a rural hotel, tells Charlie to get up and work. Only bosses get to enjoy the day of rest. And there is little love in his heart for his unfortunate slave. Later in the day the boss goes to church while Chaplin must do the chores and herd the cattle. The cross and the sampler are mere show; the actions of men do not reflect the words and symbols. The boss spends most of his time booting Charlie in the seat of the pants. This film transforms the slapstick boot into a symbol of human callousness and insensitivity.

Equally stinging are Chaplin's selections for residents of this pastoral happyland. In addition to his nasty boss, the rural ideal is represented by a fat goon, a midget, and a bearded horse doctor who overcharges his human patients. In addition, there is Edna's brother, a smiling, freckled, Tom Sawyerish lad whose smile is so permanent, whose face is so unchanging that he appears to be an idiot.

A key insight into the Chaplin method comes in the scene in which Edna does her shopping at Sunnyside's general store. Charlie must work as store clerk as well as hotel janitor, cowherd, cook, and every other job that needs doing so the genuine country residents can enjoy the Sabbath. When Edna arrives at the country store, she cannot remember what she has come to purchase. Charlie starts showing her pieces of merchandise to spur her memory. He eventually shows her a hunk of cheese, which she smells. Then Edna immediately remembers what she wants—a pair of socks. The mental process in this comic bit is truly marvelous. It goes, roughly: Cheese . . . smells bad . . . What else smells bad? . . . Socks. The scene implies a whole thought process without ever making the process specific. It also comments on country cleanliness. And in this country world, isn't "Cleanliness next to Godliness"?

Sunnyside also contains two dream sequences. The dreams that crept into Chaplin's work as early as *The Bank* become quite prominent in the First Nationals. Chaplin's first dream is an idyllically happy one. Chasing some cows that have wandered away from him, he falls off a bridge and clonks his head. Suddenly, little nymphs appear beside him, dancing in their diaphanous gowns. Charlie twirls his hair into horns and dances along with them, a devilish Pan enjoying an afternoon of fluting and flirting. But Charlie as Pan keeps tripping and falling on cactus; the painful thorns prick his dream ballet. The cactus is the painful reality behind the pretty dream—just as the whole film depicts the reality beneath the sunny rural cliché. The ultimate cactus is the reawakening as his boss and the other country goons pull his hair and lift him back to reality.

Sunnyside's second dream is a sad one. Charlie believes that Edna has fallen for the handsome city slicker who suffered an auto accident in their town. He has observed the slicker's fancy spats, his cane with a cigarette lighter in the handle, the hankie that he wears in his sleeve. So Charlie goes to visit Edna, trying to copy the city boy's style. He puts a pair of bulky wool socks over his oversized tramp shoes, to look like spats—and one of the socks unravels. He installs a candle in the head of his cane to light his gnarled cigarette. He stuffs a hankie up his sleeve, only to see his cuff fall out. After his unsuccessful attempt at being dapper, Edna, his country girl, returns his ring. Charlie sadly walks off down the road to offer his dejected body to a speeding car. As he prepares himself to feel the crash from the rear, the boss boots him from behind to wake him up. Once again, this time luckily, Charlie has been booted back to reality. But, in the course of the film, Chaplin has booted the rural idyll itself in the pants, particularly in the breach between what it supposedly believes and what it actually does.

In *The Kid* (1921), Chaplin returns to less ironic, more sentimental material. At the center of the film is the relationship between Charlie and Jackie Coogan, a little child who, like Scraps in *A Dog's Life*, is a smaller, surrogate Charlie. Although critics admire the love and tenderness in Charlie's relationship to his adopted kid, they also find grave faults with the film's melodramatic treatment of the kid's unwed mother as well as the ironic dream in which Charlie's slum turns into a pearly-white heaven. But although the Jackie-Charlie relationship is the emotional center of the film, it is not its subject. To dismiss the other sections of the film as irrelevant is to miss the intended unity. Like *Sunnyside*, *The Kid* contrasts social and moral theory with human practice.

The subject of *The Kid* is familial and paternal love. It is a subject that Chaplin, himself deprived of this love, obviously felt deeply about. The film begins with the physical mother and father because Chaplin wants to contrast official definitions of "legitimate" parenthood with more genuine, human ones. According to society, the mother and father must be married—hence the opening section showing Edna rejected by society as an unwed mother, and witnessing a wedding of two legitimate parents-to-be. Ironically, this wedding unites a pretty young woman with a rich old goat. The social ceremony defines as legitimate that which is humanly illegitimate and immoral. The mother feels so illegitimate, so guilty that she disposes of the child—though she loves him—and even contemplates suicide. Ironically, she leaves the infant in a posh automobile (she wants to give it a "good home"), which is then stolen. The two crooks in flight deposit the infant in a heap of rubbish. This metaphoric equation of child and garbage is no accident. Society's definition of the infant as "illegitimate" does not give it much hope for a richer future.

Ironically, the kid finds a better home from its trip to the garbage heap than from its ride in an automobile. For into the rubbish-filled alley strolls Charlie, another human being who feels at home with rubbish; garbage and debris fall on the tramp from every side. He selects a scrawny cigarette butt from a sardine tin, carefully picking over the lot with a glove so full of holes that it is more hole than glove. Charlie obviously is not society's idea of a respectable, legitimate father for a child or, for that matter, a respectable, legitimate anything. Charlie spies the infant. Though he feels compassion for it, his first response to the baby is not a sentimental one. Charlie's first reaction is to give the kid away; that is his pragmatic instinct. It is only after his attempts to get rid of the bundle fail—he tries to deposit it in a carriage with another baby and thinks of leaving it in a storm drain—that Charlie accepts the responsibility. He takes the baby back to his ramshackle room and contrives some implements for him. Baby's bottle is a coffee pot with a long spout; his cradle is a chair with a hole cut in it and a pot underneath to catch whatever might drip. Chaplin's familiar "transposition of objects" now serves unique and concrete purposes.

"Five years later." Jackie and Charlie live in a happy, healthy, human home—despite social definitions. They eat well; Charlie even makes sure that Jackie's ears are clean and that he says his prayers. They go out to work together; Jackie breaks a window with a rock, and Charlie, a glazier, just happens to be walking by to fix it for a fee. This view of legitimate business—that destruction and deceit produce a healthy economy—also underlies the snow-shoveling scene in *The Gold Rush*. When Jackie gets into fights, Charlie helps him out. But Jackie, it turns out, needs little help; his wiry toughness (like Charlie's) helps him beat bigger bullies. The strategy of this whole middle section of the film is to develop the meaning of the word "love." Whatever else fatherhood might mean, Chaplin defines fatherhood as love,* and whatever else their home might lack, love it has in great plenty.†

But the definitions and assumptions of respectable society catch up with Charlie and Jackie. A doctor, tending Jackie when he is ill, learns that Charlie is not Jackie's real father. The doctor decides that Jackie needs a more "legitimate" home—the County Orphan Asylum (another irony springing from Chaplin's own life). Charlie and Jackie try to fight off the cop and orphan attendant who come to fetch Jackie (again the cop is on the side of the legitimate against the right), but the odds are against them. Charlie does not give up; he keeps fighting. As Jackie is carted off in a truck, like an animal on its way to the slaughterhouse, Charlie chases the truck, snatches Jackie out of it, and the two are together again.

They hide from the forces of society in a cheap flophouse. Charlie sneaks Jackie in but must pay an extra dime for him to sleep there (another necessity that requires money). Meanwhile Edna, who has become a famous actress as well as a charitable social worker, has discovered that Jackie is her own child and wants him back. The money-hungry owner of the flophouse (unfortunately Chaplin surrenders to literary cliché— and depicts him as an obvious Dickensian Jew) sees the newspaper offer of a reward and realizes that Jackie is a means to money. For this man, money perverts any kind of human relationship. He sees a human being as a commercial product. As he reads the ad, Chaplin adds a subtle, ironic detail: A fly unmistakably crawls across the newsprint,‡ metaphoric of the

---

* There is a further biographical influence operating in *The Kid*, for in 1919 Chaplin's first child, named "the little mouse," died after living only three days.

† Brecht's *Caucasian Chalk Circle* might have its origins in *The Kid*, for it is a (later) treatment of the same theme.

‡ This fly exists in only one of the three prints of the film I have seen. My guess is that the fly was Chaplin's original idea but that subsequent retitling omitted it.

scavenging reader's flicker of greed. Another ironic detail is the sign that hangs in the flophouse, distantly observable in the rearground of the frame: "Not responsible for valuables stolen." The flophouse owner steals Charlie's most valuable "valuable" and takes him to the police, and Charlie wakes up the next morning alone.

Charlie, after wandering the streets, returns to the stoop where the two had previously sat together. As in *The Vagabond*, the lonely Charlie evokes a touching recollection of a past relationship by sitting alone where he and his love had previously sat together.

Charlie falls asleep. Suddenly, the grimy slum dissolves into pure whiteness. The houses are immaculately clean and white. Flowers deck the walls and alleyways. All the characters—Charlie, Jackie, the cop, the bully —have been reassembled, and all can fly. In a heavenly dream, men have become angels with wings and harps. Whereas *Easy Street* ended with heaven on earth passed off as reality, *The Kid* deliberately makes this absurdity an obvious dream. But as in the *Sunnyside* dream, there are cacti in this dreamland. Little devils creep in through the pearly gates. Combining medieval allegory and Méliès tricks, they symbolize sin and all the baser human emotions—greed, lust, jealousy, ambition.

Dissension enters heaven; Charlie gets into a fight and the angels' feathers fly. The result of this comic pantomime-ballet version of *Paradise Lost* is that the angel cop shoots Charlie "dead." He lies motionless on his doorstep. The contrast between idealistic wish and earthly reality is complete. For every bit of angel in man there is also a bit of devil. That is the reality that wrecks all utopias. If God could not keep Satan out of heaven, how can man do better? Earlier in the film Chaplin comically demonstrates the same point when the social worker, Edna, urges Charlie and the bully not to fight but to turn the other cheek. Every time the bully turns his cheek, Charlie bangs him in the head with a brick. Turning the other cheek would make great sense—if life weren't life.

As Charlie lies dead on the doorstoop, he is shaken awake by the real cop—as in *Sunnyside*, a brilliant use of dissolve with perfect matching. And as in *Sunnyside*, the return to reality from dreamland is physically painful—the result of a push, a pull, or a kick. The cop motions Charlie to get into a car; Charlie, his spirit broken, expecting to be taken to jail for some unknown crime that he undoubtedly must have committed, walks into the car without argument. But the car stops at a large house where Jackie and Edna greet Charlie with an embrace. They usher him into the house as the door closes.

This ending is deliberately unspecific. It is interesting and ironic that the cop, who has persecuted Charlie throughout the film, now becomes his deliverer; presumably the cop now knows from Edna and Jackie that Charlie has been a "legitimate" father. This conversion of a cop recurs in *The Pilgrim*.

But are we to believe that Charlie actually marries Edna and that they live happily ever after as Jackie's parents? This implication would indeed be the logical outgrowth of the film's plot and moral system— for Charlie has certainly earned all the rewards that Edna can shower upon him. But would Edna really marry a Charlie? And would Charlie ever be able to marry anyone and live a conventional life? The ending is deliberately vague precisely because of such domestic questions. Only in *Modern Times* does Chaplin face them fully. At the end of *The Kid* Chaplin has painted himself into a corner. The logical outcome for the Charlie character would be for him to bid a sad farewell to both Jackie and Edna, then set off down the road again. But emotionally Chaplin cannot bear to separate Charlie and little Jackie. And so Chaplin gets out of the corner by doing a disappearing act and leaving the resolution as blurry as possible.

But *The Pilgrim* (1922), the final film in the First National group, does not ignore its intentional ambivalence. In the film's contrast of morality's surfaces with its essence, the official, societal definitions of goodness and law with Charlie's human, personal, intuitive definitions, Chaplin concludes that questions are easier than answers. Charlie plays an escaped criminal who has disguised himself as a clergyman. The film's comedy centers around the contrast between his criminal's instincts and his minister's habit. Charlie as minister cannot avoid comporting himself instinctively as a tramp-criminal-drifter-guttersnipe.

But Charlie reveals another kind of instinct in the film. Although he is a lawbreaker, he again allies himself with Edna and protects her mortgage money from another crook who tries to rob her. Edna and her family (named Brown—we are back in the rural idyll) have taken Charlie in, fed and sheltered him, thinking, of course, that he is the town's new minister. Charlie is no ingrate. He repays kindness with kindness (as he did in *The Tramp* eight years earlier). He retrieves the Browns' stolen money from his own former cellmate and thereby reveals a higher sense of law than that institutionalized in the form of courtrooms, prisons, and sheriffs.

Even the town's sheriff acknowledges this higher law. He has discovered that Charlie is an escaped convict, and therefore he is obligated to send him back to prison. But he also realizes that Charlie has performed a virtuous, unselfish act by retrieving Edna's money. So the sheriff, under the guise of taking Charlie back to prison, escorts him to the international border between Mexico and the United States. Charlie is not aware of the opportunity he has been unexpectedly given; feeling himself morally responsible to the sheriff of Devil's Gulch, he does not run away. The sheriff, therefore, orders Charlie to run across the border and pick him some flowers. Charlie still does not catch on. He is not instinctively prepared for a sheriff's kindness. Charlie picks the flowers and returns across the border to hand them to the sheriff. Even the sheriff feels the formal prescriptions of law; he cannot just let Charlie go but must pretend that Charlie is legally inaccessible on the other side of the border. So the sheriff boots Charlie across the border (as in *Sunnyside*, a kick in the pants can be a charitable act) and quickly rides off.

Suddenly Charlie realizes he has been given his freedom. And now comes the remarkable touch with which the picture (and the whole First National series) ends. Charlie, realizing he is a free man in Mexico, stretches his arms upward, miming a paean to freedom. But several desperadoes emerge from the sagebrush and start shooting at each other, with Charlie caught between them. Freedom is fine, but lawlessness has its drawbacks. And so Charlie scuttles back toward the United States. Unable to make a decision, he wanders off across the plains, his back to the camera again, straddling the border between the United States and Mexico, one foot on either side. To the left of him lie the dangers of law (prisons, sheriffs); to the right lie the dangers of anarchy (murder, a jungle world of animals struggling to survive). Neither side holds much promise for the tramp; he cannot make a sensible choice.

With this ending Chaplin shows himself the supreme ironist and humanist. This straddling metaphor is at the heart of Chaplin's view of the relationship of man and society. For Chaplin, law and civilization are undeniably necessary—given those ineradicable devils in man. However, just because they are necessary doesn't mean he must worship and idealize them. Society is an unfortunate human necessity. This attitude was a rather common one in Chaplin's time. Since World War II our own feelings about society have become so insecure and so shaky that our bureaucracy and Establishment must picture society to us as a fortunate necessity. The difference between a fortunate and unfortunate necessity is the difference between Chaplin's human, ironic, perceptive humor and the euphemisms of congressmen and presidents. By the end of the First National period, Chaplin's sense of human morality and social necessity was quite firm.

Three Silent Features (1923–28)

Although Chaplin helped to found the United Artists Corporation in 1919, his slowness in fulfilling the First National commitment postponed his first United Artists contribution until 1923—a delay that did not help the new company's financial health. For his first United Artists film Chaplin decided on a daring departure—a drama rather than a comedy, a film in which Charlie would not be the focal character and in which Chaplin would only appear briefly. The result, *A Woman of Paris*, was a gift to Edna Purviance—a starring role for her as a mature woman, and her last major performance in a Chaplin film. The film exerted tremendous influence—particularly on Lubitsch—demonstrating how to tell a story with subtlety, understatement, and implication rather than overstated acting and overexplanatory titles.* Yet today *A Woman of Paris* seems more "interesting" than effective. *How* Chaplin went about shaping the effects of the film is still exciting and revealing. But *what* he set about doing in the film now seems less significant than what he did in *The Kid, The Pilgrim*, or any other of the mature films with Charlie as central figure.

Beneath all the subtlety of Chaplin's technique, *A Woman of Paris* is still merely a melodrama, a basically *Camille*-ish piece of tripe about kept women, the boy back home in the country, the conflict between purity and sin, all ending in a melodramatic death and moralistic conversion. Chaplin tries hard (and with great success) not to moralize and not to melodramatize. He does not expound on the evils of Marie's sinful Paris pleasures. He makes the characters as complex as he can—given the one-dimensional demands of the plot. He keeps the climactic suicide offscreen, deliberately downplaying its operatic effects. And yet he cannot wriggle out of the cliché at the film's foundation. The most interesting characters in the film are the sensual Gentleman of Paris (Adolphe Menjou) and a masseuse who has no name. The Woman of Paris herself, her suicidal lover, his sympathetic mother, all seem as though stuck to the pages of some book. The film is so full of observant touches that the banality of the whole almost disappears. (The same can be said about many of Lubitsch's films.) But only almost.

The plot concerns a couple, Marie and Jean, who live in a provincial town. Very much in love but forbidden to marry by Jean's father, they plan to elope to Paris. As Marie waits for Jean at the train station, his father dies from a heart attack. When Jean does not come to the station (and their telephone conversation is disconnected), Marie goes to Paris alone. One year later she is living in luxury—elegant clothes, fancy apartment, gourmet restaurants—as the mistress of Pierre Revel (Menjou). Tension stems from Pierre's impending marriage, which, he assures Marie, will change nothing. Further tension develops when Jean and Marie meet each other again and renew their love. Jean wants to marry her, against his mother's wishes. Marie also fears living in sin—for Pierre will allow the marriage but wants to continue the affair.

Jean becomes crazed, takes a pistol, and follows Marie and Pierre to their posh eating place (ironically named Sagouin's—meaning Tramp's or Slut's). After a polite chat among the three members of the triangle, Jean,

---

* An example of such overstatement in a film combining comedy, melodrama, and sexual innuendo would be any one of De Mille's so-called comedies—for example, *Why Change Your Wife?*

enraged at Pierre's power over Marie, excuses himself, walks out to the restaurant's foyer, and shoots himself. Jean's mother intends to murder Marie
in revenge, but when she sees that Marie too is unhappy and ashamed, the
two women unite. They return to the provinces, where they open a country
home for orphans. In the final scene, Pierre and a Parisian friend drive their
car on a country road. The friend asks, "Whatever happened to Marie St.
Clair?" At that moment, their auto zooms past Marie riding on a haywagon,
listening to an accordion. And the film ends.*

The moral contrasts of the film are clear: country simplicity as opposed to city sophistication, simple purity as opposed to surface luxuries,
sincere human feelings as opposed to deceit and lust. The final contrast in
the American version of the film sums it up perfectly (too perfectly, in
fact): a chauffeur-driven automobile as opposed to a horse-drawn wagon.
These oppositions are certainly consistent with Chaplin's moral system
in other films (for example, the idyllic country home in *Monsieur Verdoux*). But in *Woman of Paris*, lacking Charlie's complexly human, simultaneously funny and serious reactions that add flesh to moral cliché,
the moral system seems too pat, too familiar, too similar to every screen
and stage treatment of the same story since *The Lady of the Camellias*.

Technically, cinematically, psychologically, the film is magical Chaplin.
Its method would one day be consecrated as "Lubitsch touches." The
film provides a series of brilliant examples of how to solve certain dramatic problems and how to communicate both internal emotions and
external facts in cinematic, "plastic" (as Pudovkin would call it) terms.
To communicate Jean's discovery of his father's death, we see only the
huge back of the father's easy chair and the pipe that has fallen to the
floor beside the chair. To communicate Marie's wavering thoughts before
making a decision in the train station, Chaplin keeps the camera on Edna
Purviance's face as the streaks of light from the train cast their rhythmic
shadows on her face and the wall behind her. To communicate the class
question in the film, Chaplin shows a headwaiter groveling before his
rich customers but snapping at his underlings.

To communicate Pierre's relationship to Marie, Chaplin brilliantly
omits the year in which the relationship began and the arrangement became formalized, just as he omits the five formative years in *The Kid*;
he simply has Pierre walk familiarly into Edna's apartment, open the
drawer of her bureau, take one of his own handkerchiefs out of it, and
then arrange it in his breast pocket. To communicate the wild "Bohemian" life at a party in the artists' quarter, Chaplin depicts the striptease
dance of a girl totally covered in gauze bandages. Chaplin keeps the
camera on the faces of the audience and on the man who unwinds the

---

* Herman G. Weinberg points out (in *The Lubitsch Touch*, p. 53) that in the
European version of the film Marie does not move to the country but remains a
"Woman of Paris."

bandages, not on the girl's body as more and more of it is unbandaged. To communicate Jean's discovery that Marie has a lover, Chaplin shows Jean sitting in Marie's apartment and observing a man's collar that has fallen out of a drawer. To communicate Jean's poverty, Chaplin shows him serving Marie tea and handing her a napkin with a hole in it.

In addition to these individual touches, several whole scenes of *A Woman of Paris* are remarkable. Marie discovers that Pierre plans to marry when her girlfriends (and the "friends" in this film are a collection of vicious cats) just happen to show her a magazine with the wedding announcement and pictures in it. Marie looks at the magazine and then shoves it aside, laughing off the news. The friends go on chatting; Marie appears totally unaffected. Then after this cheery chatter, the friends leave and Marie remains alone. She hungrily picks up the magazine and devours the story in detail. This contrast between a person's pose in public and his genuine feelings when alone goes back to the first film that Chaplin directed for Keystone with the marital argument in the hotel room.

When Marie tells Pierre that Jean wants to marry her, Pierre takes it very cheerily and begins playing a saxophone. As Marie talks about the sinfulness of such a marriage, Pierre asks why and continues tooting on his horn. Marie takes one of Pierre's presents to her, a jeweled necklace, and melodramatically tosses it out the window—a symbolic act of rejection. Pierre, unimpressed, goes on tooting. Marie stands at the window, herself impressed by her grand gesture, only to notice a tramp on the street below bend over to pick up the necklace and begin to walk away with it. Instantly, Marie snaps out of her pose, dashes down the stairs, grabs the necklace away from the tramp, and rushes back into her house with it. Pierre laughs and goes back to his saxophone. Again, an ironic sequence brilliantly contrasts play-acted emotions and real ones, a person's verbal commitments and his actions. The notes of Pierre's saxophone humorously counterpoint Marie's melodramatic words (although neither can actually be heard!).

A third brilliant sequence in *A Woman of Paris* also centers about the gossip of the film's ladies. Marie's "friends" pay her another visit while she is receiving a massage. These "friends" seem to exist solely to bring each other bad news. They tell Marie that Pierre dined with a close friend of hers the night before. Chaplin keeps the camera riveted on the head and face of the bobbed-haired masseuse. Not only do the masseuse's arms sketch the curves of Edna's body in great detail, but her absolutely impassive face underlines the nasty tone of the salacious gossip in the room. The highly emotional, charged atmosphere of this scene is ironically communicated by showing no external emotion whatsoever, and by keeping the camera on a minor character who is not directly affected by the news at all. We must infer how Marie feels about this gossip. By building his film around so many inferences, Chaplin avoids showing the most melodramatic and excessive human reactions. Our projections about the characters' feelings are far more interesting and complex than any predictable shot of a wide-eyed or tear-stained face.

Discussion of A Woman of Paris inevitably revolves about its parts, not its whole. The same cannot be said of Chaplin's next film, certainly one of his greatest, The Gold Rush (1925). The Gold Rush was Chaplin's favorite film; even his nit-picking critics find it his best blend of pathos, humor, and social comment. The film returns to the premise of the First Nationals and should, perhaps, be seen as the spiritual culmination of that group. Chaplin puts Charlie into an environment where we would not expect to find him—prospecting for gold in the frozen North. The film juxtaposes the moral behavior of the little tramp and the assumptions and definitions of the alien environment. Like the earlier First Nationals, The Gold Rush reveals the superiority of Charlie's system of values to that of the superficially respectable, legitimate society.

Structurally, the film is another circle: Prologue (the trek North), the Cabin, the Dance Hall, New Year's Eve, the Dance Hall, the Cabin, Epilogue (the trek home). In the course of his circular journey, Charlie runs up against four human necessities that consistently evade his grasp but that he luckily manages to grab hold of before the end of the film—food, money, shelter, and love. Although the film is rich in brilliant comedy, tempered by an occasional moment of pathos, the comedy and pathos arise from an intellectual premise.

The most famous comic sequence in the film shows starving Charlie cooking his shoe, slicing it carefully, and sharing the meal with his pal, Mack Swain. This transposition of shoe into food is a comic Chaplin staple going back to the Keystones and the clock in The Pawnshop. But beneath the mime, the comic idea of devouring a shoe, is the fact that two men are hungry and have nothing else to eat. In a similar sequence, a starving Mack Swain sees Charlie as an immense chicken. Chaplin's transposition of the tramp into a chicken (typically using the dissolve to perfection) and Charlie's convincing mime of a chicken are very funny. But a man wanting to eat another man is not so funny. Need turns men into cannibalistic animals.

The scene where Georgia (Georgia Hale) beckons Charlie in the dance hall is another famous comic routine (reincarnated countless times in other films—for example, the opening of Zazie dans le métro). Georgia gestures toward Charlie alluringly; he does not see that a more handsome man, the man she really greets, is standing behind him. Charlie learns that he is not Georgia's object only when he starts to move toward her and Georgia walks past him, unaware that he exists. The scene is both funny and sad, another of Charlie's vicarious fulfillments of genuine emotional need. This vicariousness culminates in the New Year's Eve sequence as Charlie waits for Georgia to dine with him. Georgia never intended to accept the invitation; she is with her friends in the dance hall. The scene is a magnification of Charlie's first mistake about Georgia. As Charlie waits for her, he dreams of their wonderful party and his social success at it. But he awakens (as he does from all his dreams) to realize that midnight is past and Georgia is not coming. He remains alone. Touching, yes. But the implications about human need and human callousness go far beyond a sentimental tear.

Like the First Nationals, *The Gold Rush* puts Charlie in a morally vicious and perverted world. The "Far North" setting had become a film convention—for both serious films such as William S. Hart's and burlesques such as Keaton's *The Frozen North* and Turpin's *Nudnick of the North*. But Chaplin often took a conventional setting—farm belt, wild West—to expose the corruption beneath the surface of the convention. Of course, the frozen North was a place where men came to prospect for gold. Chaplin looked at what happens to human relationships in a place where life has only one material object. Charlie's "buddy," Big Jim McKay, is a friend only when he can afford to be or when it is profitable. He needs Charlie to show him the location of the claim; he is friendly to Charlie on the ship after they have both struck it rich. But when Big Jim is hungry, he is no friend; when their cabin teeters off the edge of a cliff, he is no friend.

Georgia is incapable of feeling love for anyone in the dance hall. That single oasis of warmth in the midst of a frozen desert is a place where one can obtain human companionship only by paying for it. Georgia likes men who bring her gold. In that environment women are merely prostitutes. Only after Georgia has left the hardhearted gold fields can she respond uncallously to Charlie.

The ultimate state of human relationships in the film is personified by Black Larsen, whose drive for gold is so great that he is willing to murder anyone who gets in his way. Significantly, Larsen ends up buried in a landslide of snow, and no one in the film ever finds him or cares enough to. Larsen is the solitary human animal—cold, alone, dead.

A corollary question that Chaplin asks about the "Far North" locale is, What happens to basic human needs and comforts in such a place? The torture endured by the human body to gather a few pieces of valuable rock underlies most of the comic routines in the film. Charlie suffers terrible comic tortures—comic hunger, comic cold, comic pursuit by beasts, comic panic in escaping from the teetering cabin. But these are tortures nonetheless. The metaphoric oppositions between cold and warmth, softness and hardness, flesh and ore, man and beast, are at the same time very clear and very unobtrusive in the film. Unlike the overstated oppositions in *A Woman of Paris,* the serious themes of *The Gold Rush* enjoy the subtlety and richness of the Charlie character who embodies or demonstrates them.

Yet Chaplin is not so simpleminded an artist that he inveighs against gold-seeking without realizing the genuine human urge that drives people to seek it in the frozen wastes. As unmaterialistic as the tramp might be, he too has wandered north. Though the rush for gold is inhuman torture, there are very few humans who would not subject themselves to it in the hope of a strike. Chaplin the man realized the lure of wealth. His childhood poverty made him a shrewd businessman and a tight-fisted spender. Unlike Langdon, Keaton, and Griffith, Chaplin hung on to the vast sums he earned. This ambivalence about gold—both its inhuman deadness and its attraction for humans—contributes to the richness of *The Gold Rush,* lifting the film out of the dominantly ironic and bitter mode of earlier films such as *Sunnyside* and *The Pilgrim* and later films such as *Modern Times* and *Monsieur Verdoux.* This shift in tone allows the film to end happily (Charlie gets both riches and Georgia) without the uncomfortable strain of the happy endings of *The Kid, Sunnyside,* or *The Immigrant.* The happy ending of *The Gold Rush* is so satisfying because for once Charlie receives what he deserves without the bubble's bursting. Perhaps the happy ending also suggests, quietly and unobtrusively, that poetic justice unfortunately operates only in fiction.

The Circus (1928), Chaplin's next film, does not end happily. Its ending is a magnification of the ending of *The Tramp,* 13 years earlier. Charlie has been replaced in the girl's affections by a much handsomer, more romantic partner, and he returns to the road, alone, bowed but unbroken. Like *The Tramp,* and so many Chaplin films, its structure is another circle—from the road to the road. Chaplin emphasizes the circle with a circus wagon that both opens and closes the film, with the circular tracks that the wagon's wheels leave in the dust, and with the piece of circus paper with a star on it. At the beginning of the film a horse jumps through a hoop covered with the starred paper; at the end of the film, Charlie crumples a piece of paper with a star on it, gives it his jaunty behind-the-back kick (the same kick he uses to dispose of Goliath's head in *The Pilgrim* and any other object toward which he feels defiance), and sets off down the road away from the camera.

Unlike the films of the previous years, *The Circus* does not drop Charlie into a setting where the tramp really does not belong. A circus is one place where Charlie might well belong, for the circus is a society of the road. But parallel to the other dominant motif of the First Nationals, *The Circus* concerns itself with exactly who Charlie is and, by extension, who he is not. The visually marvelous chase in the house of mirrors, in which there are seemingly hundreds of reflections of Charlie, is also a crucial metaphor for the whole film. Out of these hundreds of reflections, which one is the real figure and which are mere shadows? In the same chase sequence, Charlie poses as mechanical doll. Which is the man and which the machine that seems to be a man?.

One of the things Charlie is not is a conventional circus clown. Charlie is hilarious as a circus clown only when he goes about his ordinary business—trying to avoid a cop or carry a set of dishes. But when Charlie auditions to become a typical circus clown, he is dreadfully unfunny at two set routines—the "William Tell" number and the "Barber Shop" number. Charlie's comedy cannot be fit into patterns and routines. The funniest things he does at his audition are disruptions of the routine, his own improvisations and mistakes (although they do not amuse the humorless circus owner).

Another of the things that Charlie is not is a heroic lion tamer. When Charlie gets locked into a cage with a ferocious sleeping beast, he tries as hard as he can not to wake him. But of course the lion does awake; luckily the beast isn't hungry at the moment and merely sits sleepily and harmlessly next to his new companion. Only when Charlie sees there is no danger does he strike several heroic attitudes. But the beast's roar explodes his posing and sends him dashing out of the cage and up a pole.

The primary thing that Charlie is not is a heroic, romantic leading man. When Rex, a handsome, sexy tightrope walker, joins the circus, Merna's interests (Merna Kennedy) switch from Charlie to Rex. Charlie, the clown, perceives Merna's desires and aspires to become like Rex, the high-wire daredevil. Charlie carefully practices tightrope walking. He mechanically masters the physical act of the stunt—so well, in fact, that he is called on at the climax of the film to replace Rex when the heroic figure disappears. Charlie's tightrope-walking act is a combination of magnificent grace and hilarious business—exactly like his skating. Not only must Charlie negotiate the high wire without a safety device, but his trousers keep falling to his ankles (making it a bit difficult to walk the wire), and a host of little monkeys (monkeys!) keep tumbling out of his pants and winding themselves about his face and limbs. (As he did with the lion, Chaplin brilliantly personalizes the incongruous Sennett gags.) Charlie can be a magnificent tightrope walker; it is a skill he can learn. But he can simply never be Rex. And Merna doesn't love a man who knows how to walk a tightrope; she loves Rex—his suaveness, sex appeal, poise, a manner that cannot be learned or copied. The point goes back to *Sunnyside:* Charlie can adopt some of the mannerisms and props of the city slicker, but he can never duplicate his character and being.

All that Charlie can be is Charlie—and this potentiality he shows throughout the film. Charlie is extremely artful at dodging the police—and if he weren't, there would be no Charlie. He sides with a hungry and beaten Merna against her tyrannical stepfather. When Charlie finds out that his clowning is all that keeps the circus in business (the circus owner, a vicious capitalist as well as bullying parent, tries to keep Charlie ignorant of his importance), he then uses that knowledge to help both Merna and himself. And when Charlie sees that he can never win Merna's heart, he makes an unselfish act of sacrifice to secure her happiness. He helps Merna and Rex escape together, though he personally will be left alone on the road. Those are the things that Charlie can do, for those are the things that Charlie is.

CHAPTER 8

Chaplin: Sound Films

———

W HILE Chaplin was at work on his next production, synchronized sound disrupted the film industry. After weighing the possibilities, Chaplin decided to continue shooting *City Lights* as a silent film with synchronized sound effects and score. It was, perhaps, the most brilliant decision of his career—the means of preserving his personal style and method at a time when most silent-film masters lost theirs. When *City Lights* finally appeared in 1931 (Chaplin worked slowly), synchronized sound had become so standard that audiences expected nothing else. They had a surprise waiting for them.

The opening sequence of *City Lights* thumbs its nose at the audience's expectations. It also thumbs its nose at sanctimoniousness, civic pride, the glorification of dead forms and dead things at the expense of living people and living values. The scene depicts the unveiling of a horrible city statue with three figures—one representing some kind of queenly authority, another with a palm extended, a third with a drawn sword (Justice and Mercy and Strength or some such abstractions calcified into marble ugliness). But as the pretentious statue is unveiled, who should be discovered asleep (that motif again) on it but Charlie? He suddenly realizes his trouble, but every attempt to extricate himself from it makes things worse. He gets his trousers speared by the marble sword, then sits on the outstretched palm, then rests his rear on the queen-figure's nose (this marble nose up the anus is one of the slyest obscene moments in film history). Only the playing of the "Star-Spangled Banner" saves Charlie from a lynching, for the crowd must suddenly muffle its anger and snap to patriotic attention.

And that is the second kind of nose-thumbing in the scene: he thumbs his nose at synchronized sound. To underscore the ridiculous speeches of the dignitaries, Chaplin records not their words but a series of synchronized saxophone squawks and squeaks that perfectly reveal the speeches' content without a single word—all topped by the playing of the "Star-Spangled Banner." Chaplin thumbs his nose at the talkies by excluding talk.

This iconoclasm (well, he doesn't break the idol, but he does sit on it) in the opening scene is merely a prelude to a film that is much closer to the mellow spirit of *The Circus*. Like *The Circus*, *City Lights* examines what the tramp can accomplish and the conditions under which he can accomplish it. As in *The Circus*, Chaplin mixes in large doses of sentiment in the depiction of Charlie's relationship to a helpless girl. *City Lights* was his last strongly sentimental film until *Limelight*, 20 years later. Unlike *The Circus*, however, *City Lights* adds many of the ironic and caustic elements of his earlier films—the parallelism between rich and poor (as in *The Idle Class* and several others), the power of money, the contrast between fancy surface and inner emptiness, society's innate suspicion of Charlie's actions, the painful and degrading tasks that Charlie must perform if he is to succeed "legitimately."

Charlie exists as the film's equator between two social and moral poles: a rich man who wants to commit suicide and a blind girl who sells flowers. Given the Chaplin symbolism, this polarity summarizes the film's essential values. The man of wealth has every material comfort and enjoyment that money can buy—house, car, fancy friends, expensive nightclubs, arty soirées. But beneath the things he owns or can afford to enjoy, he is empty and dead. He has failed at his marriage—his wife has left him. And his view of friendship is selfish and inconsistent. When Charlie saves him from suicide, the millionaire, drunk, swears that Charlie will be his friend for life. Charlie is always the millionaire's friend when the rich man is soused. But when the millionaire returns to sobriety, he denies that he knows Charlie. (He does so three times in the film—for those who like Christian symbolism.) When he is drunk and off his guard, the rich man may have some vague sense of what it means to be human; but when he returns to reason, he is empty and cold (another parallel with a play by Brecht, *Herr Puntilla and His Knight Matti*). That coldness is at the center of his life's emptiness.

The flower seller, on the other hand, has neither material nor even physical well-being. She is not only poor but blind. She has nothing to live with or for, yet, in contrast to the millionaire's emptiness, her life is warm and full. The fullness is apparent in her love of flowers, metaphors for the beauty and vitality of nature; in her loving relationship with her grandmother; and in her ability to elicit sympathy and even love from Charlie.

Charlie walks between these two opposite styles of life and approaches to human problems. Most of the film's hilarious comedy—and there is much—comes from his clumsy attempts to imitate the millionaire's activities. Most of the film's pathos and subtle human observation comes from his relationship with the girl and his decision to help her. No more farcical-ironic combination exists than in the first meeting between Charlie and the millionaire. Chaplin juxtaposes suicide with burlesque. In the millionaire's clumsy attempts to tie a rock and rope around his neck, he mistakenly ties them around Charlie, and both fall into the river several times; this combination of physical comedy with the most serious human act of suicide is extraordinary (perhaps an influence on Beckett's juxtaposition of suicide and pants falling down in *Godot,* and certainly a precursor of Chaplin's farcical attempts to murder Martha Raye in *Monsieur Verdoux*).

Also brilliant is the nightclub scene when Charlie and his newfound "friend" go out on the town. Charlie slips and slides across the dance floor (shades of *Tango Tangles*); he confuses the flying streamers with his plate of spaghetti and carefully eats the strings of paper (typical transposition); he mistakenly believes that the male dancer in the Apache dance is injuring his lady partner and, of course, wrecks the act by stepping in to help.

Charlie's greatest comical *faux pas* is at the millionaire's musicale. Charlie, flirting with a society belle, unfortunately swallows a toy whistle. Meanwhile a tenor begins to deliver (silently) an arty aria. Charlie can't stop hiccoughing because of the swallowed whistle, and each hiccough produces a whistling squeak—a brilliant use of the sound track that recalls the use of the saxophone in the silent *Woman of Paris.* Charlie's squeaky whistle undercuts the pretentiousness of the musical solo and converts the song into a surprising duet. The sequence climaxes as Charlie's whistle first attracts a taxi and, finally, a whole pack of dogs which run into the fancy drawing room and swamp the rich manikins with their animal exuberance.

For the sequences with the flower seller Chaplin combines pathos (handled previously in *The Vagabond, The Kid, The Gold Rush,* and *The Circus*) with the subtle use of implication to convey emotional and intellectual states (brought to perfection in *A Woman of Paris*). In their crucial first meeting, she assumes Charlie is a millionaire and he discovers that she is blind. Charlie, evading trouble, has been rushing through traffic, in and out of automobiles, and has finally slammed the door of a car right in front of the flower seller. She reacts slightly to the imposing slam and, assuming the person stepping out of the car is her typical rich customer, asks if he wants to buy a flower. As she hands Charlie the flower, she drops it. When he politely stoops to pick it up, he notices that she has not seen that he has lifted the flower from the ground. He waves the flower in front of her eyes; she makes no response. The information has been communicated effectively and clearly without a word or a title.

Many of these scenes between Charlie and the girl (Virginia Cherrill) combine pathos and comedy (such as the Oceana Roll dance in *The Gold Rush*). When the girl wants to wind a ball of yarn, Charlie holds up his hands to help her. She, however, mistakenly grabs a strand from Charlie's undershirt, not from the package of yarn she has just bought. Charlie faces a difficult decision. Does he inform her of her mistake to save his shirt, or does he keep quiet to avoid embarrassing her? He makes the latter decision and allows himself to be stripped for her sake (an ironically poignant and tender use of "unbandaging" which parallels the striptease in *A Woman of Paris*). He even gives the yarn from his shirt a little helpful tug for her when it resists. His face, however, in another instance of the Chaplin balance and perceptiveness, shows that he is not entirely happy about his sacrifice. Chaplin shatters other scenes of pathos with a slapstick gag in the manner of the elbow-in-the-beans business in *The Immigrant*: as Charlie gazes lovingly at the girl, she unwittingly splashes water in his face; as he sits on her stoop wistfully, a cat knocks a flower pot on his head.

Charlie's sacrifice of his shirt is a foreshadowing of the film's final sequence, his major act of sacrifice—an attempt to get the girl enough money for the operation that will restore her eyesight. This final sacrifice is richly ironic for many reasons. First, Charlie's sacrifice contrasts with the false sacrifices of the millionaire, who only gives away what is valueless to him, and then only when he feels like it. Second, Charlie's act is such that its result can not only fail to benefit him but might do him harm. Charlie knows that her eyesight might well cost him her love (as his almost imperceptible take reveals when she says how good it will be to be able to see him).

Third, the tasks he must undergo to earn the money are very funny with a sharp underlying edge: scooping up animal droppings on the streets; prizefighting bigger, tougher opponents who are certain to beat him to a pulp. The prizefighting sequence, a personalization of the ring antics in *The Champion*, is one of the film's comic high points: Charlie's coy attempts to strike a deal with his mean opponent; the opponent's suspicions that Charlie is a homosexual; the fight itself, in which Charlie uses the ropes, the referee, the bell, anything to dance around and away from his opponent and avoid his punches. Funny, yes—but the brutality of this means of making a living is unmistakable (yet another parallel with Brecht, who also used boxing metaphorically).

Finally, Charlie gets the money as a gift from the millionaire. (That's how little the money means to the rich man.) But because there are thieves in the millionaire's house, Charlie is suspected of stealing the cash (of course). The law eventually catches up with him, and Charlie goes to prison, but not before he has given the cash to the girl. Before Charlie steps through the huge prison gates, he takes his cigarette out of his mouth and kicks it away with his jaunty behind-the-back defiance. He goes to jail, but he has succeeded in helping one human being. Once again the reward for self-sacrifice is only self-satisfaction.

When the tramp gets out of prison, he discovers the flower seller in a fancy new shop, not on a street corner. With one of his wonderful manipulations of physical detail, Chaplin lets us know that the girl can see. She looks at herself in a mirror to see if she is properly groomed. When a car door slams, the girl does a slight take and stares at the young, rich man who comes into her shop, hoping it is the "millionaire" whom she first met after a door slammed, and who gave her sight. When she finally sees the tramp, her first impulse is a charitable one—to give the poor man some money (an ironic reversal of what Charlie did for her). But as she presses the coin into his hand, she feels his palm, and then knows who her friend is (another communicative physical detail). The two stare into each other's eyes. The titled dialogue is painfully simple. "You can see now?" "Yes, I can see." And the film ends with a final close-up on Charlie's face, holding a rose next to his cheek—a look both joyful and anguished, of happiness for her and awareness that the identity of her benefactor might cause her pain, of the joy of seeing her and the fear that she might now reject him after seeing him.

The ambiguity of the ending of *City Lights*, like that of *The Kid*, is deliberate. It is far more successful than *The Kid*'s because its implications are more consistent with the reality of the world and the character that Chaplin has defined. The girl may feel committed to Charlie out of some sense of obligation, but Charlie would never want to imprison her that way. (This theme would be picked up 20 years later in *Limelight*.) The act of love and sacrifice should not become a more stifling prison than the girl's previous blindness. And yet is it possible that the girl can love him for what he is and what he has done for her? Can she separate the money and the man now that the image of the young millionaire she had clung to when blind has turned out to be an illusion? And so Chaplin, the astute artist, implies two possibilities—perhaps a necessary parting, perhaps a vital life together—without ever subjecting us to the uncomfortable specificity of either ending. The ending of *City Lights* solves the Chaplin dilemma—the joy of home but the horror of domestication—by avoiding it.

Anyway, their future is not the subject of the film. Its real subject is what sorts of human actions make human existence possible. And Chaplin's answer in the film is that the essential human action is that of love (or friendship), and that the essential act of love is giving. In the most Christian manner, Chaplin equates love with charity, and shows that it is "works," not words or "faith," that moves mountains. But the obvious

Christian motifs of *City Lights* are less obtrusive, more subtle, than the Christian symbolism of *Sunnyside* and *The Kid.*

In this Chaplin film, as in so many others, there is a contrast between the apparent and the real, the supposed good life and the real good life, the supposed civic virtues and the real human virtues. The statue in the film's first sequence, the millionaire's abuse of his wealth, the nastiness of the two newsboys who persecute Charlie with their peashooters (more like the brat in *The Pilgrim* than Jackie in *The Kid*) are all what is wrong with city life. What Charlie does for the girl is what makes life livable.

Modern Times (1936) also contrasts surface appearances and underlying realities. It compares the social conditions for human life with the internal necessities for human life. And its ultimate statement is simply that human society and human existence are mutually exclusive. The compromises that humans must make to live together are simply not human. As always, Chaplin develops his serious theme with both compassion and comedy. Each of the sequences revolves about some social institution—factory, prison, department store, domestic cottage, restaurant. Charlie and, later, the Gamin (Paulette Goddard) try to make human sense out of each of these situations, and they fail at all of them. Their ultimate solution is to take to the road together, leaving society behind them. The two end the film by walking hand in hand down the road, backs to the camera. Significantly, in this film as compared to *The Tramp*, Charlie has a partner. Further, the road is not a dusty rural one, but a modern paved road with a painted stripe down the middle. The times are indeed more modern. Charlie and the Gamin straddle the stripe—as he straddled the border in *The Pilgrim*—and walk off into the mountains, never to return. And after this film Charlie, the tramp character, never did return.

But lest this rejection seem an act of optimistic escapism, one should never forget that apparent solutions in Chaplin are inevitably not solutions. Although the logical solution to "modern times" is to "live alone in the mountains," Chaplin knows that people do not "live alone in the mountains." Chaplin, for one, did not. The Chaplin tension between logical answers and actual human choices, between wishes and realities, asserts itself in a new form at the end of *Modern Times.*

Modern Times, unlike earlier Chaplin films, shows a number of clear cinematic influences. It begins with a montage that is obvious Eisenstein. Chaplin dissolves from a shot of sheep being led into a pen for slaughter to a shot of men streaming out of a subway entrance and into a factory. Both the montage method and the animal imagery are echoes of *Strike*. The barren factory walls and the geometric patterns of machines unmistakably recall Lang's *Metropolis*. But the closest parallel is between *Modern Times* and René Clair's *À Nous la liberté*. Like the earlier Clair film, Chaplin parallels prisons and factories. The irony of *Modern Times*, however, is that Charlie is better off—better fed, better sheltered, more at peace with his fellows—in the prison than out of it. That is not Clair's point. Where Clair finds industrial society as stifling as prison in his metaphor, Chaplin finds prison more comfortable and secure than a chaotic, hunger-driven, Depression-ridden society. And if Clair's final action, in which the two friends leave society and take to the road as tramps, also recurs in *Modern Times*, it is equally true that Charlie had been turning his back on society and tramping down the road for 20 years. However, the two films seemed so similar to Tobis Klangfilms, the company that produced the Clair film, that they sued Chaplin for plagiarism. They eventually dropped the suit when Clair, honored by Chaplin's parallels, convinced his bosses that Chaplin's influence on him had been enormous.

Although even Huff, Chaplin's biographer, thought À *Nous la liberté* a better film than *Modern Times* from his perspective in 1951, that judgment does not seem valid 20 years later. There is an underlying irony and cynicism in *Modern Times* that seems far more appropriate to its social theme than Clair's naïve, fanciful optimism. *Modern Times* returns to the caustic tone of *Easy Street* and *Sunnyside*, never forgetting to be funny at the same time. Whatever may have influenced the film, it is still pure Chaplin.

Food is to *Modern Times* what money is to *City Lights* or *The Gold Rush*. A fancy new machine, designed to feed the workers in a minimum amount of time, allows them to work while eating. Charlie becomes the guinea pig for its demonstration. Charlie looks forward to a tempting meal set in front of him—soup, pieces of meat, corn on the cob, strawberry shortcake. He need only stand passively while the machine pushes the food at his face. Although the machine starts off well enough—tipping the soup gently into his mouth, twirling the corn between his teeth, shoving a cube of meat snugly inside his mouth, blotting his lips gently with a wooden dowel—it predictably goes haywire. It dumps the soup down his shirt; it grinds his mustache and face with the speedily twirling corncob; it mistakenly shoves metal bolts instead of meat into his mouth; it bashes his lips with the wooden blotter; and it climaxes by schlupping him in the face with the shortcake (the apotheosis of the Sennett pie!). Charlie, whose head is chained to the machine, cannot avoid its tortures. Even this chance to eat a delicious meal dissolves in mechanical chaos.

Whereas in this early scene a machine feeds a man, later the man feeds a machine when Charlie, who has fallen behind on the assembly line, gets sucked into the mouth and bowels of the machine at the end of the conveyor belt.

A third scene synthesizes the preceding two. Charlie and the chief mechanic, Chester Conklin (Chaplin often used the old clowns in his films), must fix a machine that has broken down. Unfortunately, the erring machine gobbles up Chester Conklin, who winds up tangled in its gears; every time Charlie pulls another lever, Chester gets swallowed a bit more.

While Chester lies in the machine's innards, his head sticking out of a huge wheel of gears, the lunch whistle blows. Since they are union men, they must eat their lunch. So Charlie feeds Chester's protruding face bits of food from his lunch pail. A man (Chester) has been fed into a machine, and a second man feeds him. Such variations reveal that Chaplin's method of circularity is again at work, just as in *The Tramp* of 20 years earlier.

Another memorable sequence also squeezes ironic laughs from food. Charlie is a waiter in a jammed café, desperately trying to serve a duckling to a customer. But in his attempts to cross the dance floor with the tray, he gets tossed like a piece of flotsam by the dancing crowd. When he finally gets across, he discovers that the duckling has disappeared from the tray. It has been speared by the restaurant's chandelier. When Charlie finally gets it down, three collegiate drunks pick up the duck and start passing it around like a football. Charlie, always the alert waiter, intercepts a pass and runs for a score. The comedy of the scene is remarkable —transposition (duck = football), instinct (what to do with a forward pass but intercept it and run for a TD?). But beneath the comedy lies the implication that these patrons are so wealthy that a precious bit of food becomes a plaything to them.

Food is so important in *Modern Times* because it is an absolute necessity for human survival—an organic material, a source of life—which has itself become enslaved by the inanimate, sterile machine. This contrast of the quick and the dead becomes especially clear when Chaplin shifts his focus from food to look exclusively at the machine.

Charlie's experience on the assembly line becomes so debilitating that he eventually snaps and, like the machine that fed him lunch, goes haywire. He begins dancing balletically all over the factory, squirting everyone in the face with his oil can, transposing his wrenches, those mechanical tools, into a satyr's horns and using them to twist any kind of protuberance (including the buttons on a lady's blouse). In contrast to the standardized regularity of the dead machines is Charlie's freedom of movement, his supple grace, his lively human expressions, his oil that helps machines function when squeezed into them but reduces people to hysteria when spattered in their faces. Charlie, the most lively, human, natural being in the factory, is judged insane by the mechanical standards of society and goes off to the hospital to recover from his nervous breakdown. People, like machines, can supposedly be fixed when they break down.

Ironically, after Charlie leaves the hospital, he is mistakenly arrested as a political agitator and radical. The prison sequences that follow contain two touches that combine realistic unpleasantness with hilarious business. In the first, Charlie meets his new cellmate—tough-looking, stocky, bristly-bearded, awesome. The tough guy, however, does needlepoint. Similarly, one of the convicts skips around mincingly throughout the prison sequence (he obviously "services" the prison)—although you have to take your eyes off Charlie to see him. The second touch centers around a prisoner who has been smuggling "nose powder" (either cocaine, heroin, or some such white powder) and disposes of it in a salt shaker at supper to avoid being caught with the goods (another food game). Charlie, of course, uses the salt liberally on his food and gets himself comically high, after which he performs a heroic action (as in *Easy Street*). But this underlying serious reference to dope in prisons was also years ahead of public awareness.

Not all the excellences of the film are caustic and seamy. There is relief from hunger, prison, and the machine. Charlie's relationship with the Gamin, the girl of nature, gives the film its tender, sensitive moments. Like so many of the Chaplin films, *Modern Times* contrasts the painful reality to a pleasant dream. Charlie and the Gamin, finding themselves in a quiet, pleasant, respectable neighborhood, dream of what it would be like to live there. In the typical Chaplin manner, the film dissolves to Charlie's dream of stereotypic bourgeois happiness—cheery home, orange tree and grapevines outside the kitchen door, a cow for fresh milk, a sizzling steak on the stove—which gets shaken back to reality by the neighborhood cop, who wonders what two derelicts are doing in that respectable section. The dream's idyllic corniness is a later manifestation of the same parodic spirit that infused the dreams of *Sunnyside* and *The Kid*.

Equally gentle is the real domestic life that Charlie and the Gamin establish in the ramshackle little cabin (another parallel that specifically echoes an earlier section of the film). Life in the cabin is no bourgeois dream—orange crates as chairs, tin cans as teacups, ham steak instead of sirloin, the walls so shaky that Charlie repeatedly falls through them and into the brackish swamp that lies beside the house. But their house is vivified by love, much more important than possessions or grapevines (a reminder of Jackie and Charlie's life in *The Kid*). However, even this haven cannot last. Charlie and the Gamin must still confront the forces of society—the need to work, to observe the law, to avoid poverty on the one hand and the police on the other. And so they must give up even this version of a conventional home and take to the road.

Endings had frequently been a problem for Chaplin in his early films. The endings of A *Dog's Life*, *Sunnyside*, and *The Kid* were painfully facile evasions—the artist's inability to come to terms with the paradox that Charlie deserved earthly rewards but that he could never possibly attain them. The endings of the films that left Charlie without the rewards, alone on the road (*The Tramp*, *The Adventurer*, *The Circus*), were consistent with the tramp's character, but they avoided the paradox by emphasizing the emotional effects of pathos, the sadness of Charlie's being left alone. The greatest Chaplin endings (in, not surprisingly, the greatest Chaplin films) force attention on the paradox itself. In *Easy Street, The Pilgrim, The Gold Rush,* and *City Lights*, the endings all look at the ten-

sion between poetic justice and earthly justice, personal morality and public definitions of morality, fiction and life, wish and reality. The ending of
Modern Times, which is also the ending of the tramp's cinematic journey,
is perhaps the ultimate ending of all. On the one hand, the ending shows
that the tramp will go on (because he is tough) and will go on with another human being (because he is loving). But the film, as a whole, has
just as conclusively shown that there is nowhere to go, that the times are
modern and that life cannot avoid those times.

Chaplin and the Sound Track

Chaplin's principle of sound synchronization in Modern Times was precisely the same as for City Lights. He used a musical score for tonal effects
—bouncy, jaunty tunes for comic sequences; a lush, romantic violin melody for the tender sections between Charlie and the Gamin. Chaplin
wrote his first major "hit" song for Modern Times, now titled "Smile,"
which parallels "Won't Somebody Buy My Violets?" the flower seller's
theme in City Lights. Chaplin also used sound for comic effects—gurgling
noises as Charlie and a prim, snobbish preacher's wife drink tea; the hum
and whir of factory machines. Interestingly, Chaplin's use of sound exactly
conforms to Eisenstein's and Pudovkin's views on the most effective function of sound in the film medium—much more closely than Eisenstein's
and Pudovkin's own sound films. Further, Chaplin's principle of using
sound would be one of the dominant methods of Jacques Tati—perhaps
the greatest of the sound director-comedians.

But Modern Times uses synchronized speech for two sequences—although both of them are also nose-thumbing comments on synchronized
sound, like the opening sequence of City Lights. In the first of them, the
factory president (like Big Brother in 1984) uses television screens all over
the factory to spy on his workers and to order them to quit slacking. When
Charlie sneaks into a gleamingly white, sterile lavatory (another pointed
contrast of nature and artificiality) for a smoke, the president's face appears on the screen and orders him back to work in synchronized speech.
His voice is booming and cavernous, slightly distorted by an echo effect.
For Chaplin to reserve synchronized sound for a tyrannical, artificial, dis-
comforting visual-vocal presence is a neat piece of irony.

Similarly, the second synchronized sequence is highly ironic. Charlie,
working in a nightclub as a singing waiter, must sing his number; however, he cannot memorize the words to it. So he writes them on his cuff.
But as he enters and takes an energetic bow, the cuffs fly off. So Charlie
must sing a nonsense song with nonsense words—a hodgepodge of various

languages and non-languages—for his audience. Chaplin seems to say to his film public, "OK, you want to hear my voice? Well, here it is." And what "it" turns out to be is silly non-talk, speech reduced to sound rather than sound clarified to speech (the usual method of the talkies). In *Modern Times*, Chaplin uses as much ingenuity as possible to eliminate talk, and when he includes talk, that inclusion is also ingenious.

But *Modern Times* was Chaplin's last battle with the talkies. His remaining films all depended on talk, more detailed plots, and a more carefully worked-out script. Where Chaplin had previously improvised whole films without writing them down, letting the germ of an idea grow into a scene, and then each scene grow into a film, the requirements of talk required a complete screenplay. Synchronized speech led Chaplin to drop the picaresque structure and adopt the carefully structured comparison and contrast, multi-plot form (for *The Great Dictator*), the *reductio ad absurdum* (for *Monsieur Verdoux*), and the Aristotelian plot of discovery (for *Limelight*). In these later talkies, the picaresque tramp necessarily disappeared, to be replaced by a different principle of characterization that was consistent with their new structures.

The three films all gave Chaplin more than one role. In *The Great Dictator*, he plays both a little Jewish barber and the dictator of Tomania (Adenoid Hynkel); in *Monsieur Verdoux*, he plays a series of different gentlemen who use different styles and methods to dispose of different women; in *Limelight*, he plays Calvero in the present and Calvero in the past, really two different men.

Chaplin had avoided speech in the two earlier sound films because he knew that Charlie the tramp was an Everyman figure, his universality a product of mime, gesture, and facial expression, which are also generalizations. Words, however, are highly specific—not only in translating general feelings into specific terms, but also in immediately identifying the speaker's education, class, level of vocabulary, and precise habits of thought. The way to maintain universality in a talking film would be for Chaplin to talk differently as different characters in the same film, to use not a single member of the species to symbolize the whole genus but several members of the species to add up to the genus.

The Great Dictator (1940) is a political cartoon—very funny, very successful at reducing serious questions to silliness.* The film combines several earlier Chaplin motifs. As in *The Idle Class*, it casts Chaplin in two roles—a social outsider and a supreme social insider who look alike; as in *Shoulder Arms* it reduces potentially serious political issues to silly stereotypes like Benzino Napolloni and Garbitsch, who parallel the parodic "Hun" of the earlier film; and it treats a serious political reality with the

---

* Again there is a striking parallel to Brecht. *Arturo Ui* is Brecht's political cartoon on the rise of Hitler, written one year after Chaplin's film.

same parodic spirit as the *Burlesque on Carmen* treats the serious melo-drama.

The film has great comic moments. The two dictators, Hynkel and Napolloni (Jack Oakie), compete in a hilarious series of one-upmanship games, culminating in a food-flinging battle at a buffet table (which would reappear in the political food fight in *Doctor Strangelove*). Hynkel's frenzied speeches are so feverish that even the microphones melt and bend. In the midst of his oratorical fury, the dictator pauses for a glass of water to cool his overheated throat. He also splashes some water down his trousers; his genitals are as overheated as his tonsils. With this gesture Chaplin implies that the Nazi mania has as much to do with the sex organs as with words, and more to do with either than with ideas. There is also a wry touch of humor in the colorful little sign, painted in old German script, bordered by quaint flowers, reading "Ghetto." (This contrast between the "picturesque" and the reality stems back to *The Immigrant*.) For the Jews who live in that ghetto, existence is neither colorful nor quaint.

There are two supreme moments of Chaplin magic in the film—and they occur back to back. Despite the fact that the film is a talkie, both moments use physical motion, the great Chaplin skill, underscored with a perfectly harmonious piece of music. In the first, Chaplin transposes the globe of the earth into a floating balloon. Hynkel, indulging in his dreams of world conquest, lifts the globe from its wooden stand and then tosses it about in space to suit his fancies. He flings it into the air, catches it, tosses it again, leaps effortlessly onto his desk to continue the game, bats the balloon-globe with his feet, his head, his rear. The dictator and his world are transformed into a performing seal with a ball, a child with a toy, a "specialty" dancer with her bubble. Chaplin's "transformation of objects" comically serves the serious purpose of psychoanalyzing and debunking the Führer's dreams of conquest. The gliding, liquid dance almost seems to be shot in slow motion. And Chaplin underscores the hypnotic slowness with a syrupy choir of violins. But the dream ends when Hynkel leaps to grasp the balloon and it bursts in his arms. Pop goes the dream (an ironic use of a typical Chaplin dream motif and the painful reawakening).

Immediately after the dream ballet, the little barber shaves a customer, accompanied by a Brahms Hungarian dance. His movements are quick, precise, perfectly synchronized with the rhythmic beats of the music. The barber's human work contrasts with the dictator's inhuman dreams of glory, just as snappy movement and music contrast with the ethereal slowness of Hynkel's dream ballet—percussion and *pizzicato* rather than *obbligato*, razor rather than lighter-than-air balloon.

Chaplin's use of speech in his first dialogue film also shows great care and cleverness. Both Chaplin characters in the film use words extraordi-

Charlie surrogates. Three of a kind—Edna, Scraps, and Charlie—in *A Dog's Life*; Charlie's reunion with Jackie in *The Kid*.

Dream and cactus—Charlie as Pan in *Sunnyside*.
Nature and machine—Charlie as Pan in *Modern Times*.

Chaplin expressionism—Adenoid Hynkel's "study" in *The Great Dictator*.

Chaplin transposition—the goal of Hynkel's studies.

The clown among his memories—past and present in *Limelight*.

The Keaton body—Buster with Big Joe Roberts in *The Love Nest*.

Buster as three musicians in *The Playhouse*.

The projection-booth window as movie screen in *Sherlock Jr.*

The montage sequence in *Sherlock Jr.*: Buster dives as the ocean turns to snow.

The escape in *Sherlock Jr.*: a single far shot makes believable the metamorphosis of Sherlock into an old lady.

Buster goes about his business—unknowingly swallowed by the Union Army—in *The General*.

Harold Lloyd as "Lonesome Luke"—with Snub Pollard and a Roach imitation of the Sennett bathing beauties in *Luke and the Mermaids*.

Harold as weakling in a "story picture"—*Grandma's Boy*.

Harold pushing his way to the top in a "situation picture"—*Safety Last*.

narily. Hynkel spouts nonsense words and non-language—shrieking sound
rather than articulate speech. This reduction of speech to sound parallels
the nonsense song at the end of *Modern Times* and reveals that Chaplin's
shift from silence to talk was more gradual and less abrupt than it might
seem. The barber, on the other hand, hardly speaks at all.

But Chaplin does run into difficulties with talk in the film's final speech.
Because the barber and the dictator look alike, the barber is mistaken for
the Führer and is forced to give the radio address that celebrates the successful invasion of Austerlich. The barber steps to the microphone, begins
hesitantly, but eventually gathers his strength to give a speech urging world
brotherhood, peace, and the future happiness of the human species. "The
Kingdom of God is within man. . . . [I]n the name of democracy let us all
unite. Let us fight for a new world—a decent world that will give men a
chance to work. . . . The soul of man has been given wings and at last he is
beginning to fly. He is flying into the rainbow—into the light of hope—
into the future, into the glorious future that belongs to you—to me—to
all of us. . . ."

The abstractions of the language, the poetic failure of the words to add
up to the grand concepts they attempt to express, represent a severe stylistic disruption in the film—from human comedy and political burlesque
to humanistic hearts and flowers. The concepts are so abstract—Marxism
sweetened with American idealistic clichés—that the speech could appear
in a film by, say, Frank Capra, who was certainly no Marxist. The speech
is in many ways like the endings of Griffith's *Birth of a Nation* and *Intolerance*—a literary formula of hope and humanitarianism. Chaplin was
again having troubles with his endings.

The most disappointing thing about the speech is that Chaplin divorces
comedy and serious comment. The disjunction between the comic parts of
the film—which contain fewer serious glimmers than usual—and the serious, breast-beating parts violates the essence of Chaplin. The speech does
have a dramatic function. In the course of his stirring oration, the previously nonverbal barber becomes strengthened and ennobled by the very
ideas he expresses. The sense and sensitivity of his words contrast markedly
with the inarticulate shrieking of Hynkel. Nevertheless, the switch from a
mimetic, comic depiction of life with serious overtones to a didactic, direct
statement of beliefs is not Chaplin.

To some extent the same fault affects *Monsieur Verdoux*. The final two
reels are explicit moralizing, summing up the values of the film in talk
rather than action. But *Verdoux* has a much more complex premise than
The Great Dictator, and the film's ironic bitterness is a return to such
unique Chaplin conceptions as *Easy Street, Sunnyside*, and *Modern Times*.
Like Welles' *Citizen Kane*, *Monsieur Verdoux* is one of those tremendously influential works which are less than a success in their own time—and

for the same reason as *Citizen Kane*: it was a sardonic and disturbing work out of temper with its times.* *Verdoux*'s mixture of horror and belly laughs leads directly to the black comedy of the last decade. If Chaplin had not withdrawn *Verdoux* from circulation after its initial failure, it probably would have been rediscovered by buffs in the 1950s and 1960s the way *Kane* was.

Henri Verdoux is a dapper, witty, cultured, sensitive gentleman. He cultivates flowers and refuses to crush even a tiny caterpillar. He is the adoring husband of a crippled wife, a devoted father to his young son. When the boy pulls a cat's tail, Daddy reminds him: "Violence begets violence." He is a vegetarian and helps out at the church bazaar. The only thing wrong with him is his business, which is marrying rich, ugly old women and murdering them for their money. This tension between what Verdoux seems to be and what he does is a typical Chaplin motif—pushed to its acid limit. There is a contrast between the surface of Verdoux and his reality. But even that opposition is complex, for Verdoux is not really a murderous person. He is indeed kind, polite, and refined. He simply must murder to survive and support his wife and child. And so the film raises further questions: What is the relationship between ends and means? What is the relationship between human morality and animal survival? Is morality a function of character or of action, wish or deed? Is moral virtue possible in an immoral world?

Yet Chaplin raises these serious questions by way of the most hilarious business. The prime materials of the plot are two actions—neither of which Verdoux succeeds in accomplishing: He tries to get rid of an old wife—Annabella Bonheur (Martha Raye); and he tries to acquire a new wife—Madame Grosnay (Isobel Elsom). His attempts to snare Madame Grosnay are burlesques of romantic conventions. As soon as he discovers she is rich and widowed, he grabs her hand, swears that their love is written in the stars, spouts poetic clichés, tries to seduce her with his sensitive eyebrows, twitching mouth, delicate flowers; he openly chases her around the room—only to climax his courtship by falling out the window.

Rejecting his forwardness, Madame Grosnay is then inundated weekly with dozens of roses from her suitor. She eventually relents. But when Verdoux finally sees her again, he remembers her so vaguely (their affair has been conducted by post and telephone) that he mistakes the maid for Madame. And on their glorious wedding day, which he finally manages to contrive, who should be one of the guests but big-mouth Annabella, whom Verdoux has not yet bumped off. He spends his wedding day trying to avoid Annabella, scurrying underneath tables and ducking into the greenhouse (an appropriate place for both Chaplin and Verdoux), eventually

---

* The film's credits even list Orson Welles as the one who suggested the idea for the film, but, according to Chaplin, Welles apparently did no more than suggest that Chaplin make a film about Bluebeard.

running off and renouncing the rich harvest he has taken so long to plow and plant.

Verdoux's attempts to dispose of Annabella are the funniest sequences in the film, among the funniest material in Chaplin's entire work. The humor stems from Annabella's character. She is, first and foremost, lucky. She won her fortune in the lottery; her luck continues in her consistent evasion of Verdoux's carefully contrived death plots. Annabella is also loud, brash, gaudy. She laughs too loudly and hoarsely. She wears obnoxious cherry-topped hats and vile feather boas, the plumes of which often creep into Chaplin's mouth. And contributing to the character that Chaplin conceived is Martha Raye's brilliant comic performance (he wrote the role specifically for her), which plays in perfect vulgar counterpoint to Chaplin's fastidious, suave, polished Verdoux-Bonheur.

Verdoux makes three attempts to dispose of Annabella, each funnier and more complicated than the previous one. In the first, he simply wants to poison her with a bit of arsenic. Unfortunately, the presence of Annette, the housemaid, interferes with his attempt. In the second, Verdoux has concocted a special new poison that cannot be traced. But Annette gets into the act again. Verdoux has poured the poison into a bottle of peroxide. When Annette starts to dye her hair, using the poison instead of peroxide, she breaks Verdoux's bottle (remember Annabella is lucky) and substitutes a new (and real) bottle of peroxide. Meanwhile, Verdoux prepares for his wife a romantic supper complete with wine (spiced with poison—except it's peroxide). Annabella loves the wine—"Very dry." She drinks and drinks and drinks with no adverse effect. Meanwhile, Annette shrieks as all her hair starts falling out.

For his third attempt, Verdoux takes Annabella out in a tiny rowboat in a vast lake (a beautiful far shot emphasizes the isolation and smallness). He has brought along a rock tied to a noose (recalling the device in *City Lights*). When Annabella asks what the rock is for, Verdoux coyly tells her it's for fishing. She stares into the lake and screams, "I see one. It's a monster. Oh no, it's me." The rest of the murder scene progresses with the same comic clumsiness. Verdoux tries to slip the noose around her neck, but she always catches him and forces him to invent some kind of explanation. When he tries to chloroform her, the handkerchief winds up on his own face, making him woozy. As they try to fish, she sees him with the noose again. "What're you going to do with that?" "Lasso him." Finally, a fish grabs the bait, yanks the line, rocks the boat, and Verdoux winds up in the lake, to be rescued by an adoring Annabella. The comic disaster of a murder attempt is a parodic comment on the climactic murder in Dreiser's *American Tragedy*.

Behind all the comic shenanigans is Chaplin's investigation of why Verdoux must murder. He was a bank clerk—a pillar of respectability in the capitalist temple—when the Depression cost him his job. The need to support his family led to his new occupation. With a perceptively funny piece of business, Chaplin masterfully shows the old bank clerk's instincts under the polish of the new Verdoux. Every time Verdoux must count some money or leaf through a thick telephone directory or ledger, he does a finger ballet, flipping through the individual sheets of paper with incredible dexterity and speed.* Throughout the film Chaplin reminds the viewer of this social-financial context. Verdoux reads newspapers whose headlines proclaim wars, strikes, depressions, layoffs, and the like. Social realities are responsible for Verdouxism.

Chaplin skillfully presents Verdoux as a man with gentle, sympathetic instincts pushed up against the wall of survival. As with Hynkel and the barber in *The Great Dictator*, he uses sound to characterize Verdoux. Verdoux's voice is high and sweet, helping to define him psychologically and morally.

Chaplin also defines Verdoux in a serious confrontation with a prostitute. Verdoux picks her up on a rainy night to try out his new poison. He figures the girl would be better off dead anyway—poor, wet, reduced to selling her body. (Despite trouble with the Hays Office, Chaplin managed to keep in the film the lines that conveyed this information.) He fixes her a nice supper (with a bit of spiced wine, of course) and talks with her before she drinks. Ironically, she loves life, despite its hardships, frustrations, unhappiness. (Here she really speaks for Chaplin, and he will return to this theme in *Limelight*.) He takes note of her optimism, which he considers naïve, but still plans to go through with his experiment, until he finds out about her dead lover. While the girl was in prison, her lover, an invalid, died. Verdoux feels kinship with her: both have loved invalids and define love as sacrifice. Verdoux takes away the glass of poisoned wine just before she drinks it, and gets an unadulterated bottle from the kitchen. His moral system will not permit him to murder this girl. (She eventually rises to become the mistress of a munitions maker. "That's the business I should have been in," says Verdoux.) After Verdoux spares the girl's life, he turns to the camera—and laughs.

This laugh indicates a crucial element of the style and technique that lets Chaplin get away with the film's macabre premise. We are partners in Verdoux's murderous activities. We vicariously experience the joy of bumping off these women—who are all repulsively old and unpleasant; we feel as clever as Verdoux, in on the game with him. Before the scene with the girl, he turns to the camera and says, "And now for the experiment." His laughter at the end of the experiment—he has learned something he

---

* Jerry Lewis also plays a bank clerk, in *The Big Mouth*. But when Lewis counts out money, he sticks his tongue out of his mouth in a series of grotesque, silly maneuvers. Chaplin counts money the way a bank clerk really would—multiplied by ten. That is only one example of what makes Lewis a schlock comedian and Chaplin a comic observer of human behavior.

didn't expect from it—is also shared with us. It tells us something about the relationship between Chaplin the creator and Verdoux the character, who are both supreme ironists. Chaplin artfully detaches us from the illusion of the film; we take the murders no more seriously than the silly ending of *Easy Street*. We accept the film as comic metaphor, not murderous reality. And because we laugh, we think. And because we think, we laugh.

We stop laughing (and thinking) when Chaplin loses this ironic objectivity in the final two reels of the film. Verdoux gives himself up to the police. Awesome figures of authority in earlier Chaplin films, they are total bunglers in this one. Verdoux deftly poisons the detective who gets wise to him (but not wise enough); and he escapes a whole gang of swarming cops simply by walking through the revolving door of a restaurant. But after demonstrating his prowess, he returns "to meet his destiny." The final sequence of the film takes place in his death cell, before the execution. Two men come to talk with him—a reporter (who wants a typical moralistic slant on Verdoux's personality that will explain his atrocities in simple psychological terms for simpleminded readers) and a priest (who wants to save Verdoux's soul). The confrontations between the condemned man and the two interviewers are reminiscent of the similar sequences in Albert Camus' *L'Étranger*.

Verdoux explicitly tells his interrogators that he is a small-time criminal. He has killed very few people compared with governments and businesses that have killed millions. "As a mass killer I'm an amateur. . . . Wars, conflict. It's all business. One murder makes a villain, millions a hero." (The film is two years after Hiroshima.) When the priest asks Verdoux if he begs forgiveness for his sins, Verdoux's reply is equally explicit: "Who knows what sin is."

This long, talky sequence may well make some wish that Chaplin had not capitulated to the talkies. The real problem of the final reels, however, is not that the talk is bad but that the ending is. The whole film is built on another of Chaplin's magnificent paradoxes: on the one hand, morality is undeniably a product of actions, not words, desires, or inclinations (always a Chaplin credo); on the other, actions are undeniably products of specific social and human pressures, not the least of which are expediency and survival. The conclusion of *Monsieur Verdoux* repetitiously states the paradox, rather than demonstrating that paradoxes necessarily continue, as the endings of *The Pilgrim*, *City Lights*, and *Modern Times* do. Before this two-reel sermon, however, the film remains one of the marvels of the Chaplin canon—a mixture of intellect, hilarious comedy, irony, social comment, psychological observation, farcical burlesque, comic performances, inquiry into human accomplishment—as dry as Annabella's glass of peroxide and wine.

Limelight bears approximately the same relation to Chaplin's work as *The Tempest* does to Shakespeare's. Both works are finales, the artists' farewells to their art—although neither could stay away after saying fare-well. Both works contrast age (which their creators feel) with youth, art with life, human accomplishment with human fallibility and mortality, being an artist with being a man. *Limelight*, like *The Tempest*, is a ro-mance rather than a comedy; a story of love, of the human will to achieve and triumph over obstacles, of the continuity of human life and the valid-ity of the human experience. *Limelight* is probably a better film in the light of the 40-year career that went before it and the public animosity that Chaplin was himself suffering at the time than it is as a single work of art. It is one of those reminders that the totality of Chaplin's work is more impressive than any individual film. *Limelight* seems the perfect film to close that totality with Chaplin's favorite figure—the circle.

Limelight's setting is London in 1914—where it all began. Here, how-ever, London is where it all ends. Chaplin plays an old music-hall come-dian, Calvero, who was a great star in the 1880s and 1890s but now is a broken, unemployed drunk. The old has-been meets a young girl who wants to commit suicide; she feels only contempt for life. She was study-ing ballet, but her legs suddenly became paralyzed; she has no reason to live. Calvero, himself without a reason to live, decides to make the girl, Terry (Claire Bloom), his reason. He saves her life, shelters her, and starts talking to her. He is sure her paralysis is psychological. He becomes her psychoanalyst. And he helps her not only walk again but become a great ballet star. During her rehabilitation he has stopped drinking and started looking for work. He plays one disastrous night at the Middlesex Music Hall. The rise of Terry's career parallels the collapse of his own.

At the end of the film's first half, Terry has become a success and Cal-vero is suddenly empty, having nothing at all but her. The problem the film now takes up is the one with which *City Lights* ended—the relation-ship of love and sacrifice, the obligation of the cured patient to her physi-cian and vice versa. Although Terry swears she loves Calvero and wants to marry him, Calvero is certain that Terry really belongs with the young, handsome musician—played by Chaplin's own son, Sydney, an irony that fits nicely into the film's contrast of youth and age, past and present. Cal-vero, not even successful as an anonymous clown in Terry's ballet com-pany, purposely pulls himself away from her, freeing her to go her own way. He becomes a street musician; after 38 years Chaplin returns to *The Vagabond* (and one of his partners is Snub Pollard). When friends ask him why he lives such a life, he replies: "There's something about work-ing the streets I like. I guess it's the tramp in me."

Terry finds him again, and she insists they stay together. She and his friends arrange a benefit night for Calvero, a gala program of stars paying tribute to the great clown, with Calvero himself taking a turn on the bill. Because they are afraid that Calvero will not be funny, they make sure there are claques in the audience. Calvero makes up in his dressing room, and who should be there with him as his accompanist and comic partner but Buster Keaton? Keaton's opening line is simply, "I never thought I'd come to this." And in 1925 Keaton undoubtedly hadn't thought he'd end up playing a has-been second fiddle to Chaplin. The film is about more than what is just in the film.

Calvero goes on for his number, despite the callousness and contempt of the stagehands. What follows is the most overpoweringly emotional moment in the whole Chaplin canon. Calvero does his routines—and they are brilliantly funny. We have known how funny they might be because of the film's dream sequences, when Chaplin magnificently demonstrates he is still the complete physical and pantomimic clown. But Calvero in front of a real audience succeeds in drawing their genuine and uncontrollable laughter—without help from any claques. After watching Calvero suffer failure, abuse, and contempt for the length of the film, this sudden proof of his comic brilliance—this sincere and loving laughter and applause which he has craved so desperately—produces a rush of emotion in a viewer who has followed the Chaplin life and career that is simply indescribable.

Calvero is such a huge hit that the audience clamors for more. He does several routines. The "Flea Number" is a tender dance-mime that creates two invisible lover-fleas, Phyllis and Henry, before our eyes. In the "Tramp Number," Charlie re-creates the tramp for us, and to show how much his body can still do (at age sixty-three), he tumbles gymnastically into a split, after which, with complete ease, he slides his legs up together and strides off. Finally, in the "Chaplin-Keaton Duet," Charlie is the violinist, Buster the nearsighted, bespectacled pianist. The sheet music falls all over the stage; Buster and Charlie cannot get their instruments in tune; the fiddle's strings break; the musicians yank out a tangle of piano wires; Buster steps on Charlie's fiddle; Charlie can't find it because it's stuck on Keaton's foot.

They finally play the song. First a mad gypsy dance, then a sad romantic song, then back to the mad dance again. Chaplin's face brilliantly reflects the tone and tune of the music, snapping schizophrenically between glee and dolor and back to glee again. The act ends when the mad music gets so frenzied that Keaton hurls himself off the piano stool and Chaplin falls into the bass drum in the pit. Calvero keeps fiddling as they carry him offstage in the drum.

But Calvero has suffered a heart attack in the fall. He is weak and near death. Still he returns to the stage, stuck in the drum, to say a few last words to his newly converted believers. Then he returns to the wings, and it is Terry's turn. She doesn't want to go on with Calvero so ill. They lie to her, saying that Calvero's injury is slight. While Calvero lies in the wings dying, watching her, she dances on stage, bathed in the spotlight. Calvero dies in the dark wings while Terry dances in the light. And as she twirls in a pirouetting circle, the film ends. The circular dance continues; the light is always there. Only the dancers change. Despite the public antagonism, the loss of his audience, the fears of losing his touch, Chaplin (in the guise of Calvero) reaffirms his commitment to life, to human artistic expression, and to selfless sacrifice for another human being, which is the ultimate act of love.

CHAPTER 9

Keaton

—

L IKE Chaplin, much of what Keaton became as an adult clown was shaped by childhood experiences. If Chaplin's childhood was a combination of homelessness, poverty, and hunger, Keaton's was quite the reverse. Although the Keaton family life was far from normal, the family did stay together—both on the stage and off. In the vaudeville act "The Three Keatons," Buster's father, Joe, held the boy's ankles and swept the stage with Buster's hair (Buster was billed as "The Human Mop"), after which he hurled his son across the stage, over the scenery, and into the flies (and, once, into the audience). Buster learned to suffer any kind of fall without injury. As an adult, Keaton injured himself seriously only once; he broke his leg when his foot got caught in one of the intricate, crazy machines that dominated his films (the moving staircase in *The Electric House*). Keaton's adult body was so resilient that he broke his neck during the filming of *Sherlock Jr.* without finding out about the injury until years afterward.

Keaton's delight in intricate machines also began in childhood. At their summer home in Muskegon, Michigan (the Chaplin family could not even afford a home, much less a summer one), Keaton and his pals rigged up various tricky devices. One of them was an outhouse whose boards collapsed at the tug of a string, exposing the busily seated occupant to the wind and world. Another was a tricky fishing line that fooled the victim by seeming to be attached to a huge fish; it was really hooked to a piling of the yacht club. (A modification of this fishing device appears in *The Frozen North*.) As a child, Keaton also discovered his love of sports—particularly baseball. As a star at M-G-M he organized a studio baseball team; and his love of baseball shows itself in two films (*College* and *The Cameraman*) in which the baseball sequences are among the funniest, most exciting moments.

Acrobatics, athletics, and machines—three essential ingredients of the great Keaton films. Buster received his nickname (he was christened Joseph Francis Keaton) from his godfather, Harry Houdini, after the infant Buster tumbled down a flight of stairs without busting himself. On a single day of his one-year-old existence, Buster caught a brick on the head, got his finger caught in the wringer of a washing machine, and got caught up in a cyclone which swept him into the air and carried him hundreds of feet through the town. The cyclone practically leveled the Midwest town, but Buster survived all three catastrophes without serious injury. (He did, however, lose a joint of one finger.) The Keaton pattern had been established while he was still in swaddling clothes—impossible physical feats accomplished with miraculous success. In his films, Keaton never performed a physical stunt with the aid of any trick. Except for using a double once (to pole-vault into the girl's window in *College*), Keaton actually performed every stunt in every Keaton film. And he often doubled for stuntmen who were less proficient than he. Unlike Chaplin, he consistently caught the perfect performance of a gag in a single take. He would have to. Such stunts did not bear frequent repetition.

Whereas Chaplin's comic technique centered about his face, hands, and legs, each of which operated as separate entities, with individual limberness and subtlety, the Keaton comic technique centered about the body as a whole, a single physical object that could comport itself in space the way no physical object ought to have the right or power to do. When Keaton takes a fall, his body doesn't merely fall. It lifts itself several feet into the air and then hurls itself down onto the ground. When he does a flip, his body doesn't merely flip. It leaps into the air, tautens itself into planklike stiffness, then tucks in its knees and tumbles over itself in mid-air. The Keaton body is alternately, indeed simultaneously, both elastic and bone, the most malleable and the most tensile of physical substances.

When The Three Keatons broke up in 1917, Buster could have gone on the stage by himself at $250 a week. Instead, he took a job in films at $40. His career in films paralleled Chaplin's. Keaton began his apprenticeship as a subordinate clown in pure knockabout farces. Whereas Chaplin began with Sennett, Keaton began with Arbuckle, a Sennett pupil, in highly Sennettesque romps. Keaton then, like Chaplin, went on to perfect his comic technique and cinematic ideas in two-reel films. Then, like Chaplin, Keaton reached his maturity in a series of features. Finally, like Chaplin, Keaton suffered disappointment, disgrace, and rejection by his public—although for reasons and under circumstances very different from Chaplin's.

The Keaton Comic World

Keaton never took the world so seriously as Chaplin did. Whereas Chaplin's films, even his individual comic bits, are pointedly social, intellectual, concerned with hunger, humiliation, justice, and freedom, Keaton's films seem pointedly pointless. Keaton as an artist was never conscious of trying to say something; he merely tried to do something that he found funny.* In his autobiography Keaton belittles Chaplin's seriousness and intellectual pretensions. Keaton constantly tried to be a "good guy" with his "team"—gags on the set, drinks with the gang at the studio or at home, playing bridge, playing baseball—things that Chaplin did not do with his employees. Keaton's surface cheeriness shines through his autobiography in his refusal to say anything nasty even about those who ruined him. He went out of his way to be nice. And this niceness exists in his films—on the surface. They seem to be purely funny collections of gags and situations.

But beneath the surface there is more. The situations that Keaton found funny, the way he comported himself in relation to objects and the world, the stories he selected, and the way he solved his comic problems successfully in those stories—all these imply an attitude toward human experience, whether Keaton was conscious of it or not. The tension between surface and depths begins with the Keaton face—where discussions of Keaton always begin. The Keaton "Great Stone Face" has itself become a stony cliché. The fact that Keaton's face reflects no reaction to any event around him—no smile, no laugh, no tear, no puzzlement, no inquiry, no anticipation, nothing—lures some into assuming that Buster neither feels nor thinks. But the Keaton character is not unfeeling; and he is certainly not stupid. The Keaton character uses far more intellect, far more long-range strategy, than Charlie does. And that strategy is a product of thought.

In *The General* (1926), for example, two little town lads tag along behind Buster as he goes to visit Annabelle, his girl. They walk behind him into her parlor and sit down. Buster, without changing the look on his face, stands up, puts on his hat, and starts to walk toward the door. The two boys, of course, stand up to follow. Buster opens the door and the two boys walk out; Buster then closes the door behind them, takes off his hat, and goes back to sit beside Annabelle, again without changing the look on his face. The objective has been accomplished. Buster has performed a sensible action in a pragmatic way. And he has not tipped off a single maneuver; he plays his cards the way cards should be played.

* J. P. Lebel makes the same point in his perceptive study *Buster Keaton* (London and New York, 1967).

This initial bit of strategy in *The General* is merely the prologue to a whole film in which similar pragmatic strategies drive the plot.

Buster's unchanging expression is another strategy that helps him survive. He does not kick, like Charlie; he feints. Behind the blank eyes and frozen mouth, the gears of Buster's brain are constantly clicking and turning. What it consistently comes up with is inevitably right in the circumstances. If the circumstances don't make any sense, well, that isn't Buster's fault. The face is a mask, a ruse, a cover for the ceaseless activity of the brain beneath.

The activity of the Keaton brain translates itself into action, not expression, as Chaplin's does. Whereas Lloyd's face shows all the mental activity that is taking place, and Langdon's face all the mental activity that isn't taking place, Keaton's body alone tells all. That Body can either be in motion (kinetic) or at rest (latent).

At rest the Keaton body is a coiled spring; its perfect poise, its tense wariness, reveals its potential—even when covered with clothes. Keaton wears costumes beautifully. Many of his films effectively and purposefully use period costumes: the elegant gray cutaway and top hat in *Our Hospitality*; the formal top hat, white tie, and tails in *The Navigator, Battling Butler*, and *Spite Marriage*; the loose shirt, ascot tie, and flowing long hair of *The General. Battling Butler* is almost a male fashion show as Buster models a series of outfits for fishing, hunting, and camping.

The latent energy of the Keaton body that shines through his clothes becomes even more obvious when he is stripped to his shorts in *College* or *Battling Butler*. In those films, Keaton's body is so physically developed, so perfectly shaped and muscled, that he throws the whole premise of both plots (that Buster is physically weak and incompetent) under severe suspicion. Whereas Chaplin in shorts (*The Champion, City Lights*) still looks like a baggy-pants, puny weakling (the shorts are indeed baggy), Keaton in shorts is an uncaged and uncased jaguar.

The Keaton body in motion is equally elegant, poised, and commanding in its apparent ability to accomplish anything with the greatest ease and smoothness. Keaton performing a stunt was apparently no more taxed than Keaton at rest. Unlike Lloyd, whose technique makes every physical stunt look as difficult as possible, Keaton makes the most impossible physical stunts look like nonchalant, everyday activities: his smooth, effortless leaping from deck to deck in *The Navigator* and *Steamboat Bill Jr.*, from car to car in *The General*; the effortless swing over the falls that snares his lady love just as she plunges toward her death in *Our Hospitality*. Like his family's lifelong friend Harry Houdini, Buster Keaton makes the impossible seem easy. Unlike Houdini, Keaton shows us his body's magic while he performs the feat.

Keaton's real personality reveals itself not in facial expression but in posture and motion. Just as Chaplin thought words more limited, less communicative than mime and gesture, Keaton thought facial expression more limited than physical posture and motion. Keaton, unlike Chaplin, plays many different characters in his films, from different eras and different social classes: Rollo Treadway, Willie Canfield, Johnny Gray, Willie McKay, Jimmie Shannon, Alfred Butler. But beneath the different names and surroundings, all these Keaton figures reveal the same habits of mind —composed, careful, pragmatic, completely certain of the task to be accomplished, wildly imaginative in accomplishing it if that is the most sensible method, extremely flexible at responding to new obstacles, dogged about reaching the goal. All of these mental attitudes are clearly expressed by the Keaton body and without the Keaton face—or rather by the interplay of body and face, for the activity of the body plays in counterpoint to the inactivity of the face, leaving the spectator to infer what is going on behind that beautiful mask. The blank face is not a comic gimmick but a means of survival in a chaotic, dangerous world. It knows much more than it shows.

Psychological interaction and human motivation in the Keaton films are much more formulaic than in the Chaplin films. Motivation is far more literary: the plot demands a particular kind of action, and Buster's motivation is clearly to accomplish it. The desire to win the girl, to prove his mettle, and especially to stay alive are the three spurring drives. These formulas are further reasons that Keaton's films, unlike Chaplin's, did not require subtle and sensitive facial interactions. What the characters want and why are the basic stuff of the Chaplin films. What they want and why are obvious in the Keaton films; how they get what they want is the business at hand. For this premise, the body in motion is more useful than the expressive face. But unlike movement in the Sennett-style film, the Keaton body in motion is always directed in a specific manner toward a specific goal. It is not miscellaneous movement.

But blank-faced Keaton had other means to express himself than the body. Although that body is the center of the Keaton film world, many things revolve about that center. The Keaton body is a single object, indeed a small one, in space. The element surrounding Keaton is not society—a social role, definition, or assumption—as in Chaplin's films, but nature itself—trees, forests, oceans, the vast plains, cyclones, fire, rivers. Keaton is not a little guy set against malignant social forces, like Chaplin; he is a little guy set against elemental forces. And natural enemies, unlike Chaplin's opponents, are not necessarily malignant and oppressive. Nature is neuter. It is huge, violent, and overpowering. But it is also conquerable. Nature has no will. Only man has will. And Keaton films consistently reveal the triumph of human will and spirit over natural opponents. The Keaton comedies are more epic than Chaplin's because they show man in conflict with traditional epic forces rather than with individual men and social attitudes.

Keaton's camera reflects the change in emphasis. There is very little nature in Chaplin's films—even in *The Gold Rush* and *Sunnyside*, which use nature as a metaphor. Chaplin's camera works very close to the human players; human faces and bodies are Chaplin's photographic subjects. Keaton's camera works much farther away from the people; even Keaton himself is often only a distant figure in the frame, a human dot surveying the horizon with his hand on his brow. The Keaton film focuses on the interplay between man and nature. Every Keaton feature includes major sequences shot outdoors on location; most Chaplin films were shot on his studio lot. Keaton films were outdoor films; Chaplin films were not. (Even outdoor films such as *Sunnyside, The Pilgrim,* and *The Gold Rush* seem claustrophobic—intentionally.) The outdoors gave Keaton the space to move and the vast panoramas to contrast with his moving body, that small piece of elastic granite. Chaplin could generate a world of excitement from a single room (for example, *One A.M.*); Keaton films needed the world.

Little man juxtaposed with big universe—this was the Keaton theme, cinematic principle of composition, and basis of story construction. It also influenced the kinds of objects that Keaton chose to play against. Huge inanimate objects and living opponents were merely a manifestation of the hugeness of nature. Keaton played against a dinosaur, a waterfall, an ocean liner, a landslide, a herd of cattle, a locomotive, the entire Union and Confederate armies, a steamboat, a Tong war, a gang of bootleggers, a storm at sea, a tribe of Indians, and the entire New York police force. In most of the films, Keaton began playing against the enormous object and ended up playing with it. The object that dwarfed him at the film's beginning became an ally that he used to defeat others by the end.

Keaton conquered immense mechanical objects in addition to conquering immense natural forces; the two conquests were parallel and interrelated. Keaton's attitude toward machines is clearly two-edged—unlike Chaplin's monolithic contempt for escalators and asesmbly lines. Machines can pulverize little people; but people run machines, not the other way round. And people make machines, not the other way round. Once the principle of machines has been discovered, they can be tamed by men. Keaton sees both the brutality and the wonder of machines.

This attitude toward machines influenced his cinematic technique and makes the union between a mind like Keaton's and a mechanical medium like the movies particularly felicitous. Keaton favored the far shot, not only to juxtapose his individual body with the natural universe, but also to provide a distant view of how a particular mechanism works. The cinematic far shot provides the means to see both cause and effect, to see all the relevant elements, to illuminate the total process of a mechanism. And that is why Keaton's far shots are so memorable and so revealing— not just a little man on the vast plains of *Go West*, or a little man falling from a rope bridge in *The Paleface*, or a little man leaping from train car to train car in *The General,* but the principle of showing how a totality works.

In both *The Haunted House* (1921) and *The High Sign* (1920), a Keaton far shot reveals all four rooms of a house (one wall cut away) and exactly how the chase progresses from one to another. In *The Navigator* (1924), a far shot reveals both decks of an ocean liner and both aisles on each deck, so we can see exactly how a ship's hugeness can keep two lone passengers from finding each other. In *The General* (1926), another far shot reveals the Union train on a bridge between the Union and Confederate sides of a river. The bridge magnificently collapses and the train slides into the river, drowning the Union hopes.

Perhaps the most brilliant Keaton far shot to reveal a process (and what a process!) is in *Sherlock Jr.* (1924). A single far shot presents (1) a room where Buster is surrounded by thugs (Keaton has dissolved its fourth wall); (2) an open window with a paper hoop that Buster previously placed in it; and (3) the exterior of the house outside the window. In a single shot Buster dashes toward the window (1), leaps through it, through the hoop resting inside the window frame (2), somehow puts on a dress stuffed inside the hoop as he is tumbling through it in midair, rights himself on the ground outside the house (3), and begins to impersonate an old beggar woman, since he is now wearing a dress. Without the far shot, it would be impossible to believe that a human being could turn himself into a beggar woman while in midair tumbling through a hoop; it would also be impossible to believe that any comic acrobat could perform such a stunt. Apart from the mechanical performance of the stunt, there is the idea behind it. Who else would think of escaping his foes in such an incredible way and with such an incredible means to an incredible disguise? Keaton's far shot makes incredibility to the third power completely credible.

No director ever used the far shot with more strategic effectiveness (rather than just pictorial grandness) than Keaton. Keaton far shots turn human processes into mechanisms (Sherlock's leap through the hoop: pure Bergson) and reveal the human causes of mechanical effects (the chase in the *Navigator:* a mechanical game). For Keaton's physical comedy is essentially a synthesis of malleable human flesh and Bergsonian encrusted machine. While his human brain clicks away its strategies, his body becomes a perfectly designed machine for carrying them out. Where Sennett converts people into pure toys and Chaplin displays a limber flexibility that abhors the mechanical and inelastic, Keaton is both machine and man at once.

Keaton's interest in machines and mechanical processes also influences the way he handles the camera, that cinema machine. Keaton was far more interested than Chaplin in the camera apparatus, and he had more fun with it as mechanical toy. In *The Cameraman* (1928) Keaton demon-

strates Buster's incompetence as a cinematographer by using double ex-
posures and split frames to show a battleship gliding down Fifth Avenue.
Buster's "newsreel" is an unintentional surrealistic joke. Perhaps Keaton's
greatest use of the cinema as toy is in the short *The Playhouse* (1921),
when Keaton plays every role on the vaudeville bill, as well as every member of the audience, with the aid of the masked lens and multiple exposure. Most delightful in mechanical terms are Keaton's impersonations
of both members of a tap-dance duo; Keaton, as both hoofers, dances in
perfect symmetry with what seems a mirror image of himself. And *The
Playhouse*'s pyrotechnics climax with Keaton's playing all nine (count
'em, nine) members of a minstrel act—from the interlocutor to Mr. Bones.
He accomplished the dazzling technical trick by shooting the sequence
nine times, with a perfect nine-piece mask over the lens (designed by
Keaton's great mechanic-designer, Fred Gabourie), and with Buster oc-
cupying exactly the right spot in the frame each time.

Keaton's greatest cinema game, his clearest realization of the cinema's
mechanical basis, is the famous montage sequence in *Sherlock Jr.* Buster
plays a motion-picture projectionist. As he falls asleep in the projection
booth, a transparent second self (double exposure) rises out of Buster's body
and walks through the theater and up to the screen. After several failures,
Buster's dream-ghost succeeds in entering the looking glass of a motion-
picture screen. (Lewis Carroll is not so far away.) Once Buster gets inside
the film screen, he finds he is at the mercy of film space and film time,
not reality's space and time. As Buster stands in a single spot in the frame,
the environment surrounding him undergoes the editing process. Buster
remains fixed; he maintains his spatial continuity. But the universe does not
as it instantaneously shifts from a desert, to an ocean, to a snowdrift, to a
lair of lions. Buster knows who and what he is; he has complete control
over himself and his actions. He merely is powerless to control the filmic
montage that instantaneously changes his physical surroundings without
allowing him to do anything about it.

This scene in *Sherlock Jr.* is very much at the heart of Keaton's style and
imagination. The mechanical perfection of the stunt is extraordinary, but
behind the mechanical ability to work the gag is the sheer marvel of even
conceiving it. Such farfetched lunacy is not what Chaplin would do at all;
it is too dependent on trick, too divorced from individual human feelings,
too much a far-out stunt. But it is precisely the kind of imagination that
Keaton reveals in film after film. However, the stunt would not have been
suitable for any screen comic or character. Despite its apparent lack of
humanness and personality it has a unique relation to the Keaton *persona*.

This relation is clear, first, in the combination of sense and nonsense in
the gag. The gag works not just because of the montage idea, but because
a human being tries to make sense out of impossibly changing surroundings;
the activities of the universe (in this sequence, a cinematic universe) make

no sense, but Keaton goes about his business trying to make as much sense of it as he can, to deal with it in the most practical way he can devise. That conflict—between senseless surroundings and sensible Keaton—is what makes the montage sequence of *Sherlock Jr.* a uniquely Keaton gag.

Second, Keaton knows that he is toying with the differences between cinema and reality, with the different ways that cinema can scramble both time and space. For *Sherlock Jr.* is, above all, a movie about a movie—a film within a film within a film. This intention is especially obvious in the film's conclusion when Buster, returned to the reality of his projection booth from his glorious screen dream, must deal with his real girlfriend. To know how to conclude his story line with her, he must look at the motion-picture screen to see how it is done in the movie. And Keaton visually parallels the activities in the projection booth with those on the screen by shooting the scene through the window of the booth. Just as there is a frame around the movie screen, there is a frame around the scene in "reality." Keaton's imaginative brain has discovered both the ways that the cinematic universe defies nature and the way nature would try to copy cinema if it could. The film's story, gags, situations, and character all proceed from the same idea—the depiction of life-in-cinema and cinema-in-life.

As a further demonstration that Keaton's far-out stunts are highly personal and not just gimmicks, the opening sequence of the short *The Scarecrow* (1920) does very nicely. In this scene, Keaton and his roommate live in an efficiency cottage. Keaton literally makes that cottage as efficient as possible. Everything is on strings—matches, stove, dining table, salt and pepper shakers, napkins, milk, refrigerator. Everything is worked by pulling a string and setting the perfect machine in motion. At least two other films use the same mechanical gag: Snub Pollard's *It's a Gift* (1923) and Harry Langdon's *Three's a Crowd* (1927). In both of these later imitations of a Keaton machine, the comics and filmmakers work as hard as possible to show how funny, extraordinary, bizarre, and ingenious such mechanizations are. In Pollard's film, the machines define him as a silly, crazy inventor. Keaton's *Scarecrow* does exactly the opposite. Keaton and his pal go about using the mechanical gadgetry as if it were as natural and ordinary as waking up in the morning, getting out of bed, and eating breakfast—which it is.* Keaton makes the unnatural perfection of his mechanical contrivances seem human and natural by showing the perfect coordination of Buster and pal in adapting to the needs and rhythms of the machine: handing each other the rolls, passing the salt and pepper, slinging the milk into the fridge. Keaton personalizes such a scene in his calm ability to

---

* Keaton's first cinematic use of a domestic machine with strings was probably the 1919 Arbuckle film *The Garage*. This film contains so many Keaton elements— the machine, Buster's acrobatics, a human ladder that would recur in *Neighbors*, the Keaton pose with hand on brow surveying the horizon—that it reveals how far Keaton developed in his apprenticeship with Arbuckle.

assimilate the extraordinary and mechanical into the routine of normal life.

Almost all the great Keaton gags reveal this synthesis of impossible nonsense and pragmatic sense. In the short *Cops* (1922) Buster thrusts out his hand to signal for a left turn. A dog bites his wrist. Next time, Buster signals with a boxing glove hooked onto an expandable towel rack. Another very sensible machine. Unfortunately, the boxing glove smashes a traffic cop in the face. Later in the same film, Buster wants to light a cigarette. An anarchist tosses a bomb onto the seat of Buster's wagon. Buster calmly picks up the bomb, lights his cigarette with the burning fuse, and then tosses the "match" away. What else do you do with an unlighted cigarette and a handy bomb? Unfortunately, he tosses the "match" into the midst of a policeman's parade. Keaton, of course, has no control over the consequences of his sensible actions. A pragmatic maneuver can produce unforeseen and disastrous results. Conversely, a simple pragmatic maneuver can have monumentally effective results far beyond the intention of Keaton's strategy—as in *The General*. Such disproportion between act and result, intention and consequence is another blend of sense and nonsense. A man can control his actions, not their consequences.

There is similar sensible nonsense in the short *The Paleface* (1922), when Buster, tied to a wooden stake, is about to become fuel for the fire. Buster, however, succeeds in getting the stake out of the ground. Now he could run away—or attempt it. But how far could he get tied to a portable stake? So Buster sneaks up behind each Red Man gathering tinder and slyly conks him over the head with the stake. Much more sensible strategy.

The plots of Keaton's features usually juxtapose the sensible and the impossible. In *Our Hospitality*, Buster must go through a series of practical maneuvers to avoid being the next casualty in the Canfield-McKay feud. In *The General* he goes through a series of tiny practical maneuvers —chops wood, uses logs, boxes, rope, kerosene lantern, and the like—and in the process singlehandedly rescues his train and his girl from the Union Army and then wins a terrific victory for the South. In *The Navigator*, he goes through a series of practical maneuvers in the process of running an entire ocean liner by himself, repairing it when it gets damaged, and fighting off a whole tribe of jungle savages who attack it. Buster performs the ultimately impossible by merely performing the ordinary—step by step, bit by bit. Eventually a series of steps mounts to a heroic plateau; individual moments of sense add up to one impossible sum.

The first two reels of the Keaton features set up some character trait in Buster that makes it seem even more impossible for him to accomplish such feats: weakness (*Go West, The Three Ages, Our Hospitality, Battling Butler, College, Steamboat Bill Jr.*) and/or bungling incompetence (*Sherlock Jr., The Navigator, Seven Chances, The General, The Cameraman, Spite Marriage*). Buster, without erasing the general inadequacy established in the opening reels, shows how he can still perform impossibly heroic acts. Thus, the Keaton features begin slowly. Unlike the Chaplin films, which can start with a Charliesque bang of a gag, the early reels of the Keaton feature must establish the character Buster plays. Then the Buster character faces what might be called "the Keaton imperative." Buster *must* do something—something that the character he plays would never do, yet somehow must. The imperative can be thrust on him specifically: you must marry by 7:00 P.M. of your twenty-seventh birthday to receive $7,000,000 (*Seven Chances*, 1925); you must become an athlete before you can woo the pretty girl again (*College*, 1927); you must be a tough physical brute to wed the daughter (*Battling Butler*, 1926). Or the imperative can be simply a problem that Buster walks into and cannot possibly walk away from (and continue to exist): saving himself from murder and the girl from the falls (*Our Hospitality*, 1923); steering an ocean liner (*The Navigator*); taking a whole herd of cattle to market (*Go West*, 1925); saving his locomotive (*The General*); saving his father from a cyclone (*Steamboat Bill Jr.*, 1927); saving himself and his wife from gangsters (*Spite Marriage*, 1929).

Buster's successful accomplishment of the Keaton imperative reveals how close the Keaton comic world is to melodrama, and how influenced Keaton was by the master of melodrama, D. W. Griffith. Many of Keaton's films culminate in variations on Griffith's last-minute rescues (*Our Hospitality, Seven Chances, Sherlock Jr., College, Steamboat Bill Jr., Spite Marriage*). *The General* is a pure chase. Buster's last-minute rescue of Natalie Talmadge from the awesome waterfall of *Our Hospitality* seems a specific glance at Richard Barthelmess and Lillian Gish at the end of *Way Down East*. And if there is any doubt about Keaton's awareness of Griffith, consider that in *Go West* Buster plays a character called "the Friendless One" and his lover's name—she merely happens to be a cow— is "Brown Eyes." Keaton loved parody, as so many of the two-reelers reveal: *The Frozen North* (parodies William S. Hart), *Convict 13* (parodies prison pictures), *The Playhouse* (parodies Thomas Ince's egotism).

Among Keaton's favorite targets for parody were cinematic plots, structures, and devices themselves. *The Three Ages* (1923) is a story of three identical love triangles in three historical periods, its structure an obvious parody of *Intolerance*. Keaton also makes the film overly symmetrical— for symmetry was another of Keaton's mechanical passions. In all three sequences (Stone Age, Roman, modern) the plots are identical (parents want girl to marry rich, strong suitor, not Buster) and the devices are identical—transportation (dinosaur, chariot, automobile); fortune-tellers; sporting contests (Stone Age golf, chariot race, football). Keaton also destroys seriousness with anachronism. When one of the dogs pulling Keaton's chariot in the big race poops out (it's snowing, so dogs are more practical than horses), Buster takes a "spare" dog out of the chariot's trunk; as the Roman fortune-teller predicts Buster's future using two huge dice (marked with Roman numerals from I to VI), four Negro litter bearers drop their passenger and run over to shoot craps.*

Our Hospitality parodies "feud" melodramas. It even begins with an apparently serious melodramatic reel to set up the feuding milieu. Although some critics have thought this serious beginning an error, what better way to begin a parody of a melodrama than by setting up your target? *Sherlock Jr.* parodies the detective story and serious cinematic versions of that Conan Doyle hero's exploits—including the close-up of the elegantly gloved hand ringing the doorbell (see Stan Laurel's *The Sleuth*, 1922, for an identical shot) and the unbelievable death plots the crooks have hatched for poor Sherlock (dynamited pool ball, poisoned wine, and guillotine-like axe poised above a chair). *Seven Chances* parodies the domestic romantic comedy in which the young man is too shy to ask his girl to marry him. It culminates in an unbelievable chase as thousands of would-be brides and thousands of landsliding rocks chase Buster all over town, all the while pressing him toward that seven-o'clock deadline. *Go West* parodies the cowboy film; *Battling Butler*, boxing heroism; *The General*, Civil War romances; *College*, college pictures; *Steamboat Bill Jr.*, Mississippi riverboat romances.

Although the features are playful, they have an underlying moral edge. When Shakespeare parodied both classical heroism and medieval romance in *Troilus and Cressida*, he raised the serious and disturbing question of whether any virtuous human action is possible in a world where both love and honor are reduced to nonsense. Although Keaton consciously dealt in the completely comic, his films suggest serious human issues that cannot be laughed away. The artificiality of the code of honor in *Our Hospitality*, which demands on the one hand that the Canfields treat the guest in their home with courtesy and, on the other, that they murder him as soon as he steps out the door, is certainly the basis of many ingenious Keaton gags —coy and subtle attempts to stay inside the house, disguising himself in a dress to leave it. But that code of honor is vicious as well as comical. It is inhuman, respecting abstract forms rather than the human spirit. The word "honor" in the film is no more than a word, divorced from the realities that created both the word and the concept.

That a human being's worth is defined in so many of the films as physical prowess or material success is also central to Keaton's observation of the separation of form and essence. Like Chaplin, Keaton contrasted surfaces with more important realities. Where Chaplin's contrasts invariably

* Keaton's racial jokes, like Sennett's, are very impolite by today's standards. They are also very funny. Actually Keaton's "sick" jokes and racial jokes are neither sick nor bigoted. They do not stem from contempt or superiority but are simply comic magnifications of human observation. Race and physical deformity exist in the world. They are, therefore, perfectly suitable comic subjects.

center on social definitions of human respectability and success, Keaton's center on personal definitions of human integrity and accomplishment. In *The Three Ages*, the girl's parents in all three ages want a rich, powerful (both socially and physically) mate for their daughter. In *Sherlock Jr.*, the man who gives his sweetheart a $3 box of chocolates is superior to the man who spends only $1—even if the gentleman stole the $3. In *Battling Butler*, the girl's family values a man in boxing trunks and despises the same man in expensive suits.

The moral culmination of the Keaton cycle is *The General*, which contains all the typical values of the Keaton canon—and more. Once again Buster earns the contempt of his girl and her family. They assume that he is a coward and does not want to enlist in the Confederate Army. The fact is that he had tried to enlist but was rejected: the Army needs his pragmatic abilities as an engineer; he is worthless to them as a romantic warrior. The Lee family is blinder than the recruiting officer. They do not respect Buster as engineer, only as potential soldier. The rest of the film reveals that being an engineer is handier than being a soldier. Further, it casts doubt on all the clichés about war and romanticism, of which the American Civil War is perhaps the most splendid historical example. *The General* is anti-heroic, anti-romantic, anti-war, turning romantic illusions into comic bits.

The consistent Keaton motif is the ridiculing of all inhuman definitions of human worth. To define a man by his uniform, wallet, muscles, or family name is not to define him as a person. In his denigration of the value of clothes (despite his elegance in wearing them) and surface characteristics as a means of defining a man, Keaton is the opposite of Brecht (*A Man's a Man*) and, therefore, of Chaplin (whose tramp's clothes *are* the tramp). What Buster accomplishes often has little to do with social and literary clichés about what certain *types* of men can accomplish. The Keaton character consistently shows how much a little, unheroic, unromantic man can do simply by going about his business in his own way, exercising his individual human abilities and will.

But beneath Buster's accomplishments there is not the same optimism, the same view of success as there is in Harold Lloyd or Douglas Fairbanks films. In several of the shorts, Buster fails to fulfill the Keaton imperative. In *Cops* (1922), his lady love demands that Buster make something of himself. What he makes is a public enemy, attracting the animosity of every policeman in New York City. After this dazzling performance in the negative, the girl rejects him for the final time. Buster walks back into the police station, choosing to suffer their physical punishment rather than the pain of his emotional loss. The film ends with a tombstone, Buster's porkpie hat hanging atop it. Similarly, in *Daydreams* (1922) Keaton's girl demands that Buster make himself a success. After his failure and her rejection, the film ends with yet another tombstone. *One Week* (1920) and *The Boat*

(1921) end with disaster: the little house and ship that Buster spent so long putting together have been smashed or sunk.

Even the features exist in the shadow of disaster and the tombstone. In *College*, after Buster has successfully mastered athletics, his bullying rival, and his lady's affections, Keaton ends with a strange series of dissolves— Buster and wife with kids, the two as a pair of old folks, and then their tombstones in the cemetery. Though Keaton may have meant to imply their living "happily ever after," those two tombstones cast doubt on the whole value of the task he has mastered and the prize he has won.

Many of the Keaton features seem skeptical about that prize. In most, doubt arises primarily from the fact that the lady Buster wins isn't much worth winning. The Keaton women are literary personages; they have names such as Annabelle Lee, Mary Jones, Mary Haynes, and Betty King. They provide Buster with a literary motivation: the striving to win them. But they have little apparent value except that Buster wants them. Keaton takes no pains to give them any value, whereas Chaplin's women, metaphors in his symbolic system, do at least smile, reveal tenderness, sensitivity, and charm. In Keaton films, the only reason he seems to care about the lady is that the plot would have it so.

Keaton's denigration of his ladies was conscious: "There were usually but three principals—the villain, myself, and the girl, and she was never important. . . . The leading lady had to be fairly good-looking, and it helped some if she had a little acting ability. As far as I was concerned I didn't insist that she have a sense of humor. There was always the danger that such a girl would laugh at a gag in the middle of a scene, which meant ruining it and having to remake it."[2] Although Lebel thinks that Keaton performs his heroic feats because he has been inspired by a lady,[3] Keaton really accomplishes the heroic because he has to, "because it's there." Keaton's ultimate feeling for his leading ladies comes through in *Go West*, when he uses a cow as the ingenue. Are we to believe that a cow actually spurs Buster's heroic impulses? Not without also seeing Keaton's sense of parody. No wonder no Keaton ingenue made more than two features with him.

The two nastiest Keaton women are the ladies in *The General* (Marian Mack) and *Spite Marriage* (Dorothy Sebastian). In the earlier film, the lady rejects Buster, the man she supposedly loves, for his lack of courage. She, like everyone else in the film, is a victim of false romantic notions. When Buster discovers Annabelle Lee in the Union Army's headquarters, she immediately makes the romantic assumption: Buster has performed all his heroics for her. Ironically, he has only been chasing his train and happened to stumble on her as a surprise bonus.

This romantic bonus almost costs him his train and his life, for Annabelle is incompetent. She runs the train in reverse when it should go forward; she starts it up when it should remain still, and vice versa. She is even incompetent at throwing pieces of wood into the engine's furnace, rejecting a perfectly good one on the aesthetic grounds that it has a hole in it, and thereafter choosing the tiniest, most genteel wood chips she can find.

But she receives poetic justice for her incompetence. Buster dumps her in a burlap sack, hauls her about like a sack of oats or potatoes, and can only imagine her pain when a heavy wooden box gets piled on top of the sack. Although Keaton's strategy is designed to rescue her, it is also designed to be as painful and undignified for her as possible. When Annabelle throws the engine a tiny piece of wood, Buster mimics her. He finds an even tinier chip, daintily hands it to her, and calmly watches as she seriously throws it into the fire. He then drops the dainty pose, grabs her by the neck, and throttles her. But he stops himself—and instantly switches from strangulation to a kiss.

The lady in *Spite Marriage* is the bitchiest of all the Keaton women. She thinks Buster a foolish idiot, but she marries him to spite the man she really loves, who has rejected her. Buster also gives this lady a dose of poetic justice. The sweet thing gets drunk on their wedding night; Buster hauls her—again the woman becomes an inanimate object—out of the nightclub and into their bedroom. Then follows a hilarious ten-minute scene in which Buster tries to hoist her insensible body onto the bed. (For once, Keaton's ingenue is a brilliant physical comedienne.) And once again Buster reduces the lady love to a piece of wood or sack of potatoes. He bounces, belts, lifts, drops, pushes, twists, hurls, and prods this human bundle.*

If Buster's ultimate rewards are questionable, the feats that he performs similarly undermine the moral homilies, "The race goes to the swiftest," "If at first you don't succeed, try, try again," "Where there's a will there's a way," and all the other pap of American idealism. Buster employs extraordinary human strategy, performs extraordinary physical feats, and enjoys extraordinary amounts of luck. The effort itself, the accomplishment of miracles by a resilient man with a limber body and a limber brain, is far more important to Keaton than the winnings. Exertion, expenditure of energy, magnificent human effort are more valuable than their result. For what comes afterward is middle age, old age, and the graveyard. In philosophy as well as comic method Keaton emphasizes action, not its consequences.

The most "serious" element in the Keaton films is this assertion of human potential, which in turn implies the imaginative potential of the Keaton mind. As in the Chaplin films, the man who conceives the comic situations and gags is closely related to the man who performs them. The same qualities that produce a character who can outwit the Union Army,

---

* This great sequence, from a rarely seen film, was so dear to Keaton's heart that he and his wife, Eleanor, performed it in Paris at the Medrano Circus in the mid-1950s.

outslug a gang of mobsters, outsmart a tornado, or outrace an entire police force also produce the situations, the stories, the business, and the machines that the character plays in, with, and against. Keaton's creative ideas as a director, his inventive stunts, parallel his ideas as clown; although many comic films copied Keaton's gags, they were never so powerful or unique as Keaton's, simply because in conception as well as execution they lacked the Keaton mind, the unique Keaton view of the human mechanism—as mechanism.

The gags themselves are, of course, brilliant. In *Convict 13* (1920), Buster walks to the gallows; Keaton's close-up shows the three strands of string that will send the prisoner to his death when severed (another parody of *Intolerance*). Meanwhile Buster's fellow prisoners sit in a grandstand watching the execution; a vendor circulates among them selling peanuts. Who else but Keaton would have the audacity to turn death into a ball game? Who else could also make the idea funny? And Keaton does not let the parallel simply hang there but tops it. As the razors slice the strings, the trapdoor opens beneath Keaton's feet, and he falls through with the drop that should break his neck. The gallows rope, however, is a rubber band, and Buster bobs up unharmed, like a jumping jack. The folks in the grandstand boo—as they would an umpire who has made a bad call or a shortstop who has made an error.

In *The Playhouse* (1921), two Civil War veterans go to see a show; one lacks a right arm, the other a left. In order to applaud an act, the two veterans must agree on who is worth a meeting of their remaining hands. Sometimes they agree; if not, one one-handed man sadistically keeps from his friend the means to applaud an act he liked. In that same film, Buster impersonates a vaudeville ape (perhaps modeled on "Peter the Great," a very intelligent ape that played on the bill with Keaton in London). Buster's imitation of a real ape is perfect—facial expressions, mannerisms, stance, posture, gestures, movements. Who else but Keaton could do it? Or would?

But great as the gags are, the best Keaton films do not rely on them alone. Although the short Keaton films are compounds of these individual, inventive gags, the Keaton features assimilate them into unified and coherent plots. Perhaps the late two-reeler *Cops* (1922) points the way most clearly toward the features. The film is tightly unified: one man gets into more and more trouble with more and more cops. The film's first shot foreshadows the action by making us think that Buster is behind bars; later a far shot reveals he is really talking to his girl from behind an impressive iron gate. Working with this suggestion, the film steadily puts Buster closer to actual prison bars. He mistakenly finds the wallet of a cop, who thinks Buster has stolen it. While trying to make an honest living as a furniture mover, he mistakenly loses a cop's furniture. He mistakenly punches a traffic cop in the face. And his biggest mistake is hurling an anarchist's bomb into the midst of a policeman's parade. Each of the mistakes is the result of circumstance; his intentions are always honest and sensible. These mistakes culminate in the precinct house. Although Buster successfully avoids the thousands of cops who have swarmed into that house after him, he walks back inside when his girl rejects him. Now Buster finally gets his bars and stripes for real.

To sustain a comedy longer than two reels, Keaton realized he needed to pay attention to plot; not a series of inventive gags, but Buster's exploits (of course loaded with gags) drive the longer works. Keaton films never used any other performer who was so interesting as Buster. (The two who came closest were "Big Joe" Roberts, in the shorts and early features, and little Snitz Edwards, in *Seven Chances, Battling Butler,* and *College.*) Buster and his individual deeds took on a new importance: "I realized that my feature comedies would succeed best when the audience took the plot seriously enough to root for me as I indomitably worked my way out of mounting perils."[4] Keaton's most successful films are those with the strongest plots, with "mounting" rhythms, mounting troubles, and an irresistible, "indomitable" drive toward the climax. Unlike Chaplin's films, Keaton's rely on drive, suspense, story, increasing complexity, and tension.*

The weaker Keaton features have great moments but weak structures from a lack of rhythmic drive. *The Three Ages,* his first feature, is more like three two-reelers than a single film. Its anachronistic gags are delightful, but it substitutes a schematic symmetry for story. *College* also is too insistent on symmetry; there are obligatory (and rather predictable) attempts by Buster to run the dash, hurl the discus, broad-jump, pole-vault, and so on, just so he can perform all the same feats in the film's climax. *The Cameraman* also seems predictable and schematic, too pat in its difficulties and their solution. *The Navigator* seems perfect Keaton up to the repair sequence and the battle with the savages, which stretch the film for gags and a climax. *Go West* also wanders about the plains rather than driving in that straight Keaton line. Again, the film's parodic premise (what other cowboy fell in love with a cow?) often obstructs its narrative drive.

But *Our Hospitality* is a driving straight line (after the prologue estab-

---

* The importance of excitement and suspense to the Keaton comedy might well seem to contradict one of the preliminary assertions that suspense and the comic climate are mutually exclusive. But as with Chaplin's uses of empathy and pathos, Keaton's use of suspense is subordinate to his overall comic aims—as well as a warning about overly rigid and inflexible definitions. Keaton's work is very close to melodrama—not only his parodies of melodrama such as *Our Hospitality,* but his use of the suspenseful rhythms of melodrama in films such as *The General* and *Spite Marriage.* But the primary difference from melodrama is indeed that Keaton uses its *rhythms* but not its *probabilities*—that is, he uses ludicrous characters, farfetched gags, incredible events, situations, and twists. Mack Sennett demonstrated the closeness of the rhythms of the comic chase and the suspenseful "race for life." It is that rhythm which drives the stronger Keaton films.

lishing the melodramatic milieu), from the effete Buster on a wooden bicycle in the "Big City" (ironically a cow town at the time) to Buster avoiding death from the old feud, to Buster saving the feuder's daughter herself from death. *Sherlock Jr.* drives irresistibly from Buster's being falsely accused of theft, to his illusionary heroism as he imagines performing exploits on screen, to his discovery of the real thief, to his use of the movie screen to show him how to end his own movie now that his girl stands in his projection booth. If the real plot of *Sherlock Jr.* is sketchier and more predictable than it might be, its imaginary "movie" plot makes up in energy, breathlessness, and dazzling surprise for any thinness in the projectionist's story.

The General drives from Johnny's rejection for military service to his pragmatic chase after his locomotive; to his heroic return with his girl, his locomotive, and a warning to his comrades; to his induction as an officer in the Confederate Army for his bravery. Interestingly, *The General* is as symmetrical as *Three Ages* or *College*. The four parts of the film—refusal for induction in the Army, chasing the Northern train robbers, being chased by the Northern Army, induction into the Army—mirror each other. The difficulties Keaton encounters on his trip north—wooden obstacles on the tracks, a loose car as obstacle, diverting the train to a side track—are repeated identically in the return trip south. But the driving structure of *The General* assimilates symmetry as an aid to narrative unity, rather than emphasizing symmetry at unity's expense. Similarly, the symmetry of *Seven Chances*—all those sevens—is absorbed by the film's driving structure rather than slowing down that structure with obligatory patterning. *Steamboat Bill Jr.* and *Spite Marriage* (an overlooked and curiously neglected delight) also drive relentlessly from Buster's effete inadequacy to his climactic success.

A driving, "indomitable" narrative line; outrageously inventive physical gags that serve both the narrative and character; a tiny human figure with an amazingly agile, acrobatic body and a constantly alert, strategic brain; vast panoramas, clever parody, melodrama, romance, costumes, elegance, grace; camera tricks and visual surprises—these are the elements that fuse to form the Keaton comic world.

A Lion's Lunch

In 1929 Buster Keaton was the comic pride of the M-G-M lot. In 1933 Louis B. Mayer fired him because Keaton preferred to attend a Saturday afternoon football game rather than show up at the studio to pose for tourists. At least that was the ostensible reason for Mayer's decision. The real reason was that Keaton's films were getting worse and Keaton was drinking more. After leaving Metro, Keaton spent most of the 1930s fighting alcoholism with various drying-out cures. He made cheap two-reel comedies for Al Christie's Educational Pictures and for Columbia. The short films kept him alive, but the great star and director of the 1920s had become a hack clown and bit player less than ten years later. Keaton spent the 1940s doing bits in films and played an occasional supporting role on stage in a stock or touring company. To these odd jobs he added gag writing for M-G-M, television appearances, commercials, several live appearances in a Paris circus, and more interesting cameo roles in films during the 1950s and 1960s. Whereas Chaplin walked out on Hollywood in anger and defiance at or near the peak of his talent and career, Keaton crawled out of Hollywood a beaten and wounded animal.

What caused the Keaton demise? The answer is neither simple nor single. Keaton's personal life was a mess. Marital troubles with Natalie Talmadge began in 1931 and continued through the divorce in 1932. As the difficulties with Natalie increased, so did the Keaton consumption of alcohol. Keaton, always a heavy social drinker, began to drink very unsocially. Unlike Chaplin, Keaton never learned from his father's example to stay off the stuff. He would show up on the set hung over and would need several belts to get going again. Although many performers have been famous for an ability to work this way, Keaton, who was dependent on the resiliency of his body, the comic alertness of his brain, and the smooth, marble perfection of his face, could not withstand the assault of so much physical poison. By 1933, in *What! No Beer?* Keaton looked 20 years older than he had in *Spite Marriage* of 1929. The eyes had sunk, the forehead had wrinkled, the voice was cracked (even more than usual), the body was sluggish, the movements seemed vacant and slow. At thirty-eight Keaton looked less able, less physically alert than Chaplin looked in *Limelight* at sixty-three.

But more than personal problems and liquor had done Keaton in. M-G-M in the 1930s was the worst place for any slapstick, physical, "coarse" comedian to be—as the Marx Brothers would find out a few years later. Although Keaton enjoyed a fairly free rein on *The Cameraman* and *Spite Marriage*, the reins got much tighter when the studio converted to sound. Even with *The Cameraman* Keaton complained about the over-scripting of the scenario department, the curtailment of his improvisation and freedom, and the fact that technicians were more loyal to the studio than to his picture. The M-G-M hand can be seen in *The Cameraman* with the sentimental close-ups of Marceline Day, shots of a type that Keaton pointedly omitted from his earlier films. *Spite Marriage* shows the usual Keaton freedom, perhaps because M-G-M was too busy worrying about sound to worry about this last silent gasp. But with the conversion to sound, M-G-M loaded Keaton down with rigid scripts, glossy "production values" (songs, dances, sets, and costumes), and a lame idea for a character named Elmer (last name Tuttle or Butts—a Midwestern num-skull in modern American dress).

Easy Go (also called *Free and Easy*), Keaton's first sound feature, re-veals all these weaknesses. The plot sends Elmer to Hollywood as press agent for a Kansas beauty queen; Buster winds up a star, and the queen winds up married—not to Buster, who loves her, but to the handsome leading man (Robert Montgomery). The film is full of useless plot twists and uneven musical numbers. Buster comically dances in four of them and sings two songs. (M-G-M apparently wanted a combination of Al Jolson and Groucho Marx.) The end of the film strives desperately for pathos when Buster loses his lady love. His face is indeed as pathetic as can be. (They wanted Buster to be Chaplin too.) But as the whole emotional relationship between Buster and the girl has been pure formula, without a single touching, evocative moment, Buster's face has nothing to be pathetic about.

Except the rest of the horrible movie. The beautiful rhythms of Keaton's silent films are absent from this one, whose poorly motivated, overly abrupt narrative cutting leaps from a shot before Buster has a chance to react. Keaton has been frozen indoors rather than allowed to move freely outside as he did in his great films. He no longer faces a life-or-death challenge—the essential motivation of the great Keaton films. He no longer plays a man with a brain; his creative powers have been confined to performance, not cinematic conception.

There are moments when Keaton shows some of his old spirit. In a comic ballet number with Trixie Friganza, Buster pirouettes, sways, falls, and dives with beautiful comic grace, playing the ballerina to Trixie's behemoth bulk. In another musical number Buster plays a marionette who pops out of a box. Buster's brilliant physical control while suspended on strings parallels his perfect control as an ape in *The Playhouse* and dancing-jack in *Convict 13*; he becomes a completely believable puppet dangling in space. But three minutes of interesting screen action is not a typical Keaton percentage.

In later films M-G-M paired Keaton with Jimmy Durante. Buster steadily became a supporting player for Durante in a string of jokes that milked Durante's inevitable mispronunciations, malapropisms, and com-ments about his nose. As Keaton's body was able to do less and less, as the plots of the films became more and more binding, Buster's sole assign-ments became taking as many irrelevant falls as he could muster, and looking dumb. For those who have seen the disastrous *Passionate Plumber* and the even worse *What! No Beer?* Mayer's dismissal of Keaton after this film might seem an act of mercy.

M-G-M was Hollywood's "toniest" studio. If M-G-M had produced *The General*, Mayer and Thalberg would have been more interested in the color of the locomotive than in what Keaton did with it. It would probably have been a white train—with sharp black trim. The glossiness that made M-G-M films seem dazzling in the 1930s often makes them seem silly today. There are limits on the amount of human passion—both serious and comic—that can take place on a birthday cake. Even the "memorable" M-G-M comedies such as *Dinner at Eight* and *Bombshell* are covered with sentimental frosting, romantic idealization, and comic overstatement—so that you can tell the stars are just kidding. Paramount was the big studio that produced the great comic talent—Lubitsch, the Marx Brothers, W. C. Fields, Sturges.

Keaton's own carelessness had put him into this impossible conflict with the M-G-M passion for sequins and whipped cream. For ten years he had left all his business and contractual affairs in the hands of Joseph Schenck, who served him fairly well from the days of the two-reelers. Keaton ran his own studio, made his own films, which were then distributed by Metro and later United Artists. But in 1928 Schenck sold Buster's contract to M-G-M, and Buster had been sold down the river.* Keaton suspected as much and tried to wriggle out of the hole, but no other Hollywood producer would fight Mayer. The Keaton imagination was buried under story departments and the M-G-M gloss. Although Keaton politely refers to Thalberg as a "boy genius" who was an innocent babe about slapstick, Thalberg's "genius" essentially consisted of turning hack, conventional tripe into shiny, well-decorated tripe. Thalberg and Mayer vetoed several of Keaton's story ideas. Perhaps because Keaton was intimidated himself by the new sound machines—and impressed by being an M-G-M star—he gave in on every issue.

On the other hand, it is questionable whether Keaton's imagination could have survived the transition to sound under any circumstances. Keaton's honky croak of a voice may have been well suited to the microphone, but was it well suited to the frozen brilliance of his face and eyes? When a blank stare said so much, what could a word do? In the sound films, the great Keaton face disappears. And the expressive body—its grace, its tense potential, its power both at rest and in motion—also ceases to function except for special moments when he does a stunt or takes a fall. The great subtlety of the Keaton silent films is that the Keaton body performs impossible stunts with the same ease and naturalness it shows at rest. Further, when Buster speaks in the sound films, his voice is fine, but he thrusts his neck forward and unconsciously bobs his head in rhythm with his words. This straining head motion further negates the expressive face, emphasizes the unnaturalness of the speech, and contorts the top part of his body in a way that is something less than elegant.

Other details of Keaton's sound films indicate that he would have had a tough time making great ones for any producer. First, the rhythms of

---

* Louis B. Mayer was an in-law of Schenck's, and Joseph's brother, Nicholas, was a major executive in Loew's Incorporated, M-G-M's parent corporation.

cutting were completely scrambled by the new sound techniques. And the flowing, rhythmic grace of the Keaton silents had been closely related to their power. As in the Chaplin films, there is a feeling of both music and dance in the visual-kinetic rhythms and flow of images in Keaton's silent films. Sound films turned this music into choppy cacophony.

Second, the Keaton stunts are deplorable when accompanied by natural sounds. When Keaton takes a fall on his back side, the sound of bam and crash do not help. When Keaton runs away from a landslide of beer barrels, the thudding barrel sounds disturb the visual concentration. When Keaton steps on one car of a train and soon steps off another in one of his beautiful far shots (*Easy Go*), the sounds of human quarreling undercut the visual comedy of the scene. We know from the idea of the shot, the placement of the camera, and the look on his face exactly why he got off the train. To tell us with words what we already know is ineffective and repetitious. Many of the jangling discordancies of natural sounds that destroy the flow of Keaton's style of comedy are clearer in the Christie two-reelers, when he went back to outdoor, anti-romantic Keatonesque situations. Those situations never included crashes, bams, thuds, and thonks.

What becomes quite clear from watching the Keaton features and shorts of the 1930s is that Keaton, like Chaplin, needed to come up with some completely ingenious, unique relationship to the sound film. And Elmer Butts was not the answer. By walking down the same road into the dialogue film, Keaton could not possibly maintain his individuality, his personal view of comedy and the world, the qualities that made him uniquely Keaton. Chaplin's initial refusal to capitulate to synchronized sound gave him a uniquely personal and ingenious approach to the sound track in the early years and allowed him to think through the best way to solve the dialogue problem in later years. Perhaps Keaton would have evolved a distinctive interrelationship of gag, character, plot, and sound track if he had had the time, the independence, and the lack of pressure. Perhaps he would have evolved something like the method of Jacques Tati or Pierre Étaix.

Perhaps, though, even given the independence and the opportunity to experiment, he would never have come up with anything. Perhaps the body was too tired, the brain too soused, the spirit too broken. The ten frenetic years of activity—19 shorts from 1920 to 1923, two features a year from 1923 to 1929—all based upon the virtuosity of his physical instrument, would have taken their toll some time. The physical instrument cannot last forever. Perhaps the disaster of 1930 to 1933 was merely a combination of new problems (sound, marriage, alcohol) and the predictable onset of physical and mental exhaustion. Perhaps.

IV

—

OTHER SILENT CLOWNS

CHAPTER 10

Harold Lloyd

—

CHAPLIN, Keaton, Lloyd, and Langdon were the four silent clowns to make successful, popular feature films in the 1920s. Arbuckle would probably have been the fifth; he already had two features in the can for Paramount when the Virginia Rappe scandal kept them from being released. Douglas Fairbanks had dropped his comic character and style by 1920 and had switched to romantic swashbuckling. Wallace Reid might also have made comic features in the 1920s; he had made polite, medium-length comedies early in the decade, combining his strong profile and his physical grace, but he died under a scandalous cloud in 1923. And so Chaplin, Keaton, Lloyd, and Langdon remained the four comic stars of the 1920s who made successful, popular feature films.

In the mid-1920s the four comics had almost equal stature, popularity, and wealth. Today it is easier to distinguish their talents. Both Lloyd and Langdon made films that remain very funny, unique, and entertaining. But their lights look much dimmer beside the brilliance of Chaplin and Keaton, whose films have not faded. Lloyd was a great comic of the surface with very little beneath; Langdon, on the other hand, had a compelling, haunting soul and not enough comic ingenuity and variety on the surface. Lloyd was a sort of Keaton in his flair for ingenious and brilliantly constructed gags—without the Keaton mind, imagination, and human perception. Langdon was a sort of Chaplin in his pathos and subtlety—without the Chaplin intellect, instinct, and comic imagination. What Lloyd and Langdon lacked was that perfect unity between soul and surface, internal feeling and external gag, comic business and serious implication, subjective reaction to human life and objective depiction of it in the film medium.

Man in the Glass Mask

That Harold Lloyd ever made it to the top of his profession (a profession that defies men to make it) is one of those American miracles which could not possibly happen, but did. When they were nineteen, both Chaplin and Keaton enjoyed international success as stars of vaudeville and the music hall. At nineteen, Harold Lloyd was an unknown performer in high-school plays and amateur theatricals in San Diego. Both Chaplin and Keaton came to the movies with warm welcomes, both began playing important featured roles immediately, and both quickly leaped from apprenticeship to stardom. Harold Lloyd began in films as the lowliest extra on "cattle calls"; he plugged away in films for six years before he made a comedy that was anywhere near the quality of Chaplin's first Essanays or Keaton's earliest two-reelers. In comparison to Chaplin and Keaton, Lloyd lacked the experience, the showmanship, the connections, and, even more important, the training and natural gifts.

Despite these handicaps, Lloyd's physical control of his body was a virtue in his earliest films. Lloyd may have lacked the delicacy of Chaplin, whose mime said so much with the tiniest gesture, or the hypnotic grace of Keaton, who defied nature with the acrobatics of his tensile frame. But Lloyd could do plenty of everyday knockabout—tumbling, falling, ducking, leaping, running, flipping, and even the famed "108" (the midair back flip that Sennett said separated the sheep from the clowns). What Lloyd's body lacked in subtlety and dexterity he made up for in energy, bounce, and push. The same could be said for his whole career.

As a young boy in the Midwest, Lloyd, fascinated by the theater, began perfecting different kinds of character makeup. This bit of childhood training would pay off. Lloyd eventually stumbled (or dragged) his way into success through makeup. His first comic ideas in films began with makeup. He felt he needed a "character" (really a costume) that would be funny. And so he tried to make himself look funny. This was in 1915, and Lloyd was clearly working in the shadow of Chaplin's tramp. Lloyd shadowed Chaplin even further by stealing a modified version of the tramp's makeup and costume. Harold's "Lonesome Luke" wore a small mustache, a tight coat, tight trousers, a striped shirt, gawky shoes, and a cane. Although Lloyd claimed he tried not to imitate Chaplin but to do the reverse (tightness rather than bagginess), Charlie always wore a tight vest and jacket, and in the early "Lonesome Luke" films Lloyd wore baggy trousers.

Lloyd's early career was obviously imitative. Not only his "Lonesome Luke" character and outfit, but the things Luke does, consciously imitate Chaplin—not the Chaplin of the Essanays or Mutuals, but the Chaplin of the Keystones. Lloyd's primary activities in such films as *Just Nuts* (1915), *Luke and the Bangtails* (1916), and *Lonesome Luke on Tin Can*

Alley (1917) are kick and get kicked, push and get pushed, duck, jump, and run. The locations of the films—parks, restaurants, boxing rings, the races—also echo the Chaplin Keystones. Even later Lloyd films, after he dropped Luke and put on the horn-rimmed glasses, are imitations. *Fireman Save My Child* (1918) echoes Chaplin's *The Fireman; Pipe the Whiskers* (1918), Chaplin's *The Cure; Back Stage* (1918), Chaplin's *The Property Man.*

Lloyd eventually found his unique, non-imitative character through makeup. He refers to this new *persona* as the "glass character." After seeing a movie about a fighting parson with horn-rimmed glasses, Lloyd decided those spectacles were just the thing. He first adopted the glasses in late 1917 or early 1918. His discovery of the glass character's character came a good year or more later. Although it might also be said that Chaplin discovered his character through makeup and costume, that discovery went far deeper than Lloyd's. For Chaplin, the tramp costume was only the superficial beginning (as he revealed when he dropped the costume and kept his *persona*). There is no question that the glasses were the starting point of Lloyd's success and style. In a sense they were also the ending point—the limit to his imagination.

"Character" for Lloyd was the rather traditional one of drama. What a man does, what he chooses to do (Aristotle defined character as *choice*), what his external traits reveal him to be—these all add up to produce his "character." Chaplin and Keaton defined the term in a different way—one much more in keeping with film's greater intimacy and identity of character and player.* Character for Chaplin and Keaton was a combination of their external characteristics with their consistent screen *personae* not specifically defined by action in the film at all. Rollo Treadway was both a rich, incompetent, effete gentleman *and* Buster Keaton the magnificent. Rollo eventually performs great deeds not because of Rollo's potential, but because of Keaton's. Similarly, Charlie is not simply a prospector for gold in the Yukon, but a prospector *and* Charlie Chaplin, who has a particular attitude toward gold, prospecting, people, and the like. For Lloyd, the *persona*'s essence is the glasses, and the character is composed only of those traits that the film specifically enumerates.

That character is usually either a weak mama's boy or a pushy go-getter. After establishing this initial trait, the film runs off a series of gags related (sometimes not very closely) to that trait, culminating in some supreme manifestation of pushiness or some supreme reversal of weakness. This technique was also typical of Lloyd's first boss, Hal Roach.† Roach, Sen-

* Whereas there are many Hamlets, there is only one Henri Verdoux or Johnny Gray.

† Lloyd met Roach in 1913 when they both worked together as extras. He went to work for Roach in 1915 when Hal bet his shoestring on a tiny film company. In 1922 Lloyd began producing on his own, leaving Roach to manage the large comedy stable that Roach had built.

nett's major rival, was far more interested than Sennett in character and logic. His films may culminate in crazy chaos (Laurel and Hardy provide the most obvious example), but they get there very clearly, carefully, and cohesively in psychological terms. Roach's notion of character, however, was limited. He would take a single character trait—and usually a rather petty one such as cheapness, spite, envy, or cowardice—and milk it relentlessly until it flooded the film at its climax.

Lloyd's "character" was pure literature. Harold is the affable boy next door, anxious to get ahead, not very good at anything, but willing to compensate with energy for his lack of talent. He is the American Dream of what a mediocre man can accomplish with a lot of hard work. He embodies all the homilies that people supposedly learn at their mother's knee, the apotheosis of Parson Weems' view of American history. In *Never Weaken*, Harold's girl tells her boss, "He can do anything he tries." The line might be the motto of all of Lloyd's films—and, ironically, of his life.

Lloyd's screen *persona* is much closer to his offscreen reality than either Chaplin's or Keaton's. Both Chaplin and Keaton created screen alter egos dramatically unlike themselves. Charlie became more kind, generous, and outcast as Chaplin gained more enemies, money, and social influence. Buster was the incompetent bungler, Keaton the physical magician; the tension between the two opposites became an essential ingredient of every film. Lloyd, however, adopted a character as close to himself as possible and then revealed nothing. He consistently cut us off at the surface.

What did Lloyd think of the American Dream's success ethic and the platitudes that his films implied? In *The Freshman* Harold learns that, to be a success in the college world, you have to "be yourself." But Lloyd hasn't shown that Harold has any self other than his pushiness. Further, he sees nothing wrong with "himself" earning a success defined by other people's standards. And what standards!—popularity, money, and athletic prowess. Lloyd deals not with the value of such standards, but only with Harold's incorrect way of trying to fulfill them.

Ultimately Lloyd comedies say nothing about life. Although his films seem to re-create familiar, everyday reality, they do not take place in the real world—which, funny and ingenious as they are, the Keaton and Chaplin films do. Rather, they take place in a literary world where banal values are taken for granted and clichés of human conduct go unquestioned.

There is something very deliberate, cold-blooded, and detached about Lloyd's hiding inside this box of literary conventions. Lloyd's character, his makeup, his goals, and his problems are intentionally superficial. The same is true of his gags. Many of them are brilliantly funny and often serve as perfect models for how to set up a gag, develop it, twist it, scramble it, then redevelop it, twist it again, and top it. They are constructed to achieve certain effects, and they succeed. But instead of coming from inside Lloyd's emotions or intellect—as Chaplin's and Keaton's do—they are cunningly plotted and built from outside. In one chapter of his auto-biography, "Recipe for a Laugh,"[1] Lloyd rather cold-bloodedly dissects a series of gags in *Speedy*. Perhaps Chaplin and Keaton could dissect their gags this way; however, their comic senses seem more intuitive. But even if they could, they did not write down their "recipes," for the same reason that a magician does not tell his audience how the rabbit got into his hat. Lloyd's mechanical control of his gag construction was so conscious that he hired someone to chart and measure (with a meter) the laughs for every gag in *The Kid Brother*.[2]

Take Lloyd's comic use of his glasses. When Harold is an infant in *Grandma's Boy*, the infant wears glasses. Babies don't wear glasses. Nor does a man playing football (*The Freshman*), a man asleep in bed (*The Kid Brother*), or a man in a fight (*Grandma's Boy, The Kid Brother*). Lloyd gets another easy sight gag out of the glasses in *Grandma's Boy* in the Civil War flashback scene. His granddaddy in the Confederate Army, played by Lloyd himself, wears antique square-cut glasses. The handling of the glasses in his films further reduces Lloyd's believability as a human being. (Chaplin and Keaton, despite the comedy, deliberately maintained an element of believability and sense about themselves and their actions.) Lloyd makes jokes of the glasses themselves rather than their relationship to either the situation or the character. For Lloyd, the glasses are his comic mask, and he hides the man behind them. Although the frozen comic mask was very useful in the amphitheater of Athens, it reveals its cracks and its coldness on the intimate cinema screen.

Lloyd's externalized definition of character led to a different kind of plot from Chaplin's and often from Keaton's. The character trait established early in the film impels the plot to its climactic reversal or culmination. Lloyd films weave character and plot in the expected, conventional method of the well-made "Aristotelian" play: Character trait produces action; clear-cut motivation produces events; consistent, credible causes produce the work's effects. For this reason, Lloyd plots often seem better-made than Chaplin's or Keaton's. *Safety Last*, for instance, seems better-made than *The Kid* or *Our Hospitality*[3] because the dominant character trait becomes clear early and that trait carries Harold into and through every stunt and scrape from first to final safety.

But in another sense *Safety Last* is much more poorly made than *The Kid* or *Our Hospitality*. It avoids the melodrama of the opening sections of the Chaplin film (essential for setting up that film's theme) and the Keaton film (essential for setting up both the theme and the purpose— parody), but it does not avoid being predictable and banal until the mid-dle of its sixth reel (of a seven-reel film). Lloyd devotes five reels to laboriously setting up the reasons why Harold, rather than his agile friend, must make the climactic climb. Who remembers anything about *Safety Last* before Harold's climb of the building? Very few critics who discuss the film mention anything else about it. This neglect is not a critical over-sight. Lloyd's shorter "high-rise" films, *High and Dizzy* and *Never Weaken*, are almost as effective as *Safety Last*. Although the skyscraper gags are less developed and less complicated in the shorter films, Harold gets up to them with much less banal ado.

The tightness of the narrative lines in *Grandma's Boy* and *The Kid Brother* is more apparent than real. The beginnings of both films are clear: Harold establishes himself as a weak sissy. The endings of both films are clear: Harold performs a heroic feat. And the motivation for the reversal is clear: Harold has been inspired by illusion (*Grandma's Boy*) or anger (*Kid Brother*). Whereas Keaton performs his heroic deeds simply because he must, because he can't avoid them, Harold only does so after getting himself all steamed up. This difference again stems from Lloyd's definition of character as an externalized trait, as well as from his pious view of what a man can do once he determines to do it. But despite this clarity at start and finish, the films wander in the middle. The plot often stops (more so in the later *Kid Brother*) for a series of gags—most of them playing off Harold's physical weakness and his social incompetence in the presence of his girl.

The Freshman, too, is not so tight as it seems. After establishing Harold Lamb's comic "flaw"—demonstrated by the silly jig step he does before shaking hands, topped with the idiotic line, "Step right up and call me Speedy"—the film makes an illogical reversal. *The Freshman* is one of those comedies that build to a comic recognition of a moral flaw—Harold discovers that he is an idiot, that people only pretend to like him, that they snigger behind his back, that they keep his company merely because he spends money, and that he is only the water boy on the football squad. After his discovery, Harold gets a chance to play in the big game and help good old Tate defeat Union State. This victory has nothing to do with the comic moral trait that propels the rest of the film (though it is a brilliantly funny sequence). After bringing victory, Harold is a hero, and the entire campus imitates his inane jig-step prologue to shaking hands. So after establishing Harold as an object of ridicule because of his excessive desire to be well liked, the film reverses itself and shows everyone accepting and imitating Harold's inhuman and false activities. Harold Lamb's discovery produces no consequences in his character; the moral principle he discovers is then negated by the film's climax. If one is going to build an "Aristotelian" comic plot—a comic flaw produces problems that lead to a discovery that, in turn, leads to a moral readjustment correcting the social imbalance (Bergson's view of comedy's moral function)—one ought to build it well.

This collapse of the moral foundation of *The Freshman* is another sign that Lloyd's comic sense of who he was, who other men were, and how he related to the social whole was either naïve, fuzzy, or dishonest. Lloyd was a great comedian, rather than an artist—like Chaplin and Keaton—who used the comic form. The one thing that Lloyd could do brilliantly was construct and execute gags—and that he could do as well as anyone ever did. But in Lloyd's sense of character, in his view of human life, in his study of the relationship between a man's aspirations and his accomplishments, in his handling of social realities, and even in his construction of whole sequences of human events, Lloyd was a schoolboy (or worse, a schoolmarm) compared to his rivals with genuine artistic vision.

From Willie Work to Harold Diddlebock

Harold Lloyd's first screen character called himself Willie Work. Lloyd remembers little about him. He is vague about when he made the Willie Work films (it must have been between 1913 and 1915), and he confuses an early Lonesome Luke film (*Just Nuts*) with a Willie picture.[4] All of these Willie Works have apparently vanished. The years before 1915 were not very auspicious for young Harold. The Willie Work films were so unimpressive that Roach refused to raise Lloyd's salary from $5 to $10 a week, and Lloyd quit. He worked awhile for Sennett, but, according to Sennett, Lloyd was not funny, and Sennett fired him. (According to Lloyd, he left Sennett to go back to work with Roach on more favorable terms.) Lloyd's early Lonesome Luke films, those imitations of Chaplin's costume, style, and comic business, were not very impressive. But Lloyd and Roach kept plugging. Between 1915 and 1919 Lloyd probably made some 200 one- and two-reel films, a staggering number compared with the 50-plus short films Chaplin made between 1913 and 1918 or the 34 shorts Keaton made between 1917 and 1923.

The Lonesome Lukes copied the Keystone-Chaplin formulas—pies, bottles of seltzer, kicking and bashing, incompetent cops, sliding on slippery floors and streets, running around in parks. There was no radical change when Harold put on the glasses. He still used running, tumbling, sadistic kicking, incompetent cops and firemen, and seltzer bottles. But gradually Harold began to define his differences from those around him. In *The City Slicker* (1918), Harold is a brash young man from the city, in glasses, straw hat, double-breasted jacket, and tie, who comes to the sticks to modernize a rural hotel. In *Spring Fever* (1919), he plays a bank clerk who hates numbers and longs to stay outside in the park—where he quickly gets into trouble. The "glass characters" of these two films clearly are specific human beings who have individual interests, personalities, and desires. This specificity was a great improvement over earlier Lloyd films in which general horseplay was the sole human activity.

In these early films Lloyd also defined his method of comporting himself in the presence of the pretty lady he loves (originally Bebe Daniels, then Mildred Davis, whom Lloyd later married). Whenever Harold saw his lady, he suddenly erupted into nervous, almost frantic activity. In *The City Slicker*, Harold spots Bebe and then jumps onto the hotel desk, smiles broadly, sits next to her, crosses one leg over the other, reclines on his elbow. For Lloyd, passion translated itself into movement. He moved, first, because his character's movement compensated for lack of strategy; and second, because he was unconsciously revealing the manly discomfort that any pure, American country boy ought to feel in the presence of a lady. Charlie raised an eyebrow; Keaton froze; Lloyd crossed his legs and got very busy. Lloyd also began giving his smiling, flirting glass character lots of close-ups. The lady remained without them.

Lloyd's career took an immense leap when he signed his first two-reel contract with Pathé in 1919. The smooth transitions in Chaplin's career from contract to contract, level to level, the smooth transition in Buster's switch from shorts to features, are in sharp contrast to Lloyd's first major film, *Bumping into Broadway* (1919), which surges forward in definition of character, construction of gags and story, and clarity and smoothness of photography. Early Lloyd films are so cinematically crude that one can say very little about them—except that we can see most of the action most of the time. *Bumping into Broadway* is a neat, smoothly shot, occasionally funny story of a meek and penniless author (a good Lloyd type of character) who gets unexpectedly dragged into a gangland gambling casino, which gets raided. There are clever gags: Lloyd avoids his landlady by masquerading as a dummy (dummy masquerades are one of his constant ploys in later films) and avoids the police by masquerading as a coat on a rack (another standard Lloyd ploy). There is a brilliant climactic chase as Harold and Mildred try to elude the police, including some terrific flips and slides as Lloyd demonstrates the old gymnastic talents that date back to Willie Work. The film is a slick, pleasant, and often funny piece of entertainment.

Compared to Chaplin and Keaton, Lloyd played a much more domestic animal. Charlie was an outsider because his integrity could not compromise with social definitions; Buster was an outsider because his farfetched imagination and extraordinary talents had no place in domestic reality. But Harold was an "everyday guy"; he developed this character in the Pathé two-reelers. In these short films, he played a husband, a doctor, a baby-sitter, an automobile owner, a salesman. He was a member of society. And his problem was not how to survive because of or in spite of society, but how to survive within society, how to succeed on society's terms without offending society irreparably. In most of his shorts there is not nearly so much at stake as in Chaplin's or Keaton's films; only in the "comedies of thrills" did Lloyd ever risk his life. Usually he risked his ego and his material success.

High and Dizzy (1920) is the first of two Lloyd films that mysteriously combine doctor gags and high-rise thrills. Lloyd is a young doctor whose business is so bad that as soon as a real patient appears in his office, he goes through a series of clever impersonations of nonexistent patients—bearded, on stilts—to make the patient think he's in demand. Then he gets drunk with a fat doctor-friend, and the two roll down the street—more great physical gags—and into their hotel. Lloyd thinks he's drunk too much when he sees his hat crawl away (a chihuahua has crawled under it), and when he looks into what he thinks is a mirror only to see a black man's face staring back.

Only in the film's final section does Lloyd start walking on dangerous heights; he has followed his patient, a sleepwalker, out onto the ledge where she is strolling; when she strolls back to her hotel bed, she locks Harold outside. Then he is in real comic trouble, and Lloyd cleverly mixes suspense and laughs with his brilliant physical control and his careful mastery of camera angle. In this film, Lloyd reveals the secret of his "comedy of thrills"—his body and the street below him both appear in every shot. If they did not, we would instantly suspect an editing trick. Although Lloyd performed the stunt while only a short distance above a protective ledge that a perfect camera angle hid from sight, he made it look as though the feat were all stunt and no trick.

Never Weaken (1921), the second combination of doctors and thrills, is more economical and more effective. In the first of two major sequences (rather than three as in *High and Dizzy*), a doctor (not Lloyd this time) again is without patients. So Harold tries to help the man out with a wild scheme. Using a professional tumbler, he tells the gymnast to fake a terrible fall and then cures him on the spot, handing out the doctor's card to onlookers. Eventually Harold is successful, and the doctor's office fills with patients. Harold, however, sees his Mildred (the doctor's secretary) discussing marriage with another man; so Harold decides to end it all. He hooks a revolver to a string that will pull the trigger when his office door opens. He telephones the janitor to come in, and then leans back in his chair, the pistol aimed at his breast. However, a light bulb falls off a cabinet and explodes. Harold assumes he is shot dead.

Then the film's pyrotechnics begin. A steel girder drifts in Harold's office window, picks up his chair, and hoists him out the window. As Harold drifts upward, he opens his eyes and sees an angel (a stone figurine on the office building); he hears angelic music (a girl practicing the harp). Then he hears jazz (a black band on the street). He opens his eyes at this devilish cacophony and looks down; then he knows he is not dead but will be if he falls off that chair. Panic. He scampers onto the girders of the unfinished building. As if he hasn't enough trouble being a thousand feet above his death, additional problems crop up. He starts to climb down a ladder only to feel the ladder pulled upward from above. He starts to walk on a girder that is then hoisted away. He sits on a girder only to miss being bashed in the head by another swinging beam. He sits on a hot rivet. And again, in every cut, Lloyd makes sure that both Harold and some reminder of the street below exist in the composition of every frame.*

Another sign of Lloyd's growing awareness of the cinematic medium in the two-reel shorts is an early sequence of *I Do* (1921). Harold and Mildred walk jauntily down the street together. A traveling shot walks with them, echoing their lively motion. If the far shot was Keaton's most effective tool, the traveling shot was Lloyd's. In films whose main character was distinguished primarily by the quantity rather than the quality of his activity, the moving camera was a very useful ally for heightening the impression of vitality. Lloyd films seem to come most alive when the camera moves. There are fine traveling shots as Harold and his fat friend rove down the street in *High and Dizzy*, exciting ones as Harold drives his car in *Get Out and Get Under*. In the features, traveling shots add zip to the exciting football sequence in *The Freshman*, and in *The Kid Brother* there is a sensational vertical traveling shot that ascends with Harold as he climbs a tree to keep his lady love in view and then falls with him when he tumbles from it.

Another kind of cinematic device that Lloyd brought firmly under his control in the early 1920s was editing. Editing rhythms are very important to Lloyd's physical stunts and gags—just as they are to Keaton's. Pace, timing, movement, suspense, excitement—all these require tight, functional, unobtrusive cutting. In addition, Lloyd, always concerned about the logical causes for the effects of his stunts, cut away from himself constantly to show something else that would soon influence Harold's activity. Lloyd's comic technique was essentially one of setting up disparate (and often highly improbable) pieces—which then fit together to influence Harold's activity. Whereas Chaplin's routines emanated from himself and Keaton's from the juxtaposition of himself and comic antagonist in the same shot, Lloyd's comedy sewed pieces together and then confronted Harold with the whole comic cloth. In *High and Dizzy*, for example, Lloyd had to cut to show the chihuahua crawling into his hat and to show the Negro valet opening the mirrored door. In *Never Weaken*, he had to cut to show the building construction in progress, to show the light bulb falling, to show a harp and jazz band playing, to show the riveters tossing rivets. Lloyd consistently used editing to skirt one of the greatest problems of the silents—how to translate sound into visual terms.

In order to keep the editing of these pieces from being distracting or ineffective (they could easily swamp the eventual comic stunt by giving

---

* Although Lloyd does not take screen credit for directing his films, like Keaton he was the captain of his creative "team" and dominated the conception and execution of each film.

too much away; they could make us uneasy by snatching our attention from where we wanted to keep it), Lloyd had to make them rhythmically perfect, long enough to provide the information, short enough so that we felt their subordinate function. Lloyd's editing of the clothes-ripping sequence in *The Freshman* is a perfect blend of rhythm and information, giving us the ripping pieces in close-up without obscuring the comic human focus of the whole.

A consistent weakness of the Lloyd shorts is lack of unity; the films are collections of disparate gags. Why should a film about attracting people to a doctor's office culminate on a skyscraper? Why should a film about a man's love for his car end in an amateur theatrical performance? There are no particularly good answers. Many of the features suffer from the same weakness. Although Keaton's two-reelers are also collections rather than unities, Keaton tightened his structures tremendously when he switched to features. But Lloyd's features are often like his two-reelers in that whatever structural braids he gives the appearance of weaving, he is really only interested in spinning gags. The great strengths of the features are the gag sequences.

The finale of Lloyd's most famous feature, *Safety Last* (1923), is his best union of thrill and gag. In addition to getting himself into dangerous elevated troubles, Lloyd turns several other screws. First, he climbs up 12 floors. With each floor, he thinks he will be relieved of climbing farther when his friend, the "human fly," takes over for him. But the friend must dodge a cop, and so Harold must keep climbing—floor after floor after floor. Then, as in *Never Weaken*, Lloyd has to contend not only with the primary obstacle (gravity) but with other bits of trouble. Pigeons coo in his face; a tennis net drops from the sporting-goods department onto his shoulders and head; the scaffolding used by the building's painters entangles his legs and body; he grabs a rope thrown to help him, but it isn't tied to anything (Lloyd's rhythmic control of cutting back and forth is very effective in this twist); a mouse (a mouse!) runs up his trousers.

When Harold, in the most famous shot in the film—perhaps in any comic film—grabs hold of the building's clock, its minute hand steadily deserts its position at nine, parallel to the ground, and slides down to six, leaving Harold clinging to a metal finger that points in a very alarming direction. Then the whole face of the clock pops out, and Harold is hanging by a thread (or rather a spring).* Once Harold finally gets to the top of the building, and to apparent safety, he gets smashed in the head by an

---

* The clock actually is hanging by threads—or rather, wires. The only observable fakery in the scene is the faintly visible piano wire supporting the clock. The wires are not easy to see unless you look for them. We can certainly forgive Lloyd the wires. The piano wires pulling the old-fashioned, rubber-band train in Keaton's *Our Hospitality* are also visible occasionally.

anemometer. He walks dizzily on the roof's ledge, unable to take the one tiny step to safety. His foot catches in a rope; he trips and swings over the side of the building, hanging by his heel. But the rope just as unexpectedly swings him back and deposits him on the roof, and Harold has reached safety at last.*

Safety Last is a "situation picture"; *Grandma's Boy* (1922), a "story picture." (The distinctions are Lloyd's own.) The gags and sequences in *Grandma's Boy* aim more at telling a story and depicting the weakling character than creating lengthy comic situations. There are wonderful comic touches in the exposition. Young Harold spends his time with his girl—churning ice cream. His tough rival tosses him down a well—and Harold climbs out, a pathetically comic giraffe in his shrunken jacket and trousers (perhaps "borrowed" by Keaton for the opening sequence of *College*). Harold is so weak and cowardly he is afraid to throw a nasty tramp off Grandma's property. So Granny goes up to him herself and shoos him away with her broom.

Later, that same tramp breaks into a jewelry store and shoots a man. Every able-bodied local is sworn in as a deputy. And that excludes Harold. When he tells Granny of his cowardice, she decides to apply a little psychological salve. She spins him a story about his granddaddy in the Confederate Army, who thought he was a coward but performed heroic deeds because of a gypsy's magic charm that protected him. Granny's story is a sort of comic *Red Badge of Courage*. In a flashback, Granddaddy (played by Lloyd) goes about bashing each Union officer over the head as they all sit at a strategy conference. Compared with Keaton's methods in *The General*, Harold's heroics are more premeditated and emotional, less mechanical and nonchalant. They are as much a part of the way Harold does things as Keaton's heroics are a part of his. Granny's story—and the Civil War flashback—ends as Granny gives Harold the famed charm that so inspired Grandpa. Harold is now himself inspired.

He dashes after the tramp (undercranked camera to add dash to the dash) on a horse, races into the vicious murderer's cabin alone, and, aided by a black cat that distracts the tramp and a horseshoe that smashes the menace on the head (diametrically opposite kinds of charms), Harold

---

* As in Keaton's comedy, suspense and excitement are essential elements of Lloyd's "comedy of thrills." And as in Keaton's, the suspense is very close to melodrama. But the improbability and ludicrousness of the people and events in *Safety Last* distinguish Lloyd's comic suspense from the tense suspense of melodrama. For example, where Harold's near-fatal, near-miss stunts produce whoops of laughter in an audience, the climax of Hitchcock's *Saboteur*—which uses the Statue of Liberty for its "high-rise" tension—keeps an audience tense and anxious. This tension forces the audience to suck air in (the cliché of "holding one's breath"), not let it out in laughter. This effect must be the consequence of some kind of intellectual awareness of comic probabilities and "climate." And although we may "know" that both protagonists (Harold and Robert Cummings) will eventually succeed, the tense melodrama actually makes us forget what we know, whereas the comedy never lets us forget it.

nabs the tramp and begins to take him back to town. But Harold must summon his zeal again when the tramp breaks free; Harold chases him, wears him out, and captures him again, wheeling him back to town in a baby buggy. Harold often conquers his opponents by simply exhausting them.

All the film then needs is Harold's discovery that the magic charm is only an umbrella handle and that all the "magic" deeds he has performed stemmed from his own spirit. Before Granny tells Harold this, Harold takes on his final foe, the nasty rival who pushed him down the well. They engage in a lengthy knock-down-drag-out fight, spiced by shots of Granny coaching Harold and dancing with delight every time he lands a good punch. The fight ends when Harold pushes his rival down that same well. The wheel has come full circle.

Despite the artificiality and incredibility of the charm device—an external motivation for Harold's actions—and despite the rather predictable consequences and reversals of character and events, *Grandma's Boy* is a well-paced, enjoyable, occasionally hilarious entertainment that holds up, from first to last, better than the more famous *Safety Last*.

But *The Freshman* (1925) seems Lloyd's best film. Despite its social banality and moral contradictions, the film has several of Lloyd's greatest gag sequences, as always the best things in Lloyd. One of the great comic sequences takes place on the football practice field. Harold, who is more successful at tackling the coach than the tackling dummy, gets kicked off the team. Then the coach has a better idea: use a live Harold to replace the battered tackling dummy—much better practice. Harold stands there, getting bashed, getting up, getting bashed, getting up—as the shadows on the field lengthen. At the end of the day a woozy Harold starts to pick himself up, grabs the leg that is bent beneath him—and can't feel anything. The leg is lifeless; it feels like straw. Suddenly Harold (and we) discover that the leg is indeed straw—it is the broken tackling dummy's, not Harold's. Harold stands up to reveal that he is still in one piece. Lloyd's brilliant camera angle keeps the dummy leg in exactly the right position to make us believe that a man could mistake it for his own.

Each of the film's major gag sequences is longer, more complex, more developed than the one preceding it. For the Fall Frolic, the big college dance, Harold has ordered his tuxedo, but the tailor is subject to dizzy spells and has been able only to baste the suit, not sew it securely. However, the tailor assures Harold that he will come along to the Frolic himself and sew anything that might happen to rip. Lloyd, as usual, has carefully planted the seemingly irrelevant and incredible seeds for this gag sequence. Now he harvests the crop.

When Harold raises his arm, the sleeve rips. When he takes the hankie out of his breast pocket, the pocket comes off with the hankie. When he pulls the jacket together to button it, the rear seam splits. The tailor thinks up a strategy. "If anything rips, I'll ring this bell." Unfortunately, every table has a bell on it, and the collegians continually ring the bells to summon their waiters. When Harold dances with a lady, his sleeve remains attached to her dress after he has left her. He chases his sleeve-turned-tail around the room. When Harold talks to another lovely, he nervously twirls a thread in his pants. The pants seam opens. When he backs over to the tailor's corner for a hasty repair job (the tailor hides behind a drape), the tailor suffers one of his dizzy spells. He falls against Harold's legs and Harold slowly feels himself dragged down under the curtain in the midst of a polite conversation.

Later Harold proposes to his girl, Peggy, and she accepts. He is so ecstatic that he swells his chest with pride—and the buttons of his suspenders pop off. Then all the buttons go, and Harold must hold his trousers up. They don't stay up for long. (Originally Lloyd was not going to use the old pants-falling-down gag, but he discovered the scene had no climactic effect without a climax.)

The big game against Union State is the film's ultimate comic sequence. Tate, Harold's college, trails late in the game, 3–0. Harold is the water boy. The Tate players are dropping like flies. There are only two substitutes left, and one is Harold. The coach beckons toward Harold on the bench. Harold expectantly runs onto the field. They order him to take off his jersey; they want it to replace one that has ripped. Harold dejectedly walks back to the bench. When the coach tells him that he is only the water boy, Harold gets mad. And when Harold gets mad, Harold does things.

Another injury finally gets him into the game. He snares a pass—which drops into his lap as he sits on the turf. As he runs out for another pass, a fan tosses a hat. Harold grabs the hat and races for a touchdown, then realizes he has only snagged a hat. Later, he refuses to heed the referee's whistle and receives a lecture on the significance of that whistle. (Many of these same gags recur in the wild football sequence at the end of the Marx Brothers' *Horsefeathers*.) Harold then waits for a punt. As the ball floats toward him, a vendor releases a load of balloons. The balloons float toward him. The ball floats toward him. Which is which? When Harold finds the real ball, he unties its string and twirls it about like a Yo-Yo. The strategy is so successful at fooling the enemy that Harold has run almost to the enemy goal. Just as he is about to cross it, a factory whistle blows. When Harold hears the whistle, he thinks the play is dead and drops the ball. A Union State player scoops the ball up, and Harold's TD is almost-but-not-quite.

But Harold does not give up. With only seconds left, on the last play of the game, Harold blocks a punt; a State player picks it up and runs. He fumbles. Harold scoops it up and runs. State players try to bring him down. Harold drags them toward the goal. The players pile up. The gun goes off. When the human jumble is unpiled, the ball lies over the goal line. Tate wins, and Harold receives a ride off the field on the shoulders of his teammates. Significantly, Harold had to be heroic not once but three times. (He really scored three touchdowns—or could have.) Similarly there are two fights at the end of both *Grandma's Boy* and *The Kid Brother* (1927). Harold's heroic reversals are magnified by multiplication.

Lloyd's film career ironically offers its own epilogue. His last film appearance was in Preston Sturges' *Mad Wednesday* (1947). Lloyd made only three appearances in sound films after 1934. His own sound films of 1929–34, attempts to incorporate thrill comedy with talking, were ingenious in spots but unimaginative as wholes—either because Lloyd's style was unsuited to sound, or because the vitality that kept the gag sequences of his silents together had dried up, or because his naïve optimism was unsuited to post-Depression America. *Mad Wednesday* begins where *The Freshman* ends—quite literally. Sturges' first reel is a film clip of Lloyd's last, ending with Harold carried off in triumph. Then Sturges' footage begins. A businessman, carried away with Tate's victory, offers Harold a job: "I am opportunity." Harold goes to work for Mr. Waggleberry. Harold Diddlebock (Harold's last name of Lamb has been purposely bureaucratized) looks forward to rising in the Waggleberry firm. He occupies his own desk in the large office and tacks up signs bearing his slogans—for example, "Success is just around the corner." Lloyd obviously parodies his own screen self, full of drive and vim and confidence that wherever he wants to go, he will get.

Twenty years later. Diddlebock is slow, broken, bent. He sits at the same desk with the same signs. His voice is feeble and cracked. Mr. Waggleberry calls him into the office. The boss doesn't even remember why he hired this do-nothing, go-nowhere hack. Waggleberry forces Diddlebock into involuntary retirement—gives him the inevitable watch, severance pay, and pension check. Diddlebock's triumph in *The Freshman* has been buried under the years of bureaucracy and the falsity of those idealistic American clichés on his wall. The remainder of the film (Harold's revitalization) has more to do with Sturges' view of spontaneity than with Lloyd (except for a thrill-comedy sequence with Harold and a lion on an office-building ledge). But the premature burial of Harold Diddlebock is a symbolic burial of the values and assumptions of Lloyd's world. It may also be a comment on the shallowness and obtuseness of those values in the first place.

Whatever Lloyd's superficialities as an artist, he was a brilliantly successful comedian, and he retired gracefully from pictures (as he predicted he would in his autobiography) to enjoy his family and the millions of dollars he had made (and kept). If he lacked the artistic vision and depth of Chaplin and Keaton, he was also spared their years of bitterness, frustration, and unhappiness. In 1952, the year Chaplin left America and the Hollywood witch hunts were at their height, the Motion Picture Academy awarded Harold Lloyd a highly political special Oscar as "master comedian and good citizen." The good citizen died in 1971.

CHAPTER 11

Harry Langdon

▬

HAROLD LLOYD'S career was one kind of American success story—the tough, determined climb from the bottom of the ladder. Harry Langdon's was the other—the meteor that appeared from nowhere, dazzled, and just as suddenly disappeared. Langdon began making films for Mack Sennett in 1924, almost a decade later than his three rivals. He was five years older than Chaplin, almost ten years older than Lloyd and Keaton—a film rookie at forty. In 1926 and 1927 Langdon was a star, earning some $7,500 a week and the critical respect of reviewers who ranked him alongside his more experienced and established competitors. By 1929 he was a has-been. After a decade of playing minor roles and making two-reel cheapies for Christie's Educational Pictures (ironically, Keaton, Langdon, and Sennett all worked for Educational in the 1930s), Langdon died broke and forgotten in 1944.

Langdon's talents, too, were the obverse of Lloyd's. Lloyd was speedy; Langdon was almost painfully slow. Lloyd was active; Langdon was passive. Lloyd was the smiling, eager dynamo; Langdon, the haunting, wistful pixy. Lloyd was a collection of clearly defined, externalized traits; Langdon was a vague, internalized mixture of shyness, immaturity, an almost subhuman intelligence, with few clear outer characteristics at all. Lloyd traveled in a clear direction toward a goal, while Langdon wandered in a tiny circle. Lloyd got, Langdon was gotten. If Lloyd's greatest weaknesses were the surface banality of his character and the manipulative cunning of his comic technique, Langdon's were a lack of range and breadth, a single kind of emotion and a single kind of pace that could become predictable and tiresome.

Langdon's comedy showed the limits of pathos. It clearly revealed that pathos was merely a by-product, not the core, of Chaplin's greatness. Chaplin was a whole human being—vulgar, clever, insightful, perceptive, instinctive, tough, sarcastic, *and* pathetic. Of the four major silent comedians, Langdon's *persona* was the most stupid, helpless, immature (despite his greater age in real life), sexless, timid, and unfit for survival in the world of men—and women. Langdon cannot do any of the "masculine" tasks well—make money, feel at ease with the guys, run his household, manage a romance. His women are domineering shrews—the bitchy henpecker in *Saturday Afternoon*, the moll in *The Strong Man*, the escaped criminal in *Long Pants*, the domineering latent lesbian in *The Chaser* who is happier fulfilling the masculine role than staying at home playing housewife. Langdon's most successful emotional relationships are with infants, stuffed dolls, and animals. Those companions best reveal his mentality and maturity.

Langdon's starting point—and ultimate limit—is his face. More than his three rivals, Langdon is a comic of the face, not the body. The Keaton-Chaplin-Lloyd faces are important, but they surmount significant bodies. If one wonders why Chaplin and Keaton surpassed their rivals, one can begin with the surpassing abilities of their bodies—another reminder that physical comedy emanates from the physical instrument. Although Langdon was an ex-vaudevillian, his body was a soft cream puff, a foam-rubber pillow, a mass of jelly. It merely stood in some awkward position, usually a clumsy variation of ballet's first, with the feet splayed and heels together.

It was the look of Langdon's body (like Woody Allen's), not its physical abilities, that contributed to his comedy. And that body always looked silly, whether it was draped in the usual Langdon costume—round, battered soft hat with turned-up brim; tight jacket with the top button fastened, the others unbuttoned, spreading open at the hips; baggy trousers; awkward boots—or in the absurd romantic or military costumes he often wore with plumes, epaulets, feather hats, and long swords. Whereas Keaton never looked silly whatever the costume, and Chaplin's costume, though comic, fit him as naturally as skin, Langdon always looked as ill-dressed as a young boy in Daddy's (and sometimes Mommy's) clothes.

Langdon's face, too, was a strange mixture of discordant opposites. Like Keaton, Langdon used white powdered makeup and heavily outlined eyes. Lacking Keaton's strong young features, the powdered face made Langdon look like a combination of clown, infant, and hermaphrodite. His skin looked more like flour or powdered sugar than flesh. The penciled eyes added a further, effeminate touch to an already asexual, amorphous face. The babyish makeup over Langdon's obviously adult face resulted in a strange juxtaposition of infancy and senility, sincerity and pretense, male and female. James Agee's concise descriptions cannot be bettered—"an elderly baby" and "a baby dope fiend."[1]

The combination of overpowered face and underdeveloped body produced the least virile and most sexless of all the comedians. Langdon is incapable of responding to a woman as a sexual being. His character is the slave of his wives. He responds to the picture of a lady on a billboard (*Tramp, Tramp, Tramp*) more successfully than he does to the same lady when he meets her in the flesh. He prefers an abstract figure of romance to the girl he is going to marry (*Long Pants*). He is successful with Mary Brown, a blind small-town virgin, in *The Strong Man* because she, like him, is physically helpless and spiritually pure. When Harry unknowingly takes a woman's breath away—one of the consistent comic absurdities in his films—he doesn't know what to do with her. When the evil queen faints from his kiss (*Soldier Man*), Harry continues munching toast. When a woman faints in his arms (*The Chaser*), Harry looks for help.

Langdon's sexual pastiness consistently puts him in the feminine rather than masculine position. In *The Strong Man*, Harry is the naïve virgin who thinks he is about to be raped by the city slicker—except the slicker is a slickeress, and Harry plays the role usually reserved for the ingenue in melodrama. In *Long Pants*, Harry gets illusions from romantic novels, in the tradition of ladies whose immorality is blamed on the ideas they devour from lurid fiction. Langdon's womanishness is literal in *The Sea Squawk* and *The Chaser* when he puts on a dress and masquerades (very convincingly) as a meek and pure lady. Chaplin in drag (*A Woman*) was a mature siren; Keaton in drag (*Our Hospitality*) was still very male; Arbuckle in drag was bizarrely perverse—a fat, sensual male who got great fun out of prancing in skirts with such gusto and believability. Langdon in drag was merely an extension of the baby-pure Langdon in pants.

Langdon's most characteristic gestures combine the masculine and the feminine, the adult and the child. The Langdon take is his most unique piece of business. These takes communicate either the joyous disbelief of the little boy who wakes to discover that his bedroom has become a candy store, or the anxious disbelief of the little boy who wakes to find his bedroom floating out to sea. Disbelief is the heart of the Langdon take, transmitting itself with almost agonizing slowness. It takes his tiny brain a long time even to register disbelief. Langdon's face and eyes (and, by implication, his brain) work in slow motion. Langdon looks. Stops dead. Frozen stare for five seconds. He blinks his eyes for three seconds, pressing the lids together with special force to make sure he is awake and his eyes are functioning. Frozen stare again, five seconds. Blink again. Stare again. The frozen Langdon face and the deliberate blink of those carefully lined eyes produce a truly infantile perplexity. That perplexity is indeed so truly infantile that Harry plays his own baby in a crib at the conclusion of *Tramp, Tramp, Tramp*. Baby's problems and reactions are identical to Daddy's.

Another Langdon gesture is his method of saying hello. Harry walks into a room, stops dead, and flips his right hand into a circle, which comes to rest palm up, frozen by his side at chest height. Harry's hello is a puppy greeting its returning master, or a two-year-old child its returning father. It is a gesture of alarming simplicity, naïveté, and lack of self-consciousness. Harry's hello is especially silly and funny when he flips it in the most inappropriate circumstances—to his shrewish wife and domineering mother-in-law in *The Chaser* after he has sneaked into the house guiltily from an evening on the town; or to gun molls, cops, and criminals. The adults usually flip him back a very different kind of response.

More like Lloyd than like Chaplin or Keaton, Langdon's character tries to survive in domestic reality. Despite his quirky innocence, Harry lives in society, not out of it or heroically above it. The tension in many of his films is between his complete incompetence at adult social behavior and his attempts to live a "normal" (in society's terms) adult life. Langdon often plays the husband and wage earner. His wife usually suspects him of lechery, and her mother often feeds her suspicions (*Saturday Afternoon, The Chaser*). Langdon's supposed promiscuity is especially ironic since he looks more comfortable performing the housewife's chores in *The Chaser* than in vamping ladies. Harry's occupations in these domestic films are purposely vague. It is hard to imagine what Harry might do to make money. Whereas Lloyd belongs in an office because he is able to perform any routine banality with both spirit and snap, Langdon is as out of place in an office as he is in a bedroom in which more than one person sleeps.

In other films Langdon plays the young man who finally gets the girl. All three of the features that Langdon made with Frank Capra use this familiar pattern of situation comedy—but with some unique twists. In *Tramp, Tramp, Tramp** Harry wins the girl, Joan Crawford, and rescues his father's shoe business by walking across country—a Keaton plot without the heroics and farfetched strategies that work; a Lloyd plot with plodding instead of dashing. In *The Strong Man*, Harry resists seduction by the evil city moll and weds the blind girl from rural Cloverdale, Mary Brown. In *Long Pants*, Harry rejects the callous lady crook and returns to his small-town family and fiancée.

The motifs in these three Capra-Langdon features have as much to do with Capra's world as Langdon's. The preference for warm-hearted, unaffected, uncallous, homey "little" people, rather than selfish, money-hungry, power-mad city rats, would return in Capra's later, personal films. The huge Burton Shoe Company (*Tramp, Tramp, Tramp*) which forces the little shoe manufacturers out of business (Harry's dad) is the ancestor of the various conglomerates that Edward Arnold controlled in *Mr. Smith Goes to Washington, You Can't Take It with You*, and *Meet John Doe*. In Cloverdale, the big-money forces have swamped the small town, converting the town hall into a saloon and smashing the horse-drawn wagons with their trucks delivering bootleg liquor. *Mr. Deeds Goes to Town* pits

---

* Capra does not receive screen credit for directing *Tramp, Tramp, Tramp*, but he claims a substantial responsibility for conceiving and controlling it.

the same two foes against each other (money versus rural peace), and *Mr. Smith* uses the same symbolism of a big truck (big business—mechanical, cutthroat, illegal) that bashes into a helpless vehicle (full of kids delivering newspapers).

The Capra-Langdon collaboration reveals a key difference between Langdon and his three rivals. Langdon began in films (like the other three) as a comic performer, merely doing the tricks, stunts, and bits his employers instructed him to do. For the four years of his greatest popularity, Langdon continued as performing clown, not film creator. When Langdon went to work for Sennett in 1924, Sennett assigned Harry Edwards, Arthur Ripley, and Capra to make something out of the vaudeville clown. According to Capra,[2] the three of them—not Langdon—developed the Langdon *persona*, character foils, gag situations, and mannerisms. Capra claims Langdon never really understood who he was or what he was playing; he merely performed what other minds thought up for him to do. When Langdon became his own director in late 1927, his films supposedly fell apart—again in Capra's opinion. His audiences went away, he lost his sense of humor, and he fell from stardom as quickly as he had risen.

The evidence is not so clear. Though audiences did not like the later films, the pictures were certainly as entertaining and interesting as the weaker Lloyd comedies. And the weirdness of Langdon's comic situations unmistakably link the films he directed himself with the films directed by Capra. Perhaps Langdon would have developed a unique cinema style if he had had more time (he had one year on his own as against Keaton's and Lloyd's decade and Chaplin's half-century), if the audience's tastes had been more harmonious with Harry's, and if sound had not come along to stifle further possibilities.

Regardless of who gets the credit for the discovery of the Langdon *persona*, "the helpless elf whose only ally is God,"* it came quickly at Sennett's studio in 1924. The gags that the Sennett team thought up for him worked with Harry's helplessness, infantile naïveté, and effeminacy— usually in a comic context in which exactly the opposite traits were required. Langdon constantly found himself in a situation demanding an adult, masculine, sensible, active response. In *The Luck o' the Foolish* (1924), Langdon generates comedy when child Harry uses the men's room on a train to shave. The idea of this womanly infant needing a shave is weirdly comic; Harry supports the idea with his bungling incompetence and childish haste in manipulating an awesome straight-edged razor. In the same film, the meek waif gets handcuffed to a vicious criminal making his getaway from the sheriff. Little Harry ducks the bullets, responding to the shoot-out as if it were a children's game.

In *The Sea Squawk* (1924), Harry the innocent runs up against genuine criminals. In *Feet of Mud* (1925), he innocently strolls into the midst of a

* Capra's terminology.

Tong war in Chinatown. The consistent device of the Langdon shorts and many of the features was to drop Harry into some situation where childish angels should fear to tread. Where Chaplin commented on an alien environment and Keaton conquered it with his cool and cunning, Harry merely wrung gags from his anomalous presence.

In *Tramp, Tramp, Tramp* (1926), Harry enters a race that demands great physical strength and courage. His participation in such an activity is as sensible as his confronting the frightening cyclone in the film's climax. As the twister heads toward him, Harry turns around, sees it, stares, picks up a few stones (small ones), and hurls them into the teeth of the twister. Amazingly enough, after receiving this barrage of pellets, the twister turns around and goes off.

This gag is the essential Langdon situation: little, unprepared man against impossible, huge opponent. Harry takes a feeble, childish, stupid action against the unconquerable foe, and the foe collapses—not because of Langdon's action, but because the foe was about to collapse anyway. There is no cause-and-effect relationship between Harry's actions and their successful results. Also essential to the Langdon style is the gag that follow Harry's "chasing away" the cyclone. Harry, in a moment of false masculine pride, demonstrates that he is cock of the walk by spitting defiantly at the retreating cyclone. The wind blows the spit back onto his jacket.

The boomerang is a recurrent Langdon gag. In his first Sennett short, *Picking Peaches* (1924), Harry strolls on the beach, picks up a basketball that some Sennett bathing beauties have lost, and hurls it back to them. The ball hits the backboard, bounces back, and clouts Harry on the head. In *Tramp, Tramp, Tramp*, little infant Harry, in a crib, tosses away a ball. It hits the wall, bounces back, and smashes Baby Harry, once again, in the head. The boomerang underscores the man's helplessness, the ineffectiveness of his actions, and the ease with which trouble and pain find him without his doing anything to encourage them. In Bergson's terms, the mechanical perfection of the boomerang, the geometric perfection of the circle, is a way of making Harry's painful experiences comic.

The boomerang is a perfect kind of Langdon gag, probably conceived as such by Capra and the other members of the Langdon gag team at Sennett. As in Lloyd films, the gag sequences in Langdon films—particularly the features—are brilliantly constructed and carefully related to the performer's personality. An example of such an extended gag sequence is the prison scene in *Tramp, Tramp, Tramp*. Harry is arrested for stealing fruit and chickens as he walks along the road across country. His theft is rather easy to discover—his mouth is stained with berry juice, a bulging chicken sticks its head out of Harry's sweatshirt, a watermelon falls to earth dragging Harry's pants down with it (another old pants gag in a new context). Whereas Charlie is a subtle and effective thief, Harry is the little boy who stole the blueberry pie that Mama just baked, and his innocent looks cannot erase the stains all over his mouth. So Harry must join a work gang.

Harry wants to do work that suits him; he finds a tiny toy hammer for breaking tiny toy rock. The prison guard demands that Harry take a man-sized hammer for man-sized rock. But when Harry picks up a large hammer, the head falls off. When Harry has trouble with other large tools, the exasperated guard hands his rifle to Harry and begins to search for a real hammer himself. He finds one—only to notice Harry pointing the rifle at him. (Harry, of course, doesn't realize what he could do with the rifle.) In a panic, the deputy grabs the rifle and thrusts the hammer at Harry. Harry, assaulted with frantic activity, drops his prisoner's ball on the guard's foot. The guard hops off in pain; Harry casually goes back to the tool pile, picks up his little toy-sized hammer, and toddles back to work on the tiny rock. A perfect gag circle.

There are three great gag sequences in *The Strong Man* (1926). In the first, Lily, a tough moll, tries to get back the roll of money she has stuffed into Harry's coat. Harry thinks she wants to seduce him. She eventually sees that Harry wraps his mind in a chastity belt; while she feels him up in a taxi cab, he eats popcorn, freezes, stares, and blinks. Lily realizes she will have to use strategy; she will have to pretend to be a weak and helpless lady. So she faints—and Harry must lug her home. He drags her apparently lifeless frame up a flight of steps; the two constantly crash down the stairs and on top of each other. (The scene may have influenced Keaton's lugging scene in *Spite Marriage* and was specifically echoed in Pierre Étaix's *The Suitor*.) When Harry finally lugs her body into the bedroom he falls asleep, cuddled up like a baby, with his head on his hands, after she knocks him over the head. He awakens to find her hands and body pawing and bumping his. He runs away from her, but she chases him with a knife. He assumes that she is after his body, and no virgin in a Richardson novel ever protected her purity with more energy than Harry. But he finally surrenders (well, if she wants him that much . . .) and allows himself to be kissed. For Langdon, a kiss is not the sexual prologue, but the finale. Harry then slinks out of Lily's room, his virtue gone (also the money).

This sequence, too, ends with a brilliant circular topper. As Harry walks out Lily's door, he notices a sign informing him that Madame Browne's Art Studios are in the same building. (He is looking for a girl named Mary Brown.) Harry wanders into a room where a nude is posing—another sexual confrontation for the innocent child. He sees the nude. Frozen take. Stare. Blink. Suddenly in a burst of frantic activity Harry rushes out the door of Madame Browne's and falls down the entire length of the flight of stairs—the same stairs that he had climbed laboriously while lugging Lily. Capra-Langdon close the comic-sexual circle.

In the second great comic sequence, Harry, on a bus, tries to ease a cold with some medication. He carefully pours some awful medicine onto a spoon, raises the spoon to his lips, holds his nose to blunt the taste, sneezes, and splatters the medicine all over the fancy suit of a dapper, nasty gentleman sitting next to him. The man threatens Harry with what he will do if it happens again. Harry looks at the man menacingly. He looks. And looks. Suddenly, he closes his pudgy hand into a fist and flicks a tiny jab to the man's chin. Harry may occasionally take a positive action, but he is still a little boy sticking out his tongue. Harry looks at the man again for a very long time. He raises his pudgy hand for another little sock—and the man bashes both the fist and Harry down with convincing force.

So Harry goes back to his cold. He starts to rub his chest with camphor. The jar of camphor gets switched with a jar of Limburger cheese, which Harry calmly rubs on his chest. Something smells. Harry picks his nose with the finger that has been in the cheese. (Chaplin's use of unpleasant, "vulgar" details is also a Langdon method.) The smell gets worse. The dapper man sniffs Harry and tosses him out of the bus. Harry tumbles down a slope and at the bottom of the hill crashes back into the bus through the roof, falling on top of his opponent. Another gag circle comes to rest.

The third major comic sequence begins as Harry substitutes for Zandow the Strong Man, who is drunk. Harry appears on stage, looking like the fruitiest Strong Man in show-business history. He poses—in a ballet position. The audience does not respond. He tries to lift a 400-pound weight —and can't. He poses again. Finally, Harry gets a reaction—by reducing the Palace Saloon and Dance Hall to chaos. He swings on a trapeze over the audience's heads, pelting them with bottles, kegs, and sprays of beer. The bootleg treasure becomes his weapon. He throws a stage backdrop over the crowd and walks on top of the billowing mass, a comic Christ walking on canvas waters (pure Capra). He starts shooting the crowd with the cannon that is part of Zandow's act. He discharges his cannon at the chief mobster, knocking him through a second-story window and down into a trash can. Its lid closes, and a sign above it reads, "Dump Trash Here" (another Capra touch). Harry, the weak man, has broken the Cloverdale mob and knocked down the "walls of Jericho" of the Palace Saloon.

Unlike the Keaton or Lloyd films, however, Harry's heroics still do not seem to come from Harry. In *The Strong Man*, the plot does not build toward Harry's heroics. The final comic sequence is self-contained, not the result of action preceding it. In fact, all of the sequences seem unrelated to each other—World War I, Immigration to America, Trouble with the Moll, His Cold on the Way to Cloverdale, Meeting Mary Brown, Substituting for Zandow and Leveling the Palace (he played the Palace with a bang), Marrying Mary and Becoming Town Cop. The Chaplin echoes are unmistakable throughout—*Shoulder Arms* (World War I), *The Immigrant* (coming across), *Easy Street* (Harry as toy cop). The structure of *The Strong Man* derives not from the story, but from the thematic contrast of the naïve and pure with the callous and crooked. In both major sequences of the film, little Harry triumphs over a person who has broken the law. In the conclusion of the film, the two meek people inherit the earth.

This thematic contrast of innocence and cunning, mildness and cruelty unfortunately presents no particular moral or social point of view, except the most obvious homiletic one—that nice people are nicer than not nice ones and finish first. The Capra influence is unmistakable. The moral system of *The Strong Man* separates good guys and bad guys into two camps. There are no surprises, no ironies, and no reversals in the film's moral definitions. Langdon's thematic film is structurally ineffective because it is thematically banal. His schoolboy simpleton provides no more than a schoolboy simpleton's view of life.

The film is as innocent as Harry—which means that its creators are lying. Some non-simple, non-innocent people conceived this film about innocence. Where Chaplin had both the honesty and the good sense to realize the tension between his artistic metaphor and his (and everyone else's) life—indeed that tension is the subject of the films—the Langdon film asks us to swallow the clichéd metaphor whole.

The final Langdon-Capra film, *Long Pants* (1927), is very much like *The Strong Man* in its strengths and weaknesses. A vague thematic unity links its sequences, each contrasting romance and reality, daydreams and life. Harry the dreamer must make a realistic choice between Bebe Blair, the hypnotically beautiful, tough moll, and Priscilla, the sweet home-town girl. For example, in one of the film's greatest gag sequences, Harry, who has dreamed of shooting Priscilla on a walk in the woods, slyly asks her to walk there with him just before their wedding. A genuine murder attempt seems a sensible way to get rid of Priscilla so he can join the girl of his dreams. Unfortunately, Harry has trouble bumping Priscilla off. Every time he raises the pistol (comically large in his pudgy fist), Priscilla turns around, and he must quickly put the gun back in his pocket. Then he gets the idea to play hide and seek, so that he can shoot her while she isn't looking (another combination of childish game and adult activity). She turns around and begins counting to 500. First, Harry can't get the gun out of his pocket. Then he loses it in a pile of leaves. When he picks up what feels like the gun, it turns out to be a stake to which a horse is tied. The horse gallops off, and Harry takes a flying fall. He finally gets hold of the gun and aims, but he starts shaking. Then he sees a sign, "No shooting." Well, he can't disobey a sign; the obedient child in him is more powerful than the murderer.

Then the sequence reverses itself. Harry has renounced his murder attempt but must now suffer comic poetic justice for his nasty intentions. As Priscilla continues to count, Harry suffers a series of painful indignities. He tosses away a horseshoe Priscilla had found, but it rebounds to crack him in the skull. A low-hanging branch bashes his top hat over his eyes. He blindly gets tangled in barbed wire and his own suspenders; he catches his foot in a bear trap and is clobbered by the tree to which the trap is attached. Worse yet, when Priscilla finishes counting, she finds the gun on the battered Harry. But she merely thinks that Harry wants to play another game. And so she starts target-shooting practice—using a newspaper picture of Bebe as the target. Bebe's picture, not Priscilla, gets "murdered" in the woods: a perfect gag circle.

In another extended sequence, Harry runs off to San Francisco (this film's "big city") to help Bebe avoid her police pursuers. She climbs into a large box, which Harry must lug about, encasing the lady of romance and reducing her to a comic corpse (a parallel to the lugging scene in *Strong Man*). Harry sets the box down for a moment near the stage entrance to a theater; when he returns, he sees what he thinks is a policeman sitting on the box. The policeman is actually a ventriloquist's dummy in a policeman's outfit, but Harry doesn't know that. He stops dead. Stares. Flips the "cop" a "Hi." Stares. Turns. Sits on the curb. Throws the "cop" another "Hi." Nothing.

Harry decides he must do something to get the "cop" off the box. He runs to the "cop" and pretends there is a terrible emergency. The "cop" doesn't move. He pretends to be robbed in a doorway. No reaction. He runs and falls dead of a stroke in front of the box. The "cop" does nothing. (However, a storekeeper comes out and throws water on Harry.) Then Harry sees a stagehand pick up the dummy-cop and carry him into the theater. Stare. Blink.

But the gag doesn't end here. When Harry leaves the box again for a moment, relieved that the cop was only a dummy, a real cop walks in and sits on the box. Harry returns. He smiles at what he is sure is a dummy. He playfully picks up a brick and hurls it at the cop, who leaps up to pursue Harry in earnest. Again, the film contrasts the real and the illusory.

The tension created by these contrasts is resolved when Harry sees the dream girl, Bebe, for what she really is. He sees her belt another lady in the face and then belt down a drink. Dream ladies don't belt. The camera remains frozen on the back of Harry's head and neck (a brilliant strategic choice—and the kind that Capra makes continually in his later films) for an agonizingly long time. Bebe sits down beside Harry. He stands up (translating emotion into physical action), turns, gives Bebe a withering stare (not his perplexed one), blinks (as if to chase the sleep from his eyes), and tells her he's through. He goes back to the woods, picket fences, and family dinner tables of his home town, Oak Grove.

As he walks in the door, Ma, Pa, and Priscilla sit at the table praying (what else?). Harry quietly sneaks into his old chair. When they look up from the benediction, in their great joy to see him they push the dinner table over on top of him.

Langdon After Capra

According to the box office, Capra, and tradition, later Langdon features deserted comedy for greater doses of pathos, weirdness, and an insane craving to out-Chaplin Chaplin. *Three's a Crowd* (1927) has so many Chaplin echoes that "echo" becomes a euphemism. The story itself is Chaplinesque. Harry, an outcast and childish bungler, longs for a wife and child of his own (symbolized by the rag doll for which he feels affection). He finds a woman in the snow and takes her in. He later discovers that she is pregnant, and soon Harry has two charges. The woman's husband is a drunkard and dissipater, so Harry plays father. But the real father reforms, returns to find his lost family, and retrieves them from Harry's hovel.* Harry is left alone.

There is also plenty of Chaplin in individual sequences. The film begins at 5:00 A.M., when Harry must get up to work—a typical Chaplin necessity that often ruins the tramp's sleep at the beginning of a film. The boss is a Chaplinesque slave driver (but not, as in Chaplin, emblematic of the necessity to work in our society). When Harry takes the baby from its mother, he realizes it is wet (as in *The Kid*). Harry treats baby's diaper like a pie crust, rolling it flat with a rolling pin—typical Chaplin transposition. And when Harry is left alone, he remains motionless, pathetic, in his doorway, a clear evocation of a similar pathetic doorway scene in *The Gold Rush* when Georgia leaves Charlie alone on New Year's Eve.

In Langdon's defense, it must be said that many of the sequences and gags in *Three's a Crowd* are pure Langdon. The scene in which Harry finds the doll and lovingly plays with it while Harry's boss plays with his living son (effective cross-cutting) is a combination of whimsical comedy, touching pathos, and psychological aberration. This juxtaposition of the infantile and adult is typical Langdon. So is Harry's discovery that his lodger is pregnant. When he sees the baby clothes she is carrying, he stops dead. Stare. Blink. His mouth drops open. In a panic Harry suddenly races around his room like a short-circuited toy. The mixture of frozen slowness and ecstatic frenzy is a Langdon technique. So, too, is Harry's reaction when he first walks into his room and sees the infant in

---

* In *The Kid*, there is no reconciliation between the legitimate parents, another sign that Chaplin discarded the kinds of obligatory moral clichés that Langdon keeps.

the mother's arms. He stops and simply stands there, looking at mother and child. He stands. And stands. And stands. Slow fade.

Three's a Crowd lacks the great extended gag sequences of the three earlier features, and it certainly mixes various styles rather indiscriminately—Langdon pathos and childishness, Chaplin tenderness and social commentary, Keaton string machines, symbolism, red-herring gags and plot points (some nonsense about a fortune-teller), and an expressionistic dream sequence that is more Strindberg than Chaplin. But Langdon is trying to do something different and personal, reaching much further than Capra tried to take him, but unfortunately without stylistic mastery or intellectual control.

The same is true of *The Chaser* (1928). This film has an extremely strange premise. Harry is such a flirt (!) that the judge, rather than granting Harry's wife a divorce, decrees that Harry must wear women's clothes and do the woman's chores for 30 days while the wife adopts Harry's "masculine" role and duties. The film's sexual reversals (doubly strange given Langdon's sexual amorphousness), its grotesque caricatures of wife and mother-in-law, and the unprepared-for haste in the judge's bizarre decision all give the film the flavor of a dream or nightmare.

At the same time, the film has several brilliant gag sequences. In one, Harry, cooking breakfast, tries to get an egg from a chicken—but he hasn't the slightest idea of how chickens make eggs. He takes his frying pan out to the henhouse, pulls a hen out, sets her on it, and waits. Nothing happens. He tries to get the lady to cooperate. He wheedles, prods, begs, tickles, makes faces, waits. Nothing. But unseen by him, another chicken has walked behind him and laid an egg. Harry gives up on his chicken, starts to stand up, and sees the egg under his haunches. He suddenly feels ashamed and tries to hide the egg in the bushes—the little boy who has made a nasty poo-poo where he shouldn't and wants to cover it up. This is a perfect Langdon childish gag—and a great comic reversal as he suddenly doesn't want an egg after waiting five minutes to get one.

Then the first chicken relents and gives Harry a desirable, "unsullied" egg. But as he walks carefully with it into the house (wife sits at the table in a suit and tie, forcefully demanding his/her breakfast), he trips and falls. The egg lands on Harry's rear, caught in the folds of his skirt. Harry searches desperately for the egg, gives up, sits on a chair—and then discovers where the egg is. Perhaps this lengthy egg gag is a bit too anal for many, but it fits both Langdon and the situation perfectly.

A second masterful comic sequence in the film is Harry's suicide attempt. He feels worthless as a man (a belated awakening). The bill collector has tried to put the make on Harry, and the iceman kissed him on his way out the door. Harry writes a suicide note and tries to do himself in. First, he uses a pistol. But he can't decide where to aim it so that it will do the most good without scaring him too much. He aims at his head, his rear, his ankle. Then he decides the pistol is too big and gets a smaller one. (Langdon always defines himself in terms of tiny things.) Harry pulls the little trigger. Splurt. It is a squirt gun.

So he gives up guns for poison. But he mistakes a bottle of castor oil for the bottle of poison (a variation on the camphor-Limburger mistake in *Strong Man*). Harry swallows a whole glass of castor oil, bids goodbye to the world, lies down on the kitchen floor, and covers himself with a sheet. There is an unbelievably long take, perhaps a full minute, of a completely motionless sheet. Suddenly, the sheet springs to frantic life; Harry races out from under it and dashes upstairs. The camera remains downstairs, merely implying where Harry might be going. The scene fades out. Again the scene may verge on the tasteless, but its juxtaposition of suicidal despair and farce is truly remarkable. Three years later Chaplin used the blend in *City Lights*. (It is only fair to point out when Chaplin borrowed from Langdon—the blind girl in *Strong Man* is another instance—as well as the other way round.)

There are other comic touches in *The Chaser*. In a gentle scene, Harry flirts with a group of girls who are on a camping trip (another bevy of very masculine damsels). Harry's flirtatiousness is so tentative that when he finally screws up his courage to wink (feebly) at a camper, he then hastily looks around to make sure no one has caught him in the act. There is brutal comedy in the sorrow of Harry's wife when she believes he has committed suicide. The mascara mixes with her tears and runs down her cheeks, producing one of the ugliest and most insanely grotesque close-ups of a leading lady's face in the history of cinema. (Like Chaplin and Keaton, Langdon the man had plenty of trouble with his wives—four of them.) Although *The Chaser* is weak in its narrative unity, very hesitant in examining marital relationships with consistency or seriousness, and gropingly eclectic in its style and development of gags, many things in the film are uniquely and quirkily Langdon, and the work is not many cuts below his most respected films.

Langdon's career was not long enough to give him a grasp of the film medium. His cinematic style was more like Chaplin's than like Keaton's or Lloyd's. It was deliberately unobtrusive, and he used cutting with great caution and economy. For example, Langdon plays a tender scene in a cradle with a baby in *Three's a Crowd* in a single long take, identical in principle to the Oceana Roll dance in *The Gold Rush* and the Murphy-bed duel in *One A.M.* Langdon even slowed down Chaplin's functional editing. He purposely drew out the pace of scenes, leaving the camera riveted on Harry's eyes and face for seeming minutes while the whole world (except for a flicker in the eyes) came to a dead stop. This slowness suits Langdon. His mind and emotions seemed to work in slow motion; quiet slowness seemed the proper tone for such a gently comic world; and the minuteness of Harry's reactions needed time to become manifest to our eyes and brains.

If any kind of cinematic composition is especially unique to the Langdon films, it is probably a particular use of screen depth, with Harry and the object of his attention playing contrapuntal roles in the frame's rear- and foreground. A good example is the shot in *Soldier Man* (1926) when Harry looks with perplexed fascination at a cow's udder. The body of the cow frames the shot at the top and sides, the udder hangs prominently in the foreground at screen right, and Harry's wide-eyed amazement dominates screen center behind them. The udder and Harry's amazed eyes both share the frame. Another effective use of the same principle is the dummy-cop scene in *Long Pants*. The dummy sits on the box in the foreground, only its back showing. (The audience, unable to see the "cop's" face, accepts the childish absurdity of Harry's mistake as credible.) Harry, reacting, stands in the center rearground of the frame. The composition allows the dummy, Harry's body, and Harry's expressive eyes to share the frame throughout the sequence, always revealing both cause and effect. As in Chaplin's compositions, the camera has found the only place from which to film the sequence effectively. And as in Harold Lloyd's high-rise stunts, keeping Harry and dummy, cause and effect, together in the shot was crucial to its comic effect.

Langdon was certainly no cinematic innovator. A sameness of style and tone makes his films better when seen occasionally than in a group. They lack the fertile inventiveness and variety of Chaplin and Keaton, who could build amazingly diverse and individual films on the same character and premises. (Lloyd, too, is deficient in variety, and his films do better one at a time than bunched in "festivals.") But Langdon's gentle pixy of a character stands alone in film comedy for his absolute sweetness, helplessness, and passivity. Every other screen comic (even Chaplin and Stan Laurel, who were the two closest to Langdon) contains some measure of snap, scrap, toughness, or sadism; Langdon is pure jelly. And Langdon's films, perhaps more impressive in their parts than in their wholes, are unique in their haunting wistfulness and the hilariously comic perplexities of this boy-man, male-female fleshy pillow.

CHAPTER 12

More Fun Shops

ALTHOUGH Mack Sennett was the most famous producer of silent comedies, and Chaplin, Keaton, Lloyd, and Langdon were the most celebrated comic performers, there were scores of other comics and thousands of comic films produced in the 1920s. The quantities suggest both the popularity and the fertility of physical comedy in the final decade of silence. The renowned comic masters were merely the tip of a very large iceberg. Among the other comics and companies were such as Earl Hurd, Lupino Lane, Sunshine Comedies, Campbell Comedies, and some two dozen others—all long since consigned to oblivion. The minor clowns made two-reelers (although the one-reel form also survived), which Hollywood supplied to support the more grand and grandiose feature presentation. Today the shorts seem far more entertaining than the often ponderous feature that was the primary attraction.

These minor comics never achieved the stature and stardom of the great four. Perhaps their styles were unsuited to more than 20 minutes of gags, or their personalities did not seize the imaginations of the public, or their approach to comedy was not unique, personal, and human enough to lift it above the level of the delightful and impersonal gag. Nothing is more revealing of the personal style of the greatest comedians—particularly Chaplin and Keaton—than to see their business in the hands of less imaginative clowns. The funny business remains, but the human slant on that business does not. Chaplin was especially gifted in his ability to take the stock vaudeville-burlesque gags (and the more minor comedies you see, the more you also see how stock Chaplin's bits were) and elevate them, not only by using his personal comic style but also by creating a particular human context. The minor clowns are interesting, however, because they were better at making good gags than good films and because they reveal how the greatest comedians transcended mere gags to make comic works of art.

Doug

No discussion of American silent comedy should omit the comic films of Douglas Fairbanks, although most do. Fairbanks was making comic features (or near features) years before Chaplin. That those films look good today is surprising, because the legend surrounding Fairbanks is that his films were ornate, gaudy costume spectacles (remember Gene Kelly as "the dueling cavalier" in *Singin' in the Rain?*). The early Fairbanks comedies of 1916 to 1920, however, still seem clever, entertaining, and charming. In them, Doug was, like Harold Lloyd, an American: energetic and eager, anxious to succeed, and athletic in his efforts to make his eagerness and schemes pay off. But in addition to Lloyd's hustle, Doug had his own masculine good looks, suave charm, and underlying virility and human strength (like Keaton), whatever the external character. When Fairbanks gave up comedy, his assets went in two different directions: to Wallace Reid went the suave, graceful charm; to Harold Lloyd went the American push and "git."

The cleverness of Fairbanks' films owes its origin as much to the ideas of his "team" as to the incredible feats of his body. Anita Loos wrote the scripts for the Fairbanks comedies; her husband, John Emerson, directed them; and Victor Fleming (later known for *Red Dust, Gone with the Wind, The Wizard of Oz,* and others) photographed them. In the last two years, Loos and Emerson began writing together, leaving Fleming to direct. Their starting point for the Fairbanks film was parody. They delighted in parodying popular film types—the Western (*Wild and Woolly, The Mollycoddle*), the detective mystery (*The Mystery of the Leaping Fish*), the Middle-European spy story (*Reaching for the Moon, His Majesty the American*), the stranded-on-a-desert-island story (*Down to Earth*). Unlike the Sennett parodies with Ben Turpin, Fairbanks' parodies did not burlesque specific hits and stars, but genres. And like the Keaton films, Fairbanks could parody a story and keep you interested in the character's fortunes at the same time. The parody was never so obvious that it destroyed the film's continuity, pace, and tension.

In addition to parodying the movies themselves, the Fairbanks films also parodied some human trait—the effete Easterner's divorce from nature and the free human spirit (*The Mollycoddle, Down to Earth, Wild and Woolly*); the American adoration of aristocracy (*Reaching for the Moon, His Majesty the American*); the American hunger for success and

Harry Langdon in *The Strong Man*. Preparing to sock the mobster (William V. Mong); preparing for feats of strength.

Harry and friend in *Three's a Crowd*.

Douglas Fairbanks as the smiling American in *His Majesty, the American* (with Lillian Langdon).

Charley Chase attempting to scare the cashier out of the hiccoughs in *Movie Night*.

A publicity portrait of Larry Semon.

Stan and Ollie as their own kids in *Brats*.

The kiddies out on the town. Stan, Ollie, and Charley Chase in *Sons of the Desert*.

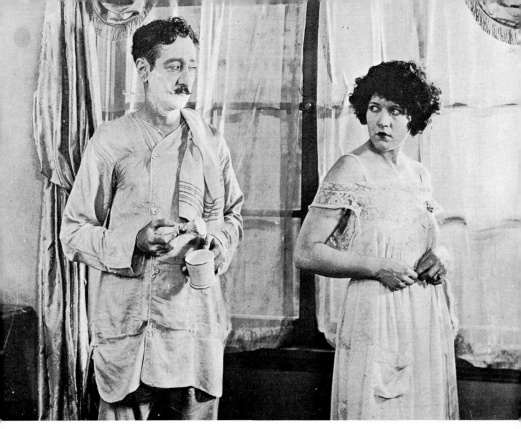

Tension in the bedroom. Professor and Mitzi Stock (Adolphe Menjou and Marie Prevost) in *The Marriage Circle*.

Dr. Giraud (Monte Blue) chokes on a very concrete lie in *So This Is Paris*.

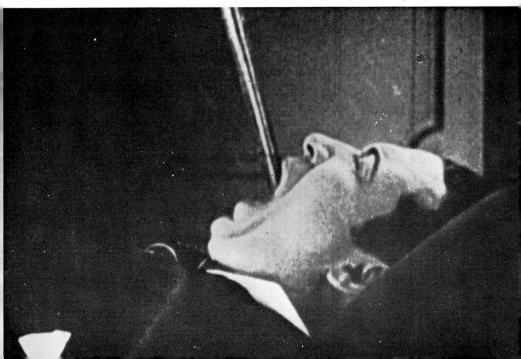

The deception of appearances in *So This Is Paris*. M. and Mme. Lallé (André Beranger and Lilyan Tashman) as sheik and victim; Lallé as nude in the window.

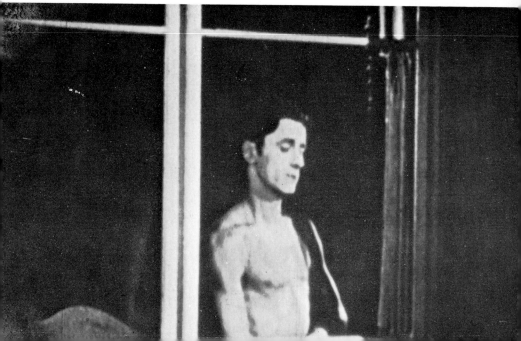

Courtesy of Contemporary Films—McGraw-Hill

The sterility of social ceremony. The deaf wedding guest sleeps through a violent argument in *The Italian Straw Hat*.

Clair cleverness. The contrasting occupants of three different beds in split screen—in *Les Deux timides*.

Courtesy of Contemporary Films—McGraw-Hill

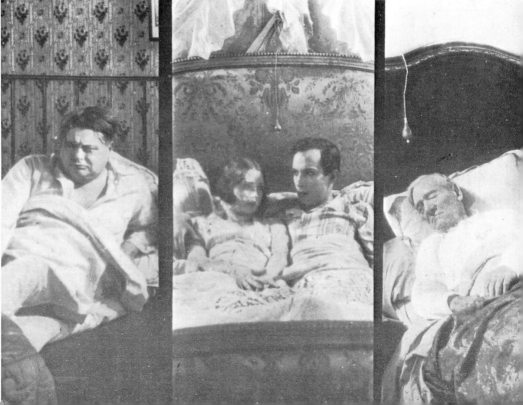

Clair's visual parallels. The factory as prison in À *Nous la liberté*.

Clair's ideal of friendship. Capitalist and worker as Laurel and Hardy in À *Nous la liberté*. (Henri Marchand and Raymond Cordy)

publicity (*His Picture in the Papers*); pacifism (*In Again, Out Again*); the power of positive thinking (*Reaching for the Moon*). Doug's personality was uniquely suited to this human parody. Sometimes he embodied the trait that the film ridiculed—and Doug was so energetic, so frenetic, so able to run extremely fast in the wrong direction that he was the perfect figure to embody a human trait gone frenziedly wrong. But often he played the opposite role, the healthy embodiment of a positive trait that overcame the erring ways of those misguided folks who crept unknowingly in the wrong direction: Doug raced about, collided with the erring wanderers, and smashed them back into the path of sense and sanity. Doug's physical energy was the perfect center for fast-moving, breezy films that took the business of making films rather lightly and showed how easily human error can be corrected with a little zest, a little effort, and a lot of jumping around.

Many of the moralistic sentiments in the Fairbanks films are dated and banal. These films were made in the age of Griffith, whom few would exempt from the same flaws. Fairbanks' comedies constantly lauded American openness as opposed to European duplicity (Europeans were consistent villains); physical exertion as opposed to laziness, drinking, smoking, and eating; the West as opposed to the East; masculine forthrightness as opposed to effeminate deviousness; home and family; strong body and clean mind; imaginative, forceful attempts to achieve the worthwhile and possible as opposed to daydreams about the unattainable.

At least one myth that Fairbanks had the honesty and insight to avoid (Griffith did not) was that the poor are happier than the rich. Significantly, Doug's films never debunk the desirability of money. Fairbanks himself was making enough of it, and besides, money is the primary ingredient of the American Dream that Doug personified. In most of the films, Doug plays a wealthy man. The problem of money in Fairbanks films is how to be rich and stay natural rather than becoming affected. Money is fine, but it is no excuse for a man to drink, become a snob, abuse his body, women, or other human beings who are less fortunate. Doug is a democratic plutocrat.

If these moralistic obsessions seem distasteful, the charm, energy, pace, and cleverness of the films make them acceptable—or at least forgivable. For one thing, there is the Fairbanks body. As physical trickster, Fairbanks rivaled Keaton in his ability to make the physically difficult look gracefully easy. Fairbanks' body was another of those great physical instruments that moved so hypnotically in the silents; its movements were smooth and effortless, as well as smoothly and effortlessly related to the films' plots. It bounded up staircases, swung on ceiling beams, raced up steep slopes, tumbled down ravines, leaped from cliff to tree branch, flew through the air to tackle an enemy, vaulted over rooftops. Doug could ride a horse, twirl a rope, swim a river, and perform countless other specialized and spectacular skills. And he did not look simply interesting or athletic doing his fancy stunts. He looked as graceful as a ballet dancer. The films helped him by not milking his physical stunts but using them only when a burst of physical steam exactly suited the increasing pace and momentum of the story.

The strength of the Fairbanks stories and the cleverness of their comments and contrasts are further virtues of these early comic features. Their favorite cinematic device is the cross-cut. Seven years before *Strike*, Fairbanks' *Wild and Woolly* (1917) begins with a satiric montage of cuts, contrasting the past and the present—horse-drawn carriage as opposed to a streetcar, a stagecoach as opposed to a train. Four years before *The Last Laugh*, Fairbanks' *The Mollycoddle* (1920) uses a subjective, moving-camera shot of a blurry, dizzily spinning stoke hole into which a woozy, exhausted Doug has been shoveling coal. There is plenty of ingenuity and imagination in these films. Although the imagination does not take the form of gags—as in Keaton, Lloyd, and Langdon—it exists in the very construction of the plot and the characters who perform it. The Fairbanks comedies were the best-*written* early comedies.

The beginnings of the Fairbanks films are often arrestingly clever. *The Mollycoddle* begins with a series of cross-cuts that contrast the Indian civilization of Arizona to the millionaire playground of Monte Carlo. After a series of shots of Hopi houses on rocky mesas overlooking the desert, and the great casino on its rocky cliff overlooking the Mediterranean, a title asks, "What's under them both?" Answer: "Just rock." The contrast between uncorrupted nature and corrupt civilization (Fairbanks is a sort of American Rousseau who also believes in the flag, Mom, and money) returns in the film's closing montage—an Indian drummer as opposed to a jazz drummer; an Indian dance as opposed to the shimmy. If the idea behind such contrasts isn't particularly new or engaging, the cuts themselves are active and visually interesting.

The Mystery of the Leaping Fish (1916) is a parody of Sherlock Holmes in which Doug plays the detective, Coke Ennyday. He opens the film by shooting himself full of cocaine and drinks gallons of booze round the clock. Coke eventually solves the caper by getting himself hopped up with dope and then disposing of the criminals by throwing the powder in their eyes. This plot may sound a bit strange for 1916, but Chaplin also used a syringe of dope to pep himself up in *Easy Street*, one year later. Part of the strangeness might be explained by the fact that Tod Browning, not Anita Loos, wrote the script. (Browning's bizarre perversity would emerge later with the Lon Chaney films, and with *Dracula* and *Freaks*.)

Wild and Woolly contrasts East and West again; this time Doug is not a mollycoddle but an imaginative Easterner who longs for the openness and excitement of the West. Doug, again a plutocrat, gets his chance when he must go to Arizona to transact some business for his father's railroad. The irony of the film is that the Arizona town of 1917 is calm, peaceful, modern, civilized, exactly as placid and respectable as the cities back East. But the residents, hearing of Doug's mania for Western clichés, do up their town (false building fronts, false misspelled signs) and themselves (cowboy gear with chaps, spurs, and guns rather than their ordinary business suits) to suit Doug's fancy. When Doug gets to Arizona, he is delighted with all this Western costumery. Anita Loos fills the title cards with fake Western expressions like "ain't" and "a-walkin'" and "a-worryin'" and "a-skeered."

In *Reaching for the Moon* (1917) and *His Majesty the American* (1919), Fairbanks presents a Hollywood comic interpretation of European monarchy. The monarchs are besieged with enemies; the nobles are jealous; the countries seem to exist only for the purposes of spying and counterspying; revolution is in the air; no one trusts anyone else. Underlying this comic exaggeration is the clear implication that in the good old USA, where we have "democracy" rather than kings and nobles, none of these nasty, treacherous cabals exists. (At the time, American boys were fighting in Europe to "make the world safe for democracy.") The picture-postcard naïveté of both films makes the kingdoms look like a cross between Venice, Paris, Vienna, and Lower Slobovia. If the comic kingdoms seem expressions of American jingoism, they are not so very far away from Freedonia of *Duck Soup*, Klopstokia of *Million Dollar Legs*, and "Russia" of *Never Give a Sucker an Even Break*. Not only are the Fairbanks comedies amusing in their own right; they are very much a part of the American comic tradition that distrusts all forms of artificiality, affectation, and pretense.

Hal Roach

Hal Roach was Mack Sennett's major competitor. By the mid-1920s Roach had probably surpassed his more famous rival, in style and comic ingenuity if not in earnings and popularity. The early Roach career is inextricably bound up with the career of Harold Lloyd (and vice versa). They began imitatively, copying Sennett's formula of chases and rhubarbs in parks, streets, restaurants, and beaches; on cars, horses, motorcycles, and speedboats. But the development of Lloyd's comic character—and its eventually spectacular success—began to turn Roach's ideas in a different direction. He began thinking more in terms of character than zany non sequitur, carefully structured gags rather than speed, logical plotting rather than cumulative romping; a slower pace and a more personalized use of the camera to pick motivation and decision out of chaos.

When Lloyd left Roach in 1922, Roach had already begun to drift away from the Sennett mayhem into his own particular kind. By the end of the silent era the Roach method had perfected itself so well that it can be seen with equal clarity in films featuring very different comic personalities. For example, a Laurel and Hardy short, You're Darn Tootin', a Charley Chase gem, Movie Night, and a less familiar classic with Stu Erwin and Edgar Kennedy, A Pair of Tights, all produced in 1928–29, share similar characteristics (they also share the same creators behind the camera—Leo McCarey and George Stevens). The films build from carefully developed (if also rather petty) character traits. The camera takes the time for frequent close-ups of human faces to show minds working and feelings translating themselves into action. Gag sequences are lengthy, carefully constructed, and smoothly polished. Rather than Sennett's string of fast gags, each of the three two-reelers uses three or four carefully developed long sequences, each with a beginning, middle, and end.

A careful unity links the sequences: in You're Darn Tootin', the musical instruments; in Movie Night, the hiccoughs; in A Pair of Tights, the girls' hunger, their beaux' cheapness, and an angry cop. Finally, from sequence to sequence, there is a careful build in tension and momentum, an increase in pace and frenzy, a magnification of the human vice presented in the early moments. The Roach films often end in as much pandemonium as Sennett's ever did, but they reach it in the most logical, psychologically clear way—irritation by irritation, mistake by mistake.

The Roach films are full of comic people (as opposed to Sennett's Bevans and Turpins and such, who are comic non-people and not of this earth): Stan Laurel—the weeping, puling, blank-brained, sleepy-eyed kid —and Oliver Hardy—the florid, fussy, self-satisfied, fat brat—are the most familiar Roach types. But there were also Charley Chase—the fastidious husband and father with tiny mustache, fussy mannerisms, brilliantine-slicked hair; James Finlayson—squinty-eyed, nose-puckered, prune-faced, impatient and testy, short-fused; Edgar Kennedy—master of the slow burn, absolutely motionless as the circumstance and injury speak for (and often slurp all over) his face; Anita Garvin—cold, haughty, contemptuous, with a frozen, piercing stare; and Specs O'Donnell—the obnoxious freckle-faced kid whose cute adolescent blotches don't fool anyone about the genuine venom in his heart.

The great Roach films roll these comic people into a perfect Bergson "snowball." Perhaps a man delivering pies slips on a banana peel. He retaliates by pushing a single fallen pie in the face of the man who dropped the banana peel. That man vengefully grabs another pie to hurl at the pie man, unfortunately missing him but hitting a bystander across the street. The bystander retaliates by striding to the pie truck, of course loaded with pies, and firing in the direction of his attacker. He, of course, also misses his target, but the new pie-bashed innocents want to get their hands on more pies to avenge themselves on their assailants. And so forth until the street is filled with flying pies.

In Roach films, pies are not carelessly thrown (as they were in Sennett's). The bizarre act of throwing a pie takes careful preparation, for people do not ordinarily throw pies, and Roach would have us accept his world as some version of reality. Further, Roach films never use one pie or a few isolated pies (as Sennett's often did), but take one pie and then build the oneness to infinity. There is less improvisation and far more gag construction in Roach than in the Keystones. But this pie-sequence example (the film is the famous *The Battle of the Century*, with Laurel and Hardy) shows the Roach structure at its most effective and rhythmic. For examples of the same structure without the essential momentum, compare Laurel and Hardy's *Bacon Grabbers* with their *Big Business*, or *Below Zero* with *You're Darn Tootin'*, or *Wrong Again* with *The Music Box*. The former of the pairs fail to move properly and fall flat; the latter are perfect stairways to insanity.

Hal Roach's most important players (after Lloyd's departure) were Our Gang, Will Rogers, Snub Pollard, Charley Chase, and Laurel and Hardy. The Our Gang comedies reveal that Roach's touch was gentler than Sennett's: children rather than adults, attention to faces and human traits rather than bodies and non sequitur gags, developed and constructed gag sequences, more rounded stories, affectionate ethnic humor, whimsy, tenderness, and cuteness. Will Rogers' silent films synthesize the qualities of Douglas Fairbanks and Ben Turpin. Like Fairbanks, Rogers was adept at physical stunts—leaping, jumping, running, falling, tumbling—as well as Western tricks of the trade—riding, roping, bulldogging, bronc-busting. Like Turpin, Rogers parodied popular hits and stars. But rather than being an exaggerated, out-of-this-world burlesque of film heroes, Rogers was amazingly adept at giving a convincing impersonation of the popular star. Turpin's parodies are funny because the cross-eyed idiot looks silly trying to be von Stroheim or Valentino or Tom Mix. Rogers' parodies are funny because he fools us with the accuracy of his look, style, and gestures. Perhaps the difference between Rogers and Turpin is also a sign of the difference between Roach and Sennett.

Snub Pollard signals something else about Roach. Snub began working in Harold Lloyd's earliest "glass character" pictures. When Lloyd left the Chaplinesque Keystone imitations for domestic reality, the goony-looking Snub no longer belonged in Harold's universe. So Roach made Pollard a star of his own films, and Snub carried on the Sennett style of insanity at the Roach lot. But just as Pollard eventually no longer had a place in the Lloyd world, he also lost his place in the Roach world of the mid-1920s. Pollard left Roach—whose style had evolved toward a more domesticated reality—to make his own films.

Pollard would have been much more at home with Sennett. He both looked and acted like a goon. His trademarks were the huge mustache, so long that its ends dripped over his chin at left and right, the tiny, beady eyes, derby hat, string tie, striped shirt, white gloves, and white collar. His look was in the Sennett tradition; he could easily have been a Chester Conklin or Billy Bevan, both of whom he resembled. So was his costume—consciously goofy, evoking memories of both Charlie and Lonesome Luke. And his comic style and manner of playing were also strictly Sennett. Snub was simply not of this world, and Roach films in the 1920s gradually decided that this world was where they wanted to be.

Pollard's early comedies were very Sennettesque in style. In 1920, almost the same year in which Roach began turning out the smooth, slick, realistic Lloyd two-reelers, Roach produced a Pollard one-reeler, *All Lit Up*, that looks far more like Sennett than Lloyd. Snub plays a butterfly collector. His daffy looks and style required him to play daffy characters rather than any version of real human beings. Snub races around chasing butterflies, using Sennett's undercranked camera for comic speed, Sennett's parks and restaurants as comic locations, and Sennett confusion between husbands, wives, lovers, robbers, and children as its vague story line. Equally Sennett is *Waltz Me Around*, also 1920, in which Snub and his pal, the black child actor Ernie Morrison, make fun of arty, fruity ballet dancing (rather similar in spirit to Sennett's parodies of "artistes," such as *Cursed by His Beauty* of six years earlier).

Later Pollard films at Roach tried to find some kind of character that Snub might approximate and impersonate. The decision was to turn Snub into a daffy inventor. Of course inventors were crazy, and Snub could play the mastermind dreaming up crazy (and funny) new machines. And so "Inventor Pollard," as he came to be called, served as comic foil to a series of insane gimmicks and gadgets that were supposedly the fruits of his so-called brain. In *The Big Idea* (1922), Snub's Rube Goldberg inventions are the envy of his competitors, who send spies out to snoop on his furtive ideas. His new invention turns out to be an automotive pavement polisher that looks like a cross between a street cleaner and a Pershing tank. It succeeds more in bashing things down than in polishing things up.

Pollard's funniest film is *It's a Gift* (1923), which is crammed with Rube Goldberg machines (borrowed from Keaton, but funny nonetheless). In the first sequence, Snub wakes up in the morning. His alarm clock is a feather that tickles his feet; he pulls cords to light the stove, put the eggs on the fire, perk the coffee. A tug of a cord lifts his bedcovers onto the window to serve as curtains; another tug of a cord lifts his trousers up his legs; another raises the bed up into the wall, which converts into a cheery hearth and fireplace—ablaze with a warm fire.

Then Snub walks out of his house to a garbage can. A flick of a slat covers the "b," changing "garbage" to "garage"—and out comes a little car, shaped like a large mortar shell on four tiny wheels. The car uses not an engine but a large magnet. Snub sticks out the magnet, and off his bullet car goes, towed by its magnetic attraction to some other vehicle. Of course, Snub's magnet car runs into difficulties when it starts attracting the wrong kinds of metallic companions. Eventually Snub arrives at the oil conference where he demonstrates his non-explosive, fireproof gasoline. One tiny drop makes all the autos and flivvers go completely mad—careening and racing uncontrollably in chaotic patterns (the Sennett use of undercranking, multiple exposure, stop-action, and shooting in reverse). Snub escapes the melee by climbing into his bullet car and pressing the button that makes it spread its wings. He flies off into the clouds, away from the havoc he has wreaked on earth.

The early Pollard films consistently used the one-reel form; their silly gimmicks and gadgets were best suited to a single reel. When Pollard left Roach to make his own two-reel films, he perhaps revealed Roach's wisdom in limiting him to a single reel. The films consistently begin with a dazzling, delightful gimmick—and then degenerate into plot clichés. For example, *The Yokel* (1927) begins with a brilliant trick shot —a skinny post with Snub's legs and arms appearing incongruously and impossibly on one side of the post or on the other, his torso completely obscured by the post. But later sections of Pollard films use purely Sennett material—the country rube vamped by the city gal because she thinks he has money, pie-slinging and dish-breaking chaos in a restaurant, chases on automobiles and motorcycles. Pollard tried to use the ingredients of 1915 Keystone comedy in 1927—years after both Sennett and the audience had begun to prefer other ingredients.

Perhaps the most popular and important star at Roach through the 1920s was Charley Chase. Roach passed the Lloyd mantle to Chase, and the Chase comedies are quite amazing in their ability to evoke the Lloyd style, techniques, and situations, yet be original comic films in their own right. Like Lloyd, Chase was of the American genus and the domesticated species. His aim was simply to survive comfortably and securely with a family, job, and friends. But Chase played an older man than Lloyd (although both performers were exactly the same age). Whatever his youthful dreams of success might have been, Chase has given them up to try to exist as quietly and uncomplicatedly as possible. He knows he is not going anywhere in life; there is no ladder of success to climb. He usually wants to sit at home and eat a quiet dinner, take his kids to the zoo, go to the movies, enjoy a ride in his car. Compared to Lloyd, Chase has much less dash, zip, and fervor; he is more cranky, more fastidious and fussy, more irritable. Whereas Lloyd has his smile, Chase has his twitching nose, pursing mouth, and dancing mustache. His greatest emotion is exasperation, and the situations in his films exasperated him constantly.

Chase was a much bigger man than his more famous rivals. He was not a little dwarf unsuited to reality but the normal-sized, everyday person who was as suited to reality as anyone could be. He embodied the domestic failures, frustrations, and difficulties of the audience—not their fanciful wishes as Lloyd did. Yet another physical difference that really counted between Chase and his rivals (and physical differences always count in physical comedy) was that Chase's body was not remarkably gifted. Its most comic kind of maneuver seemed to be a bouncy, jaunty dancing (and many of the Chase films purposely used dancing). Chase's pratfalls often fall flat themselves. (There are obligatory pratfalls in *Movie Night* that are the most ineffective and false notes in the entire film.) Although Chase began with Sennett's knockabout troupes in the Keystone years, he never really distinguished himself in such early Keystones as *Settled at the Seaside* and *A Versatile Villain* (both 1915), because Sennett merely used him as a nondescript juvenile who did a lot of running and falling. But with Roach, Chase could cultivate his two greatest talents—comic facial reactions and a consistent comic temperament—which were precisely suited to the Roach style.

Chase's *All Wet* (1924) is a superb example of both Chase's affinities with and differences from Harold Lloyd. Like Lloyd's *Get Out and Get Under*, *All Wet* is a film about a man's relationship to his automobile. As in the Lloyd film, Chase plays an ordinary, domesticated American male (by the name of Jimmie Jump, Chase's usual screen name) with an ordinary errand to perform. Unlike Lloyd, Chase feels no particular affection for his automobile; he simply needs to use it on an errand. And unlike the Lloyd film, *All Wet* is not a series of potential disasters that threaten to afflict the beloved auto, but a series of frustrating domestic tragedies, each worse than the one before. Whereas Lloyd triumphs over the dangers in *Get Out and Get Under*, and his automobile survives in one untarnished piece, Chase, at the end of his film, ends up with a totally wrecked car and a traffic ticket for illegal parking—and, to make the domestic tragedy even more frustrating, he has run his disastrous errand on the wrong day.

The film builds its frustration and failure with great care. When Jimmie Jump receives a telegram to pick up some puppies at the train station, he sets off in his car. On the way he sees another man's car stuck in the mud. Jimmie, the good neighbor, stops, tows the man's car out of the mud, and finds that his own is stuck. The man Jimmie helped refuses to push or tow Jimmie's car. But another neighbor, Garibaldi, comes along and offers to help—for a dollar. Jimmie hands over the dollar, Garibaldi pushes the car, and Jimmie watches his car slide slowly out of the mud and then into a puddle of water five feet deep, where it sinks with agonizing slowness—a beautiful far shot with no movement except the car's slow envelopment by the murky pool. Garibaldi hands Jimmie back his dollar.

A tow truck pulls up, attaches a rope to Jimmie's axle, tugs, and pulls the axle out from under Jimmie's car. Someone must now dive under the water to re-attach the axle and towline. Guess who? Jimmie dives, and in a far shot we see only a wide pool of water, the tow-truck driver sitting lazily on the bank of the pool, Jimmie's hand emerging periodically from the muddy depths to grasp a tool and return another. After all this grimy effort, Jimmie gets the axle and line attached, the tow truck tugs again, and this time pulls itself off its own axle. So Jimmie takes a trolley to the train station. A cop sees Jimmie's car "parked" illegally, dives into the muddy pool to find the license number, and then emerges to write out a citation. Meanwhile, Jimmie discovers he has arrived at the train station one day early. Finally, as he stands by the cage of a lion delivered to the train station, the beast reaches out its paw and claws off Jimmie's pants. He runs off as the film fades out.

Other films accumulate and multiply Jimmie's frustration and failure. In *Rat's Knuckles*, Jimmie Jump has invented a humane mousetrap that no one will buy. He eventually throws himself into the river as the result of his frustration. In *Be Your Age*, Chase plays a bashful, brilliantined bank clerk who tries to woo a rich, fat old millionairess—without success. In *Fluttering Hearts*, Chase plays an effete rich gentleman who gets his clothes ripped off in a department-store linen sale, and who must protect himself in a speakeasy by dancing with a manikin and then using the manikin to flirt with "Big Bill" (Oliver Hardy), the tough gangster (a variation on Chaplin's manikin bit in *A Dog's Life*).

Perhaps the greatest of the Chase shorts is *Movie Night* (1929), one of the last silents that Roach produced. The film makes full use of Chase's irritable fussiness, his facial reactions and grimaces as they show his steady loss of dignity and control to the forces of frustration and humiliation. The film is built around the device of hiccoughs (a wonderful premise for a silent film, in which a disturbing sound must be communicated in purely visual terms). In the first sequence, Charley's little daughter has the hiccoughs at the dinner table, and Charley does everything in his power to cure them. He eventually scares her so effectively (by dressing as a ghost) that the child faints.

In the second sequence, the ticket seller at the music house has the hiccoughs. Charley scares them away by impersonating a robber and using his umbrella handle as a pistol. Neither the woman nor the nearby cop appreciates this bit of masquerading. In the final sequence, inside the movie theater, Chase magnifies the frustration by setting the hiccough scene in a packed movie where everyone is intently trying to concentrate on the film. Chase sets up these tensions with his initial difficulty of finding a seat, his need to disturb everyone and tread on toes to get to it, his further embarrassment when he must go back and forth several times to take his daughter to the pottie.

But the frustration climaxes when Charley himself (of course) gets the hiccoughs in the crowded theater. When the manager passes him a glass of water—across a row, with some six people handling the cup while trying to watch the film—Charley spills it with a hiccough. He spills the next cup, and the next, and the next. The manager pulls Charley out of his seat and pours the entire pitcher of water down his throat. Charley's one pleasure in life—the weekly night at the movies—has been ruined.

Chase was no longer a star comedian in the sound era, but he made frequent appearances in featured roles. Perhaps his most memorable was as the obnoxious practical joker at the Shriners' convention in *Sons of the Desert* (1934). Chase perfectly captures a species of American vulgarity— the man who does the most vicious and sadistic things under the guise of joking, then squeals with laughter when his victims get bit, boffed, kicked, or terrified. Chase also directed films—under his real name of Charles Parrott. But the most interesting thing about Chase's work is his silent ability to suffer torments of comic frustration that build with magnificent control and increasing complexity to drive Jimmie Jump farther and farther up the wall.

This admirable control of intensity, rhythm, and structure, which had become a comic science at Roach by 1925, culminated in the films of Laurel and Hardy, the most famous comics (after Lloyd) to work for Roach and the most artful practitioners of the Roach structure of accumulation. Although Capra vividly recalls that Leo McCarey directed Stan and Ollie in 1924 when Capra worked for Roach, his memory is very vivid indeed,[1] for Laurel and Hardy never worked together as a team until 1927 (another reminder that anecdotes and memories owe no loyalty to historical fact). Ollie played minor roles in Roach comedies through the 1920s, usually a bully, an overgrown brat, a heavy, or some such combination of indolence and nastiness. Stan, like Chaplin a former member of the Karno Pantomime Troupe, was a very gifted physical clown and pantomimist; he starred individually in many Roach films that used his funny face, limber body (for example, sliding all over soapsuds in *Collars and Cuffs*), and pantomimic skills. (Stan's miming of "Samson and Delilah" in *Slipping Wives* rivals Chaplin's miming of "David and Goliath" in *The Pilgrim*.)

It was this film, *Slipping Wives* (1927), a rather weak parody of Lubitsch and von Stroheim marital tensions, that brought the fat man and thin man together—although not yet as a team. Perhaps the Roach decision to pair the two was influenced by the best thing in *Slipping Wives* (in addition to Stan's pantomime routine), the comic tension between Ollie as the disdainful, bullying, fastidious butler and Stan as the droopy house painter who is asked to pretend to be Madame's lover so as to make her husband jealous. This short comic scene between Stan and Ollie contains many Laurel and Hardy ingredients: a veneer of politeness with an underlying contempt and hostility; Ollie's clear assumption of his own superiority; Stan's befuddled incompetence that unintentionally reveals Ollie to be the fool.

Between 1927 and 1929, Stan and Ollie paired to make a series of brilliant physical comedies featuring their funny faces and bodies and their childish and foolish human reactions. The Roach strengths—masterfully constructed gag sequences, careful control of pace and rhythm, mounting intensity—reached their culmination in these films. Between 1929 and 1932 Stan and Ollie made a series of sound films—some two-reelers, some short features—that were less even as a group but occasionally reached the control and effectiveness of their silent masterpieces. After 1932 the pair made features that were consistently sloppy, completely lacking the tension, rhythm and unity of the earlier films, and interesting (if at all) in their parts rather than as whole films. With sound and without McCarey or Stevens, Laurel and Hardy were not what they had been.

At the base of the Laurel and Hardy method is the essential Roach premise—a clear, one-dimensional, petty, magnified psychological trait out of which all things in the film grow. Laurel and Hardy enjoyed the advantage of being able to use two basic human traits—one for each of them—as well as a shared attitude toward others and human experience. The starting point of every Laurel and Hardy film is that they are overgrown children. (They even play their own children in *Brats*, in which the two brats act exactly like their bratty fathers.) As overgrown children, they are incapable of sensible, competent adult activity—like Harry Langdon. But unlike Langdon, both Stan and, especially, Ollie assume they are the opposite of incapable, incompetent children. And the films consistently puncture their illusions and pretensions to maturity—especially Ollie's.

The two clowns are simply incompetent at any human task. They are terrible carpenters (*The Finishing Touch*), terrible salesmen (*Big Business*), terrible automobile drivers (*Two Tars*), terrible musicians (*You're Darn Tootin'* and *Below Zero*), terrible process servers (*Bacon Grabbers*), terrible furniture movers (*The Music Box*), terrible escaped convicts (*Pardon Us*), terrible soldiers (*Beauhunks*), and terrible husbands (*Sons of the Desert*). Their total incompetence at every occupation increases both their own exasperation and that of the people they serve (but good).

Ollie is the more sure of himself, certain he is able, clever, strong, and smart. He is florid in his gestures of preparation to perform a task and dogmatic in his insistence to "Let me do it," or "I'll take care of it"—both in word and in gesture. And for his greater pretension to competence, Ollie gets slammed harder with his insufficiency. He always suffers more crushing and crunching physical pain than Stan, primarily because he has been so insistent about taking the burden on his shoulders in the first place. Stan, making less ado about his adult abilities, faces every difficult scrape with the most childish ploy of all—he simply breaks down and weeps. If Langdon was the sweet child in a naughty adult world, Stan and Ollie are naughty children in a world they mistakenly think they can outbully and outshove.

Not only are Stan and Ollie nasty children in their incompetence and spitefulness, but the world itself in their films is populated solely with brats. The childish spite of the central pair runs up against the equally childish spite of their opponents.

The Laurel and Hardy films show that even the most respectable people —homeowners, landlords, professors, European princes, Shriners, police-men, nurses, dentists—are just as vain, pompous, and vengeful as the mad protagonists. James Finlayson and Edgar Kennedy, two respectable home-owners, are as petty and irrational in their human responses as the pair who attack their homes. The Professor in *The Music Box* (Billy Gilbert) thinks he has the right of way on a flight of stairs simply because he is a pro-fessor with a string of degrees. Despite his education and vocation, Laurel and Hardy provoke him into childish screaming and willful destruction. Stan and Ollie can convert a group of normal people into a mass of pie-slingers, shin-kickers, and pants-pullers. They bring out the worst in every-body. And to bring out the worst in folks is to belittle human pretensions to anything better.

One of the most striking psychological observations in the Laurel and Hardy films is the quiet deliberateness with which these child-adults go about their petty revenges. People in Laurel and Hardy do not hurl pies, bricks, and sticks at each other inadvertently in the heat of passion; they do not rip up each other's houses, cars, and clothing in frenzied haste and irrationality. They perform these vicious and childish actions with the greatest slowness, calm, and reason. They think very carefully before com-ing up with the next atrocity. They want to make sure that the atrocity is atrocious enough. The Roach method provides plenty of time and plenty of close-ups for the minds behind the faces to come up with the next piece of insanity. The camera lingers on Ollie's face while he thinks about what to break next. Then he nods. Then he calmly walks off to break a window or fender. Then, the destruction accomplished, the camera often moves back to the face of Stan, who gives his nod of approval: "That'll show you."

This rational insanity is another indication of the childish premise of the two main characters and their entire world. The destruction and chaos could never mount so high if one bad turn didn't provoke another. Domi-nating the films is a childishly barbaric equation of revenge and justice. If a man breaks your window, the just thing is to break his window. Or rather, two of his windows, because he should be taught a lesson. And if two of his windows get broken, he will have to do the just thing and break two doors, for he cannot be outdone in revenge. In a sense, the Laurel and Hardy comedies are unintentional comic parodies of the Revenge Tragedy —reduced to childish spite. The greatest of the Laurel and Hardy films— *Two Tars* (1928), *The Battle of the Century* (1928), *You're Darn Tootin'* (1928), *Big Business* (1929), *The Music Box* (1932), *Brats* (1932) —work on this equation of spite, revenge and justice.

Yet another childish Laurel and Hardy trait is their passionate attachment to their hats. They may be incompetent at every task, but they are perfectionists at trying to keep their hats on. The implication of this devotion to their hats is simply that as feeble and ridiculous as their activities are, they would be incapable even of them without their hats. In *The Music Box*, they interrupt their arduous task of getting a heavy piano up an immense flight of steps and into a second-story window specifically to fish their hats out of a pond and get the right one on each of their empty heads.* Ultimately, their hats become a nuisance and give them more to worry about and combat. The hats are as annoying and troublesome as all the other objects and people in their world. But the hats belong to them. And they are going to keep them on—come what may.

In the Sennett world, human activity looked insanely bizarre because it moved with such frenzy, illogic, and randomness. In the Laurel and Hardy world, human activity looks insanely bizarre because human motivation and passion have been so rationally and realistically reduced to such a petty, vengeful, vicious norm. The Sennett and Roach methods fuse in their similar assumptions about human greatness, human potential, and human accomplishment.

"Educational" Pictures

A third film company devoted to comic fun was Al Christie's Educational Pictures, a misnomer if there ever was one. Educational's comedies lack a distinctive style; they have neither Sennett's random romps nor Roach's careful accumulation and multiplication. Christie's studio seems to have had the same relationship to the two comic "majors" as Monogram, Republic, and pre-Capra Columbia had to the major Hollywood studios. Educational made comedies cheaply and quickly. They copied the successful formulas of their more celebrated and adventurous competitors. The Educational style seemed to be a cross between Sennett chases and Keaton machines. Perhaps the most striking characteristic of Christie's company

---

* The hat-passing game in *Waiting for Godot* and Lucky's inability to think without his hat on are two obvious Beckett derivations from Laurel and Hardy—a substitution of form for essence, covering for reality.

is its longevity—and the irony that he employed the same comics in the 1930s whom he had imitated in the 1920s.

Educational's most important star of the 1920s was Larry Semon. Semon, one of the strangest-looking comedians of the silent era, looked as if he ran a kosher delicatessen on Mars. His most distinctive features were a hideous horse-face (huge hooked nose and high forehead, thin hair pasted down with brilliantine) surmounted by a seeming pinhead. Semon used the camera's wide-angle lens to distort his comic features even more. His black-lined eyes (the liner made them look even more like bulging saucers) and his powdered, pasty-white skin added to the other-worldly ugliness of his face. And yet the plots of his films consistently put him into the romantic juvenile role—the young man trying to win the girl of his dreams. The role was comically and intentionally inconsistent with Semon's patent ugliness.

In addition to a distinctive face, Semon had a unique physical style. His movements were militarily precise, smart, crisp. He seemed to be worked by strings. He was not a fluid human being but a mechanical toy —toddling about the world in short jerks. This mechanical, puppetlike precision enhanced the strangeness of his comic ugliness to create a being who was not quite of this planet.

As a pure comic technician, Semon was often considered the "comedian's comedian." Keaton paid Semon the compliment of saying that Semon's films were as funny, as stuffed with great gags as anyone's. But he also noted that Semon's films were highly forgettable since they seemed to be nothing but collections of gags.[2]

Keaton's assessment of Semon's weakness is quite valid—as well as an indication that Keaton perceived the interrelationship of gag, character, and structure in a truly successful comedy. Semon's films were full of great gags—all products of other people's styles. There were Sennett chases in autos, planes, and boats; Sennett's use of frightened Negroes; Sennett's undercranking and camera games; Keaton's great leaps, falls, and stunts; Keaton's effete-rich-man characterizations; Keaton's melodramatic plots about performing some heroic task to win the girl. All of these ingredients were packed into two reels and seasoned with speed, speed, speed. (Appropriately, one of Semon's best films is Kid Speed (1924), about a race-car driver.) Semon especially milked chases and stunts. (The Stunt Man, 1927, is simply a series of stunts that Larry performs for a movie studio, each one more dangerous and difficult than the previous one.) Semon's comedy was merely that of a funny and funny-looking character who pulled any familiar joke out of the film gag bag. His films prove that great film comedy is a blend of a particular kind of peculiar, funny man who gets into a particular kind of comic trouble, who performs a particular kind of comic gag, and whose comic activities add up to a particular vision of human experience. Semon is peculiar but not at all particular.

Perhaps the same can be said of the Christie product in general. His goal was to pack as much into two reels as he could—regardless of the quality and consistency of the material. Another of his 1920s stars was Bobby Vernon, a tiny, blond, baby-faced boy who studied his comic trade with Mack Sennett—usually as Gloria Swanson's partner and protector. This use of Vernon was ironic, since Vernon was only a little larger than Gloria, and she was only five feet tall. In the Christie movies the petite, pretty-featured Vernon is easily frightened and always dwarfed. But he smiles sheepishly and somehow comes through his troubles. In *Broken China* (1926) Bobby gets mixed up in a Tong war in Chinatown (that motif again). Most of the film plays off Bobby's frightened reactions to Keatonish trick stairways and trapdoors that evoke *The Haunted House*. (Perhaps Keaton collected the debt by using a Tong war in his later *Cameraman*.) As with the Larry Semon films, Bobby Vernon's comedies were fast and funny with no distinct and consistent personality—except for a scared little boy's reactions to scary, dangerous things.

Christie silents strove to be fast and furious. Perhaps the best and most enjoyable of them is one actually called *Fast and Furious* (1924), a breathtakingly fast film starring Lige Conley (a bland straight man who was impersonally suited to miscellaneous gags) and directed by Norman Taurog (who directed mediocre Hollywood comedies for 40 years after his Christie apprenticeship). *Fast and Furious* combines wild comic antics in a rural general store (recalling Arbuckle's *The Butcher Boy*, Chaplin's *Sunnyside*, and Langdon's salesman mistakes in *Picking Peaches*), camera tricks and animation (two delightful eggs that dance a hula), a plot about a manager who robs his own store (shades of *The Floorwalker*), and a breathless, climactic chase that tries to outdo *Sherlock Jr. Fast and Furious* hasn't an original comic idea in it, but is undeniably exciting fun. The film is a testament to the rich cross-fertilization in 1920s comedy, to the vitality and energy of a genre in which any new comic idea (a tramp, an intricate machine pulled by strings, a breathless chase) and any effective comic motif (Tong wars, Limburger cheese, parodies of melodrama, drunken chaos) quickly produced dozens of imitations before the year was out. The film also pays silent tribute to the consummate artistry and control of the greatest comic imaginations that could transform the same zany, impersonal gags into a personal comic universe.

Christie's sound shorts were not fast and furious; they were slow and heavy. The best moments of the Keaton or Langdon Educationals are those which briefly (and usually silently) evoke a memory of their star's greatness in the 1920s: Langdon's *Hooks and Jabs* (1933), Keaton's *Allez Oop* (1934), *The Gold Ghost* (1934), and *Tars and Stripes* (1935). There may be a few moments in each of them when a sequence reveals a glint of the old genius or a gag develops itself into a comic idea that is a lot better than the film as a whole deserves. But Christie's sound comedies ghoulishly pick bits of gold out of comic corpses. Christie, Keaton, and Langdon together joined the living dead; Charles Lamont, a name fortunately not yet resuscitated by *auteurist* scavengers, directed most of these grim revels.* The very style of physical comedy—not just the individual comic talents—had obviously died. For those who love the physical comedy that in the 1920s so completely fulfilled the potential of 1895, the Educational sound pictures are a depressing parade of ghosts and zombies —a cemetery for a dead art.

* Lamont continued showing his "flair" for comic deadness at Universal by directing the very worst of the Abbott and Costello, Ma and Pa Kettle, and Francis the Talking Mule films.

V

—

SOUND
COMEDY

CHAPTER 13

Sound and Structure

—

ALTHOUGH the end of the last chapter might have seemed the overture to a typical singing of either the blues or a requiem for the passing of screen comedy, screen comedy did not die. A particular kind of comedy died. Film comedy—like film art in general—radically changed its emphasis and aesthetic. Although an occasional newspaper or journal article still asks where are the Chaplins, Keatons, and Lloyds of today, it might just as well ask where are the leech doctors or pardoners. Or title-card artists. There are no Chaplins or Keatons today because the sound film has no use for them. One of the reasons great physical comedians developed in the teens and twenties was that the potential of the medium demanded their services. The physical comedian who communicated personality, social attitudes, and human relationships by physical means—gesture, stunt, the expression (or lack of it) on a face—was an outgrowth of a medium whose only tools were movement, rhythm, and physical objects and surfaces.

Sound comedy is structural, not physical. It is *written* comedy. Perhaps a better term might be conceived, or shaped, or planned, or constructed. The comedy—its action, meaning, values, effects, gags, character foils and balances, ironies, and implications—are carefully molded in advance by the film's creators. In the best sound comedies, if the director is not his own writer, the director and writer work carefully together to shape the final product—Capra and Riskin, Renoir and Spaak, Carné and Prévert, Lubitsch and Raphaelson, Wilder and Diamond, Hawks and Hecht or Lederer, and so on. Conversely, the most important collaboration in silent comedy was between comic and director, or comic and cameraman—Chaplin and Totheroh, Keaton and Bruckman, Lloyd and Newmeyer/

Taylor, Langdon and Capra. Whereas the silent comedy seems simply to flow from the central clown, the sound comedy carefully builds a whole society of human beings. Most sound comedies are comedies of manners, not comedies of motion. Whereas silent comedy is most concerned with *how* the comic goes about his actions and *who* he is, sound comedies focus on *what* the action is and *why* it should be so.

The apparent exceptions to this aesthetic rule merely prove its validity. The Marx Brothers, probably the most delightful physical clowns of American sound films, were dazzling in films written by S. J. Perelman, Arthur Sheekman, George S. Kaufman and Morrie Ryskind, Bert Kalmar and Harry Ruby (*Monkey Business, Horsefeathers, Duck Soup,* and *A Night at the Opera*) and sputtering in films written by Irving Brecher, Sid Kuller, Hal Fimberg, Ray Golden (Who are they? you may well ask), and Frank Tashlin (*Go West, At the Circus, The Big Store*). The Marx Brothers films *seem* to be comedies of clownish personalities, but they are really comedies of conception and construction, brilliantly executed by the zany threesome or foursome.

Conversely, W. C. Fields and Mae West are the exciting central clowns of generally inept films. They give us delightfully unforgettable moments that sparkle in the dreary, formulaic, sloppy settings that the clowns themselves have often carelessly devised. Similarly, Jerry Lewis, a *cause célèbre* of comic controversy, is a funny man (usually less funny than he tries to be) in a boring and banal film universe. Lewis' inabilities as a writer—to manage a plot, to construct revealing oppositions and contrasts, to twist ironies and incongruities—plague his films. And the comedies of such personalities as Abbott and Costello, Danny Kaye, Red Skelton, and Bob Hope reveal the conflict and contradiction between a funny character and an inadequately conceived structure.

Woody Allen, a genuine comic personality, is, however, a more effective screenwriter than clown. *Take the Money and Run* and *Bananas* seem to chronicle the exploits and activities of the nebbish-schlepper that Allen plays. But these films actually communicate their ideas through the creator's brain, not the clown's body. Rather than putting a central clown through a series of physical adventures, these films combine conceptual parodies (some dazzling, some forced)—of social attitudes and psychological stereotypes, of television and film genres, styles, and conventions, even of specific film sequences and television programs—with surrealistic gags, jokes, wild situations, unlikely characters, and anything else that seems to occur to Allen at the time. The adventures of Woody in *Take the Money and Run* and *Bananas* are unfathomable and absolutely irrelevant. The real material of both films is the comic style that Allen conceives for depicting and commenting on each event in the "plot."

These two Allen films more closely capture Sennett's style and spirit than any of the more conscious attempts (*It's a Mad, Mad, Mad, Mad*

World, *The Great Race*, *Those Magnificent Men in Their Flying Machines*). Both Sennett's and Allen's films have an apparent structure (the story) and a real one (a dizzy symphony of miscellaneous goofing). Both "riff" and "goof" in a string of fast, discontinuous gags; if you don't like one, there's another right behind it. But where Sennett's goofing takes physical form, Allen's takes conceptual form. This difference is the essential one between silent and sound comedy. (Interestingly, when Allen wants to develop a more believable character and a more coherent human story [in *Play It Again, Sam*, 1972], he drops his riffing pace and structure and adopts the typical device of sound comedy—coherent dialogue scenes of social intercourse between two or more people, or non-people.)

Silent comedy creates the mind by means of the body, the mental by means of the physical: Chaplin's kick, Keaton's leaps, Lloyd's hustle, Langdon's slowness. In sound comedy, the mental process reveals itself in the structural pieces that the creators have elected to include. The work's intelligence reveals itself, not in the course of the physical performance, but in the prior selection of components that are then performed. For example, *The Pilgrim* reveals its "mind" in Charlie's mime of the David and Goliath story; but *The Rules of the Game* reveals its "mind" by paralleling masters and servants who do similar dead things in similar silly ways. *The General* reveals its "mind" in Buster's sly method of conking a Union enemy on the head; but *Bananas* reveals its "mind" by cutting to a shot of a baby carriage rolling down a flight of steps after a revolution has taken place. In sound comedy, structural conception, not physical gesture, implies idea and intention.

Even the films of Jacques Tati and Pierre Étaix reveal the same principle. Tati and Étaix try very carefully to follow the method and evoke the spirit of silent comedy. They almost obliterate talk from the sound track. They perform physical stunts and business, concentrate on motion and visual gags. And yet the very decision to evoke this silent world is itself a deliberate, intellectual conception. They do not perform physical comedy because it is their era's natural cinematic milieu but deliberately because it is not. They make a purposefully unnatural, self-conscious choice to fulfill their intellectual conception—much like Prokofiev's choice in writing a "Classical Symphony." Tati's and Étaix's films are far more self-conscious, directorial "style pieces" than Keaton's or Lloyd's. In the same way, Chaplin's *Modern Times* is far more self-conscious in its technique and style than *The Gold Rush*, because his silent film assumed certain conventions for mirroring reality whereas his sound film had to posit its own unusual (for 1936) conventions. Significantly, Tati's self-conscious approach to sound uses *Modern Times* as its model.

Why did comedy change its direction? Why is the physical comedy of a central personality incompatible with the sound film's aesthetics? The addition of sound obviously eliminated a key difference between the silent-film world and the real world. The world in silent film was a world without noise or talk. It has often been said that art is a function of limitations, that the province of art is precisely that gap between nature and the way nature can be imitated in the work of art.* A work seeks symbolic, artificial means—conventions—to compensate for that gap. And in those symbolic means art emphasizes and isolates elements of nature that normally we do not so fully perceive because we take in nature as a unity. The silent-film world increases our awareness of the purely visual, shapes and textures, space, the motion of bodies in space and time. Its exclusive concentration on the visual increases our visual concentration, turning the film experience into a hypnotic succession of moving images.

The silent film is as much ballet as realistic drama. Although its milieu looks like realistic rooms or the familiar outdoor world of trees and seas, human beings glide through that milieu like dancers. The balletic motion is underscored by fluid, rhythmic, or contrapuntal cutting and (most like ballet) a musical underscoring that supports the movement with an appropriate succession of tunes and tones. Lacking natural sound, the silent film works on the ear solely by means of the effects of cutting and motion on the eye, increasing the visual hypnosis still more. The movement of physical comedy—dizzily fast like Sennett's, fluid like Keaton's, magnetically supple like Chaplin's, dreamily slow like Langdon's—perfectly suits the silent visual hypnosis. Few non-comic silent films can match the emotional effectiveness of the comedies, simply because the serious emotions did not readily take to communication by pose, motion, and gesture.†

Natural sound not only destroyed the hypnotic effects of visual, physical motion; it destroyed the balletic convention for imitating reality, the balletic world in which the physical comedy was played.‡ The sound film did not simply add sound to the silent film. It did not simply (as Bazin claimed) make the film *more* like reality. It altered the way the film translated reality. Rather than taking place in a ballet world of motion, the sound comedy necessarily took place in a world that looked more like everyday reality. Rather than underscoring motion with music, the sound comedy is necessarily committed to such underscorings as traffic noises, banging doors, chirping crickets and birds, ringing doorbells and telephones, wind, waves, explosions, crackling fires, and so on. If the world of sound films is to be accepted as objective reality, every visual composition

---

* Rudolf Arnheim has said it specifically about film in *Film as Art*.

† "Serious" emotions—love, hate, desire, greed, envy, anger, joy, etc.—looked fake in early silent films simply because they could not be communicated by the physical tool (the human body and its parts) alone. They required editing—montage—to create a specific "objective correlative" for the emotional attitude of the body.

‡ Perhaps the recent explosion in American ballet—in both quantity and quality—is a reawakening of our hypnotic attraction to the visual underscored by rhythm and music.

must be accompanied by the natural sound that such a sight would generate.

Filmmakers rather quickly learned that sound could be used asynchronously, could be obliterated, or that action could be underscored by appropriate tonal music. Images and sound need not work in unison—as they did in the silents. Sound and picture could use the principles of harmony and counterpoint as well. But such possibilities for integration of picture and sound demanded that someone devise them—conceive, shape, sculpt them. This need to create a kind of conversation between sound and image became as important to the sound film's success as the sequential flow of moving images was to the silent film's.

The more the creator uses counterpoint, divorcing the literal relationship of sound and image, the more his film departs from mirroring conventional reality. Ultimately he can create a completely balletic, metaphoric dream world (as Chaplin did in *City Lights* and *Modern Times*, Clair did in *Le Million* and *À Nous la liberté*, and Tati and Étaix did two decades later). But such special uses of the sound track run contrary to the conventions that the sound film uses to imitate reality; they deliberately imitate unreality. For the purpose of reflecting social reality (still the commercial motion picture's primary intention), the film creator has limited asynchronous, contrapuntal, or tonal effects of sound to those special moments when his film requires or can sustain emotional underscoring.

The new definition of reality in sound films also changed the kinds of people films could depict and the kinds of action those people could perform. Buster, Charlie, Harold, and Harry were heightened essences, archetypes of certain kinds of human behavior. The actions of their films focus exclusively on the archetypes' reactions to metaphoric situations. The central archetype is a giant in his own films, almost the only inhabitant of his world. How many other distinctive, developed, memorable personalities are there in the hundreds of films of Chaplin, Keaton, Langdon, and Lloyd? Incredibly few. The silent clown was a solo, virtuoso performer.

But realistic social comedy requires pairs of people (Tracy *and* Hepburn, Cooper *and* Arthur, Grant *and* Dunne, etc.). Human communication and meaning do not really flow from the mime and gestures of a single being. They are dependent on social intercourse—conversation, eye contact, "vibrations" between two or more people. The comic sound performer had to communicate in the film world the way people communicate in society and nature. He could not simply freeze his body into a human statue or wink his eye while nibbling on a rose. The primary thrust of sound-film aestheticians—André Bazin, Siegfried Kracauer, Stanley Cavell—has been to elaborate the consequences of the major premise that sound film mirrors reality much more literally, much less metaphorically, than silent film. As a result, the human beings in a sound comedy must be closely related to the kinds of people one would expect to meet in society and nature. If they do crazy, "screwball" things, it must be for comprehensible, psychologically credible reasons: she is trying to snare her man; she is scatterbrained; he is cynical and egotistical; he is sexually insecure, or whatever. The players of sound comedy are not heightened, but ordinary. If the central comic personality is a bizarre type, heightened above the ordinary, his film world requires the same magnification. He cannot walk through a series of ordinary domestic problems and solutions. (Compare, for example, the successful Marx Brothers and W. C. Fields films with the unsuccessful ones; compare Woody Allen to Jerry Lewis.)

And once again we come to the importance of the writing, of the overall conception of sound comedy. If the comic personality at the film's center is not a representative of reality, the writer (or writer-director, or *auteur*) must create a film world to fit him. If the film's human focus and social milieu are familiar and domestic, then the creator's mind must supply the exaggeration that comedy requires in the selection of the total society of human beings and the diverse kinds of choices they make; in the contrasting of their talk with their actions; in the juxtaposition of material objects with the human beings; in providing surprising twists in the chain of events; in the integration of comic devices of music, noise, cutting, and composition. In a sound comedy, John Jones and Mary Smith usually go about their realistic, comprehensible business. The creator's mind shapes the slant and comment on that business. That mind, not the performer's, becomes the sound comedy's dominant personality.

Most great sound comedies are played with utter seriousness. (The exceptions are the purposely zany, irrational ones like the Marx Brothers'.) Katharine Hepburn in *Bringing Up Baby*, Michel Simon in *Boudu Saved from Drowning* and *Bizarre, Bizarre*, George C. Scott and Keenan Wynn in *Doctor Strangelove*, Jean Arthur in *Easy Living* do not try to be funny. They merely try to *be*. Few performances in great comic sound films ever scream, "Look at me, I'm funny." (The Marx Brothers do, and they only get away with it until 1937; Jerry Lewis does, and that is one more reason his comedies seem tasteless, overstated, and unconvincing.) The human being who proclaims his funniness and cleverness in a sound comedy is the wry mind behind the camera, not the performer in front of it.

In silent comedy a funny, clever mind dwelt both behind and in front of the camera. It was usually the same mind. In the sound comedy only Chaplin, Fields, Tati, Étaix, Lewis, and Allen frequently dominate both sides of the camera. This divorce of comic performer from comic *auteur* occurred partly for the aesthetic reasons enumerated above and partly for concrete, practical reasons. Except for Chaplin, the silent comedians, who mastered their craft in the days of casual improvisation, never successfully made the transition to sound. Whatever theoretical knowledge Chaplin, Keaton, Lloyd, or Arbuckle originally lacked about the movies, they gradually picked up by experience in the sheer quantity of films they made. The new sound comedians lacked not only theoretical knowledge of the medium but the opportunity to learn through experience. Chaplin made more films in 1914 (if short ones) than the Marx Brothers did in their entire 20-year career. Jerry Lewis alone absorbed his craft from a busy, productive comic apprenticeship. Tati, Étaix, and Allen learned their craft from study of the older masters. Fields almost purposely never learned any craft at all. Given the inability of the clown to manipulate his antics from behind the camera and before the shooting began, the fertile comic intelligence shifted to the brain who wrote the script and/or manipulated the camera and who had learned that control in various kinds of writing-directorial-photographic apprenticeships.

This discussion of sound comedy will not follow the chronological path traveled through silent comedy, because chronology, artistic influence, and aesthetic discovery play much less significant roles. The evolutionary process that wedded traditional comic forms to the new motion-picture medium required a discussion of early forerunners as well as the mature masters. The study of silent comedy reveals a process of discovery—both about comedy and comedy in the cinema. However, sound comedy in 1932 was as mature and complex as sound comedy in 1972. (Some, in fact, would say it was more so.) After discussing three early masters of sound comedy, the study will trace the three major traditions in which comedy, the motion picture, and synchronized speech have been successfully wedded.*

* That the discussion of sound comedy is only half as long as that of silent comedy does not imply the cliché that sound comedy is only half as good. Two obvious facts about silent comedy have necessarily influenced this study. First, the gulf of 40 years provides a useful evaluative distance. The critic and historian can indeed feel some confidence about what has survived. Second, silent comedy is an entity with a beginning, middle, and end. Because its evolutionary process is complete, it is easier today to distinguish between the pioneers, the imitators, and the grand masters. For the same reason, one can discuss the comedy of the 1930s with more confidence than that of the 1960s.

CHAPTER 14

Ernst Lubitsch
and René Clair

—

THE talent of Lubitsch was to turn the trivial into the significant; the talent of Clair was to turn the significant into the trivial. If Chaplin provided one kind of transition between silence and sound by bringing the principles of silent comedy into the sound era, Lubitsch and Clair provided another. Both Lubitsch and Clair began in the silent era to develop what were to become the most valuable tools for sound comedy. Lubitsch and Clair made director-crafted and -conceived comedies of manners in the silent era, films in which the ingenuity and intelligence of the director dominated any single performance by an actor. Lubitsch and Clair worked with whole societies, not single clowns; they emphasized their directorial control with careful and clever uses of decor, physical details, comparisons and contrasts of human behavior, ironic twists of plot, ironic parallels of character and structure, control of the camera and cutting—all the essential ingredients of sound comedy.

Lubitsch and Clair make for interesting comparisons. They were contemporaries; there was a good deal of cross-fertilization between their films; and they had similar gifts. Both had a sense of lightness and fancy; both mixed seriousness and froth; both had a feeling for music; both had strong senses of decor; both enjoyed comic understatement and irony in which the viewer infers the meaning and values for himself. Lubitsch was highly influenced by the Chaplin of *A Woman of Paris*; Clair, by the Chaplin of *The Kid* and *The Gold Rush*. Although a generation ago Clair seemed the more significant of the two directors, the passing of time has perhaps altered their reputations. Whereas Lubitsch could turn gooey Lehar into something vital, fresh, psychologically perceptive and revealing, Clair could turn Karl Marx into gooey Lehar. Clair films can still inspire respect technically—for succeeding so cleverly and masterfully with a new medium that had ravaged the aesthetics of 30 years' experience. Lubitsch films (as clever technically as Clair's) look as good as they ever did—or better.

The "Lubitsch Touch" and the Lubitsch Brain

Lubitsch's art is one of omission. It is an art of "not"—what is not shown, what is not heard, what is not said. It invests most of its screen time in objects—buttons, canes, briefcases, swords, wallets, hats, fans, corks, place cards, piano music, handbags, and so on. Yet the interest in things is never for the thing itself, but the thing's relationship to the human being who owns it, uses it, wants it, or wants to get rid of it. The physical object is the concrete expression of human feelings and desires. Lubitsch's method is a brilliant demonstration of Pudovkin's theory of the function of the "plastic material."* In fact, when Lubitsch saw Pudovkin's *Storm Over Asia*, one of his friends referred to devices in the religious scene (when Pudovkin cross-cuts between the religious ikons and the political bigwigs, both of whom are getting dressed and polished for a gala ceremony) as "Lubitsch touches."[1]

Lubitsch's "not" technique also reveals itself in his composition and camera placement; he consistently shows less than he might, implies more than he shows. Lingering shots on the outsides of doors, views obscured by windows and hedges and chair backs, shots aimed higher than the players so that only an occasional head bobs into the bottom of the frame —all of these were ways that Lubitsch used to transform Hollywood clichés of emotion and interaction into startlingly believable human terms, or to transform subtle, salacious, or sensual feelings into terms that offended neither the censor nor the audience. When Lubitsch added sound, he also compounded the methods of "not"—we listen to a scene we cannot see, or see a scene we cannot hear.

With such tools Lubitsch transformed melodramatic and sentimental tripe into credible human stuff and forged deeper into sexual desires, needs, frustrations, and fears than most of his contemporaries (and descendants) dared to go. In addition to this dominant method, Lubitsch

---

* Pudovkin defined the "plastic material" as any concrete physical object that can be used to illuminate the internal feelings, thematic ideas, or social values of a character, scene, or whole film. For a fuller discussion, see *A Short History of the Movies*, pp. 207–19.

brilliantly controlled every other technical cinematic device—montage, superimposition, masking, soft focus, dissolve, split screen, freeze frame, tonal lighting, cavernous interior far shots, intimate close-ups, tilts, blurs, asynchronous sound, musical motifs. Forty years ago Lubitsch was using most of the cinematic gimmicks of the 1960s and 1970s—and in his films they look completely natural.

Lubitsch's brilliance as a technician—probably the greatest in the American cinema after Griffith—tempts many to treat him as pure technician. Many other great American technicians—Griffith, Hitchcock, Welles, Kubrick—receive the same treatment. But technique is no more than a way of looking at the material and can never be divorced from what the material is and why the artist has chosen to look at it as he does. Lubitsch is one of the few great unromantics in the history of the American film (along with von Stroheim, Keaton, Hawks, Hitchcock, and Kubrick). He is a gentle cynic who chuckles at all the sentimental platitudes—the purity of woman, the sanctity of marriage, the idealization of love, the animal baseness of sex, the nobility of the poor, the depravity of the rich, the dignity of work, the redemption of social sin by internal virtue. All of the moral assumptions of American romantic films—even very good films like Griffith's, Ford's, Chaplin's, and Welles'—are the targets of his affectionate cynicism.

Unlike the films of his romantic colleagues, good and evil are absent from the great Lubitsch films. There are no moral blacks and whites. There are only people who want what they don't have, or can't get, or shouldn't want (but do), or have what they don't want (but should) or shouldn't have. There are contrasts of human behavior without moral evaluations of the behavior. There are conflicting human desires, conflicting human intentions, without judgments on the conflicting characters.

A great irony of these unromantic films is that they appear to take place in a romantic, operetta world (many of the films were originally operettas or operettaish plays), decked out with birthday-cake decor. But beneath this veneer the director defines people, not by the romantic's categories, the good and the bad, but by the cynic's, the clever and the foolish (also the seemingly clever fools and the seemingly foolish clever). The prime distinction between people in the Lubitsch world is not virtue but intellect. Despite its frothy exterior, the Lubitsch world is a region of thought. The harmony between the clever thinker behind the camera and the clever thinkers in front of it becomes clear. The Lubitsch technique rarely seems gimmicky because the kind of mind that is the subject of the film is also the kind of mind that controls the view of that subject.

Yet another irony of the Lubitsch film is that although it is devotedly and consciously intellectual, its primary subject is love. But love in the Lubitsch world is nothing like LOVE in the traditional American, romantic film world. The usual separation in the American film is between LOVE and

SEX. The distinction between the Dear One and the Friendless One in
Intolerance recurs in Chaplin, Ford, and even in films of the 1970s (*The
Graduate* and *Carnal Knowledge*). For Lubitsch, LOVE and SEX are not
opposites, but allies; the two passions are inseparable. Love between human beings is not a sacred rite but a combination of attuned minds and
bodies. Sex is not mysterious for Lubitsch; he does not personify it as a
Theda Bara or some other eye-shadowed sorceress. Sex is something personal, and charming, and decidedly human. That is why he shows sexual
attraction through such commonplace objects as popping jacket buttons,
dropped silverware, the chiming of a clock, or the closing of a door. Sex
is everyday, not strange; domestic, not foreign. Of course, the foreign settings of most Lubitsch films add an exotic touch to the domesticity. Perhaps Lubitsch could get away with his sexual frankness by pretending that
this open lasciviousness was indigenous only to decadent Europeans, not
to pure Americans.

There are many ironies about Lubitsch the filmmaker. It is ironic that
the little Jewish director—whose first success was in a series of German
short films as a Jewish ethnic comic named Meyer—should become the
personification of European sophistication and suaveness. It is ironic that
this bourgeois should become Hollywood's most successful chronicler of
the lives of the European upper class and nobility. It is ironic that the man
who was invited to Hollywood because of his lush, romantic historical
films should be Hollywood's most cynical deflater of the very romantic
world he depicted.

Lubitsch had been in films in Germany since 1909, first as an actor, then
as director, until he first attracted international fame with *Carmen* (*Gypsy
Blood*), made in 1918 but not released in the United States until 1921. In
the early 1920s, a series of his German costume-historical-spectacle pictures
—*Madame DuBarry* (*Passion*), *Anna Boleyn* (*Deception*), *Das Weib des
Pharao* (*The Loves of Pharaoh*)—impressed audiences on both sides of
the Atlantic with their careful decor, their sexual-romantic interpretations
of history (note how the American titles blunt history and emphasize melodrama), and their exaggerated melodramatic passions (so popular in the
early 1920s). There is little of the Lubitsch wit or intellect in these films,
but some of their traits recur in a more refined form later.

Underlying the films was the premise that the great public moments of
history are the products of private moments, that behind the greatest human events lie the most ordinary motivations and explanations, and that
behind every great man's deeds there is inevitably a woman (often not so
great). In the Lubitsch histories, the French Revolution and the political
machinations of Henry VIII are the products of sexual desires and jealousies. Lubitsch himself almost seems to have parodied his own conception in the American *Forbidden Paradise* when a woman (Pola Negri—
also practically parodying herself in the earlier films) almost causes the

Russian Revolution (or some such Hollywoody sort of Slavic revolution).

In the German historical films Lubitsch first reveals his careful control of design and decor. *DuBarry* is convincingly eighteenth-century France; *Anna Boleyn* is even more magnificently convincing as Renaissance England. Lubitsch's control of lighting gives the wood of sets and the faces of people the glow of Renaissance painting—aided by Lubitsch's ingenious use of bizarrely shaped masks for the frame (arches, oblongs, ovals, hexagons, circles, trapezoids), which further convert the screen into a painting. Lubitsch begins to use the "plastic material" effectively in these films too —the comically grotesque faces of the common people in *DuBarry*, the blindfold on Louis XV as he plays blind-man's buff with his courtiers while the political storm gathers, a snuffed-out candle to symbolize the deaths of Louis, Armand, and DuBarry. (Two years later Fritz Lang's *Destiny* would use the same symbol.) *Anna Boleyn*, the later of the films, shows even firmer control. For example, Anna meets Henry when her tennis ball flies into Henry's lap (a typical sexual Lubitsch touch).

Lubitsch came to America to direct Mary Pickford in *Rosita* (1923), another romantic costume picture. Pickford wanted to play an adult woman (she had outgrown her curls and short skirts), and Lubitsch's *Carmen* seemed the perfect model for her own story of a Spanish dancer. But Pickford was not Pola Negri; although the film made money and received critical praise, Mary as a woman would never enjoy the popularity of Mary as a girl. She fought with Lubitsch continually—and called him a director of doors, not people.[2] It was a perceptive and prophetic comment, for Lubitsch was to get more and more interested in doors (and other such objects) in the near future. What Miss Pickford did not know was that a human being's relationship to a door can depict a powerful emotion more credibly and convincingly than those soulful, teary-eyed close-ups that dominated the 1920s films.*

Rosita closed Lubitsch's first period, his apprenticeship. *The Marriage Circle* (1924), Lubitsch's next film, was an absolute break with romanticism. His new style and interests have been attributed to a single cause— Chaplin's *A Woman of Paris*. Chaplin's method—of using objects to illuminate people, of saying little and implying much, of telling a sexual story without moralizing—seemed the natural way to convey genuine passion beneath domestic, ordinary exteriors. But there were other influences on Lubitsch. Domestic, marital comedies of flirtation and jealousy were popular in the decade. Von Stroheim had made successful studies of marital tension and sexual need that also depended on concrete details and objects. Lubitsch had seen De Mille's *Why Change Your Wife?* and *Forbidden Fruit,* and perhaps he had also seen Stiller's *Erotikon*—all of them

---

* Pickford's frustration with Lubitsch parallels Sylvia Sidney's later difficulties with Hitchcock. She too accused him of being more interested in objects than actresses. Hitchcock's use of the "plastic material" in sound films was second only to Lubitsch's.

marital comedies of sex and manners, of suspected, potential, or actual infidelity. This was to be the dominant Lubitsch material for the next ten years, his peak period of popularity and creativity.

The Lubitsch plots in this period were of two primary types. The first was a marital much ado about nothing. This plot was another sign of Lubitsch's "not." It ended essentially where it began; nothing had actually happened. But plenty had threatened or seemed to happen. These plots were combinations of mistakes and false suspicions, seasoned with a grain of truth. What seemed to be happening was not; what was really happening was not perceived. In *The Marriage Circle* Frau Braun thinks her husband is wooing Fräulein Hoefer; he is really being wooed by Mizzi Stock. In *So This Is Paris* Mrs. Giraud thinks her husband has gone to prison; he is really at the artists' ball with Georgette Lallé. When Mrs. Giraud goes to the ball to retrieve her drunken husband, he thinks he is flirting with a seductive coquette—who happens to be his own wife. Appearances lead to false inferences; the real problems remain ironically hidden.

The endings of these films clear up the errors and return the characters to their original positions. They climb off the carousel where they climbed aboard. But though original relationships are restored, the characters' experiences have led them somewhere. They have a greater understanding of their own fallibility. They are more aware of tensions, ironies, and faithlessness. They learn that best friends can betray, that people lie, that lies can be accepted as truths and truths as lies, that certain feelings and events necessarily remain secrets and can never be shared. The process they live through in a Lubitsch film, though circular, is also educational. And the films imply that the process continues, that the characters will go through it again and again, and that the very process itself is an inevitable component of human relationships and social life.

The second kind of Lubitsch plot, more common to the sound films, is one in which something does happen. The central sexual figures, not married at the film's beginning, eventually get together by the end. The usual obstacle to their union is a conflict between personal desire and vocational commitment. Prince Danilo (*The Merry Widow*) is committed to "Girls, Girls, Girls"; Sonia is committed to her dead husband's memory. They eventually shift their commitments to one another. Gaston Monescu (*Trouble in Paradise*) is committed to his thievery. Ninotchka is committed to Karl Marx, Leon to money. Queen Louise (*The Love Parade*) is committed to her queenship and country. This conflict of personal and public commitments (*Angel* uses it as well) is a descendant of the pageants Lubitsch made in Germany, which also contrasted the public and private sides of a historical figure's life. Sex and money, sex and politics, sex and social position are the primary oppositions in the films where sex (or love, since they are inseparable for Lubitsch) wins the battle.

The Marriage Circle (1924) was the first of the films in which nothing really happens, in which the central couple is, except for their new knowledge and awareness, the same at the end as at the beginning. Yet Lubitsch could make nothing seem so clever and charming. Early in the film Charlotte Braun sits at her piano, singing Grieg's "Ich Liebe Dich," a sentimental song of love, for her husband (his favorite song). The ideal happiness of the Braun marriage has been cleverly defined. Later Mizzi Stock, Charlotte's best friend and the film's sexual aggressor, bursts into the same room. She sits near the piano and sees the sheet music of the love song on it. Her immediate impulse is to fold the music and thrust it aside with a look of disdain. Sentimental love is not her dish of passion. But when Dr. Braun comes into the room, Mizzi's attitude toward the music changes. She picks up the sheets and holds them up so the attractive doctor can clearly see the title—"I Love Thee."

Later Mizzi, pretending to be ill, awaits a visit from Dr. Braun. She carefully powders herself and arranges the furniture, deliberately removing the chair next to the sofa so Dr. Braun will have to sit next to her. When Braun enters, he just as deliberately picks up the chair and returns it to its original spot (although he didn't know it had been moved). In a later seduction scene, Braun again repulses Mizzi's advances and angrily starts to leave her apartment. Mizzi melodramatically reaches for a pistol and aims it at her breast. Franz and Mizzi wrestle feverishly for the gun. After Franz wins the match, he discovers there are no bullets in the chamber. (Lubitsch uses another suicide ruse in *The Love Parade*.) Being revealed as a fake, Mizzi breaks down and sobs. Braun refuses to buy this second ploy; he strides out of Mizzi's room. Mizzi continues sobbing briefly, notes that Braun has gone, and calmly begins to file her nails.

Then Mizzi's own husband (Adolphe Menjou—a further indication of the Chaplin influence) strides in. Mizzi and Professor Stock detest each other—brilliantly established in the opening scene as Stock does his calisthenics in their bedroom, thrusting his buttocks in his wife's face. From the film's beginning he has been looking for proof of her infidelity so he can divorce her. To cover up the traces of Braun's visit to her apartment, Mizzi seizes her husband's wrists passionately and embraces him warmly— the erring, prodigal wife hoping to return to her husband's heart. Meanwhile, a sly close-up reveals her kicking the telltale revolver under the sofa.

These sequences are only a few of the seemingly endless collection of clever events, observations, objects, and character twists in *The Marriage Circle*. But despite the obvious cleverness of the film, the mental vitality and technical control, the exercise is somehow trivial and banal. "Exercise" is perhaps the proper word. The virtuosity is akin to the playing of difficult cadenzas. The film's human problems are melodramatic clichés; its mistakes and plot twists, red herrings. It is less about life than about how other films handle the same melodramatic conventions. The film's characters are all versions—with a twist—of their cousins in less clever films: the faithful husband (who still feels the attraction of other women); the faithful wife (who is not so faithful that she doesn't feel flattered by another man's attentions); the vamp (who uses her brains rather than her eyeshadow); the outraged husband (whose outrage never keeps him from showing the iciest, most rational good form); the man in love with his best friend's wife (but not so much in love that he won't accept an invitation from the vamp). The twists, surprises, and reversals seemingly exist for the sake of twist, surprise, and reversal themselves.

Among the Lubitsch films that are parodies of other films are *Forbidden Paradise, So This Is Paris, The Love Parade, One Hour with You,* and *The Merry Widow.* The parodic premise ultimately limits them to being stunning fluff. *Forbidden Paradise* (1924), with Pola Negri, parodies the "woman in history" genre of which Lubitsch himself was the master and Negri herself the woman. Again the film's most perceptive (and amusing) moments center on the cold-blooded, clear-sighted cunning and unabashed vanity of the key figures. Pola as Czarina is more interested in the bed than the throne. Each of her serious, sad, or melodramatic reactions is fake. She collapses sadly into a chair and then consults her mirror to check the effect; she faints against her lover's chest and then (in another of those great Lubitsch close-ups) pushes a stool closer with her foot so she can collapse nearer his lips.

As usual, Adolphe Menjou is one of the most interesting people in the film. As the Czarina's prime minister, he watches the store while she attends to the boudoir. He also watches her boudoir—through a keyhole —so faithfully that he pays for his voyeurism with an aching back. At another point the minister coolly walks into the camp of the revolutionaries, wearing his top hat and smoking his cigar, to buy them off. When the rebel leader reaches for his sword (close-up technique again), Menjou (another close-up) reaches for his wallet. The other hand relaxes its grip on the sword. The wallet is mightier than the sword.

There is one image in *Forbidden Paradise* that is a cut deeper than the usual Lubitsch style of delightful mockery. As Captain Alexis (Rod La Rocque) and his virginal lady love (who is ironically the Czarina's lady-in-waiting) exchange romantic beatitudes in the palace garden, Lubitsch captures the scene by shooting their faces in a reflecting pool. Ordinarily, reflecting-pool shots verge on the trite. But as these two romantic faces glisten in the shimmering pool, our eyes are suddenly captured by a darting fish beneath the shiny surface—whose movement eventually diverts our attention from the lovers' mirrored faces and holds us with its hypnotic wriggles. This wriggling fish is more metaphor than symbol; it does not lend itself easily to any single meaning—hence its effectiveness and haunting elusiveness. The fish suggests many things: the sexual reality beneath the shiny, romantic surface; the twists of human energy that resist

static definitions and frozen conventions; the Captain's unconscious long-
ings for the Czarina; restlessness, furtiveness, human elusiveness.

Significantly, the fish-pool scene casts its spell on the next and assumes
even greater import. Alexis leaves the garden to meet the Czarina in her
boudoir. She throws herself at him. His first impulse is to leave. He starts
toward the door. And stops. And starts. And stops. And stays. (Lubitsch
shoots the whole scene behind the Captain's back; his movement, not his
face, reveals his indecision and emotion.) The Captain's decision to stay
with the Czarina must be interpreted metaphorically as a second triumph
of the wriggling fish over the placid pool of surface romance. The lady-in-
waiting still waits for him in the garden.

So This Is Paris (1926) is yet another brilliant style piece—part parody,
part serious domestic relationships, part comment on Hollywood clichés—
that is more surface than substance. As in *The Marriage Circle* there are
two married couples—one that gets along well (Dr. and Madame Giraud),
one that does not (M. and Georgette Lallé). Lubitsch pares the fivesome
of the earlier film down to four. The happy couple is not so perfectly,
idealistically happy; the imperfect one, not so nastily incompatible. And
so the two couples themselves serve as each other's complicating rivals—
Lallé with Mrs. Giraud, Dr. Giraud with Georgette.

The film begins with an overwhelming parodic assault. Lubitsch had
consistently begun to open his films with dazzling surprises that set the
whole tone and slant of the film—a method that carried into the sound
films with the fake suicide in *The Love Parade*, the grandiose wedding in
a rainstorm in *Monte Carlo*, the garbage gondola in *Trouble in Paradise*,
the oxen disrupting the parade in *The Merry Widow*, and the Hitler
pantomime in *To Be or Not to Be*. The film's opening seems to be the
climax of a Valentino sheik-type film, much in vogue at the time. A man
and woman, clad in Arabian-style costumes, look at each other with over-
acted passion and menace. The gentleman raises a dagger and stabs the
Arabian vamp. She melodramatically expires. Then she scratches her head
(shades of Chaplin's *Carmen*). The camera pans to reveal a pianist accompanying the Arabian passion with a musical score. The Arabian beauty
and her murderous paramour are merely a husband and wife practicing a
dance routine. Lubitsch's parody of romantic passion and romantic conflict—as they appear in the movies—has magnificently begun.

It continues in this opening scene when Giraud's wife, in an apartment
across the street, sees the turban-clad Lallé in the window and is immediately struck by his romantic magnetism—for two reasons. She is reading
an "Arabian Nights" romantic novel. And Lallé, who has taken off his
shirt, appears to be walking about naked in the window frame that coyly
covers those anatomical regions below the windowsill. Mrs. Giraud's reaction, despite her obvious titillation, is to demand that her husband go
across the street and teach some propriety to that sensuous gentleman.

She pretends to be offended by the sheik's possible nudity. Out of these early lies grows the rest of the plot, which is a tissue of lying—to others and to themselves—that passes for domestic relations.

In a film with hundreds of delightful touches, a single concrete object—Dr. Giraud's cane—dominates the film. The cane is a material object. Its undeniable physical presence consistently shatters the lies and pretenses that emanate from the human brains and mouths. And like the fish in *Forbidden Paradise*, the cane has no pat, simple meaning. It is elusively metaphoric. It is a symbol that raises questions about the sexual relationships in the film rather than answers them. It is also highly functional. Giraud first carries it over to the Lallés' apartment, responding to his wife's request to teach the man some manners. Giraud pretends to beat Lallé with the cane and returns to tell his wife that in his fury he broke the cane into three pieces. However, Giraud has merely forgotten the cane at the Lallés', distracted by his flirtatious reunion with Georgette Lallé, an old flame. Then M. Lallé pays a return visit to the Girauds', on the pretext of returning the cane. Mrs. Giraud then knows that her husband has lied to her and thrusts the cane beside her sleeping husband. He awakes to see the cane inexplicably beside him—and dozes back to sleep. In his dream he sees the cane dangling before his eyes—or rather, before his mouth. The cane dances in space, thrusts itself into Giraud's mouth, and then rams itself down his throat. As he swallows the cane in his dream, he leaps (understandably) awake. He has choked on his own lie. And the phallic evocations of that cane make Giraud's discomfort with swallowing that lie painfully, startlingly, comically clear.*

The cane continues its travels through the film—inexplicably (for the characters, not for us) making its journey across the street from the Lallés' to the Girauds' and back again. Lubitsch uses a brilliant recurring far shot of the street separating the two houses, with the houses balanced at the right and left edges of the frame, as each husband, carrying the cane, repeatedly crosses that sexual-moral-physical-societal gulf between the two domestic establishments. In the final scene of the film, Mrs. Giraud has discovered her husband's lies, including the one that he has gone to the artists' ball with Georgette, not to prison. She rages moralistically in a tirade against his perfidiousness. To emphasize her point, she unconsciously reaches for an emphatic tool—the cane. As she lifts the cane, she realizes that it is concrete proof of her own recent visit from M. Lallé. She hastily covers her brief confusion and tosses the cane into the fire—disposing of the evidence. Then she continues her tirade. Lubitsch once again shows the contrast between moral façade and genuine feelings introduced in the

---

* Lubitsch was born into the era and culture of Freud. He was also devoted to Schnitzler, who similarly used canes, cigars, candles, swords, etc. for explicit sexual puns in his plays.

opening scene. And as opposed to the Hollywood view of grandiose passion and romantic entanglements parodied by the film's "Valentino" opening, Lubitsch shows that genuine passion and romance are matters of unvoiced yearnings, tiny lies, and ordinary domestic objects—a cane, not a dagger.

Lubitsch strove for seriousness in several silent films. *Three Women*, for example, yet another Lubitsch film of 1924, is a melodrama (it builds to a murder), of all Lubitsch's films the one closest to *A Woman of Paris*. Despite its melodramatic premise, it scores its most interesting points comically and ironically—in the typical Lubitsch manner. Perhaps the most brilliant Lubitsch sequence in the whole film—one of his amazing syntheses of cynical comedy, perceptive psychology, and technical control —is the scene in which Mrs. Wilton, an aging but lascivious matron (Pauline Frederick), prepares to meet her dashing suitor—a man who only wants her money (Lew Cody). She tries to make herself as desirable as possible. Each time she consults her mirror (a typical Lubitsch sign of vanity), she notices the cracks of time. So she decides to arrange the lighting in her boudoir to make the cracks less noticeable. She turns off a light. Then another. And another. Lubitsch, of course, controls the lighting to show the set growing darker and softer. But even more clever in cinematic terms is that, with each dimming of a light, he increases the blurriness of the lens for Miss Frederick's close-ups. With each cut the lens gets hazier and hazier, gauzier and gauzier—the perfect subjective equivalent of Mrs. Wilton's feelings.

But isn't Lubitsch also parodying Hollywood's own notion of beauty and the use of the haze-lens by countless movie queens? The haze-lens had been a Hollywood staple for dreamy close-ups since the Griffith era. It continues to be used for close-ups of actresses who are not quite so young as the plot and the public expect them to be. Lubitsch snickers at the dream in both the scene's action and its camera technique. The snicker grows even louder in the piece of business that ends the sequence. Lew Cody, the dreamboat for whom all these lights have been dimmed, strides into the darkened boudoir and snaps on all the lights, totally obliterating her care and efforts. He wants Mrs. Wilton to sign a contract to lend him some money. That is also an economical statement of the film's central contrast of love and money.

Lubitsch scored his greatest points comically, deftly provoking both laughter and intellectual recognition from an ingenious piece of business, editing, sound, or composition. His morally conscious films usually separated their comic sections from their moral consciousness. There are two exceptions, and they are perhaps Lubitsch's two greatest films for that reason. *Lady Windermere's Fan* (1925) synthesizes the best elements of the marital comedies and the silent melodramas without falling into the trivia of the former or the heavy-handedness of the latter. As in *The Mar-*

riage Circle and *So This Is Paris,* there is a happily married couple at the center of the film; sexual tensions, jealousies, suspicions, and rivals—both real and imagined—all threaten to tear the marriage apart. They do not succeed. Like *Three Women,* the film interweaves sexual desire, social propriety, and financial realities.

But unlike *The Marriage Circle* and *So This Is Paris, Lady Windermere* never suggests that all the human lies, social hypocrisies, and sexual tensions are merely good fun. The film is undeniably conscious of the sadness beneath these social games, of the viciousness of gossip, hypocrisy, and propriety, of the inhuman damage that social lies inflict on people within the society. Lubitsch does not preach; he does not draw moralistic conclusions and deduce clear answers (like De Mille); he simply presents the sad societal carousel with a steely, intellectual music.

One of the magnificent scenes of the film takes place at the race track. In this scene, a box full of proper, respectable ladies and gentlemen pay no attention to the races at all, using their field glasses for observing the activities of Mrs. Erlynne (the supposedly shady lady), her gaudy plumed hat surrounded by nothing but male top hats. The gossips snicker behind their programs to each other, their eyes revealing their catty assumptions about where and how she gets her money. Then one male member of their party defends Mrs. Erlynne (for reasons that we understand, but they do not). Suddenly, all gossip in the box stops. The faces freeze. Their assumptions (about why any man should defend this stained woman) show on their petrified faces. Furtively, they take refuge in their programs, hiding their faces and their looks from each other, ashamed yet delighted to be in possession of such an intimate secret. Between watching Mrs. Erlynne and burying their faces in the programs, they see very little of the horse races.

In a second major sequence, Lord and Lady Windermere give a dazzling evening party for society's beautiful people. Mrs. Erlynne, of course, is not invited, but she blackmails Lord W. for an invitation. (He knows she is his wife's mother, and will do anything to keep that scandalous fact a secret.) Mrs. Erlynne majestically strides into the Windermere house and quickly attracts both a circle of male admirers and a circle of the old biddies' gossiping tongues. But while these "beautiful" social formalities take place indoors, less public intimacies take place outdoors in the garden, in the freeness of the open air, shielded from sight by the high and awesome hedges. Various lovers and would-be lovers steal (or are stolen) out to the garden for displays of passion more sincere than those inside the house. The two domains—house and garden, indoors and out—brilliantly summarize the film's tension between form and feeling, appearance and emotion.

Further, the garden itself synthesizes the film's tensions. It is a *formal* garden (of course), perfectly, geometrically planned. But behind its high hedges people play less formal games without being discovered—if they keep their heads and voices down. Further still, although the garden is of great beauty (like the society itself), it is also icily cold and emotionlessly regular. The hedges are too high, too smooth, too square. Lubitsch emphasizes the coldness of the garden's beauty by his use of a blue tint for the outdoor scenes at night—pale, chilly silver-blue.

In *Lady Windermere's Fan* Lubitsch permits himself a moral comment on the society in which the games of *Marriage Circle* and *So This Is Paris* are played. The tone is far closer to Schnitzler than to Lehar. Perhaps the greater cynicism and moral insight stem from Lubitsch's use of Wilde, who was, like himself, a cynical sensualist in a moralistic-sentimental era. Most of Lubitsch's other plot sources are hackneyed representatives of Sardoodledom. But *Lady Windermere's Fan* is a scathing denunciation of the society's moral shams (its "rules of the game")—what people really do and what they pretend to do. The hypocrisy causes great human pain— if it does not destroy completely. The *haut monde* that Lubitsch depicted so delightfully and so deliciously in the trivial comedies was hollow and rotten beneath its surface. In *Lady Windermere's Fan* he switches his focus from the surface games and lies to the underlying reasons for the games and lies. This contrast between surface appearance and underlying reality is also the essence of Chaplin, Keaton, the Marx Brothers, Fields, and many other American comedies. (It is the essential theme of the European comedies as well—Renoir, Ophuls, Clair, and others.)

Lubitsch's best sound film similarly contrasts surface and essence, appearance and reality. It, too, gracefully depicts beautiful people whose lives are rotten beneath their elegant veneers. In fact, *Trouble in Paradise* (1932) literally begins with the juxtaposition of garbage and beautiful surface. A garbage collector in romantic Venice throws a pail of refuse onto his gondola and glides gracefully through the picturesque canals, singing "O Sole Mio." In its delicate cynicism, *Trouble in Paradise* is the companion piece of *Lady Windermere's Fan,* carefully sticking a pin into the pretensions of high society. And yet the pin prick is so sly, so subtle, so delicate that you cannot even hear the air escaping.

At the center of the film is the fact that its most polished gentleman is a thief. He is accepted as a gentleman by gentlemen (and gentlewomen), and that puts him in a very good position to make off with their weighty goods. In contrast to the brilliant thief is the society of genteel nincompoops, represented in this film by Charles Ruggles (a bumbling, stuffy, pompous fool), Edward Everett Horton (a bumbling, flighty, scatter-brained fool), C. Aubrey Smith (the "faithful" family retainer who has been robbing the family business faithfully for 40 years), and Kay Francis (a perfume heiress who is foolish and rich enough to fall in love). The thief, Monescu (Herbert Marshall), manipulates these toy people simply by knowing the mechanical principles by which they work—suave manners, polished speech. The paradise is in trouble because it is a clockwork toy. Those who are intimidated by the toy's power (the servants and working classes), those who are incensed by the toy's beautiful possessions (the frantic Marxist who hurls his "phooeys" at Madame Collet with impunity), have already lost to the toy. To beat the toy, Monescu (with Lubitsch as his ally) merely knocks the workings out of it.

Although the film appears to be a slick, shiny escapist comedy about rich people in Europe (while real-life Americans battled the Depression and greeted the New Deal), Lubitsch's "not" gives the film a dimension that it does not appear to have. A further irony of the film's paradise is that it has lifted itself to a utopian cloud in the midst of a worldwide depression. Lubitsch, though never stating this irony directly in the film, never allows you to forget it. The film is far more sensitive to mature political realities than, say, Capra's *Mr. Smith Goes to Washington*—an explicitly political film. As Chaplin would do 15 years later in *Verdoux*, Lubitsch, in the most Marxist way, equates property with theft. Monescu steals because he has no job, no preparation for any other vocation, and no other means of eating. His family has lost their fortune in the financial crash; he is "a member of the *nouveau* poor."

But the other Paradiseans are also thieves. One literally, but the others in that they are frivolous with money that could fill a family table. They buy servants, automobiles, gloves, hats, jewels, purses, clothes. When Madame loses her expensive jeweled handbag, both of her suitors (Ruggles and Horton) go to a chic store to buy her another. She can have three jeweled handbags; they don't cost enough to matter. François (Horton) is so luxuriantly wasteful that he requires a suite of four hotel rooms while other members of the society can't even afford a bed. He deserves to be robbed. Even Madame Collet's business—a perfume factory —is totally frivolous, dedicated to vanity, amour, luxury, not human essentials. Although the social-realist milieu never intrudes into the film (except for Comrade Phooey), it always hovers alongside it—even further ridiculing the wasteful emptiness of Paradise.

Lubitsch, though proletarian and Jew, does not take his social realism or Marxism very seriously (as *Ninotchka* would show). Whereas Chaplin's *Verdoux* is acid and (eventually) specific about its social seriousness, *Trouble in Paradise* dances along the shiny comic surface without an apparently serious thought in its head. The delights, the gags, the comic business, the brilliant dialogue, the technical grace and ingenuity of camera, cutting, and sound have never been surpassed by any Lubitsch film. And yet every witty touch is itself a product of the film's essential moral contrast of is and seems. When Monescu robs François, he poses as a doctor and dresses in evening clothes. Clothes do make the man in this film.

In a lengthy early scene, Monescu poses as a baron while wining and dining a wealthy countess—whom he plans to swindle. She, however, is really a thief herself who plans to rob the "Baron." Each discovers the other's identity as they sort out all the goods they have pilfered from each other while chatting suavely and sipping champagne. In addition to being a brilliantly comic contrast of surface and essence and a brilliant parody of romantic Hollywood clichés, the scene is one of the most effective love scenes in Lubitsch's entire career, simply because the two reveal that they are made for each other by their mutual accord of minds and talents rather than sentimental abstractions.

Many other bits in the film have become deserved classics: Lubitsch's deflation of the opera (another sport of Paradise) by showing how little opera means to the people who attend it and how silly staged opera passions sound when you can't see them; the montage of yes-men to show Monescu's rising power in Madame Collet's establishment; the scene with the doors and clocks when Madame must decide whether to stay with Monescu or go to her dinner party; the consistency of the anti-sentimental ending, in which Monescu and Lily not only leave Madame without regrets but also with her money, necklace, and jeweled handbag.

But one tiny cinematic device in the film—easy to overlook because it seems so easy—reveals how steady Lubitsch's technical hand had become with sound. Edward Everett Horton must explain the robbery to the Italian police. He speaks English (ironically his English is supposed to be French); the police speak only Italian. So Horton needs an interpreter (the hotel manager) to carry the police's questions to him and his replies back to them. Lubitsch shoots the sequence in a single long take without Horton and the police ever sharing the frame at the same time. Lubitsch shoots the police asking a question in Italian, then pans with the manager over to Horton, who answers in English, then pans back with the manager to the police with the translated answer, than pans to Horton again, then to the police again, and so on. The panning shot is the perfect cinematic equivalent of the linguistic gulf between the two parties. As such, it is a parallel in the sound film to the brilliant street shot in *So This Is Paris* that shows the communication and the gulf between the two houses.

Most of Lubitsch's other sound films in the 1929–34 period are, like the delightful silents, more interesting because of how rather than what. *The Love Parade* (1929) is a dazzlingly masterful sound film for a first try. Its theme—the reversal of sexual roles, the dominance of queen-wife over sensualist-husband—is a typical bit of Lubitsch cleverness. Lubitsch made the transition to sound without losing an ounce of the wit, intelligence, style, and grace of his silent world. Ironically, the film's musical numbers (many of which he shot silent with all the old silent-camera freedom and then dubbed for music later) are less interesting, more inert than the film's dialogue sequences, which delightfully say less than they show or show less than they say. The musical sequences are often bothersome interruptions, breaking the Lubitsch flow of desire that takes the form of intellect, intellect that occupies itself with desire.

Monte Carlo (1930) shows even further control over the techniques of sound filming, and better integrates its musical offerings into the duels of wits. For *Monte Carlo* is an operetta that is at the same time a parody of an operetta. The most famous sequence in the film is the "Beyond the Blue Horizon" number in which the rhythms of the melody, the churning, chugging sounds of a train, the circular movement of the train's wheels, the thrusting forward movement of the locomotive, the percussive toots of the train's whistle, and the visual rhythms of Lubitsch's cutting all work in perfect harmony. This visual-aural symphony of music, natural sound, composition, and cutting is as complex and perfect an example of montage-in-sound as Eisenstein's editing devices in *Potemkin* were of montage in the silents.

But for sheer cleverness, the film's final sequence in which Jeanette MacDonald goes to the theater to see a schmaltzy operetta (a play within a film, or rather an operetta within an operetta) about a barber who falls in love with a noblewoman is a pure marvel. First, the operetta on stage perfectly mirrors the plot of the film itself (Jack Buchanan, who is really a nobleman, poses as Jeanette's barber and falls in love with her) and actually serves to help resolve that plot. Second, Lubitsch uses the staged operetta to parody operettas. (The onstage actors wear absurd silks and powdered wigs piled to the rafters; they deliver their hokey lines with as much woodenness as possible.) But, in so doing, he is also parodying his own film, which uses an identical plot, the same revelation that the barber is really of bluest blood, and the same motivations for the two central lovers.

Third, Lubitsch contrasts the greater humanness of his real characters to those on the stage by showing that the "real" operetta people, in addition to their operetta story and passions, indulge in psychological games that are never played on an operetta stage—witty strategies; fits of pique; moments of genuine lust. There is a scene with a series of keys that Jeanette uses to lock Jack Buchanan out of her own bedroom that could never have been made three years later—for the real sexual threat is not the aggressive male, but Miss MacDonald's own inclinations. There are humanly petty attacks of vanity, spite, and selfishness. Those are not the kinds of feelings that dominate operettas.

The primary contrast in *Monte Carlo* is between the real and the operettic illusion. The film's central figures appear to be bluebloods, but they are simply people. He appears to be a barber, but he isn't; and she responds to him not as a barber but as a man. She appears to be a woman who cannot love (she runs away from every one of her fiancés), but she really can. And, as usual, Lubitsch establishes the central contrast in the first sequence of the film—a grandiose wedding that does not take place, a marriage ceremony that looks more like a funeral (and really *is* a kind of funeral) because of the need for black umbrellas in a drenching downpour. *Monte Carlo*, especially in its final operetta sequence, produces the usual Lubitsch ambivalence that both asserts its human seriousness and laughs at the attempt to be serious, that both mocks operettas and constructs one in the same film.*

Design for Living (1933) is most interesting for what Lubitsch added to Noël Coward, particularly the bumbling Max, played by Edward Everett Horton with his usual sexless, nasal foppery. In a delightfully sly scene, Lubitsch reveals the marriage plans of Horton and Miriam Hopkins by showing them on a shopping trip—for a double bed. Lubitsch tiptoes past the censors when the salesman measures the width of the lady's body, then the gentleman's, and then stretches the tape measure to the combined width, looking for a mattress of that size. Lubitsch also indicates his opinion of the new Hollywood Production Code with Miriam Hopkins' opening word (after a long silent scene on a train)—"Nuts"—one of those vulgar Americanisms which the already written code would ban within a year. But the film as a whole lacks the sparkling vitality of *Trouble in Paradise* or *Monte Carlo*, imprisoned by its stagey script.

The Merry Widow (1934), the film with which Lubitsch's great frivolous period ends, is, like *Monte Carlo*, a stunning surprise—because one doesn't expect anything from this old war-horse and because the film was a commercial flop. Whereas von Stroheim concentrated on such seamy details as the merry widow's not so merry first husband—a deformed cripple—and on the sexual perversities of her other suitors, Lubitsch concentrates on *how* a sensual hedonist (Maurice Chevalier) agrees to submit to one woman and how he discovers that the woman is not one of his Maxim "girls" (euphemism for whores) but a rich countess on whose checkbook his country's political future depends.

In *The Merry Widow* Lubitsch played wonderful games with Hollywood conventions, as he had for ten years—especially since he had a new official foe in the formal Hollywood Production Code. Lubitsch's ability to interject *verboten* sexual material into this glossy operetta (as in *Monte Carlo*) is truly amazing. He manages to imply that Prince Danilo is sleeping (adulterously) with the queen—as the king attempts to put his sword around his fat waist only to discover that it belongs to some slenderer body that has taken it off and left it in the royal bedchamber. Then there are lines of dialogue: "Have you ever had diplomatic relations with a woman?" In a scene in a private dining room in Maxim's (and Lubitsch implies what transpires in these salons in the most Schnitzlerish fashion), the Countess sees a picture of Napoleon and informs Danilo, "His downfall— he attacked too early." And one of the most ironic sexual scenes in all of

---

* The final operetta sequence of *Monte Carlo* also probably influenced Clair's onstage opera sequence in *Le Million* of one year later.

Lubitsch keeps the camera on the faces of Danilo (Chevalier) and the Countess (MacDonald) as they sit at a table calmly, suavely, coolly chatting about what he is doing to her legs and feet underneath the table (and beneath the camera's frame). Lubitsch's "not" (what is said, not seen) glides him effortlessly past the censors.

Conversely, *Angel* (1936), one of Lubitsch's last films at Paramount, sneaks past the censors because what is shown is not said. This film, a more serious contrast of romance and politics than *The Merry Widow*, builds its plot around the scandalous fact that the Russian Countess' "salon" is actually an elegant brothel. Lubitsch conveys this essential information without ever using the word "brothel" or any of its synonyms, without ever showing that kind of business being transacted (there is a distant shot from outside a window—of course—of men standing at a bar), and without ever showing a single customer in its elegant white hallways—merely a butler traveling from "salon" to "salon" with calling cards on a silver tray. Without ever using the word or showing any overt act of prostitution, Lubitsch constructs a film about one man who is willing to admit that a whore can be an angel and a second who must deal with the fact that his apparently angelic wife is a former whore.

In the late 1930s the Lubitsch touch began to get heavier. The war was approaching, the Depression lingered, Lubitsch was aging, Paramount—that center of iconoclasm and lunacy—was in financial trouble. Even *Ninotchka*, Lubitsch's best film of the post-Paramount era, shows signs of decline. Although the film is perhaps Lubitsch's most famous, it is not his best. It is perhaps Garbo's best, simply because for the first half of the film Lubitsch freed her from the M-G-M star-system schmaltz. Her Spartan severity as a devoted Bolshevik was itself a comment on Hollywood gloss and glamor without Hollywood's (and Mayer's) knowing it.*

Ninotchka's first half—up to the famed point when "Garbo Laughs"—is a Lubitsch gem, cynically debunking the claims of both communism (the commissars really enjoy Western decadence, and Ninotchka is an inhuman machine) and capitalism (Leon is a sleazy, selfish con man who is willing to do anything for money). Ninotchka herself betrays love for money. Politics in the film becomes another garbage heap. Only love—the film's primary opposition to politics—is of value. "Lovers of the world, unite. . . ." But in his portrayal of this notion of love, Lubitsch had fallen away from the more credible sort (like that between Lily and Monescu in *Trouble in Paradise*), adopting the very Hollywood emotional clichés that he had spent his career parodying. The emotional intensity of the scene in which Garbo laughs when Leon falls on his rear is never equaled by any of

* Iconoclastic directors and writers enjoyed playing little tricks on M-G-M. In *Dinner at Eight,* itself part comic jewel and part schmaltz, we see a shot of a lion in M-G-M Leo's usual position. Suddenly a hand enters the frame and swats it. "Leo" starts shaking like jelly. "Leo," in fact, *is* jelly—the aspic mold for Billie Burke's party. Later, Leo-in-aspic falls on the floor and never makes it to the dinner table.

their later romantic duets. The laughing scene is one of those great Lubitsch love scenes which doesn't appear to be a love scene. The obvious love scenes in *Ninotchka* are romantic clichés—complete with dreamy, "hazed" close-ups. Similarly, the first sexual encounter, in Leon's apartment, when Ninotchka reduces sex play to biochemical mechanisms (another brilliant Lubitsch stratagem for getting past the censors), is much more vital than the second romantic, sentimental one. The moral synthesis of *Ninotchka* is closer to *Lost Horizon* than *Trouble in Paradise*—a vague, dreamy, romantic wish. Lubitsch reconciles irreconcilable differences and difficulties in the most optimistic Hollywood fashion.

The later Lubitsch films contain masterfully ingenious moments. For instance, there are the dazzling parallels between theatrical masquerade and political realities in *To Be or Not to Be* (1942). *Cluny Brown* (1946) offers devastating parodies of the political naïveté of the British upper class and of the provincial prudery of the British middle class, as personified by the local druggist, who talks obnoxiously through his nose, and his mother, who obnoxiously doesn't talk at all but merely clears her throat and coughs up mucus.

But these later Lubitsch films make their moral questions quite specific —love and politics (*Angel, Ninotchka*), art and politics (*To Be or Not to Be*), class differences and international politics (*Cluny Brown*). A sign of Lubitsch's painfully overt moral and social consciousness is that beginning with *Angel*, Lubitsch maintains that human beings *grow* (Herbert Marshall comes to accept his wife's present sexuality and past profession). The earlier Lubitsch films imply continuing human foolishness, not recognitions, reconciliations, and conversions. This moral consciousness led to the dampening, softening, and sweetening of Lubitsch's sharp, hard wit. With the passing of Lubitsch's self-conscious cleverness and awareness that the purely frivolous was not purely frivolous also passed his greatest contribution to the comic-film tradition.

Musical Marx

René Clair is on the one hand more consciously and pointedly serious than Lubitsch and, on the other, more frothily escapist. Clair consistently condemns the inhumanity that stems from money, the petty selfishness of material greed, the shams of social assumptions, the pretenses to social propriety, the slavish worship of dead, inanimate things. But Clair's is a world where men turn into statues, dreams turn into reality, reality evaporates into dreams, and everybody (even the flowers) sings. Ghosts fraternize with mortals, men see into the future, and the devil grants a man's innermost wishes. Whereas Lubitsch's world is clearly reality seen through a very clever and unique eye, Clair's is a balletic dream kingdom presented with apparent objectivity. Whereas Lubitsch's people are obviously people, Clair's are marionettes or clowns or dancers, twirling through their paces in a filmic never-never land.

Clair's method is to combine a dash of Lubitsch, a dash of Chaplin, a dash of his own surrealistic apprenticeship, and a large measure of his early interest in dance and song. Lubitsch's influence on Clair is clearest in *The Italian Straw Hat* (1927), a silent comedy of manners that scores its points by concentrating on concrete objects and physical detail. If Lubitsch could break the four theater walls with the Sardou–de Najac farce, *Let's Get a Divorce* (*Kiss Me Again*, 1925), Clair could do the same with another *boulevard* farce of the same period by Labiche-Michel. But Clair's method in his sound films is also strikingly parallel to Chaplin's. Like Chaplin, Clair decided to keep the balletic principle, the movement-in-space aesthetic, of silent films in his early sound films. And the only way to preserve that visual hypnosis in the sound world was to use sound contrapuntally rather than synchronously, unnaturally rather than naturally. There is more singing than talk in the early Clair sound films (they could never be called "talkies"); the world on film is more like an operetta than like reality. His sound track and picture are often independent entities. Clair's later American and postwar French films seem scrawny compared to his earlier films simply because they try to inject fantasy into a realistic world instead of rejecting reality altogether, as his greatest films did.

Into this ballet fantasy world Clair introduced serious human themes. His central moral belief is in Friendship (or Brotherhood). The loyalty between two men consistently overcomes the obstacles that tempt them to betrayal. This solidarity in fellowship becomes, for Clair, emblematic of the potential unity and brotherhood of man, freed from the social organizations, definitions, and assumptions that have corrupted man's nature. Society and nature are very much enemies in the Clair world. In *À Nous la liberté* (1932), Clair prefers a singing flower to a recorded melody, an afternoon in the sunlight to laboring in a prisonlike factory. It is man's nature to be friendly, to love his brother, runs Clair's argument. He demonstrates this nature in all three of his greatest sound films —significantly they are his first three. In *Sous les toits de Paris* (1930), the friendship of Albert and Louis transcends their antagonism as jealous rivals for the same woman. The two men band together against the vicious gangster who wants to take her away from both of them. When the time comes for the two friends to decide which of them will get Pola, they try to work up a fight—without success. Instead, they roll the dice for her. Friends to the end.*

---

* Albert and Louis are rather obviously Truffaut's prototypes for Jules and Jim. Clair's two friends resemble Truffaut's in appearance, character differentiation, and emotional entanglements.

In *Le Million* (1931), the two friends manage to heal the wound that money has cut in their friendship. Eventually both friends—and seemingly the entire city of Paris—join in the singing-dancing celebration that results from finding the lottery ticket. In *À Nous la liberté* the two friends (originally cellmates in prison) bridge the gap of social class and position. The now-wealthy factory owner and the little member of the proletariat who works for him unite at the end of the film to march off down the road together as tramps (like Charlie), singing their hymn to freedom. Even in Clair's very late film, *Gates of Paris* (*Porte des Lilas*, 1957), the friendship between the bum (JuJu) and the "Artist" is the moral core of the story.

This film, a lyric melodrama like *Sous les toits* and *The Fourteenth of July* (1933) rather than a comedy like most of Clair's films, presents a different kind of challenge to brotherhood. Rather than money, social position, or love, *Gates of Paris* disrupts the central friendship with a conflict of moral commitments. To shelter an escaped criminal from the police, the friends necessarily drive a human wedge into their own relationship. But to betray the criminal is morally impossible. The dilemma can only be resolved when the criminal demonstrates his own immorality (in Clair's terms of brotherhood) by toying with another human being and using her affections selfishly to gain money and a means of escape. Once JuJu perceives the escaped man's inhumanity, he does not betray the criminal but destroys him. The original friendship then returns to where it began.

Given the male centers of these Clair films, it follows that women and romantic love play subservient roles. Unlike Lubitsch films, Clair films have very little to do with love (in the physical-romantic sense), and sex becomes a convention of the plot that is never very deeply felt or developed. Love for Clair is a metaphoric abstraction that unites humanity, not a personal union between two hearts, heads, and bodies. Whereas Charlie walked down the road with a woman at the end of *Modern Times*, two male friends (more evocative of Laurel and Hardy in this respect) walk down the road together at the end of *À Nous la liberté*. In the same film, Clair contemptuously reduces the two primary women characters to agents of social and emotional bondage. The wealthy man's wife is unfaithful and nasty; she likes her husband only for his money and social position. The little worker's ideal of romance is herself the slave of idealistic clichés; she falls in love with a handsome, romantic figure, not the little guy who idolizes her (another Chaplin parallel).

Opposed to the need for human fellowship are the inhuman and unnatural demands of society. First, money. Clair's first film, *The Crazy Ray* (1923), laughs at the stupidity of the few unparalyzed Parisians whose idea of enjoying life (now that the rest of the world has been frozen and paralyzed) is to steal plenty of money and jewelry. But money and jewels are mere symbols of wealth. They have no value except as defined by society. Why else is a dollar bill worth more than a sheet of foolscap, or a diamond clip worth more than a glass splinter? With society asleep, the conventional symbols of social wealth that the characters steal and hoard have no value.

Money also propels the mad chase in *Le Million*, in which two men go to comic lengths to find a winning lottery ticket. Even more pointed in the film is the reversal of the neighbors' attitudes after they discover that the artist has won the million. Before the lottery, they hound him to pay his overdue bills and abuse him with strings of invective: "Scoundrel!" "Murderer!" "Artist!" After he becomes a millionaire, they gather at his apartment and honor him with a brass band, a formal oration (mechanically and stutteringly recited by a perplexedly smiling, brainless ten-year-old girl), and a congratulatory bouquet of flowers. They value their neighbor as a millionaire, not as a man (and especially not as an artist).

Second, material possessions. Property is money's cousin, a more tangible mark of material success. *The Italian Straw Hat* is Clair's most devastating attack on property. To define the unnatural, inhuman process of the social ceremony of marriage, Clair's close-ups concentrate on the shoes (too tight) that must encase the feet, and the gloves (perpetually misplaced) that must sheathe the hands. The wedding is merely a pretext for gathering gifts (ugly and useless—symbolized by the two grotesque, identical clocks that different guests give the bridal couple). When the wedding seems about to be canceled, the guests' first impulse is to snatch back their gifts. But when the bride and groom finally conclude the match and march into his house, the groom's servant carefully collects the gifts again from each of the guests making off with them. An angry gentleman intimidates the groom by threatening to toss all the gifts and furniture out of the groom's house. The intimidation is so successful that the fearful groom sees (in a slow-motion vision) all of his possessions floating out his window to their doom.

In *The Italian Straw Hat*, marriage is not a human event but an accumulation of inanimate possessions. Similarly, the wealthy factory owner of *À Nous la liberté* is surrounded by a houseful of expensive possessions—so expensive that they attract the interest of a group of bandits who are his former prison mates (yet another Chaplin motif). One of the most striking of these possessions is an immense portrait of himself, lifeless and pretentious—the conversion of life into an inanimate object (like his record business itself, which freezes song into a profitable artifact). Life in the wealthy man's house is as dead as his picture.

Third, all social forms. Social abstractions of class, proper human conduct, appropriate social ceremonies and behavior are close relatives of money and property, which are similarly defined social goals and goods. At the center of Clair's zany, surrealist *Entr'acte* (1924) is a burlesque of a funeral. The mourners wear white; they follow a hearse drawn by camels; they eat bits of the funeral wreath like pretzels; and they run madly after the uncontrollable hearse in a wild chase when the unco-operative corpse decides to break loose. *The Italian Straw Hat* later reduces marriage to the absurd. For Clair, marriages and funerals are society's essential (and laughable) means of trying to harness those chaotic, natural, antisocial phenomena of love and death.

Clair's greatest reduction of social ceremony to the absurd is the frantic chase after the wind-blown francs during the pompous dedication cere-mony in *À Nous la liberté*. The human beings drop their dignity, their formal poses, and their formal wear to chase madly after the unexpected money floating down from heaven. Clair consistently uses the energy, exuberance, and visual chaos of the chase to expose the deadness of the social form. Ironically, this chaotic chase is itself the product of a social form (money).

Clair snickers at social forms in other ways. In *Le Million* he especially enjoys deflating the police, representatives of social order. Clair treats his cops with a combination of Sennett burlesque and Chaplin bitterness. In the police station, the cops are most concerned that the prisoners remove their hats (another social form, recalling Chaplin's *The Immigrant*). In the opera corridor, the police race around and cause a lot of frenzied activity, but they are no more competent at catching their man than the Kops at Keystone. And in a truly ironic touch, Père Tulip (the film's elegant boss of the Paris underworld) reprimands a policeman for smoking backstage in clear sight of a big sign that reads, *"Défense de Fumer."*

But where Clair denigrates his cops, he romanticizes his crooks (in *The Crazy Ray, Sous les toits de Paris, Le Million, À Nous la liberté, The Fourteenth of July,* and *Gates of Paris*). Père Tulip is a warm, friendly, amiable fellow—more song-and-dance man than gangster. He is so dapper and elegant in his formal clothes that the cops fail to recognize the crook beneath the covering. A suit of tails and a white tie make Tulip and his gang (as well as the factory owner in *Liberté*) look as respectable at a social gathering as everyone else. In Clair's view they are indeed just as respect-able.

But after debunking these social pretensions, Clair's films invariably and incongruously end with sunny and fanciful optimism. His characters celebrate the winning of the lottery with dance, song, and champagne. The friendships heal, the marriages take place, the poor composer turns his dreams of success into reality (*Beauties of the Night*, 1952), and even Clair's comic Faustus can miraculously void his pact with the Devil and preserve his life, his soul, his youth, and the lady of his dreams (*Beauty and the Devil*, 1950). In the most idyllic and optimistic ending of all (*À Nous la liberté*), all labor in the society stops, leaving men perfectly free to dance, lie in the sun, fish in the river, or sing on the road. Clair's endings never cut so deeply or so sharply as Chaplin's. The straddling image of *The Pilgrim*, the wandering down the road of *Modern Times*—these show the filmmaker unable to heal the social and human sores he has exposed.

Clair does not really wound society in his films; he merely stings it a little. His Chaplin model is more the ending of *The Gold Rush* than *The Pilgrim*, *The Circus*, or *City Lights*. A happy solution in Clair never has the same feeling of uneasiness that it has in *The Kid* or *Sunnyside*. In *Le Silence est d'or* (1947), in which Clair's milieu is the early French film industry itself—the days of Méliès and Zecca—Clair creates a pioneer filmmaker (Maurice Chevalier) who clearly speaks for Clair himself: "I like happy endings." So if there is Chaplinesque social consciousness in Clair, there is also Capra optimism. Clair is confident that if you allow people to be their natural selves, human life will become a happy song and dance. There are none of those devils that Chaplin depicts in the nature of man himself. Even Renoir's parallel belief in the natural spirit of man is much more somber and paradoxical than Clair's. In his pure optimism, Clair is probably the most romantic and the most American of the French ironists—which probably accounts for the fact that the films Clair made in America during the war (*I Married a Witch*, *It Happened To-morrow*, *And Then There Were None*) were certainly no worse than the ones he made in France after it.

Clair's two most stinging films are *The Italian Straw Hat* and *À Nous la liberté*. Although the marriage ends "successfully" in the silent gem, the whole notion of success has been so tarnished and warped by the tawdry display of bourgeois conventions that we know the two "lovers" will never recover. The happy ending of the farce merely underscores the fact that the social process has indeed been a farce. The characterlessness of the two lovers, the film's lack of attention to their emotional relationship, increases the impression of deadness and emptiness about their marriage. (Clair's inability to treat love convincingly works in his favor in this film.) No genuine human relationships are possible in a society in which we are all deaf marionettes (as exemplified by Clair's brilliant use of the deaf wedding guest) responding automatically to the social gestures that everybody else uses. *The Italian Straw Hat* is not only Clair's best silent film; it may also be his best film, his best synthesis of comedy and pointedness.

À Nous la liberté becomes a better film if we interpret its ending as ironic—like the endings of *Easy Street* and *A Dog's Life*—rather than optimistic. The film has identified property with theft, work with slavery, and modern society with mechanical monotony. The factory looks like a prison; foremen look like prison guards; the lunch hour looks like the prison mess. Modern society deadens the free human spirit, the imagination, the beauty of nature, and the passions of love. Wouldn't it be nice *if*, the ending seems to say, machines could work for people while people could relax in total freedom all day?

But there is still something fuzzy about the "if." What do real humans do, given the actual necessity to work? It is nice to wish work away (just as it is to create a Shangri-La). What does Clair suggest men do with the reality? Chaplin is unmistakably clear about the gulf between fanciful wishes and realistic life choices. Besides, isn't Clair's view of work and prison an oversimplification? Could men really be happy lounging around all day in the sun? Aren't there other human urges—most of them absent from the Clair world? Perhaps it is because genuine human needs, urges, and drives never interfere with Clair's abstractions of humanity, friendship, and nature that many of the films seem schematic and thin.

Clair spices with technical cleverness the syrup he passes off as thought. His frothy comic style spreads a candy coating over his Marxist-humanist pill. But unlike Chaplin, Keaton, or Lubitsch, Clair does not always ally his comic subject with the comic style. For instance, Lubitsch's clever uses of sound, though controlled by the camera and sound track's point of view, are strictly natural. We can't hear the sexual anecdote that Chevalier tells the chamberlain in *The Love Parade* because the camera is outside a closed window, which would naturally keep the sound from us. Further, that stylistic touch—silence—itself comments on the scene's content. But Clair's clever uses of sound are merely artificial, unnatural stunts. To juxtapose the noises of a football game with the tussle for a jacket is ingenious, but gratuitous. (Chaplin, by contrast, does not use the sound track this way in the football game with the duck in *Modern Times*.)

Some of Clair's ingenious tricks are more natural. To deflate romance, he makes the music slow down and groan to a stop (*Liberté*) or stick in a repeating groove (*Sous les toits*), a trick that is indeed motivated naturally by a nearby phonograph. To juxtapose the passions of two real lovers with the fakey aria of two operatic lovers, while stagehands scatter fake leaves and rose petals from the flies (*Le Million*), he seats the lovers behind a set onstage at the opera. But since Clair's real lovers seem just as wooden and "literary" as his operatic ones, how does his depiction of real love "contrast" with operatic love? The intention of Clair's device is clear; the genuine feelings and thoughts that it tries to generate are more blurred. (When Lubitsch contrasted operetta passions with real ones in *Monte Carlo*, the real people—primarily because of their vanity, wit, peevishness, and sensuality—indeed seemed more convincingly real than the operetta figurines.)

So too, Clair's visual technique is often too consciously clever. Like his use of character, story, and sound track, Clair's use of the visual intentionally denudes the film world of its natural human texture. The director does not re-create reality (even a filtered or magnified reality) as Lubitsch does. For example, in *Ninotchka,* the two grotesque hotel rooms—the baroque, French-provincial gilt and curlicue of the Paris Ritz, the Moorish, wood-paneled white stucco of the Constantinople hotel—reveal the director's attitudes toward the cultures by showing two rooms that undoubtedly could (and do) exist in all their tasteful-tasteless garishness. But Clair interprets reality by distilling it and retaining only those details which produce his intended meaning. In À *Nous la liberté*, for example, his most controlled sound film in its handling of decor, every setting and human configuration carefully emphasizes horizontal or vertical lines—the horizontal implying the repetitive sameness of lines of people (reduced to points on a line), the vertical implying that all life is a prison and we are universally behind bars.

But the exaggeration of parallel decors becomes a purely fanciful stunt in a later Clair film, *Beauties of the Night*, in which the echoing of architectural shapes (for instance, a provincial café dissolves into an Arabian harem) is used only for the fanciful effect of parallelism. Although in the later film Clair is trying to show how a human mind can blur reality into its fancies, his fascination with decor for decorativeness' sake seems so striking that it reveals the hollowness underlying the technique. The danger of Clair's pure devotion to clever surfaces reveals itself in those disastrous failures which Clair made at the peak of his success and powers, *Les Deux Timides* (1928) and *The Last Millionaire* (1934), both of which fall off the delicate line between satire and whimsy to become heavy-handedly clever—and consequently empty. In one sense, À *Nous la liberté* may be Clair's best sound comedy, because his fanciful approach to the material seems most consistent with the life of fancy that the film advocates. In another sense, *Le Million* may be his best sound comedy because its pure comic inventiveness never ventures into a region of ideas where it does not belong.

CHAPTER 15

Jean Renoir

—

THE comedies of Jean Renoir provide the fullest and most impressive examples of the ultimate potential and style of sound comedy. They combine a staggeringly complex structure, a social microcosm of parallel classes and contrasting individual human choices, an ironic sense of detachment and understatement, a comic intellect that converts the deadly serious into the farcically silly and the farcically silly into the deadly serious, and a technical control of the cinematic medium—luminous visual compositions in depth, brilliantly moody or ironic uses of sound and music, haunting and evocative uses of dialogue—all of which do not blatantly call attention to themselves but work unobtrusively to underscore the film's comic and intellectual being. Although Renoir is not usually considered a comic filmmaker, his cold irony gives the films a quality of detachment that works much better to create a comic climate than a serious, more highly charged emotional one. Although the Renoir films consistently support the powers of feeling over the faculty of reason, no director's films are more carefully reasoned, more carefully developed intellectually than Renoir's. The Renoir intellect dominates the films (whether they were scripted by Jacques Prévert, Charles Spaak, or Renoir himself), and that intellect cannot prevent itself from viewing human action—even the saddest, sorriest kinds—with the detached chuckle of the grimly comic ironist.

Like René Clair, Renoir was heavily influenced by Chaplin. Renoir traced the beginnings of his decision to leave ceramics for the cinema to seeing Charlot.[1] But whereas Clair could cull only Chaplin's fanciful wish to turn his tramp's back on the stifling artificial conventions of society, Renoir perceives the double edges of Charlot's sword. Society's corruption is itself a function of human beings. Ironically, human life within society is unsupportable, but apart from society, human life is impossible. Like Chaplin in *The Pilgrim*, Renoir straddles the line between societal enslavement and anarchic license.

Also unlike Clair, Renoir never contradicts his own premises to surprise his protagonists with optimistic and fanciful reprieves. The contract with the devil cannot be voided; the devil must be given his due. Human actions produce inevitable and unavoidable consequences. This inevitability reveals another of Renoir's fusions of serious and comic, for many of his films combine the implacable consequences of tragedy with the wry irony and detached amusement of comedy.

A second of Renoir's major influences, Erich von Stroheim,[2] similarly fused inevitability and irony, social convention and natural desire. Yet it is a mistake to find Renoir's influences in the cinema alone. Renoir brought to the films an immense cultural background—a familiarity with painting, music, the drama, with thinkers and writers as diverse as Voltaire, Zola, Beaumarchais, Marx, Gorky, and Flaubert. The richness and texture of Renoir's intellect—its assimilation of 200 years of European civilization—contribute to the intellectual richness and texture of Renoir's films.

In his integration of comedy and film, Renoir brings the classical comic traditions of the French theater—Molière, Marivaux, Beaumarchais, Feydeau—into the French cinema (quite consciously in *The Rules of the Game*). That film is perhaps a perfect example of Renoir's application of the devices of classical comedy to bitter and ironic ends that transcend mere laughter. *The Rules of the Game* uses the typical comic parallelism of masters and servants (especially evoking Molière's spirited and sensible maids), the Feydeau contrivance of a single house jammed with conflicting buffoons who must be parceled into separate rooms (and all hell breaks loose when the door to one of those rooms is mistakenly opened), the essential comic subject of requited and unrequited love—and the consequent follies of misinterpretation and jealousy—and the classic device of turning the action on a superficial prop (Lisette's cape) that misleads a character into identifying one beloved as another.

The film is even built in five acts: I. Paris; II. Arrival at La Colinière; III. The Hunt; IV. The Party; V. After the Party. Significantly, where the traditional comedy would end with "The Party," Renoir adds his intentionally anticlimactic, bitter final "act." Similarly, where in Shakespeare's *Much Ado About Nothing* the mistake in identity occurs in the middle of the play and the rest of the action aims at clearing up that mistake, in Renoir's black comedy the mistaken identity becomes the subject of the film's final "act," and the result of that mistake is not a feigned death, as in *Much Ado*, but a real one.

And yet Renoir treats that death as if it were feigned. The murder takes place in a dimly lit garden; the camera records the scene in a distant far shot, its view further obscured by the blackness of the night and the thickness of the shrubbery. Renoir never permits us to see the reaction on the slain aviator's face or even to glimpse his fallen corpse. Renoir drains that death of all human compassion, texture, and pain. The rabbits in the hunt scene died more agonizingly and sympathetically. And after André's death, the rest of the characters indeed treat the incident as if it were much ado about nothing—"a regrettable accident." This integration of classical comic structure and comic devices with a bitterly ironic tone and serious social and human issues was Renoir's primary contribution to the comic film tradition.

The dominant Renoir theme is, like Clair's, the contrast between the sterility of social obligation and the potential freedom of natural responses and personal choices. That theme spans Renoir's immensely long and fertile career. *Boudu sauvé des eaux* (1932) contrasts the ridiculousness of Lestingois' bourgeois "humanism" with the anarchic naturalness of the bum-animal-"troglodyte," Boudu. *Picnic on the Grass* (1959), 27 years later, contrasts the spontaneity of the provincial French girl with the sterility of the scientist-politician who intends to become president of Europe, to wed a sexless general of Europe's girl-scout troops, and to inflict a program of artificial insemination on the population of Europe. *The Crime of Monsieur Lange* (1935) contrasts the formerly stifling, unhappy, inhuman publishing house under its capitalist owner, Batala, and the happy communal perfection of the institution under its new leader, Lange. *A Day in 'the Country* (1936) contrasts the false romanticizing of the Parisians, who can spend only one day a year in the country, with the casual intimacy between man and nature of the people who actually live there. *The Rules of the Game* (1939) contrasts the natural passion of love with the conventional rules and games that have been devised to express that passion. *The Golden Coach* (1953) contrasts the sterile assumptions of the Old World with the natural vitality of the New.

The key structural principle for Renoir is indeed contrast. But whereas Clair simplifies his contrasts (Clair is perhaps more interested in parallel than contrast, similarity than opposition) into a simple, obvious dichotomy, Renoir surrounds the central opposition with layers of related complexity— differences in social class, differences in nationality, differences between individual human needs and general social goals, differences between art and reality. As Renoir reveals these contributing and conflicting layers of meaning, we experience a work of art that is morally clear yet ambivalent, undeniably committed yet aware of the ironies and contradictions of commitment. The intellectual maturity of Renoir's films contrasts with Clair's moral naïveté in much the same way that Chaplin's and Keaton's awareness of paradox contrasts with Harold Lloyd's American Dream.

Renoir's view of nature is, at the same time, more visually beautiful and more thematically cynical than Clair's in the final scene of *À Nous la liberté,* where everyone sits beside a river in the sunlight. Renoir films constantly evoke the beauty of nature with shots of trees against the sky, often viewed from stirringly awesome upward angles. These shots of tree touching sky imply the unity of nature, and also the upward yearn- ing of the natural spirit (as compared with the men anchored to the earth below). The striking upward shot of Boudu and his fellow tramps march- ing with their faces against the sky, the upward shots of the trees in *A Day in the Country, The Rules of the Game,* and *Picnic on the Grass* all show Renoir's feeling for the vital world of nature that plays such an important metaphoric role in his films. In Renoir films, nature genuinely lives. He delights in trees moving in the wind; he indeed endows them with a life of their own. Renoir increases this impression of movement with moving-camera shots, circular pans of tree and sky. But in the final scene of *À Nous la liberté,* nature (like everything else in Clair) is posed. It is a tableau, not a living presence.

On the other hand, nature can also be a source of ugliness and coldness for Renoir. On a beatuiful placid lake, Toni's wife (*Toni,* 1934) attempts to commit suicide. In a beautiful wooded forest, a group of aristocrats (*Rules of the Game*) mercilessly murder every pathetically defenseless ani- mal in sight. The dominant natural image of *Grand Illusion* (1937) is snow and ice. And in *The Golden Coach* (1953), Felipe, one of Camilla's suitors, offers her an idyllic, utopian life with the uncivilized and uncorrupted na- tives of the New World who still commune perfectly with earth, trees, and sky. Although his idyllic offer may perhaps be closest to Renoir's own per- sonal philosophy, in the film it has no more power or validity than any of the other romantic offers that Camilla receives.

For Renoir, nature is (to use Camus' phrase) benignly indifferent. It exists in its beauty and vitality. Man is obviously a part of it. But the key question about nature in a Renoir film is not what it means abstractly (as in Clair) but how a man feels in relation to it. If man is out of tune with the natural harmony—like the aristocrats in *Grand Illusion, The Rules of the Game* and *The Golden Coach,* the scientist in *Picnic on the Grass*—then nature can become ominous, murderous, or barren. Even sillier (and more comic) for Renoir are the false idealizations of nature by those who have no contact with it but think they do. In *Boudu,* Lestingois, a bookseller, turns nature into a book, a series of literary conventions, seeing it solely in terms of Pan, nymphs, Chloe, and Priapus. The bourgeois Parisians who leave the city for one day to commune with trees and grass in *A Day in the Country* of course want to eat a real lunch *du pays*—outdoors on the grass. The country innkeepers are aware of this touristic desire and arrange their business (as well as their prices) to take advantage of this urban idealization. Ironically, the people who live in the country eat indoors.

The concrete relationship of man and nature is more important to Renoir than the metaphoric meaning of nature in the abstract. And yet another difference between Renoir and Clair is that people (rather than puppets) are an important element of the Renoir world—in fact, *the* important element. Whatever the complex structural balances, parallels, and contrasts, whatever the levels of social classes and layers of reality, the Renoir film revolves around human beings. There are strikingly memorable performances in Renoir films—Michel Simon, Jean Gabin, Marcel Dalio, Erich von Stroheim, Anna Magnani. The magnetic presence of these performers helps shape the Renoir film. Renoir claims that he made *Boudu* especially for Michel Simon and *The Golden Coach* for Magnani (and improvised the structure from that starting point), and that the overpowering presence of von Stroheim necessitated essential changes in the original script of *Grand Illusion*. And these three films are among Renoir's most complex and careful structural wholes. Renoir builds structural complexity from a very human center (exactly like Chaplin) rather than conceiving the entire structure first and then plugging any suitable performer into it (as Clair did).

If *The Rules of the Game*, despite its brilliance, seems one of Renoir's most despairing and oppressive films, it might be because the film is structured around a society of dead souls embodied by wooden actors, lacking a vital Gabin, von Stroheim, or Simon. The characters of *The Rules of the Game* are among the least human and most puppetlike in Renoir's entire canon. The most morally attractive figures in the film (André Jurieu and Octave) are cowardly or ineptly naïve fools; the least morally attractive figure (Marquis de la Chesnaye) is the most maturely competent human being; the actor who plays him (Marcel Dalio) gives the most interesting performance. The lady of romance who inspires the passion, desire, and conflict (the Marquise, played by Nora Grégor) is as haunting and bewitching as a plaster giraffe. And most of the other players (excepting the two servants, Lisette and Marceau) are effete, corrupt dolls playing at life and death—especially death. The premise of *The Rules of the Game* is to reduce human beings to the same kind of clockwork puppets as the Marquis' birds and music boxes. That intellectual conception gives the film its coldness as well as its acid brilliance.

The Renoir eye is as impressive and perceptive as the Renoir intellect. Throughout the films that eye reveals itself in the luminosity it sees in nature. It also reveals itself in his famed use of depth of field. In *Toni*, for example, seven years before *Citizen Kane*, Renoir consistently shot scenes through windows, doorways, and trees, creating visual tension between foreground and rearground, between shaded interior in the foreground and bright outdoor sunlight in the rearground. The visual method performs several important functions. In *Toni*, it functions as a metaphor for the film's contrast of confinement and freedom, domestication and passion, social regulation and personal desire. It also heightens the emotional tension between the married partners, whose feelings are antagonistic to each other and antithetical to what they are supposed to be.

In *A Day in the Country*, on the other hand, the shot of two men eating lunch indoors while, through the window, we (and they) see two women in the sun quickly and effortlessly establishes the future direction of the men's interests. And throughout the Renoir films, the shot in depth adds texture and fullness to the screen world, convincing us that despite the deliberate ironies and structural artifices of the film, we are looking at a rich, complex reality.

Although the Renoir eye has received frequent attention, the Renoir ear has been surprisingly overlooked. That ear is one of the most remarkable in the sound film, more subtle, more evocative, and perhaps even cleverer than Clair's (whose ear earns him much of his praise). Renoir controls the atmosphere of each film with a primary musical motif. This musical coloring not only contributes to the emotional tone of the film, but often comments on the film's values and action. The dominant musical motif of *Boudu* is a mellow, sad, non-chromatic passage played by a single thin, breathy flute. The flute serves several functions in the film. It signifies passage of time and shifting of attitudes; Renoir uses sound for transitions, as well as the usual visual methods of dissolve, fade, and montage. It comments on the airy pretensions of the bookseller to culture and humanity. It adds a sad delicacy to the rather burlesque tone of the film's comedy, deepening the film into a human experience that is sad as well as silly. But the flute's notes are so delicate, so light that the sad and serious overtones merely float along the surface of the film's comic ideas. That flute's lightness might be seen as emblematic of Renoir's mind and method as a whole, floating ironies and ideas toward us rather than shoving them in our faces.

The dominant musical motif in *French Cancan* (1955) is the French ballad "On the Steps of Montmartre," which creates the lilting, breezy warmth of Paris life in the 1890s. As opposed to this music of vitality, the dominant musical motif of *The Rules of the Game* is the elegant Mozart minuet, a perfect synthesis of polished beauty and sterile, rigidly regular form. The cold detachment of the minuet is the perfect tonal companion for the cold detachment of the society that the film studies.

Similarly, *The Golden Coach* uses the graceful, formally perfect music of Vivaldi. Again, the choice works for Renoir in several ways. The elegant music is the perfect accompaniment for the elegant Spanish aristocrats and theatrical conventions of the *commedia dell' arte*. It adds a touch of exquisite polish to the entire film, which is itself to be taken as a polished piece of theatrical entertainment, a play within a play. Finally, there is irony in using this most civilized, highly structured music from the Old World in a film that takes place in the uncivilized, unformed New World.

That irony is also the central one in the film. The gulf between the Indian culture of South America and the culture that produced (and can appreciate) Vivaldi is at the core of the film's social comment.

Music is also important in *Picnic on the Grass*—perhaps too important. The film uses musical motifs to contrast artificiality and nature. Renoir symbolizes natural responses with the reed instruments, particularly the flute of the old shepherd, Gaspard, which exerts a magical control over nature. As Gaspard plays his airy flute (a clear parallel with *Boudu* of 27 years earlier), a liberating wind sweeps through the society, scattering the elegant, artificial "picnic" paraphernalia (tables and tablecloths, chairs and china, silverware and serving dishes) across the countryside, and converting the proponents of artificial insemination into lecherous nymphs and satyrs. A chorus of other wind instruments—clarinets, oboes, flutes—accompanies the visual winds that sweep across the screen. In contrast to the winds, Renoir uses the cacophonous noises of percussion instruments—usually with syncopated jazz rhythms—to signify the disorder and chaos of the artificial, sterile social life. The film's musical battle between reeds and percussion is an exact parallel of the intellectual opposition in the film's plot and characters.

Renoir uses music for clever comment as well as to establish a film's tone and texture. *Boudu sauvé des eaux* contains, like the later *Picnic on the Grass*, its own little cacophonous musical battle. In addition to the dominant flute, Renoir uses an occasional crash of the trumpet and brass band. The cleverest of these touches is his use of a trumpet in the scene when Boudu seduces Madame Lestingois. As Boudu and Madame fall out of the frame (onto a below-frame bed), Renoir tracks in to a shot of an etching—a military bugler blowing a trumpet (decidedly a Lubitsch touch!). As the depicted figure blows that trumpet, a trumpet actually is heard on the sound track, only to erupt into the raucous march of a brass band. Shortly thereafter we discover that the real trumpeter is a member of the band that has come to pay tribute to M. Lestingois' heroic rescue of Boudu from drowning. (Unlike Clair and like Lubitsch, Renoir relates his clever sound effects to reality.) Hence, the trumpet is not only a wry way of depicting Boudu's sexual success but an ironic sign of the very bourgeois idiocy that honors idealistic clichés of virtue so fully that it succeeds in cuckolding itself. The trumpet's blast is both more real than the airy flute (a concrete sexual seduction rather than a succession of airy nothings) and more false (a salute to false ideals rather than to the elusive human feelings signified by the flute).

Renoir's ear also works with his mind in *Rules of the Game*. The tinkling mechanical tunes of the Marquis' music boxes are as formally perfect yet mechanical and dead as his society. There is Renoir's ironic use of Saint-Saëns' "Danse Macabre" at the Marquis' evening party; that scene (and, indeed, the rest of the film) is a dance of death. And there is the ironic use of a piano on the sound track, swelling in volume, as Octave explains his youthful musical ambitions to Christine, an ambition that was dissipated by laziness, failure, and the past, leaving him only the illusion as he lifts his hands to conduct an invisible orchestra and a mere piano on a cold and empty night. And for sickening horror, there is the scamper of rabbit feet in the hunting scene—a scamper that ends abruptly with the offscreen crack of a rifle.

Music and sound are so communicative in Renoir's films that he can replace whole sections of dialogue with them, effectively and functionally using them to convey his ideas. Indeed, Renoir's ability to be both intellectual and emotional, clear and subtle is partially a function of his avoidance of explicit (and banal) dialogue that discusses (and inevitably overstates) intellectual issues.*

Despite Renoir's technical control of sound, camera, structure, and human performance (montage is not one of his consistent tools—although he occasionally uses it to brilliant effect, as in the hunting scene in *Rules of the Game*), the most striking of his talents is his ability to subordinate his technical skills and cleverness to the overall effect of a film (unlike most of Clair and much of Lubitsch). *Boudu sauvé des eaux* is a perfect structural circle. Boudu begins his circular journey sitting outdoors, shabbily dressed, devouring a rough, hard piece of bread, sharing that simple food with an animal companion, and singing (although his song is more an inarticulate grunting noise, an animal growl rather than a human tune). Boudu ends his journey sitting outdoors, shabbily dressed, eating bread, sharing it with an animal companion, and grunting his animal song. Between these two identical points, Boudu, the pure man of nature, comes into contact with Lestingois, the pure man of bourgeois culture. The conflict and contrast of the two produce the film's comedy as well as its serious point.

Lestingois, culture's representative, is a bookseller. And books are, of course, one of culture's ultimate products. Books are a testimony to culture itself, for what use have they except in the contemplation of culture's ideas and assumptions? Lestingois also talks like a book. He sees nature in terms of literary models. He converts one of his young customers into "Youth" in the abstract. He talks and talks and talks. He justifies his adulterous affair with the maid by allegorizing it in literary terms. And he rescues the drowning Boudu for all the humanistic, literary reasons that a man ought to rescue a man attempting suicide. Ironically (and the word "irony"

* This is perhaps an aesthetic maxim of the sound film in general. The most thoughtful sound films contain as little of that thought in dialogue and as much in other structural and cinematic devices as possible. The maxim is patently true in Chaplin, Renoir, Carné, Kubrick, Antonioni, Fellini, Truffaut—as well as in Kramer, Preminger, Richardson, Kazan, and other directors whose "ideas" are often explicit banalities. Bergman's films also support the maxim in that his worst tend to be his talkiest, and his best, the most visual and structurally interesting.

is pervasive in any consideration of Renoir), Lestingois gives his Youthful customer a free copy of *Candide*. (The student is too poor to buy it, and Lestingois again makes the humanistically appropriate gesture.) But Lestingois' view of life is far more Pangloss' than Voltaire's. Although Lestingois is a bookseller, he is not really aware of the ideas in the very books he worships and sells.

Lestingois rescues Boudu from the river and insists that the apparently downtrodden piece of human refuse move into his house. Lestingois' neighbors salute his virtuous sentiments and honor his sacrifice with medals, testimonials, and brass bands. But Lestingois' self-conscious humanism begins to cause him trouble. His "sacrifice" begins to demand genuine sacrifices. Boudu, whom Madame Lestingois calls an animal, is incapable of living in a civilized house. He prefers the floor to a bed; he wipes his filthy hands on the curtains and bedspreads; he spits on the floor, and, when instructed not to do so, he spits in M. Lestingois' precious books (ironically, *The Physiology of Marriage* by Balzac). Even worse, Boudu drives Lestingois and his mistress apart, for Boudu wants the maid for himself—and neither hides that desire nor gilds it with pastoral poetry. Boudu also sleeps in the hallway outside Lestingois' room—preventing the bookseller's clandestine nighttime meetings. When the maid, Anne-Marie, asks Lestingois, "Are you sorry you saved him?" Lestingois answers, "At night I am." Lestingois' misery culminates when Boudu seduces Madame Lestingois, and not only reveals the existence of that affair to the bookseller, but uncovers the bookseller's own adulterous game with Anne-Marie—when one of those classically comic doors that separate the various sets of lovers unexpectedly bursts open.

But if Lestingois suffers from Boudu's presence, Boudu's dip into civilization causes the tramp plenty of discomfort, too. The circular plot is a process of Boudu's acculturation. He learns to eat bread with butter, to drink wine, to wear a suit and tie, to trim his beard and hair, to shine his shoes. He even tries to learn to sell books—although he does it badly. When a customer asks for a copy of *Les Fleurs du Mal*, Boudu informs him that it is not a flower shop. By the end of his stay in the Lestingois home, Boudu has been thoroughly acculturated. He has acquired the two absolute requisites of bourgeois life—a wife, Anne-Marie, whom he has been forced to accept to smooth over the adulterous wrinkles in the Lestingois ménage; and money, which he won in the lottery. (Renoir uses several Clair motifs in the film in a much sharper, more ironic way than Clair ever did.)

Boudu sits in a boat with his wife and "friends." He wears white tie, tails, and a bowler hat—the ultimate symbols of respectability. As the wedding party glides on this second river, a band plays Strauss' "Blue Danube Waltz"—the appropriate musical partner of derbies and tails.

And as Boudu reaches for a water lily, a reminder of his former life of nature, the rowboat tips over and spills the group into the river.

Boudu decides to take advantage of this opportunity to "unsave" himself. Ironically, the others are too busy saving themselves this time to worry about altruism. Boudu calmly and casually floats on the water and reaches the shore with no difficulty at all. Boudu is in such harmony with nature that he floats on the waters instead of sinking beneath them. He tosses his bowler back into the lake to imply his demise by drowning and trades his formal clothes for the rags of a scarecrow. He finds companionship with a goat, sits, eats, and grunt-sings. He strips himself of all the social freight that seemed to rescue him but only drowned him in quite another way. In the film's final stirring shot, we see Boudu marching with his fellow tramps, a magnificent up-angle shot, his head silhouetted against the sky. Boudu doesn't need "saving"; he ironically saves himself by pretending to be drowned.

The film derives most of its comedy from Renoir's burlesque of bourgeois assumptions. If M. Lestingois is ridiculous for his poetic drivel, Madame is ridiculous for her bourgeois class-consciousness:

"Why do you have a piano since no one plays it?"
"We have a piano because we're respectable people."

(This sort of burlesque recurs as late as *Elena et les hommes* [1956], when the bourgeois shoe manufacturer insists on inviting an opera singer to his party because every respectable party has one. Ironically, the shoe manufacturer is the only one at the party who remains to hear her sing.)

Madame Lestingois is very concerned about what "the animal" does to her pretty possessions. "This has gone too far," she says. "One should only rescue people of one's own class." The parallel final straw for M. Lestingois is when Boudu spits in his books (and, ironically, Lestingois is the one who insisted that Boudu not spit on the floor). Boudu is not the only one who spits in the film, for through him Renoir also vicariously enjoys spitting on the whole history of Western civilization—and its culmination in bourgeois respectability.

The venomous energy of Renoir's spitting, the iconoclastic joy of the film, is partly responsible for the greater impact of Renoir's burlesque of the bourgeoisie than Clair's humanistic whimsy in *Le Million* and *À Nous la liberté*. Clair's films contain a lot of Lestingois abstractions. Part of the energy of *Boudu* must also be traced to the convincing, vigorous performance of Michel Simon. His animal vitality, his unsoftened lechery, his physical clumsiness in civilized surroundings magnificently convey a human spirit as well as Renoir's almost allegorical theme. Simon staggers about the respectable house, more ape than man. As he slowly adopts the surfaces of civilization, he gradually begins to walk like a civilized being.

Simon's physical presence and control inject life into Renoir's intellectual comedy.

Renoir also tempers the film's burlesque and complicates its moral paradigm by using a recurring image that does not fit very easily or precisely into the schematic opposition of society and nature, bourgeois artificiality and animal naturalness. The image is the visual partner of the film's flute. And just as the flute music is both light and haunting, mellow and playful, this image—of a magnificent church spire reaching toward the sky—is ambivalent. The spire (the Sainte Chappelle) is endowed with that consistent positive trait in Renoir—the urge to soar above the earth. Renoir increases the impression of that urge with frequent up-angle shots of the spire that precisely parallel the up-angle shots of the men at the end of the film. In fact, the film ends on a freeze-frame of that church spire, after the men have marched past it.

On the other hand, the spire is a product of man, not nature; of civilization, not animal spontaneity. For Renoir, the church might function as the height of civilized decadence, since it was built by arduous human labor paying homage to a false civilized ideal. Or perhaps the spire is a sign of a magnificent civilized spirit that has passed away. Instead of awesome churches, society consecrates itself to bourgeois homes full of useless possessions and misunderstood books. Perhaps Renoir is implying the petrifaction and shrinking of civilization in the modern era—just as Voltaire has been corrupted into a bookseller's platitudes, magnificent music into a Strauss waltz. Whatever the precise intention, the church spire (like the flute) does not have a single or simple meaning in the film.

Yet another enriching complexity of *Boudu* is that to identify Renoir with Boudu is to overlook a sharp irony that lurks behind the comic conception.[3] Although Renoir delights in Boudu's contempt for civilization and shows the perversity of "acculturating" him, Renoir knows that he himself is as much Lestingois as Boudu. Like Lestingois, Renoir lives within society, not out of it like Boudu. Like Lestingois, Renoir is a man of culture and books. Like Lestingois, Renoir converts the natural (a tree) into the artifice of "poetry" (the image of a tree on the screen). Michel Simon's dynamic performance may give the film's comic and rhetorical victory to Boudu, but Renoir's philosophic argument lies poised evenly between the two extremes. Renoir, like Chaplin, feels the confinement and artificiality of society, but also knows that most men (including himself) live within society—especially such socially dependent men as filmmakers, whose entire production of art is itself a massive social activity.

This ambivalence also enriches *The Rules of the Game* and prevents the film from being a simple indictment of a corrupt social system. The system is indeed corrupt; its ultimate act is death, and its related acts are sponging, loafing, poaching, lying, and lovelessly loving. But despite this

human (or inhuman) corruption, there is also something perfect and beautiful about the society's rules and forms. Like La Chesnaye's mechanical
pets, they are dead but perfect. The warbler chirps every 20 seconds. The
intellectual argument of the film is not simply that mechanical responses
have been substituted for more vital human expression. It is (as Leo
Braudy notes) that the perfect mechanical order of the eighteenth century no longer functions in the twentieth, with its upheavals—scientific
(the airplane and motorcar), political (the offscreen presence of the Nazis
implied by the brief discussion of anti-Semitism), and social (the new
money of La Bruyère, the new heroism of Jurieu, the new social status of
La Chesnaye—a Jew). To prefer the rules of the game to living spontaneity is undeniably deadly, but Renoir does not present the prisoners of
that fact with an alternative.

A third clear yet complex Renoir comedy is *The Golden Coach*. This
late comic masterpiece, like the earlier two, is magnificent in its structure,
in its overwhelming web of ironies, in its mixture of comic and serious,
and (like *Boudu*) in its captivating central performance. It is also magnificent in its use of color—another great virtue Renoir's eye revealed when
he turned to color cinematography in the 1950s. *The Golden Coach* has
been curiously neglected in America. Curiously, because the film brilliantly
pulls together many of the strands of the artist's themes and thoughts and
because it is as good as his most respected films of the 1930s—certainly as
good if not better than Ophuls' heralded *Lola Montès*, which it predates
by a year (and with which it has many affinities). Both *The Golden Coach*
and *Lola* are built around the romantic exploits of a central sensual
woman; both raise questions about the relation of life to art, love to social
custom; both use an artificial, theatricalized setting; both use color magnificently. But Renoir's film uses Anna Magnani rather than Martine Carol
as its central seductress—which is quite a difference! The Renoir film also
has the Renoir brain, which subordinates decor and romance to its overall
intention rather than luxuriating in them as the Ophuls film tends to do.

The Golden Coach is a play within a film—or rather a play within a
play within a play within a film. The film begins with the curtain's rising
on a stage setting (reminiscent of *Children of Paradise*). It ends with the
curtain's coming down and an epilogue summarizing the play-film's values.
But within this stage world, the film is about a troupe of actors who travel
about, putting on their shows for the populace (another parallel with the
Carné-Prévert film). But even those characters in the film who are not
actors are "actors" playing a game in their own "theater"—which they
call life. The Spanish nobles are players—with their silken costumes, wigs,
dance numbers (the minuet), and even a *scène à faire* (the confrontation
between the viceroy and his subordinates over the golden coach). Even
the coach is a stage prop—both in the film's action (who is going to get

it?) and in the Spaniards' political strategy (its function is symbolic, theatrical—to impress the natives with its magnificence). The bullfighter is also a player with a costume, pose, prop (the bull), and theater (the bull ring). This theatricalizing of the film universe and all the characters' aims and actions makes the separation of life and art, reality and theater, a Pirandellian impossibility. The levels of "play" and "real" are so interwoven that it is impossible to untangle them.

This entanglement governs our responses to the film's political questions. The politicians blindly play roles and put on a show. They do not realize that their activities are no more real, important, or absolute than the performance of a play on a stage. (But Renoir's control of parallels makes sure we see it.)

The film's cultural clash gives it yet another level and dimension. Underlying the film's action is the irony that the rulers of the Old World have brought to the New World their culture, their aristocratic prejudices, their decadent exploitation of the weak and poor, all in the guise of saving the savages from their uncivilized corruption. The Spanish nobles carry on their lives as if they were in Castile, not South America. They have imported court intrigues, gossip and rumor, parties and balls, silk costumes and wigs, and a golden coach. They consider banning from the palace any visitor who is not descended from at least eight noble ancestors. That palace itself is an architectural stew of Versailles, a Castilian house, and the conventional hacienda of the New World. This elegant palace stands not on a tiled plaza but on a dirt square. The most interesting view from its windows is of the cemetery. The palace is an isolated and alien island of Old World "charm" (that is, decadence) in the midst of a vast, uncorrupted, natural land. The familiar contrast between nature and corrupt civilization in *Boudu* recurs in a new form in *The Golden Coach*—as it does in almost every major Renoir film.

Like the nobles, the actors have brought their culture and customs from the Old World to the New. They have brought the *commedia dell' arte*, that theatrical descendant of 2,000 years of Western dramatic tradition, to the Indians of the New World. One wonders what those Indians are to make of the Harlequins, Pantalones, and Columbines—and of the elegant Vivaldi music played on such strange-looking instruments as lutes and recorders. The actors' original attitude toward this New World is the same as the snobbish assumptions of the ruling nobles. When the master of the troupe asks Camilla (Anna Magnani), "How do you like the New World?" she replies caustically, "It will be nice when it's finished." When he remarks, "No streets paved with gold," she answers tersely, "No streets." And yet, such is the power of art and the sensitivity of the artists that their strange theatrical entertainment is capable of genuinely captivating the Indian audience. The universality of art transcends cultural boundaries.

The "troglodyte" in a bourgeois kitchen. Boudu (Michel Simon) flirts with Anne-Marie (Severine Lerczynska) in *Boudu sauvé des eaux*.

The theater as life. Camilla (Anna Magnani) onstage in *The Golden Coach*.

Courtesy of Contemporary Films—McGraw-

Artifice and nature—*Picnic on the Grass.*

The first greeting. All four Marx Brothers in *The Cocoanuts.*

Courtesy of Universal Pict

Debunking the learned and the cultured. Groucho as professor in *Horse Feathers* and with Margaret Dumont in *A Night at the Opera*.

Scenes from small-town life. W. C. Fields with blind Mr. McGonigle (Charles Sellon, with Tammany Young) in *It's a Gift* and surrounded by his new opulence in *The Bank Dick*.

Courtesy of Universal Pictures

Courtesy of Universal Pictures

Fields in Hollywoodland. Story conference interrupted by the cleaning lady (with Minerva Urecal, Mona Barrie, and Franklin Pangborn); drinking spiked goat's milk in an exotic, highly Spanish "Russia" (with Leon Errol) in *Never Give a Sucker an Even Break*.

Courtesy of The Walter Reade Organization

Courtesy of Contemporary Films—McGraw

Mr. Hulot (Jacques Tati) playing tennis in *Mr. Hulot's Holiday*.

Mr. Hulot at home in the old quarter of *Mon Oncle*.

Jerry Lewis conducting an invisible orchestra in *The Bellboy*.

Lily Garland (Carole Lombard) and Oscar Jaffe (John Barrymore) "playing a scene" in *Twentieth Century*.

Hawks' battle of brains and the sexes. Katharine Hepburn playing a gun moll for Cary Grant in *Bringing Up Baby*; Cary Grant playing Ann Sheridan's bride in *I Was a Male War Bride*.

Courtesy of Columbia Pictures

The world of children. For Capra, James Stewart surrounded by innocence in *Mr. Smith Goes to Washington*; for Sturges, the mink-clad Jean Arthur surrounded by the dried spinsters of "The Boys' Constant Companion" in *Easy Living*.

Courtesy of Universal Pictures

The world of wealth. James Stewart in Edward Arnold's corrupt temple of
Mammon in *You Can't Take It with You*; Jean Arthur in the white elegance
of the Imperial "Suit" in *Easy Living*.

Courtesy of Columbia Pictures

Social progress. Lionel Barrymore and Edward Arnold play "Polly Wolly Doodle" in *You Can't Take It with You;* Eric Blore outfitting Joel Mc-Crea as a starving tramp in *Sullivan's Travels.*

Courtesy of Universal Pictures

Courtesy of Howard Hughes Productions

Victims of the bureaucracy. Harold Diddlebock (né Lloyd) going "mad" in *Mad Wednesday* (with James B. Smoke, Frank Moran, Jimmy Conlin, Franklin Pangborn, Arline Judge, and Torben Meyer); Jack Lemmon marching to his desk in *The Apartment*.

Courtesy of United Artists

Reversal of the sexes and romantic clichés. Sugar (Marilyn Monroe), Josephine-Joe-Cary (Tony Curtis), and Jerry-Daphne (Jack Lemmon) in *Some Like It Hot*.

Vigo's world of imagination—the child's-eye view of *Zéro de Conduite*.

The midget, the dignitary, and the honorable guests of wood in *Zéro de Conduite*.

Courtesy of Contemporary Films—McGraw-Hill

The texture of reality in the British "little" comedies. The native men of the sea in *Tight Little Island*; Alec Guinness and Stanley Holloway surrounded by artifacts in *The Lavender Hill Mob*.

Courtesy of Contemporary Films—McGraw-Hill

Doctor Strangelove. Keenan Wynn does battle with the Coke machine;
Dr. Strangelove (Peter Sellers) takes his place at the conference table.

The Spanish rulers, incapable of this transcendence, never get close to the people they theoretically rule. And eventually Camilla, most cynical about the "unfinished" New World, becomes converted to its openness and opportunity.

Beneath the elegant cultural exercises of the performers and aristocrats is the basically perverse drive that has brought them all to this uncivilized land—gold. The grandees own gold mines; although these mines remain offscreen, they, like the Nazis in *Rules of the Game,* are an undeniable influence in the film. The grandees base their public policies on protecting those mines. Indeed, they tolerate the New World only so they can drag the gold out of the virgin land, defending this robbery with both an army and an assumption that the original owners of the land are barbarous, worthless savages. Like the European colonists who, at least as early as the Crusades, have clothed their plunder with the raiments of righteousness and cultural superiority, the Spaniards are ironically more barbaric than the "savages" they exploit. The actors have also come to the New World for gold. Gold, one of the recurring metaphors of the film (as the title implies), is merely a cold, dead metal—except to the society that makes it a symbol of wealth and power.

Tying together these diverse intellectual levels of meaning and commentary is a strong human story. That story revolves about Camilla and her four loves. The film could perhaps have been called *Camilla et les hommes.* Three of Camilla's loves are men. Each offers her a different kind of life. Each has a particular kind of attraction. Structurally, the film chronicles Camilla's flirtation with each of the three men, culminating in a climactic and (as usual with Renoir) farcical confrontation of the three —after which Renoir (through Camilla) synthesizes the individual appeals into an ultimate statement. Felipe is Camilla's first love. An idealist, he offers Camilla sincere, simple affection and, after his experience with the natives, a free, natural life in an uncivilized El Dorado. (*Candide* lurks behind this film, too.) Felipe, an aristocrat of the Old World, converts to the values of the New.

The Spanish viceroy is her second love. He offers Camilla, herself a commoner with a wide streak of vital vulgarity, a life of material wealth and social prestige—the ideals of European society. He gives her gold— coins, a necklace, the golden coach. Ramón, the bullfighter, is Camilla's third love. His vocation is also imported from Europe. Ramón offers Camilla romantic fire and public glory—"the King of the bull ring and the Queen of the stage." To his romantic wish that they ride on horseback in glory among the populace, Camilla cynically replies, Can he find her a nice, gentle horse? And circulating among all these choices is that golden coach—tremendously functional in the film, not just a dead metaphor. With the viceroy, Camilla can ride in the coach. With Ramón, she does not need the coach but a fiery horse. With Felipe, she cannot use the coach, because there are no roads in the utopian mountains where it can travel.

What becomes of the coach reveals Renoir's synthesis of the three choices. Camilla disposes of the coach with a grand, theatrical flourish. To save the lives of her three suitors, each of them brought to the edge of the gallows by his love for her, Camilla gives the coach away to the powerful bishop of the province—who is yet another kind of actor in another kind of theatricalized pageant. The coach is to become one of his new stage props—the means of taking condemned prisoners to the gallows, offering them the final consolation of the Church before their ultimate journey. This melodramatic gesture earns the bishop's pardon for all three male offenders. Camilla plays her last scene like a saint or Madonna, the strumpet redeemed by religious conversion—and Renoir photographs her in beatific poses and angles to intensify this new role.

But it is merely a role. Camilla's fourth love (indeed, the one that triumphs) is not a human being, but an abstract vocation. She loves acting and the theater. She loves the public in the "two little hours" onstage when she makes them all love her in return. It is Camilla's brilliance as an actress (and Magnani's fire as a performer) that brings the whole society—rich and poor, noble and peasant, viceroy and bullfighter, sensualist and priest—to her feet. Of all Camilla's loves, only her love for the stage is unalloyed and uncomplicated. Her most sincere declarations of love come after the thundering applause of her audience proves that they love her in return. She loves the stage more than Felipe (in defiance of whose wishes she insists on keeping the viceroy's golden gift). She loves the stage more than Ramón. When the bullfighter diverts the attention of the audience from her stage entrance to his entrance into her theater, she angrily stops the performance and scoffs at the bullfighter's magnetism. "Back to your cows!" And he loves her for that defiance.

In the film's epilogue, performed in front of the theater curtain, we learn that Felipe, Ramón, and the viceroy all have disappeared. Camilla stays where she really belongs—on the stage, where she can exist fully in those "two little hours." In this solution, the film summarizes the potential superiority of the stage to life, of art to reality. And indeed Renoir himself seems to be summing up his own attitude about the relation of his life and art—much as Chaplin did in *Limelight* two years earlier. (Might this have been an influence?) *The Golden Coach* becomes the filmmaker's *apologia pro vita sua*. The attractiveness of art is that in it a human being can live many different roles and experience fully all of life's many choices. Camilla can taste each of the loves and choices offered her by Ramón, and Felipe, and the viceroy. But in life a person must make *one* of these choices—and any choice necessarily excludes the others. Camilla, the actress, can love all her suitors with equal commitment and sincerity. And indeed the film never provides evidence in favor of any one of them. But life does not permit this experiential freedom.

There is also a bit of sadness and ambivalence about this chameleonlike relationship of the artist to life. The film ends with two haunting words. The master of the troupe asks Camilla if she misses Felipe, Ramón, and the viceroy, who have all disappeared from her life. Loving all of them, she cannot ever hope to attain one of them. Her answer to his question is a simple admission that implies much more than it says: "A little." In that little there is obviously a lot, including the Renoir consciousness that in accepting one value, a person necessarily loses its antithesis.

That Renoir was using his late films to put together the pieces of his own life in art shows clearly in his next comic film, *French Cancan*, another magnificent jewel of color, music, movement, structure, and human performance (and probably Renoir's last masterpiece). Like *The Golden Coach*, *French Cancan* is about the relationship of life (or love) to art (or vocation). The film is a comic, Technicolor, non-agonized examination of the same question as Fellini's later *8½*, set in Paris of the 1890s. A nightclub entrepreneur, Danglard (a surrogate for Renoir himself), successfully fights a series of difficulties—social, financial, personal—to open the famed Moulin Rouge. He is a successful artist and producer because he is capable of inspiring love in many people, of using that love to refine their raw talent into gold, and then cutting the lover loose, moving on to another to begin the mining and refining process again. Although Danglard realizes that his artistic commitment makes him a very faithless lover, he also knows that he must live according to his definitions of value and meaning. His life belongs to his creations, not to a single lover; he loves the dance, not any one dancer.

The parallels with *The Golden Coach* are striking. The film differs in tone as the cancan differs from the *commedia dell' arte* (the joy and exuberant motion of the dancing are the counterpart of the elegant gestures of acting in the earlier film), as French impressionism differs from baroque painting (the two films use these contrasting visual and color styles), and as a Montmartre *chanson* differs from Vivaldi. That the world of *French Cancan* was very close to Renoir, a more personal, less distant treatment of the questions in *The Golden Coach*, is obvious in its depiction of a man who produces whole universes of art (not just shows, but self-contained, atmospheric worlds—like films); in its use of Jean Gabin (who was so important to the Renoir films of the mid-1930s) as that middle-aged producer; and in its use of the world of Renoir's father and youth as the film's cultural milieu—just as Chaplin used 1914 London in *Limelight*.[4]

Indeed, the parallels with Chaplin are so striking throughout Renoir's work that one is tempted to treat Renoir as the legitimate Chaplin heir of sound comedy. Whereas Clair's parallels with Chaplin are limited to the surface—themes, motifs, characters, business, plot points—Renoir's parallels are closer to the essential spirit of Chaplin (and to that of any great comic artist). First, there is Renoir's awareness of paradox, ambiguity, and ambivalence, the realization that it is easier to raise comic questions about human values than to answer them. Second, there is Renoir's firm sense of himself as comic artist, the way he relates as a human being to the universes of art he has created. Renoir is as much a character in his own films as Chaplin is in his. Camilla and Danglard, both artist-creators, are obviously surrogates for the filmmaker. Boudu and Lestingois, philosophical opposites, are projections of Renoir's own warring halves. And, of course, Renoir literally appears in his own films—most memorably as Octave in *Rules of the Game*.

But this role of Renoir's (as well as the earlier role of the poacher in *La Bête Humaine*, 1938) provides a unique insight into Renoir's view of himself as both man and artist. Octave is a failure, an unsuccessful artist. He is a coward, a sponger, a "parasite" (to use his own description). He is incapable of seizing Christine for himself, withdrawing instead from the competition to give her away. He is an orchestrator of human events (like a filmmaker), not a human participant. And he is a poor orchestrator, for his *mise-en-scène* ends not with the triumph of love but with the horror of death. In portraying himself as such a man (as well as splitting himself into the incompatible halves of Boudu and Lestingois), Renoir seems to doubt his vocation, to doubt the value of his works in the abstract and their relevance to his world's suicidal course, which he is powerless to alter.

But the Renoir of the 1950s—through the voices of Camilla and Danglard—seems to have grown more comfortable with his vocation. He still realizes the human failings of the artist, but he is surer of the artist's compensating powers. He realizes that the commitment to art is not *the* choice, but it is *a* choice—and certainly *his* choice. Looked at in such a way, Renoir's comic works present a spiritual autobiography of the artist and his relationship to both art and men. Chaplin's spiritual autobiography is perhaps the reverse of Renoir's—from the tough assertiveness of *The Tramp* to the fears and doubt of *Limelight*. But the important fact for both comic artists is that their works present a sincere kind of self-awareness and self-consciousness, for if the business of comedy is an examination of human foolishness, it is essential for the comic artist to realize how he relates to that race of fools.

CHAPTER 16

The Dialogue Tradition

—

THE first of the three major traditions of sound comedy is the American film that generates its comedy through talk. Creating within the confines of the Hollywood studio system, several directors made distinctive, clever, and intelligent comedies that, like most American films of the 1930s and 1940s, were dialogue films in which pictures primarily supported talk. But if the talk was good, the pictures pleasant and functional, the performances energetic and compelling, and the structural conception careful and clever, the comedy could be very entertaining indeed.

Because the dialogue comedy was so dependent on talk and structure, it was equally dependent on the scriptwriter who devised the talk and structure. The dialogue comedies were *written* comedies, and the writer played almost as great a role in shaping the film as its director. The scripts of Ben Hecht, Preston Sturges, Robert Riskin, Dudley Nichols, Herman J. Mankiewicz, Charles Lederer, Garson Kanin, and Ruth Gordon frequently overwhelmed the weak director, exerting far more influence over the film than the director's "auteurial" style. If that fact seems to contradict the assumption that the director is a film's prime mover, it is equally true that in the best dialogue comedies the insight of the writers fused perfectly with the style and attitudes of the director, who expanded the sharp script into the full and final comic conception.

Underlying the best of the dialogue comedies was usually a subtle and silent rebellion against the very studio system and values that produced them. Most of these films slyly bit the hand that fed them, but the bite was very coy and the teeth were often capped with the same tinsel and rhinestones that Hollywood so adored. The comedies developed a unique aesthetic for destroying Hollywood assumptions and conventions while appearing to subscribe to them. Their primary targets were the familiar movie definitions of love, sex, success, and propriety. And by shredding the Hollywood clichés, the comedies frequently implied a more human, sensible, and sensitive system of emotional relationships and moral values. As in the earliest American comedies, the sting of raucous, vulgar sincerity popped the balloon of pretentious gentility.

Howard Hawks

Although he is not predominantly a director of comedies, no Hollywood director made better comedies than Howard Hawks. Like his non-comic films, Hawks' comedies refuse to sentimentalize or moralize. They show bizarre, lunatic people doing "screwball" things without ever explicitly telling us why they do them and without ever saying (or even implying) that underneath the surface lunacy they are just plain folks. Hawks never apologizes for his comic characters and never strips away the veneer to let them bare their souls. They remain unswervingly true to their bizarre schemes, hopes, and interests. In a Hawks comedy the characters do not play at being silly; they are so consistently, believably, devotedly silly that their silliness itself becomes a serious, believable, consistent way of life.

The dominant psychological trait in Hawks' comedies (as in his non-comedies) is ego. If his characters seem loony, it is simply because they are wrapped up in their own heads. They can't see beyond their own intentions—and they don't want to. This selfishness is a striking psychological characteristic in an era when the conventional protagonist was distinguished by his selfless concern for people and principles outside himself. The supremely ironic twist in Hawks' comedies of ego, however, is that they are also comedies of love. That seeming contradiction is precisely the starting point of a comic Hawks plot.

The problem for a Hawks character is to let his egoistic guard down enough to see that he loves someone else and to let that someone else see she is loved. And vice versa—for Hawks doesn't sentimentalize the women in the comedies either. Like Lubitsch, Hawks doesn't put his women on pedestals but shows them to be at least as aggressive and conniving as his men. And unlike Frank Capra, Hawks does not solve the romantic conflict by revealing the cynical girl's soft heart beneath the layers of toughness.

For Hawks, as for Lubitsch, the human moral center is the brain. (For

Capra it is the heart.) Hawks resolves sexual conflicts without betraying his characters' intelligence or competitiveness. Though his lovers perceive their need for each other by the end of the film, they do not make any conversions as a result of that perception. The endings of the films imply that the future union of the central couple will be as antagonistic and competitive as their strange courtship. The literary ancestors of Hawks' sexual attraction-antagonism are Shakespeare's Beatrice and Benedick and Shaw's Jack Tanner and Ann Whitefield, two pairs of intellectual opponents who also happen to love each other desperately. The cinematic ancestors of Hawks' egoistic lovers are perhaps Monescu and Lily of Lubitsch's *Trouble in Paradise*, who can't help competing as thieves despite their union (both sexual and vocational).

The Hawks characters love each other precisely because of their strong-willed, independent minds. They do not fall for sexual clichés on the one hand or romantic clichés on the other. One strong mind feels attraction to the strength and integrity of another. For Hawks to change either or both of these minds in his sexual resolution would rob the couple of the very basis of their relationship. As a result, Hawks' lovers fight more than they love; but without the underlying attraction and mutual respect, they woudn't bother to fight at all. Their feelings are almost never verbalized; the lovers are rarely nice to each other. In *I Was a Male War Bride*, Ann Sheridan commands Cary Grant, "Get out of here, Henri, or say something nice." Grant stumblingly replies, "Well, I don't know, Catherine . . ." "That was nice, Henri," she sincerely answers. That inarticulate mumbling is as nice as Hawks comedies get.

Twentieth Century (1934) is the most ego-centered and the most cynical of all the Hawks comedies. It is full of sentimental speeches and scenes —all of them feigned. For in this story about two people of the theater, the fighting lovers live life as if it were the theater. And all human emotions—the need for love, the sorrow of death, the disappointment of failing in a career—are merely pretexts for some play-acted scene. The two central players, Oscar Jaffe (John Barrymore) and Lily Garland (Carole Lombard), are incapable of responding to each other offstage except as performers on some imagined stage.

The film's plot is a Svengali-Trilby story. Jaffe, a great Broadway producer, takes an unknown named Mildred Plotka and turns her into a star named Lily Garland. After Lily reaches stardom, she finds her mentor is her master—ironically, more confining to her theatrical ambitions than to her personal life. She lies, deceives, and plays several "staged" scenes to get away from him. Jaffe, in financial trouble, needs to get Lily back to save his career, reputation, and skin. He lies, deceives, and plays several "staged" scenes to snare her. He wins, and the film ends as it began, with Jaffe, the martinet, ordering Garland exactly where and how to walk on a stage. If there is a single serious, underlying emotion in the film, other than selfish ambition, it is the fact that somehow these two people are a matched set, incomplete without one another to play off and against.

The film springs from the total egotism of these two actor-people. It also parodies the egotism of actor-people. The uncompromisingly cynical and iconoclastic Ben Hecht–Charles MacArthur script uses theatricalization to burlesque Hollywood clichés of both "nice people" and "theater people."* The film is probably Barrymore's most successful self-caricature in his ten-year film career of parodying himself. In one viciously delightful moment, Barrymore sits on a train playing with his putty nose. (He has just disguised himself to get away from the Chicago cops). Hawks shoots this nose play in profile—for, after all, Barrymore is "The Great Profile." And as The Great Profile plays more and more with the nose putty, his nose, like Pinocchio's, becomes a larger and larger distortion of itself. By the end of his nose doodling, The Great Profile is a hideous caricature of its greatness. Then Hawks tops the caricature: Barrymore sticks his finger up that grotesque putty nose to pick it.

Such anti-romantic, anti-genteel, and anti-stereotype attacks pervade the film. One of the brilliant Hawks-Hecht-MacArthur touches in the film is the crazy old revivalist on the train who keeps pasting his religious warnings to repent all over the train's windows and doors and all over the passengers' hats, coats, and suits. Later this moralistic old gentleman is carted off to the nut house. Hawks-Hecht-MacArthur imply that the mad house is exactly where such people belong—just as actors belong on a stage. By refusing to bow (or even nod) to a single Hollywood sentimentality, Hawks keeps his comedy moving at a tremendous pace, gives it a psychological and moral consistency that creates a unique world with its own clear laws and principles, and provides his audience with one delightful surprise after another.

The mastery of *Twentieth Century* becomes much clearer when it is compared with similar films. Victor Fleming's *Bombshell* (1933), another story of the contrast between acting and life, peddles the cliché that great stars are just people underneath. Every one of Jean Harlow's egotistical, self-worshiping scenes is balanced with a sentimental one in which Harlow wishes she could find a husband and start a family. The film's performances treat the material as a joke (whereas in Hawks the egotism is deadly serious). Frank Morgan, as Harlow's father, gives one of the worst performances of his career, simply because he is so insistent on showing us that he is not playing a human being. The result of *Bombshell's* timidity is that, unlike the Hawks film, it doesn't contain any psychological or human truth and it isn't very funny.

A later Ben Hecht script, *Nothing Sacred* (1938), screams out for a

---

* One of Hecht's first observations about Hollywood films was that the only characters to have any fun in them were the ones who weren't nice. He decided to write all his films for the not-nice characters.

director like Hawks. Unfortunately, it got William Wellman (under the thumb of David O. Selznick). The result is a battle between the cynicism of the script and the cowardice of the filmmakers. The story is a comic study of the fake sentimentality surrounding death. Hazel Flagg (Carole Lombard), a citizen of Warsaw, Vermont, is supposedly dying of radium poisoning. A newspaper imports her to New York so she can have a grand last fling before her ultimate departure. Also it hopes the stunt will sell more newspapers. The film ironically shows that death can provide the girl with the key to the city and can provide the public with a nice pretext for calling up a few heartfelt, sentimental tears in the midst of its city's pursuit of fun and profit. The film is also an ironic reversal of the Frank Capra big city–small town comparison, for the small-town Vermonters in *Nothing Sacred* are money-hungry, unfriendly, and crooked. They actually wind up taking the big-city folks for a ride. (Hazel is not ill at all.) But despite this potentially funny, anti-sentimental premise, *Nothing Sacred* looks tepid beside *Twentieth Century* because Wellman-Selznick, on the one hand, add sentimental sides to the main characters and, at the opposite extreme, so overstate the film's ironic, cynical points that the action seems not natural but farcically forced.*

Hawks' *Bringing Up Baby* (1938) also begins with an anti-sentimental premise. Although the title seems to promise some nice domestic comedy (along with its evocations of the comic strip, "Bringing Up Father"), the "Baby" in this script by Dudley Nichols and Hagar Wilde is no human infant but a tame leopard which responds with special affection every time he hears his favorite song, presumably because he hears his name in its first line, "I Can't Give You Anything but Love, Baby." In the course of the film, Baby wanders off and must be caught. Unfortunately, Baby gets confused with another leopard, an escaped mad killer, who does not think much of "I Can't Give You Anything but Love" or any other human song. In addition to chasing leopards, the characters also chase after dead animals, for the film is about a zoologist who is assembling the skeleton of a brontosaurus. One crucial bone, the intercostal clavicle, has disappeared. It has disappeared because George, an antisocial terrier, has sniffed it, taken to it, and buried it.

Apparently a mad chase after leopards and bones, the film is really Katharine Hepburn's hunt for her man, the scientist, played by Cary Grant. Katharine is far more predatory than Baby. The reason for *this* chase is that Cary Grant doesn't want to be caught—for two reasons. First, he is nearsighted, figuratively and literally, and doesn't see that he is Katharine's prey. Second, Cary is engaged to marry a dry, sexless, stiff woman who would seem a more appropriate mate for a dry, stiff scientist

---

* The film also contains one of the ugliest and least functional uses of Technicolor ever seen. Selznick was apparently experimenting for the following year's *Gone with the Wind*.

than the bubbling, bizarre, unconventional Katharine. So all the fighting, chasing, and lunacy in *Bringing Up Baby* are merely a surface deception for the film's real action—Katharine's efforts to put Cary, not a leopard, in a "cage." The film literally does cage him, for in the course of the chase Cary ends up in jail. But Katharine also wants to free him: she succeeds in springing him not only from jail but also from the emotional prison that has enveloped him.

As is typical in a Hawks comedy, the tension between surface madness and underlying feeling is implied but never stated. Katharine never verbalizes her feelings or her intentions, but Hawks conveys them in a brilliantly cinematic way. One sequence of *Bringing Up Baby* reveals Hawks' command of cinematic distance and composition. Hepburn's first close-up in the film comes almost 30 minutes into it—at the moment when she first learns that Cary is engaged to be married. As she hears this news, Hawks cuts to an unexpected close shot of her face, and the action and dialogue suddenly pause. After a few vague flickers of conflicting feeling on her face, the fast-paced talk and action resume in a longer shot. Hawks' usual reliance on fast pace and the middle-distance shot gives great power to those special moments when the pace slows and the camera leaps very close.

The comic power of *Bringing Up Baby* emerges by comparison. Leo McCarey's *The Awful Truth* is also a comic contrast of surface and depths, of apparent battle and underlying love. But McCarey's film is a softer, sweeter, less funny, and slower-paced treatment of the contrast. The couple is, first of all, a married couple seeking divorce—so we know (according to Hollywood definitions) that they really love each other. The animal in the film is not a music-loving leopard, dinosaur, or mischievous terrier, but a cute, sentimental terrier named Mr. Smith which brought the couple together originally. And the potential lovers that the squabbling couple dig up—a dumb, vulgar Southern belle for Cary Grant; a plodding, stupid Oklahoma millionaire for Irene Dunne—cannot be seen as serious, credible threats to their relationship. When these sentimentalities and implausibilities in the script that McCarey and Viña Delmar wrote are wedded to McCarey's slow pacing of the dialogue and unrhythmic cutting, the result is a film that looks more like fooling around (often quite enjoyable fooling) and less like life than *Bringing Up Baby*. Hawks reveals that the comic spark of life can only emerge from the creation of a consistent, credible world in a film, not a world in which the characters seem to know that they are making a comic movie.

The comic perfection of *Bringing Up Baby* becomes clearer from yet another comparison, with a much later film that attempts to duplicate the Hawks style and method, Peter Bogdanovich's *What's Up, Doc?* (1972). Several essential differences between *Bringing Up Baby* and *What's Up, Doc?* account for the comic life of the earlier film as opposed to the sputtering, occasionally funny comic business of the later one. First, pace. The Hawks comedy moves with breathless rapidity; the Bogdanovich film constantly slows down to provide the stars with glamorous close-ups or to emphasize human and comic details that don't require emphasis. The Hawks film never stops moving; the audience picks out the relevant details for itself as the story whirs dizzily by. As early as Mack Sennett (and, of course, such classic stage farces as Feydeau's) it was clear that a furious pace is one way to confer the breath of comic life on a sequence of events that is incongruous and improbable.

Second, the Hawks tension between surface and depths, a tension that is the real human material of *Bringing Up Baby*, does not exist in *What's Up, Doc?* What is not voiced in the Hawks film—that Katharine wants Cary—is one of the first sentiments to leap out of Barbra Streisand's mouth, followed by long, obvious close-ups that reveal (and reveal and reveal) everything about the direction of her affections. Where *Bringing Up Baby* is apparently a chase after a comic object (the leopard) but is really a woman's chase after her man, *What's Up, Doc?* is apparently a woman's chase after her man but is really a chase after a comic object (suitcases). Despite *Bringing Up Baby*'s surface absurdities, it is a film about an internal emotional process; despite *What's Up, Doc?*'s explicit emotional statements, it merely manipulates comic gimmicks and superficial absurdities.

Third, lacking this tension between surface and depths, the Bogdanovich film also lacks the egoistic tension between male and female, between two strong minds. Grant's intellectual drive and Hepburn's romantic drive, which communicate themselves in the driving hardness and crispness of their talk and movements, are replaced by the softness and warmth of Barbra Streisand and Ryan O'Neal. If one can speak of the unanimity of director and writer in the dialogue tradition, *Bringing Up Baby* is a reminder that the stars must be added to this synthesis. The surface coldness and crackle of the Hepburn-Grant style is completely suited to the story's dizzy pace, its contrast of cold surfaces and warm depths, and its battle between two strong minds. Both Hepburn and Grant are "intellectual" actors who successfully convey the impression that their heads, like their mouths, are not stuffed with cotton.* But the warmth and obvious vulnerability of Streisand and O'Neal—qualities that make them stars of the 1970s—make them completely unsuited to "screwball" comedy, which must race along a cold, slick surface if it is to live at all. Further, although it is possible to accept the premise of Barbra's blatant sexual attraction to Ryan, it is not possible to accept the premise that Ryan O'Neal (*a*) is an intellectual; (*b*) if he were an intellectual, could

---

* Cary Grant's pace, drive, and intellect make him the ideal Hawks comic hero. When Hawks used the warmer, softer, slower Gary Cooper (*Ball of Fire*, 1941), the result was much less dazzling than the three Hawks-Grant comedies. Ironically, Grant's serious performance for Hawks, in *Only Angels Have Wings* (1939), seems far less successful than his comic ones.

acquire a Eunice for a fiancée; and (c) knows anything at all about igneous rocks except how to pronounce the word. Cary Grant may not be very credible as a zoologist, but the sheer speed of his performance diverts us from considering this potential incredibility.

Finally, the collapse of dramatic and comic tension between the central pair of What's Up, Doc? leads Bogdanovich to shift his comic focus from the stars to the supporting players and to impersonal cinematic gimmicks (the comic chase echoing Mack Sennett, Bullitt, and The General, among others). Where character players like Charles Ruggles were delightful and yet obviously subordinate in Bringing Up Baby, the comic doings of minor figures overshadow the central pair in What's Up, Doc? The spiteful machinations of Ryan O'Neal's musical rival, the pseudo-hip pretentiousness of the head of the Arts Foundation, the hypochondriac sadist who serves as judge of the night court, and especially the sexless, nasal, sanctimonious, bitchy, henpecking Eunice become the film's major comic interests. The sexless fiancée rarely appeared on screen in Bringing Up Baby, a strategy that did much for that film's credibility, since we never had to wonder why our hero was attached to such a woman. But Eunice becomes a major figure in What's Up, Doc?—simply because she is funnier and more interesting than anything else in the film.

Hawks' film owes its success not just to comic devices, but to his ability to find and develop the human source of gravity that pulls comic incidents and business together to form a complete comic world. The success of Bringing Up Baby (particularly in comparison with the unevenness of What's Up, Doc?) provides a concrete example of the theory of comic sprezzatura discussed in Chapter 3, and of the ways rhythm and emphasis produce (or fail to produce) that sprezzatura.

His Girl Friday (1940) is another brilliant Hawks comedy built on the tension between surface and depths. Hawks and Charles Lederer add a new dimension to the Hecht-MacArthur Front Page by turning the two warring journalists into members of opposite sexes. Although His Girl Friday is apparently a story about a newspaper's covering an execution (the remnants of the original play), it is really the story of Walter Burns (Cary Grant again) trying to win his former wife (Rosalind Russell) back to both his bed and the newspaper business (no pure sentiment here either). The film is concerned with several kinds of unvoiced conflicts—male versus female, vocation versus love, words versus feelings—typical of Hawks comedies.

Like Twentieth Century, the plot is based on egoistical strategies and counterstrategies, lies and counterlies. Indeed, the film is built on two essential lies: first, that Walter Burns only wants to keep Hildy Johnson in the newspaper business, when he also wants to keep her as a human companion; second, that Hildy Johnson wants to leave the turbulence of Walter, the newspaper business, and the big city to settle down with a schleppy insurance salesman in Albany, New York (played by the perennial schlepp, Ralph Bellamy). Hildy's lie to herself—that she doesn't need Walter or her vocation—is the biggest lie of a film that is filled with lies. And that is what she finds out by the end of it. By reversing the sex of Hildy Johnson, Hawks and Lederer inject a sexual conflict into *The Front Page* that completely dwarfs the original slice-of-journalistic-life conception (which the film could perhaps do with even less of).

To minimize the tension between the melodrama of the play and his own sexual comedy, Hawks plays the melodramatic sections of the plot with incredible speed (especially Molly Molloy's incomprehensibly throwing herself out a fourth-floor window as a diversionary tactic)—thereby reducing their seriousness. Hawks takes the original script as a pretext for the lark he is having with his new one. Part of this lark seems to be parodying *The Awful Truth*, which won McCarey an Academy Award three years earlier: using Cary Grant; beginning the action with a marital separation (though Hawks has the guts to make it an actual divorce); casting Ralph Bellamy as "the other man," whom no one can take seriously as a threat (except a cockamamie character with a name like Molly Molloy).

The lark extends to self-conscious parody of the film's own stars—like *Twentieth Century*. When Walter Burns sends a blonde floozy to vamp the insurance salesman (Bellamy), she asks, "What's he look like?" "Like that guy in the movies—Ralph Bellamy." When the corrupt mayor (and Hawks has more larks with the corrupt officials in the film) tells Walter Burns, "You're through," Burns answers, "The last person to say that to me was Archie Leach" (Grant's real name—which certainly *was* through). Having found his human comic center, Hawks could indulge in such jokes, for the cleverness of the creators matched the cleverness of the central characters (just as in Lubitsch comedies).

I Was a Male War Bride (1949) is another breezy lark built around the reversal of the sexes and the clash between sex and vocation. In the first part of the film, Henri Rochard (Cary Grant yet again), a member of the French Army, and Lieutenant Gates (Ann Sheridan), a female member of the American Army, work together on one of their many missions in postwar Germany. After a series of mistakes and arguments, all of them revolving about the question of who wears the pants, the two not only fulfill their mission, but fulfill their relationship and decide to marry. In the second part of the film, the new Mrs. Rochard tries to get her husband home with her, a problem that can be accomplished only if Henri claims to be his spouse's bride—for the only way for a soldier to get his (her) mate home is under the provisions of the War Bride Act. After several arguments and mistakes, all of them revolving around who wears the skirts and how the bureaucracy works (or doesn't work), Henri and Catherine finally get a room together on a ship to America.

The film's structure is a wonder of balance and symmetry. The sexual tensions and reversals begin early. When Henri protests about working with Gates again, his superior (also a lady) asserts, "She's your man all right." As the two journey by motorcycle and sidecar toward their objective, Ann must do the driving—a regulation, for only she has the permit to drive. Ann puts on the pants—literally and figuratively. This action is perfectly matched toward the end of the film when Cary must put on a skirt to masquerade as "Florence"—another ploy to satisfy bureaucratic regulations.

The film is a comic sexual war, with the director refusing to take sides but merely noting its sexual ironies and clichés. And as always in Hawks, the sexual tension accompanies the clash of egos, for the two soldiers also fight bitterly about whose military strategies and plans are more effective. Both are pigheaded and both receive comic punishments for their stubbornness—but especially Henri, for woman is still officially the weaker sex according to social (and bureaucratic) clichés. Henri's primary comic pain is being unable to find a bed and losing one night's sleep after another, in both parts of the film. The culmination of this running gag is his pronouncement that women are the stronger sex—because they get enough sleep.

Hawks' comic denunciation of the bureaucracy, the primary matter of the film's second part, also begins early. Cary walks into Army headquarters to look for the proper office, only to be greeted by a bewildering series of letters on the doors—"WAIRCO," "SSPDDP," "CDMTWR," "LADIES" (another gag combining bureaucracy and sex). Bureaucratic inefficiency culminates in the second part of the film as the married couple encounters a bewildering series of forms and applications, as they must go through the marriage ceremony three times in three languages, and as Henri must pretend to be a woman (eventually, quite literally) to fulfill the requirements of bureaucratic regulations. The horrifying thing about a bureaucracy is that it is totally unprepared to handle the unusual and the exceptional. Hawks subjects Henri to this comic horror—without explicit moralizing, without sentimentality (when Henri makes his most sincere expression of love to Catherine, she isn't there to hear it), and without commenting that this is a loony comedy played with breathtaking pace against the background of a country in postwar rubble.

The decline of Hawks' comic style should probably be seen as parallel to the decline of black-and-white and the small screen. Hawks' comedies in color and CinemaScope (for example, *Gentlemen Prefer Blondes*, 1953) seem clumsy, visually ugly, and leaden (like Chaplin's *Countess from Hong Kong*). The pace and spirit of the Hawks comic world required the detachment of black-and-white and the picture-framed distance of the smaller screen. The hugeness and consequent emphasis on pictorial texture and detail of the wide screen work against the dialogue film (yet another stylistic difficulty of *What's Up, Doc?*), an aesthetic fact that has much to do with the withering of the dialogue tradition since World War II.

Frank Capra

Capra was Hawks' opposite—the supreme master of the comedy of sentiment, moralizing, and idealization. The rise of the comedy of Capra coincided with the decline of the comedy of Lubitsch. And this simultaneity was no accident. With the Depression at their backs and World War II staring them in the face, Americans demanded entertainment that would help them affirm their own beliefs, ideals, and mission. Capra believed that eventually the "little people" would triumph over hypocrisy, selfishness, and moral chicanery, that political problems could be solved if we all treated each other as neighbors and friends, that eventually kind hearts and human justice would triumph over economic miseries, political corruption, wars, and dictatorships. The Capra comedies are among the most valuable sociological documents in the history of the American cinema, reflecting an era's idealized view of itself. Capra's films demonstrate a striking skill in depicting lively, energetic, and compelling people, but, in the light of today, they also demonstrate a striking naïveté in their handling of complex political, social, and moral issues.

After Capra's early success on the Langdon features (too much success to suit Langdon's egomania, according to Capra),[1] he landed a job with the small and struggling Columbia Pictures Corporation. For several years his Columbia pictures were drab and undistinguished. His *Platinum Blonde* of 1931 is a leaden, overstated story of a tough newspaperman who gets snared by wealth; and as late as 1933, his *Bitter Tea of General Yen* is a piece of plodding Oriental hokum (which foreshadowed the same kind of exotica in *Lost Horizon*). But 1933, that crucial year of the New Deal, the legitimization of the Nazis, and the Hollywood Production Code, was the year of Capra's first great personal success—*Lady for a Day*. And for the next eight years the Capra comedies (with scripts by Robert Riskin) were the most energetic and stylish expressions of the American audience's hopes, beliefs, and ideals.

The consistent targets of the Capra comedies were the obstacles that kept people from responding sincerely, warmly, and kindly. Money was one of them. Both Claudette Colbert and her father in *It Happened One Night* (1934) allow money and its social influence to interfere with their natural human responses. The lure of money perverts the New York society that Mr. Deeds encounters when he leaves Mandrake Falls (a lovely pun), Vermont, with his 20 million dollars. Money corrupts the "Silver Knight," the once-honest Senator Paine in *Mr. Smith Goes to Washington* (1939). Money has robbed Mr. Kirby of all his friends and human feelings in *You Can't Take It with You* (1938). In *Meet John Doe* (1941) money drives Barbara Stanwyck into the grasp of the Fascist plutocrat D. B. Norton and goads her into manipulating the honest warmth of John Doe.

But money is only one kind of obstacle to human warmth. Another is cynicism and sarcasm. Many of the Capra pictures center around newspaper people, simply because for Capra, newspaper people have seen so much corruption, so much abuse of money and its by-product, power, that they erect a cynical fence around their feelings to protect their jobs and self-respect. Clark Gable, the cynical reporter, is as incapable of responding to the runaway heiress in *It Happened One Night* as she is to him. Only by escaping from their two sheltered worlds—his newspaper and her money—can they establish a human relationship. Jean Arthur is the cynical, sophisticated newspaperwoman in both *Mr. Deeds* and *Mr. Smith*. She can laugh at the film's central simpleton as long as she thinks him a phony. When she discovers his genuine kindness, her kindness also surfaces. Through the influence of John Doe, Barbara Stanwyck eventually shakes off both her callousness and her material greed. In the process of converting the films' ladies, Messrs. Deeds, Smith, and Doe also convert several peripheral cynics—for example, wisecracking reporters Thomas Mitchell in *Mr. Smith* and James Gleason in *John Doe*. Beneath the veneer, these people have hearts.

The heart is the ultimate human instrument for Capra. The golden rule of his Shangri-La is "Be kind." When Longfellow Deeds tries to be kind by giving all his money away, the cynics (especially those who want that money) accuse him of insanity. But at the hearing, the judge, to the delight of Deeds' many friends, finds him the sanest man who ever appeared in that courtroom. In Capra films, a man's wealth is measured by the number of his friends. Grandpa Vanderhoff in *You Can't Take It with You* is so kind to everyone that he has hundreds of friends with him in court. Kirby, the millionaire, pays four lawyers to be there; he must buy his "friends." John Doe has thousands, even millions of friends, while Norton, the millionaire, spends Christmas Eve alone, accompanied only by the carolers who sing, obligatorily, outside his window. Capra summarizes his view quite explicitly at the end of *It's a Wonderful Life* (1946), the story of a man who has given his whole life to helping others and then wonders if it has been worth it. George Bailey learns: "No man is a failure if he has friends."

Two accompanying motifs of Capra's friendship are music and Christmas Eve. The people on the bus in *It Happened One Night* build their camaraderie by singing. Mr. Deeds plays the tuba, Grandpa Vanderhoff the harmonica; and John Doe and his friend the Colonel play duets on harmonica and ocarina. Music helps to bridge the human gap when words fail. Christmas Eve is essential to both the plots and the themes of *Lady for a Day, Meet John Doe,* and *It's a Wonderful Life.* Christmas is an important symbolic time for Capra because it is a day for the reunion of families, for a man's pulling together all the pieces of his life to see what he has achieved. Christmas also is the season of Christ's birth, and for Capra this symbolism is very important indeed.

All three of Capra's simpletons—Deeds, Smith, and Doe—are Christ figures. (George Bailey is a fourth.) In Capra's view, the essential attributes of Christ were worldly innocence and human kindness—precisely the starting point of Deeds-Smith-Doe. In all three films, a character observes, "They're crucifying him," when the simple man runs into worldly trouble. The problem with Capra films intellectually, however, is whether the comic tales support the symbolic freight, whether Christian parables mix well with contemporary political issues. Will a courtroom full of friends overrule the machinations of four lawyers? (Indeed, should they?) Will a selfish, brutal munitions maker convert to niceness after hearing one snappy chorus of "Polly Wolly Doodle"?

Capra's problem as a self-conscious maker of "significant" political films is that he cannot solve political problems without flying away (figuratively and literally) to Shangri-La. By making the heart the center of moral (and political) virtue, Capra excludes the possibility that two perfectly nice people might hold conflicting intellectual views. The problem with Capra's films intellectually is his inability to divorce moral character and ideological principle.

This problem is especially clear in *Meet John Doe,* by Capra's own admission his most ambitious film.[2] The film is the story of a folksy bum whom a newspaper has scooped off the streets and paid to mouth various political platitudes that protest the injustices of modern society. The stunt begins as an angry reporter's practical joke against the newspaper that fired her; it evolves into a commercial campaign to sell more newspapers; it finally becomes a vicious, subversive political maneuver to mask the ambitions of the plutocrat who owns the newspaper.

The primary tension in the film is between the simplicity of Doe and the corrupt drive for money and power of the people who manipulate him. Doe is a pure American. He is a former minor-league pitcher who has fallen on hard times because his arm went soft. He accepts the masquerade as a means to make enough money for the operation on his arm that will allow him to continue playing at America's national pastime. When Doe orders food, he asks for hamburgers, milk shakes, and apple pie. And Doe is played by Gary Cooper—the folksy American raised to the nth power. Although Capra condemns the vicious, selfish, corrupt way that D. B. Norton, with his army of Black Shirts, manipulates this sympathetic fool of a Doe, what does Capra think of the Doe platitudes themselves? The film is obviously an allegorical conflict between Christ and Hitler in modern America. But does Capra see that his Christ's sentimental idealizations are exactly parallel to Hitler's own?

The answer in the film seems to be yes and no. There is a cynical anti-idealist in the film, Doe's close friend, the Colonel, played by Walter Brennan. Brennan is the foe of money and the advocate of a Chaplinesque rejection of society and civilization (he is, perhaps, the film's "Marxist" spokesman). For the Colonel, society is in the hands of the "heelots"—translation, a lot of heels. He tells Doe directly that the John Doe speeches are merely a collection of platitudes. When Doe voices his hope that all neighbors will tear down the fences dividing them, the Colonel answers, "Tear down one picket of your neighbor's fence and he'll sue you."

But Capra is noncommittal on the Colonel's cynicism—admiring the man's pragmatism but never accepting his view of humanity. In the most cynical moment of the film—perhaps in all of Capra—Doe poses for the press photographers, holding aloft two midgets, one in either arm. These midgets are ironic and brutal symbols of "the little people." But Capra persists in treating the scene as a commercialized perversion of the idea of "the little guy." So though the film almost suggests that platitudes are dangerous, Capra's ultimate statement is that the real danger comes from the nasty people who have the money, the newspapers, and the radio stations to manipulate platitudes so as to serve their own selfish ends.

This ideological vagueness and contradiction within the film itself left it without an ending. Capra discussed how many different endings he tried to give the film—all of them unsatisfactory.[3] The story could have no ending because Capra had dug himself into an impossible hole. Doe is reviled by all his followers after Norton exposes him as an imposter. (Doe had earlier decided to expose Norton.) In order to show his sincerity, Doe decides to jump off a building on Christmas Eve, as "his" first letter to the editor originally promised. Doe intends his death to be the birth of the people's new faith in him and themselves, just as Christ's birth was the birth of faith. (Capra is telescoping Nativity and Crucifixion here, but no matter.)

If Doe actually jumped, the act would be consistent with the film's premise (after all, Christ *was* crucified) but a horrible violation of poetic justice, Capra optimism, Hollywood convention, and our emotional sympathy with Gary Cooper. If Doe doesn't jump but merely settles down with Barbara Stanwyck and forgets the whole political business, none of the film's ideological issues will be resolved and the evil D. B. Norton will suffer neither exposure nor conversion. Doe doesn't jump. He walks off with Barbara in his arms, presumably to some domestic Shangri-La. The John Doe movement may or may not begin again and may or may not win a victory over the D. B. Nortons, who either can or cannot be defeated. The film's inconclusive conclusion is a perfect example of the antagonism between political issues and sentimental assumptions, between epic myth and folksy reality, between tragic inevitability and comic reprieve.

There are other questions about *Meet John Doe*. If Christ failed to transform mankind 2,000 years ago (for if he had succeeded there would be no D. B. Nortons in 1941), how can a simple American mini-Christ succeed? And even if everyone does decide to put the charity of Christ in his heart, will that put men back to work, put supper on the family dinner table, and solve such economic problems as a worldwide depression? And how can a D. B. Norton ever be stopped, since even John Doe has failed to defeat him? The unanswerable questions that Capra's film unintentionally raises and, hence, never even considers show the limits of Capra's artistic intellect.

Despite their ideological mush, many of the Capra comedies are charming, entertaining experiences. They consistently compel respect for their vitality and wit regardless of one's opinion of their ideas. In *Meet John Doe*, for example, the baseball pantomime in which Doe and the Colonel play the game with an imaginary ball is a delightful piece of physical action and human comedy, regardless of one's view of this ultra-American symbolism. The breathlessly fast pace of the opening scene, the overwhelming rapidity of the crackling dialogue are an effective, entertaining way of establishing crucial information and the premises for Barbara Stanwyck's later actions—as well as a clear sign of Preston Sturges' and Howard Hawks' influence on comic technique. The scene in which Doe first spouts his populist platitudes on a radio broadcast is very clever—for Capra can include his pet ideas and, at the same time, comically show the commercialization of those ideas in the many difficulties that Doe encounters with the microphone, the audience, and the technicians. The climactic convention of the John Doe clubs is an ironic marvel. It takes place in a baseball stadium (Wrigley Field), where the main speaker would feel more at home on the mound than on a political platform. And it takes place in a pouring rain where the black umbrellas of the huge crowd turn the meeting into an impressionistic funeral rather than a celebration. The ironies and ideas that are unspoken in a Capra film are consistently effective.

Capra also handles his most sentimental, emotional scenes with a wonderful delicacy and insight. In both *Mr. Deeds* and *Mr. Smith* Capra shoots the climactic *scène à faire*, the inevitable moment when the innocent discovers the overwhelming corruption of the world, from behind, in silhouette. We cannot see the figure's face, only his back looming out of the darkness (a dark hospital room in *Mr. Deeds*, the darkened Lincoln Memorial in *Mr. Smith*). Capra seems to have realized that specific attention to emotions on the face would be melodramatic, overstated, and unconvincing. Our imaginations are more powerful than any concrete depiction of the man's feelings could be.

Capra's greatest strength remains the natural warmth, internal logic, and inner vitality of his people. *Mr. Deeds Goes to Town* (1936), perhaps Capra's best film, is paradoxical in that the characters' thematic functions are banally obvious, yet at the same time those characters are charming in their human warmth and comic integrity. *Mr. Deeds* delights the viewer (or, at least, this viewer) with what he knows is intellectual drivel because at the same time it is so enjoyable. Of course, Longfellow Deeds is the representative of small-town friendliness—uncorrupted and incorruptible, selfless, committed to his fellowmen rather than to Mammon and the golden calf. He writes trite (but supposedly sincere) poetry for greeting cards; he plays sappy (but happy) tunes on the tuba; he wants to give away all his money to the poor folks who need it. For, as the film's theme song repeatedly informs us, "He's a Jolly Good Fellow." What could be cornier?

And yet Capra can sustain an almost 150-minute film on this premise because the jolly good fellow who embodies that sap, Gary Cooper, is completely convincing, sympathetic, and affecting and because the comic contexts in which Deeds demonstrates his virtues are clever, sharply paced, and warmly textured. Gary Cooper, an actor of the heart, is as important to the comedy of Capra as Cary Grant, an actor of the head, is to Howard Hawks'. The Capra comedies with James Stewart rather than Cooper (*Mr. Smith, You Can't Take It with You, It's a Wonderful Life*) miss Cooper's ability to call up these deep springs of warmth, which Stewart cannot quite duplicate. Jean Arthur, the woman of brain with a heart beneath, is also a Capra necessity. If *Mr. Deeds* seems Capra's best film, perhaps it is also because it is the only one with both Gary Cooper and Jean Arthur. As in the comedy of Hawks, the human truth beneath the Capra surfaces ultimately sustains the comic work.

Capra's ability to capture this underlying human texture makes his films look particularly good in comparison with Leo McCarey's, his primary rival as a director of sentimental-moralistic comedies. McCarey consistently subordinates his people to issues (and those issues are no less banal than Capra's). In *Ruggles of Red Gap* Charles Laughton and ZaSu Pitts rise above McCarey's conception, but Charles Ruggles gives perhaps the worst performance of his career in trying to demonstrate the wild, woolly exuberance of the American West. McCarey comments on his characters, and his players demonstrate that comment rather than live it. Capra's people live without commenting on themselves. Even Edward Arnold, that consistently rich, nasty, unfeeling man, plays his villainy as seriously and sincerely as the plots will allow. And Capra furthers that credibility by giving Arnold comparatively little screen time, another sign of his awareness that less often does more.* Because Capra people live in his films with complete sincerity and seriousness, his film world seems saturated with human and comic (if not moral) truth.

Like Hawks', Capra's later comedies show a decline. But where the decline of Hawks' comedy was tied to changes in cinematic techniques and pictorial values, the decline of Capra's was also tied to changes in economics and moral values. *It Happened One Night* and *Mr. Deeds Goes to Town* owe much of their lively spontaneity to their cheapness, to the fact that they were "sleepers" out of a minor, "quickie" studio. But with *Lost Horizon* Capra began to surrender to two Hollywood temptations: he started taking himself too seriously (like Griffith and De Mille before him), and he started visualizing his films more grandiosely. Capra was genuinely proud of the millions of dollars he pried out of Harry Cohn for *Lost Horizon*. Both *Mr. Smith Goes to Washington* and *Meet John Doe* are heavier and more self-conscious than the earlier *It Happened One Night* and *Mr. Deeds*. Capra's film translation of *Arsenic and Old Lace* (1944) is lighter, livelier, and funnier than his late-1930s films—perhaps because of wartime economies and the wartime pressure to take the audience's mind off serious troubles. After the war, Capra's subtle human comedy was squashed under the weight of banal intellectual self-consciousness (when audiences no longer wanted or needed heartfelt sermons) and glossy, expensive production values (when sagging box-office grosses demanded modest budgets for modest, non-spectacular films).

Preston Sturges

Preston Sturges would seem to be another of Frank Capra's opposites—cynical rather than sentimental, a satirist rather than an apologist, an advocate of the sharp tongue and brain rather than the warm, soft heart. But Sturges was not so distant from Capra as the surfaces would indicate. Like Capra, Sturges was better with comic scenes than with explicit ideology and had as much trouble as Capra at combining funny incidents and serious issues in the same film. And despite his belief in the brain, Sturges' most affectionate and sympathetic people, like Capra's, have sincere hearts beneath the tough exteriors.

No one made better dialogue comedies than Sturges, primarily because no one wrote better dialogue. Sturges is one of those filmmakers whose one-liners are often as memorable as his whole films. In *Easy Living* (a

* Lionel Barrymore plays the villainous miser, Potter, so successfully (and so fleetingly) in Capra's *It's a Wonderful Life* that he is totally unrecognizable as kindly, lovable Lionel.

Sturges screenplay that completely dominates its director, Mitchell Leisen), Jean Arthur is sitting on a Fifth Avenue bus when a sable coat descends from the skies to land on her head. She angrily turns to the man behind her, a Hindu wearing a turban, and snaps, "What's the big idea, anyway?" His answer, "Kismet." Ironically, the joke also functions in the film, for Kismet, fate, is the driving force in the film's plot.

In *The Great McGinty*, a crooked politician remarks, "If it wasn't for graft, you'd get a very low type of people in politics." When McGinty subsequently runs out on his wife, he tells her about the money he stashed away "to send the kids through college—without selling magazines." And the most brilliant collection of Sturgesisms opens *Sullivan's Travels*, as an idealistic director discusses a socially conscious film with his money-minded producers:

"You see the symbolism of it? Capital and Labor destroying each other."
"It gives me the creeps."

"It was held over a fifth week at the Music Hall."
"Who goes to the Music Hall? Communists."

"It died in Pittsburgh."
"What do they know in Pittsburgh?"
"They know what they like."
"Then why do they live in Pittsburgh?"

The Sturges emphasis on dialogue determines his film technique, which relies on the conventional American two-shot to capture the faces and features while the characters talk, talk, talk. But it is such good talk—incredibly rapid, crackling, brittle—that the film has plenty of life. Like Hawks, Sturges was a master of the lightning pace. When Sturges uses special cinematic devices, he inevitably turns them into self-conscious bits of trickery and gimmickry that harmonize well with the parodic spirit of the film. His favorite game with the sound track is to use musical backgrounds that comment parodically on the action in the scene. The opening of *Sullivan's Travels* uses melodramatic "movie music" that underscores a stagey, predictable gunfight on top of a speeding train. We later discover the scene was indeed part of a melodramatic movie within the movie. *The Palm Beach Story* opens with the William Tell Overture to underscore a breathtakingly funny pseudo-melodramatic montage sequence that finally brings a future husband and wife to the altar. The film's final use of music is just as clever. While Rudy Vallee serenades Claudette Colbert with "Goodnight, Sweetheart" (complete with full orchestra) outside her window, the sweetheart takes refuge in the arms (and, by implication, bed) of her husband inside the room. Rudy's romantic singing drives her into the arms of his rival. And perhaps Sturges uses music most effectively and wittily in *Unfaithfully Yours* (1948) when an orchestra conductor imagines three separate strategies for handling his adulterous wife, each perfectly correlated with the musical feeling of the piece he is conducting.

Sturges also reserves his manipulation of editing and the camera for the occasional tricky effect. *Christmas in July* uses a comically obtrusive zoom shot accompanied by a whistling kazoo to achieve its final miraculous solution. *The Lady Eve* combines jarring shock-cuts and screaming train whistles as comic punctuation for each of Eve's "revelations" of her previous affairs to her innocent husband. The opening sequence of *The Palm Beach Story* is a dizzying, almost illogical montage that parallels a melodramatic murder in a closet with a wedding (breaking out of the closet?). Sturges similarly punctuates his scenes of talk with an occasional bit of physical, slapstick comedy (the automat scene in *Easy Living*, the racing land yacht in *Sullivan's Travels*, the escape from prison in *McGinty*, the rifle-shooting sequence aboard the train in *Palm Beach*) that cunningly—sometimes too cunningly—injects motion into his motion pictures.

Sturges' cleverness also shows itself in the unconventional, unexpected people and situations with which he filled his films. His crazy foreigners—Louis Louis in *Easy Living*, the Boss in *McGinty*, Toto in *Palm Beach*—are burlesques of the Hollywood cliché. Where most of Sturges' contemporaries contrasted the pure, natural American with the corrupt, suave European (Henry James in Hollywood terms), Sturges' foreigners parody American ideals by trying to imitate them. Louis tries to open a huge, grotesque hotel rather than remain a brilliant French chef. His aspirations to gentility and class are undercut by his vulgarity and pronunciation—the Imperial "Suit" (suite), "phenonemom," "inwisibles." The Boss explains his American success by referring to the romantic tradition of the robber baron and by pointing out that, if it weren't for him, "everyone would be at the mercy" (but he never says at the mercy of what). Toto is the looniest foreigner of all, a slimy gigolo, ugly and wormlike, whose sole functions seem to be to parade around in a series of different costumes, to intrude into conversations with his single coherent word, "Greetings" ("His English is a little elementary"), and to chatter in some stew of languages that makes it impossible to tell to which tongue he owes his original allegiance.

Among the other wonderful Sturges caprices is "the Wienie King" in *Palm Beach*, a gruff, testy, deaf old gentleman who still loves the ladies and who can carry on whole conversations without understanding a single word. To Sturges we owe the comic and rare opportunity to hear Eugene Pallette, the human bullfrog, sing "For Tonight We'll Merry Merry Be" in *The Lady Eve*. *Easy Living* features a youth magazine called *The Boys' Constant Companion*. Ironically, this magazine is staffed entirely by prune-faced, moralistic old maids and misters. And about this magazine Sturges sneaks in a wonderfully sly bit of obscenity (Sturges, like Lubitsch, was a master at ducking the censor) when the rich businessman mistakenly refers to the publication as *The Boys' Constant Reminder*.

Sturges also delighted in showing apparently conventional Hollywood characters and scenes in a very unconventional light. The conventional boy and girl in *Christmas in July* engage in verbal battles that no Hollywood juvenile and ingenue ought to have. (He even tells her to shut up.) *The Lady Eve* contains two seduction scenes in which the lady throws herself at the recalcitrant gentleman, who insists on protecting both her and his virtue. The idyllic, conventional life of the rich receives rough treatment in the opening scene of *Easy Living*, when the wealthy husband and wife fight (almost to the death) over her newest sable coat. The Hollywood clichés of loving father and daughter get a tough beating from the continual violent arguments between Diana Lynn and William Demarest in *The Miracle of Morgan's Creek*. *Sullivan's Travels* reverses the clichés of city sensuality and country purity as a fat, lecherous farm widow does her utmost to enjoy the physical pleasures of Sullivan's young, firm body. The best things in the Sturges films are these surprising pieces of reversal and burlesque.

As for their wholes, each of the Sturges films begins with a parodic premise. *The Great McGinty* (1940) parodies both Hollywood "flashback" stories and the American ideal that anyone can rise to greatness; *Sullivan's Travels* (1941), Hollywood production values and the Hollywood iconoclast's urge to say something significant; *The Lady Eve* (1941), shipboard romance and virginal innocence; *The Miracle of Morgan's Creek* (1943), small-town Americana, the sanctity of motherhood, and patriotism; *The Palm Beach Story* (1942), marital tensions; *Unfaithfully Yours* (1948), marital infidelity; and so forth. The best Sturges films never desert delicate, fast-paced parody for moralistic, sentimental conclusions.

The Great McGinty is unrelentingly ironic. It begins with a delicious red herring, a framework story that seems to promise the tale of an erring bank clerk in a South American "banana republic." But the film couldn't care less about this bank clerk. The real story turns out to be about the bartender (Brian Donlevy), the man who stops the clerk from shooting himself. The bartender (only several reels later do we discover his name is McGinty) tells of his rise from hobo to governor. He begins his political career as a two-dollar voter for the political machine of some big city, substituting for those registered voters who are no longer alive to vote for the machine candidates. In his zeal, an ironic burlesque of "get out and vote," the hobo votes 37 times, earning himself $74. That is American ingenuity and gumption doubled and redoubled.

From this auspicious beginning the hobo rises through the machine's ranks. He first shakes down the shady businessmen (and women) who don't want to pay protection; for example, Madame LaJolla (pronounced "Hoya"), a "fortune-teller," must come up with $250 or "Madame La-

Jolla doesn't jolla any more." Then Dan McGinty wins his first office—alderman. He develops more refined methods for plucking higher sums. Finally, after acquiring a wife and kids, McGinty becomes "reform" mayor. (The Boss ironically runs the "Reform Party" as well as the machine.) In each of McGinty's steps up the political ladder, his style gets smoother (he even grows a mustache), his clothes get slicker (from hobo rags to a ridiculous plaid suit referred to as a "horse blanket" to a dapper three-piece business suit to a top hat and tails).

But McGinty gets into trouble when he falls in love with the woman he married for political convenience. She suddenly feels qualms about McGinty's "municipal improvements" (euphemism for graft) and the grafters who support him—slum landlords, owners of sweatshops. She urges McGinty to institute genuine reform, to buck the party, to make the world safe for the children. McGinty has his doubts. To his wife's sentimentalities about the "dark, airless factories," McGinty retorts with his own sentimentalities: the factory where he worked as a kid was clean and neat, a place where he labored profitably "instead of playing on the streets learning a lot of dirty words." But the wife's sentimentalities triumph—and Sturges clearly parodies yet another political cliché, the woman behind the man. (These were, after all, the years of Franklin D. and Eleanor.) Ironically, McGinty's one honest moment costs him his family, his power, his wife, and his fortune. When he bucks the Boss, the Boss bucks back, and the two of them end up in the "banana republic," continuing their long feud over who exactly is boss.

The unadulterated cynicism of *The Great McGinty*, its burlesque of the democratic political process and its reduction of an ideal—America as "the land of opportunity"—to the absurd would never have been accepted by audiences one year later. During the war years Sturges had to worry not only about the censor but also about stepping on the sensitive moral toes of a country sacrificing its young men to preserve the very ideals that *McGinty* burlesques. Sturges' greater consciousness of audience values is clear in *Sullivan's Travels*, in which the cynicism is tempered by an uplifting moral affirmation. The plot of this film springs from the tension between an intellectual film director who wants to make a "significant," socially conscious film, *Oh Brother, Where Art Thou?* and the producers who want him to keep making the escapist fluff at which he excels, *Ants in Your Pants of 1941*. The first part of the film convincingly demonstrates that a man with a college education, swimming pool, alimony payments, butler, and a troop of publicity men on his tail is incapable of capturing the desperation and misery of the poor and suffering. (There is perhaps a conscious reference to Ford's *The Grapes of Wrath* and the Pare Lorenz documentaries in the film's depiction of starving tramps and government camps.)

But the second half of the film takes Sullivan and the audience in a very different direction and toward a very different conclusion. Through a series of bizarre accidents, Sullivan winds up truly wretched and helpless, an inmate of a brutal Southern prison (evoking the Hollywood chain-gang genre). In the midst of his misery, Sullivan goes to the movies; the prisoners are guests of a black congregation on its movie night. Sturges shows the parallel misery of both blacks and prisoners; as the convicts shuffle into the humble chapel wearing chains, the blacks sing, "Let My People Go." After this rather idealized display of social misery, the movie flashes on the screen (the third film within this film about films), a Walt Disney cartoon with Mickey Mouse and Pluto. And all the downtrodden members of the audience respond in unison to the funny film—with laughter. From this demonstration, Sullivan concludes (after he gets out of prison as bizarrely as he got in) that *Oh Brother, Where Art Thou?* is not worth making. He directly proclaims, "There's a lot to be said for making people laugh. That's all some people have. It isn't much, but it's better than nothing in this cockeyed caravan." After the explicit proclamation, only slightly softened by the fancy metaphor, Sturges ends the film with an equally explicit montage of laughing faces.

Christmas in July also insists on a moralistic ending, for the young man learns that his own ability is a stronger asset than any windfall (after which Sturges gives him the windfall). *Hail the Conquering Hero* ends with the young man's confession of his dishonesty to the whole town, a greater act of personal heroism than the very clichés that forced the man into his initial lie (after which the town elects him mayor). *Mad Wednesday* ends with the implication that it is better to be "mad," spontaneous, and free than to be chained to a stifling, deadening routine (and after Harold Diddlebock's lesson in spontaneity, he discovers he has miraculously won both riches and the hand of the woman he loves).

So many of the Sturges films end with these "miracles"—like those sextuplets which are the miracle of Morgan's Creek. Such miracles are cop-outs. Despite their obvious parodies of Hollywood success stories and the Hollywood homily that the rewards go to the virtuous, Sturges' endings, like René Clair's, are incapable of tracing the implications of the issues that he himself has introduced. Either Sturges sells out to Hollywood's commercial necessities, or he is a lazy, sloppy thinker who cannot refuse the easy road (as James Agee suggests), or, like René Clair, he simply "likes happy endings"—whether they make intellectual sense or not.*

The absence of these moralizing and miraculous solutions in Sturges' domestic films perhaps accounts for their greater unity and consistency. *Easy Living, The Lady Eve,* and *The Palm Beach Story* do not desert

---

* Agee parallels Sturges and Clair, finding Clair less guilty of the Sturges evasion than I do. See *Agee on Film,* pp. 75–6, 343.

irony and satire to give the audience an obligatory piece of optimistic inspiration. In its own way *Easy Living* is a much better film about the Depression than *Sullivan's Travels,* simply because it plays on the irony that for some people a $58,000 sable coat is so valueless that it can be thrown away like a piece of trash, and for others a $58,000 sable coat is so valueless that it can't provide a nourishing meal or a necessary job.

Despite the Sturges toughness, his scorn for fakery and poses, his ridiculing of false ideals, it is more difficult to see what he accepts than what he rejects. If there is a positive Sturges ideal, it can be seen more easily in his people than in the moral summaries that conclude so many of his films. The members of the Sturges troupe—the character actors he uses over and over again—say much about Sturges' values. William Demarest is Sturges' alter ego; tough, cynical, anti-sentimental, he owes no allegiance to abstractions, but is always loyal to his friends. Jimmy Conlin—the owlish flea, nervous, squeaky-voiced—usually comforts those in trouble. Eric Blore, a man of words and poses, knows how to twist appearances to make people accept the fake as real. Robert Greig, the inevitable butler, enjoys the luxury of being a butler and is a loyal cynic who refuses to romanticize the class question. Edgar Kennedy—bartender, private detective— never lets his gruff voice and appearance interfere with his human compassion. And so forth. Most of the Sturges players are mixtures of toughness and softness (even the mincing Franklin Pangborn), scornful of idealistic clichés, usually responsive to each other as people.

In his attack on sentimental and pretentious clichés, Sturges is clearly part of the great American comic tradition that stretches back to the earliest comic jests. Like Lubitsch, Hawks, and Ben Hecht, Sturges disguised his contempt for the Hollywood beatitudes with cinematic conventions that looked very much like the usual Hollywood product. For most members of the audience, *Easy Living* was a wonderful chance to indulge fantasies about incredible luxuries dropping from the skies. The ornate, lavish sets—particularly the Imperial "Suit"—looked exactly like the gaudy settings of their favorite M-G-M films. But for a few members of the audience, the film was a chance to see the grotesque excesses of wealth, the immense gap between rich and poor, and the instability of a stock market that could rise and fall crazily on the whims of a dizzy lady. Further, the film coyly exposes the importance of sex in our supposedly puritanical society; Mary Smith derives all her power from everyone else's assumption that she is sleeping with the powerful financier. In his delightful games with Hollywood expectations, Sturges' cleverness and iconoclasm are more impressive than the depth and complexity of his vision. Sturges very quickly ran out of that iconoclastic energy in the years following the war.

Billy Wilder

Although Billy Wilder reached the peak of his comic career more than a decade after Lubitsch, Capra, Hawks, and Sturges, he was a product of the same tradition and represented the last of that line. Like Sturges, Wilder was a screenwriter who turned director. Like the films of Capra and Hawks, the Wilder comedies were collaborative fusions of the minds of clever writers (I. A. L. Diamond and Charles Brackett) and controlling director. Like Hawks, Sturges, and Lubitsch, Wilder enjoyed ridiculing the Hollywood clichés of success, love, and sex. And like all of Capra, much of Sturges, and the late Lubitsch films, Wilder usually introduced specific moral questions into his comedies, issues embodied by the film's characters, who worked them out in the film's action.*

The best Wilder comedies are a blend of tough, witty dialogue, a serious moral question examined with intelligence and without overstatement, lively and engaging performances, and clever scenes of comic human interaction that reverse the usual Hollywood expectations. Wilder hit his stride in about 1950, when he began combining the exposure of human callousness and moral corruption of his earlier films with a comedic structure. In the decade between 1950 and 1960, Wilder directed ten films which today seem quite remarkable for their consistency, intelligence, vitality, taste, and cleverness—particularly, *Sunset Boulevard* (1950), *Stalag 17* (1953), *Sabrina* (1954), *Love in the Afternoon* (1957), *Some Like It Hot* (1959), and *The Apartment* (1960).

Significantly, this great Wilder decade is bracketed by two films about Berlin—*A Foreign Affair* in 1948, *One, Two, Three* in 1961. The two Berlin films shed an interesting light on the Wilder decade between them. *A Foreign Affair* focuses on the corruption, squalor, and rubble of postwar occupied Berlin. Love becomes merely a commodity that, like anything else, can be bought, sold, or traded. *One, Two, Three*, on the other hand, is a study of the new Berlin that grew from this rubble, using the American dollar as its manure. The new Berlin is slick, skyscrapered, and bureaucratized, retaining very little of its original German soul, capitulating completely to the dollar, the bomb, and Coca-Cola. To some extent, the Berlin journey in Wilder's two films also mirrors the journey of the former Berliner who made the films, from iconoclastic comic moralist to slick, superficial humorist.

Many of the themes, traits, and devices of *A Foreign Affair* returned to dominate the films in Wilder's great decade. Wilder consistently juxtaposed comedy with moral corruption, human insincerity, and a perversion

---

* Wilder's films grew very specifically out of the late Lubitsch films, for Wilder worked on the screenplays for both *Bluebeard's Eighth Wife* and *Ninotchka*.

of the social and emotional relationships that make life livable. The typical conflict in the films is between love on the one hand and money or success on the other—prostitution and the black market in A *Foreign Affair*; the lure of Hollywood success in *Sunset Boulevard*; the marriage that is really a business merger for the manufacture of plastics in *Sabrina*; the converting of an apartment into a brothel in the hopes of promotion in *The Apartment*. As in Chaplin's *Gold Rush*, prostitution is an implicit motif in the Wilder films (quite explicit in *Irma la Douce*); a man (or woman) prostitutes feelings, body, values, possessions—anything for some kind of material success.

A corollary corruption is lying, deceit, and masquerade, for the prostitute usually must lie to others—as well as to himself—to protect himself. Captain Pringle lies to Congresswoman Frost (Jean Arthur), and his German mistress, in turn (Marlene Dietrich), lies to Pringle in A *Foreign Affair*. There are lies in *Sunset Boulevard*, in *Sabrina* (Linus at first pretends to love Sabrina only for business reasons), and in *The Apartment* (Baxter lies to his neighbors, his co-workers, and himself). Wilder uses deceit ironically in *Stalag 17* in which the apparently callous, selfish prisoner (William Holden) lies only to camouflage his escape operations. And *Some Like It Hot* is built on the immense sexual lie that the two male stars are women.

The plot of the Wilder comedy brings the central liar—who is basically a sympathetic, perceptive person—to a moment of crisis and decision. He eventually renounces the lie and confesses his human crime to the person his lies have most injured. Linus (Humphrey Bogart) confesses to Sabrina (Audrey Hepburn); Joe confesses to Sugar, and Jerry gives his absurd mock-confession to the millionaire in *Some Like It Hot*; C. C. Baxter (Jack Lemmon) tells off Mr. Sheldrake (Fred MacMurray) in *The Apartment*. For his moral deceit the Wilder character usually receives two kinds of poetic justice: the psychological discomfort of admitting his mistake openly; the physical pain of a bust on the jaw.*

Beneath the Wilder films there is a very clear moral system, usually implied but occasionally quite explicit. In *The Apartment*, Miss Kubelik (Shirley MacLaine) articulates the Wilder moral philosophy—the theory of the takers and the taken. There are those who take and give nothing, and those who give and get nothing. In at least three of the Wilder films, the "taken" women try to take their own lives. Yet one of them, Norma Desmond (*Sunset Boulevard*), merely tries to take it as a strategy for taking someone else. So, although all the Wilder films work with those verbs of taking, giving, and getting, Wilder uses them ironically. The absolute takers (Norma Desmond or Mr. Sheldrake) end up getting very little.

---

* In the comedies he receives a sock in the jaw; in the non-comic films, a fatal gunshot wound—*Double Indemnity, Sunset Boulevard*.

The absolute taken (Sabrina, Miss Frost, Miss Kubelik, C. C. Baxter, Jerry) all wind up getting something. And most characters in the Wilder films are neither absolutely takers nor taken. They try to take but end up giving; or they seem to take but are really giving. Wilder reveals both his artistic maturity and his human sense by setting up the two polarities and then collapsing them, for neither life nor art lends itself to facile dichotomies.

Most of these moral values reveal themselves in Wilder films in his use of the triangle—an appropriate geometric figure for both his attitudes and for comedy. The central figure wavers between his commitment to the other two members of the triangle, eventually choosing the partner who will make his life meaningful. Such obvious triangles as von Schlüttow–Pringle-Frost, Norma-Joe-Betty, and Joe-Sugar-Jerry come to mind. But Wilder's use of the triangle can be even more complex. The obvious triangle of *Sabrina* is Linus-Sabrina-David, but the implied triangle of "plastic"-Linus-Sabrina is equally important to the film. And in *The Apartment* there are three interlocking triangles—the romantic one for Miss Kubelik (Baxter-Kubelik-Sheldrake), the conflict between love and money for Baxter (Sheldrake-Baxter-Kubelik), and the insincere commitment to both mistress and wife for Sheldrake (Kubelik-Sheldrake-wife).

Out of these triangles and the choices of the protagonists come the positive values of the Wilder world. His system is a sort of hybrid of the Sturges-Lubitsch-Hawks cynicism and the Capra idealism. On the one hand, Wilder ridicules clichés of human morality and conventional Hollywood definitions of the good life. On the other, he asserts that the essential human function is feeling, and that life without love is very poor indeed, regardless of money in the bank or position on the corporate ladder. By the end of *The Apartment* both Baxter and Miss Kubelik have rejected the lures of Sheldrake. They sit together in the apartment, playing gin rummy; the warm, sincere interaction of the two people in that room have converted a place of prostitution into a place of human love. The apartment is a home, not a room. Baxter verbalizes his feelings for the first time in the film: "I love you, Miss Kubelik." She replies with both charm and vigor: "Shut up and deal." The actions, not the words; the companionship, not just the sex are important to these people and to Wilder.

As a cinema technician, Wilder takes his style from the late (less flamboyant, less self-conscious) Lubitsch pictures. Rather than relying on devices of editing and the camera, Wilder depends on the vitality and suggestiveness of his actors' performances (for example, William Holden is the definitive taker and Jack Lemmon the definitive taken) and on the power of the "plastic material." Wilder's use of physical objects provides the dominant visual accompaniment for his dialoguey scripts.

In *A Foreign Affair*, for example, there is a brilliant scene built around file cabinets. The scene not only is interesting to watch, but is also a precise metaphoric translation of the moral issues in the film—the conflict between sincerity and deceit, the spiritual and the material. The crusading Miss Frost searches through the files to find Fraulein von Schlüttow's dossier. Captain Pringle wants to keep her from finding that dossier. So he uses the file cabinets to "romance" her—hemming her into a corner by pulling out drawer after drawer, arousing her fear and passion, taking her mind off the search. Pringle merely pretends to love Miss Frost—and he uses material objects to convey this false feeling. At the end of the film, after Pringle has decided he loves Frost and vice versa, there is a wonderful reversal of the file-cabinet scene. As Pringle tries to escape her, she hems him into a corner with wooden chairs. Her planting of chair after chair mirrors his earlier pulling of drawer after drawer. And this time the material genuinely mirrors the spiritual.

This awareness of the power of objects—both to evoke an emotional response and to communicate plot material in an economical way—recurs throughout the Wilder canon: the dictaphone in *Double Indemnity*; the whisky bottle in the light fixture in *The Lost Weekend*; the grotesque house, car, and photographs in *Sunset Boulevard*; the trunk in *Stalag 17*; the plastic plank, the champagne glasses, and the umbrella in *Sabrina*; the toothpick, the spats, the hearing aid, and the bass fiddle in *Some Like It Hot*.

Wilder's use of the physical in *The Apartment* is especially effective. His shot of the immense office—the geometric rows of desks, the regularity of the ceiling's fluorescent lighting, the clicking sound of business machines, the visual patterns that reduce people to mechanisms—has become a classic example of the use of composition for the wide screen. Within this immense physical landscape, Wilder pivots the action around tiny objects. One of them is a makeup compact—with a broken mirror—that identifies Miss Kubelik as Sheldrake's mistress. The other is a key. Baxter reveals his subservience to the system and its corruption in the early parts of the film by his willingness to put the key to his apartment in an inter-office envelope. And his final decision to reject both Sheldrake and the system also takes the form of his surrendering a key—this time not to the door of his apartment, but to the door of the executive washroom, the place (and an ironic one) that he has worked so long to reach.

Wilder's best film, certainly his funniest and probably his most effectively subtle at examining social and human values, is *Some Like It Hot*. The film is a rich, multilayered confection of parodies and ironies. It is a parody of gangster films—complete with George Raft as the mobster and Pat O'Brien as the cop. And it is a parody of sexual love and romance—with Tony Curtis as the male idol and Marilyn Monroe as his female counterpart.* But beneath the obvious parodies of these two genres of Hollywood films, Wilder plays some very clever games.

As funny as the gangsters are, they do a lot of killing. Wilder constantly allies them with death. The alliance begins in the opening scene in which the truck that transports the bootleg booze masquerades as a hearse and the liquid cargo masquerades as the corpse in the coffin. The comic use of death recurs in the speakeasy, which masquerades as a funeral parlor, complete with orchids and organ. And the shadow of death returns to the film when the mobsters gather in Florida for a "convention," masquerading as music lovers—the "Friends of Italian Opera." The film is carefully and cleverly constructed, for the two real musicians in the film are also masquerading in Florida—as women—in order to keep out of the same kind of coffin with which the film opened. And just as the coffin in the film's opening was riddled with machine-gun bullets (an ironic killing of a corpse), Jerry's bass fiddle is riddled with machine-gun bullets during the St. Valentine's Day massacre.

The final association of the mobsters with death is the fancy banquet when the "Friends of Italian Opera" do their own singing—"For He's a Jolly Good Fellow." Right after their serenade, a machine gunner pops out of the immense birthday cake (the expected inhabitant of a cake is some kind of sexual treat) to murder the guest of honor, Spats Columbo, for whom the song has been sung. Indicative of the irony in Wilder's handling of these murderous clowns is one gangster's final advice to the assassin climbing into the dessert with the machine gun: "Don't mess up the cake. I promised to bring back a piece to my kids." As in so many of the Wilder films, human beings have been reduced to things. The cake is more important than a human life.

Wilder's game with sexual stereotypes also burlesques the way Hollywood conventions reduce people to bodies. Rather than playing off the male-female reversals as Hawks does in *Male War Bride*, Wilder uses female impersonation to comment on the inhuman stereotyping of sexual roles. As men, both Tony Curtis and Jack Lemmon are distinct sexual *types*—the one sexy, suave, virile (Joe is Wilder's "taker"), the other weak, passive, helpless (Jerry is "the taken"). But when they dress as women, they switch personalities. Joe becomes Josephine—soft, seductive, demure, genteel, refined, the kind who gets "her" man. Jerry becomes Daphne—spunky, vivacious, full of life and pep, the kind who laughs and then cries at parties. Tony Curtis, both as male and female, plays the sexual cliché; Jack Lemmon, both as male and female, plays the sexual departure—too passive as male, too aggressive as female.

* Wilder frequently uses stars whose roles consciously refer (either by parody or by reversal) to the types they created in their other films—Jean Arthur, Gloria Swanson, Bogart, Cooper, Curtis, Monroe. Although the method might seem to "brutalize" them (see Sarris, *The American Cinema*, p. 166), their great charm as people and stars not only aids Wilder's acid films, but reveals precisely why they are indeed stars.

But into this ironic sexual pattern Wilder interjects Marilyn Monroe—herself a cliché of female sensuality. And Marilyn plays the cliché completely—she is weak, soft, vulnerable, stupid, so often hurt that she carries a hip flask in her garter for comfort. She has a stereotypic weakness for saxophone players—who inevitably do her dirt. Her name—Sugar Cane (ironically, née Kowalcik)—reveals her sweetness. She is a thing, not a person, a soft pillow suitable only for supporting some male body. All of the characters in the film play parodies of themselves in other films, thereby exposing the inhumanity of the cliché.

Wilder then gives the Curtis-Monroe-Lemmon parody another twist. Both Joe and Jerry would like to have Sugar (and Wilder is vague about the way they'd like to have her). But both of them are masquerading as female stereotypes themselves, which makes the having of her rather difficult. They must remain in disguise to protect their lives. And in addition to the prying eyes of the mobsters, there is the suspicious scrutiny of "Sweet" Sue (leader of the orchestra, "Sweet Sue and Her Society Syncopaters"), who is as sweet as a scorpion. Despite the cliché implied by her label, "Sweet" Sue is the opposite female stereotype—mean, nasty, businesslike.

Predictably, Joe (Josephine) gets farther with Sugar than Jerry does, for he is the appropriate sexual type for a Sugar. And he plays the saxophone. But in order to possess all of Sugar's sweetness, Joe needs to get out of his female disguise. So he adopts a second disguise—another male stereotype. He pretends to be a millionaire yachtsman, a society snob with horn-rimmed glasses—the ideal of any lady named Kowalcik. He affects an English accent that sounds exactly like Cary Grant's. In fact, he tries to be Cary Grant (another cliché of male desirability). In response to this incredible accent, Daphne (Jerry) angrily snaps, "Nobody talks like that."

On "his" borrowed yacht, Cary-Josephine-Joe wines and dines Sugar, and Wilder executes yet another sexual reversal. Cary-Joe pretends to be suffering from a psychological trauma that makes him incapable of responding sexually to any woman. He spins an incredible story. The first time he kissed a girl, his first and only true love, she immediately fell to her death off the rim of the Grand Canyon (a delicious parody of Hollywood's depiction of the power of a mere kiss). Because of this traumatic memory, Cary-Joe is incapable of making love to Sugar; she must seduce him. (Yes, she is that dumb.) And so the male disguised as a female redisguised as a male plays the conventional female sexual role, as the female disguised as a love goddess redisguised as a female stereotype must play the conventional male sexual role and seduce him.

These sexual circles are reduced to the absurd by Jerry-Daphne's own love affair with Osgood Fielding (Joe E. Brown), the conventional dirty old rich man (yet another sexual stereotype). Daphne plays the vamp (complete with tango and a rose in the teeth), eliciting both a diamond bracelet and a marriage proposal (which, stereotypically, "go together like a horse and carriage") from her rich suitor. And when Daphne-Jerry works up the courage to confess her-his lie to Osgood (this confession follows Cary-Joe's obligatory confession to Sugar), the millionaire is not at all upset that his bride is a man. His answer, "Nobody's perfect," is perhaps the least conventional (although it plays on an obvious cliché) and most flexible human response in the film. Indeed this deliberately incongruous, inconclusive conclusion seems the most honest ending in all of Wilder. As in Sturges films, one wonders if Wilder's uplifting endings (A Foreign Affair, Sabrina, and The Apartment) are really consistent with the director's acid temperament and the human corruption he has depicted. Wilder, like so many of the comic iconoclasts who declare war on Hollywood's clichés, usually signs an uneasy truce for the final fade-out.

Beneath all the wonderful fun, Some Like It Hot implies that stereotypes hurt and kill. In a haunting sequence, Sugar-Marilyn sings, "I'm Through with Love." Although the song may be a parodic comment on the inevitable blues for a lost love, it is also genuinely moving and tender. Like Miss Monroe's whole performance, the song slices through the film's wonderful silliness with its own kind of unspoken, unmistakable appeal. That slicing—as well as the clever and complex silliness—is the very best of Billy Wilder.

Among the other contributors to the dialogue tradition are some directors whose comedies seem less distinctive, less personal, or less consistent than those discussed in detail. Leo McCarey was a masterful comic technician in the silent years with Hal Roach and in his early years at Paramount. Duck Soup (1933) and Six of a Kind (1934), in their unself-conscious unseriousness and control of comic timing, are masterful pieces of comic entertainment. Ruggles of Red Gap (1935), The Awful Truth (1937), and Going My Way (1944) seem the forced works of a comedian yearning for significance, McCarey striving to be Capra without the Capra feeling for human warmth and spontaneity, and without Capra's skill with dialogue—for McCarey seems more comfortable with physical business than with words. (McCarey's two primary additions to the script of Duck Soup were the mirror scene and the battle between Edgar Kennedy and Harpo as lemonade salesman and peanut vendor—both of which were essentially silent).[4] Obviously, stylish dialogue comedies require a stylish sense of dialogue.

George Cukor had that stylish sense. Cukor made so many entertaining dialogue comedies—Dinner at Eight (1933), The Philadelphia Story (1940), Adam's Rib (1949), Born Yesterday (1950), Pat and Mike (1952)—that it is hard to find anything wrong with him as a director of crackling talk and the comic conflict of temperament except that he is not so psychologically perceptive as Hawks, so clever as Lubitsch, so parodic as Sturges, or so complex with structure as Wilder. Among the many other entertaining films in this dialogue tradition are Vincente Minnelli's *Father of the Bride* (1950) and *The Reluctant Debutante* (1958); George Stevens' *Woman of the Year* (1942) and *The More the Merrier* (1943); Gregory LaCava's *My Man Godfrey* (1936); Harry D'Arrast's *Laughter* (1930) and *Topaze* (1933); and George Axelrod's *Lord Love a Duck* (1966).

Since the mid-1960s, with the demise of dialogue and the rise of the cinematic experiential metaphor, the comic-dialogue tradition has been sustained by cinematic translations of Broadway comedies or films by directors (or authors) of Broadway comedies. Mike Nichols' *The Graduate* (1968) and *Carnal Knowledge* (1971) both exhibit strong control over comic human interaction and dialogue and much less consistent control over the cinema's means of recording them (which accounts for the disaster of *Catch-22*, much more ambitious cinematically and, unfortunately, much less dependent on extended scenes of interaction between two people in a room). Alan Arkin and Jules Feiffer's *Little Murders* (1971), which seems better suited to the claustrophobia and unity of place of the stage; Woody Allen's *Play It Again, Sam* (1972), which suits the film medium fairly well since it revolves around a film freak's cinematic fantasies; and the filmed versions of Neil Simon's plays, which are as close to television situation comedy as Broadway and the movies can get, all represent the remnants of a once vigorous dialogue tradition.

CHAPTER 17

The Clown Tradition

T HE second major tradition of sound comedy is the film built around the physical, facial, and verbal assets of the central comic performer or performers. The few film clowns to surmount the limitations of talk were those with a unique and personal relationship to the very use of talk and synchronized sound, to the manipulation of whole film structures, and to the very formulas and conventions of picture-making.

The sound-clown comedy is a hybrid form, combining elements of radio, vaudeville, the nightclub, and, later, television. Many of the most commercially successful sound comedians were equally successful in these other forms—the Marx Brothers, W. C. Fields, Mae West, Abbott and Costello, Red Skelton, Danny Kaye, Martin and Lewis, and Bob Hope. But American sound comedians have been more successful at creating comic character than at combining that character with a unique comic structure and a unique approach to creating comedy *through cinema* W. C. Fields was the same muttering misanthropist in films, on the stage, or when he made a guest appearance on the Bergen-McCarthy radio show. His funniest lines can be appreciated by listening to a phonograph record. The Marx Brothers tested their sketches on the vaudeville stage with a live audience before shooting for the inanimate machine. And most clowns were not even so successful as Fields and the Marx Brothers in using the cinema uniquely.

As an extreme example of the distance between comic character and a cinematic comic conception, take George Burns and Gracie Allen. Burns and Allen were (in my opinion) hilariously funny. But they were equally funny—and in exactly the same way—in vaudeville, on the radio, on television, and in films. No one thinks of Burns and Allen as film comedians, although they made almost as many films as the Marx Brothers and were brilliantly delightful in several of them—particularly *Six of a Kind* (1934) and *Damsel in Distress* (1937). Burns and Allen (and Hope, Skelton, Abbott and Costello, Lucille Ball, Joan Davis, etc.) were comedians in films, not masters of the comic-film form. The less important sound clowns often succeeded at creating comic characters, but not at creating unique sound-film structures in which those characters could cavort.

The Anarchists

The Marx Brothers and W. C. Fields were the legitimate descendants of the American iconoclastic tradition. Like John Bunny, Mack Sennett, Chaplin, and Keaton, these comics made films that ridiculed the sweet, the nice, the polite, the acceptable. Significantly, their films ridiculed other films as well as social customs. As the silent filmmakers had earlier discovered, to parody "serious" films was also to parody the values on which those films (and society as a whole) were built. Although more famed as masters of comic performance, the Marx Brothers and W. C. Fields performed in films with very personal and individual conceptions. Lacking complete control over their material (and, later in their careers, not even interested in such control), the Marx Brothers were dependent on their writers. And at Paramount those writers gave them very surprising, iconoclastic things to do. The Marx Brothers films were far closer in both spirit and method to the dialogue comedies than to the later funnyman sound films. Fields, on the other hand, gained complete control over the writing of his own films at Universal. And their deliberate sloppiness was Fields' own kind of statement about the pretentious gentility of the well-made film.

The Marx Brothers' three best films at Paramount—*Monkey Business* (1931), *Horsefeathers* (1932), and *Duck Soup* (1933)—all hurl comic mud at the gleaming marble pillars of the American temple. The target of *Monkey Business* is money and high society; the rich society snobs merely happen to be gangsters who made their money from bootlegging. The target of *Horsefeathers* is the university; knowledge and the pursuit of it are reduced to thievery, bribery, lechery, and foolishness. The target of *Duck Soup* is democracy and government itself; grandiose political ceremonies, governmental bodies, international diplomacy, the law courts, and war are reduced to the absurd. All three films also parody popular "serious" genres—gangster films, college films, and romantic-European-kingdom films. The implication of this spoofing is that the sanctified institution is as hollow and dead as the cinematic cliché; the breezy, chaotic, revolutionary activities of the comic anarchists give society's respectable calcifications a much-deserved comeuppance.

The Marx Brothers could get away with subversion because of their sheer madness. The brothers, like Ben Turpin in the silents, were pure loons, creatures from some other world, and this distance from reality gave them powerful privileges. To sustain a full-length film (the parodic silents with loons like Turpin and Snub Pollard were purposely shorts), the Marx Brothers' pictures capitalized on diversity. Each of the brothers had his distinct comic style—Groucho's brazenly nasty double-talk, Chico's artfully stupid malapropisms, Harpo's startling physical horseplay. Zeppo added a fourth dimension in the Paramounts as the cliché of the straight man and juvenile, the bland, wooden espouser of sentiments that seem to exist only in the world of the sound stage. The Marx Brothers' Paramounts added up these four kinds of human comedy—plus musical numbers (some parodic, some not), plus the central parodic idea of the films, plus the individual pieces of intellectual and visual parody. They overcame the sound film's limitations on the single comic performer through multiplicity and addition rather than unity.

The Marx Brothers also overcame the problem of the talkies by revealing individual relationships to talk. Groucho talks so much, so rapidly, and so belligerently that talk becomes a kind of weapon. He shoots word bullets at his listeners, rendering them (and the audience) helpless, gasping for breath, trying to grab hold of some argument long enough to make sense of it. But before anyone can grab a verbal handle, Groucho has already moved on to some other topic and implication that seems to follow from his previous one—but doesn't. Groucho's ceaseless talk leads the listener in intellectual circles, swallowing us in a verbal maze, eventually depositing us back at the starting point without knowing where we have been or how we got there. Groucho's "logic" is really the manipulation of pun, homonym, and equivocation. He substitutes the quantity of sound and the illusion of rational connection for the theoretical purpose of talk —logical communication.

Chico's relationship to talk also substitutes sound for sense and the appearance of meaning for meaning. To Chico, "viaduct" sounds like "why a duck," "wire fence" like "why a fence," "shortcut" like "short cake," "sanity clause" like "Santa Claus," "dollars" like "Dallas," "taxes" like "Texas." He alone can puncture Groucho's verbal spirals by stopping the speeding train of words and forcing Groucho to respond to his own erroneous intrusions. Groucho cannot get away with his coy substitution of sound for sense when Chico makes different (but similar) sounds out of the key terms in Groucho's verbal web. Chico's absurd accent (this Italian burlesque would be considered very impolite by later standards) makes him hear Groucho's words as if he, the Italian who speaks pidgin English, were speaking them.

The substitution of sound for sense reaches its perfection in Harpo, who makes only sounds. Harpo substitutes whistling and beeps on his horn for talk. Ironically, he communicates in the films as well as anybody. He communicates especially well with Chico, who understands Harpo better than Groucho does. Chico continually interprets Harpo's noises for Groucho. The irony that a bumbling foreign speaker renders a mute clown's honks, beeps, and whistles into English so it can be understood by the supreme verbal gymnast plays a role in every Marx Brothers film.

Harpo also substitutes the language of the body for speech. In this system of communication, Harpo uses two powerful allies—props and mime. He gives the password ("swordfish") that admits him to a speakeasy by pulling a swordfish out of his pocket. He impersonates Maurice Chevalier by miming a Chevalier song to a phonograph record, produced out of his coat especially for the occasion. Or he orders a shot of Scotch in the speakeasy by snapping into a Highland fling. In these early talkies, talk became one of the comic subjects of the films as well as one of the primary comic devices. As in the early Chaplin sound films, the Marx Brothers made talk an ally simply by treating it so specially.

Sex and love are also subjects of these films. In an era of glamorized or purified sexuality, the Marx Brothers said something about both clichés. Groucho carries most of the comic love interest in the films, and his love takes two different shapes, depending on whether the object of his affections is shaped like Margaret Dumont or Thelma Todd. Margaret Dumont—fat, matronly, but rich—is one kind of sexual cliché, the lady whom Groucho plans to use. He wants to take her for her money. Unfortunately, he also has to take her along with her money. And so Groucho inevitably tries to romance her, using the poetic verbal clichés of love as his bait. But in spinning his romantic web, Groucho can never get away from his habit of using words as weapons. In their first film together (*Cocoanuts*, 1929), Groucho sets the pattern: "I can see you tonight. You and the moon. You wear a necktie so I'll know you." Why does the rich matron put up with so much abuse? Perhaps the fact that this question has no sensible answer is one more element in the film's parody.

Thelma Todd, on the other hand, is the sexual siren—blonde, curvaceous, young, pretty, and no purer than she ought to be. When Groucho romances her, his object is more pleasure than business. They dance the tango in Thelma's stateroom in *Monkey Business*. In fact, they dance it on her bed. And in *Horsefeathers* Thelma plays a parody of blonde sexuality in general and Jean Harlow specifically—including the famed beauty spot (which wanders from cheek to cheek and is inconsistently present from take to take). In this film, Thelma pulls the reversal on Groucho;

she pretends to romance him, but is really intent on using her sexuality to get something away from him. In a specific parody of Harlow in *Dinner at Eight,* Todd begs Groucho to let her see the "secret signals" for the big football game, using Harlow's baby talk and baby whine as her means of turning sex into tool.

But Groucho is not one to be taken in by romantic drivel. As they glide along in a canoe (Thelma rows, Groucho merely sits and plays his uku-lele), he listens to Thelma's baby talk, glances at a fake-looking duck idyllically swimming beside the canoe, and asks: "Did that come out of you or the duck?" When she continues with her baby talk, he responds in the same language: How would she wike him to push his big foot wight down her widdle thwoat? So much for sex symbols and romance.

Harpo also reduces sexuality to the absurd. Where Groucho's seductive-ness (such as it is) takes the form of talk, Harpo is much less subtle. He simply chases and grabs, wrapping his arms around whatever attractive lady happens to pass. He is pure satyr. He makes no pretenses about his drives or his intentions, for he is the man of nature. He eats anything—buttons, telephones, pencils, any of society's tools or machines. He drinks ink. And what he doesn't eat, he destroys. He spends most of his time in *Duck Soup* with a pair of scissors, cutting people's clothing to shreds. His special target is that symbol of propriety, the necktie. And nothing so dis-arms Harpo's opponents as his constant urge to press his stomach against theirs or to hook his knee around their hands and arms. This intimate physical contact is violently antisocial, violating social codes of distance, propriety, and masculinity.

A key question about the Marx Brothers films is exactly how much of them the brothers conceived. When Groucho sings "Whatever It Is, I'm Against It" in *Horsefeathers,* he concretely summarizes the social atti-tudes of the films. But was it the brothers, the film's writers (Bert Kalmar, Harry Ruby, S. J. Perelman, and Will B. Johnstone), the director (Nor-man Z. McLeod), or the iconoclastic producer (Herman J. Mankiewicz) who decided to turn the line of professors sitting behind Groucho during his song into the chorus line of a minstrel show? Whose idea was it to build the scene in the "widow's" apartment—she is a loose, unprincipled seductress—around the deliveries of the "iceman," with the sexual impli-cations of that term? Whose idea was it to turn the two rival colleges into those intellectual colleague-rivals, Darwin and Huxley? And whose idea was it to end the film with the absurdity of all three Marx Brothers mar-rying the widow? Were the Marx Brothers aware of the fact that every self-respecting comedy ends with a marriage and every movie "widow" ends with either marriage or tuberculosis?

Duck Soup is even more striking in the thoroughness of its conception —again written by Kalmar and Ruby, produced by Mankiewicz, and di-rected by Leo McCarey in his pre-self-conscious salad days. Every action in the plot is a burlesque of some important governmental function—selecting leaders, collecting taxes, spying, enforcing the law, carrying on diplomatic relations with other countries, making war. The film climaxes when Sylvania declares war on Freedonia ("the land of the free") for some absurd breach of etiquette (a comment on society's worship of honor and propriety as well as the enormous effects of diplomatic trifles). The immense war that follows is a multilevel parody: of musical styles, using operetta, jazz, spirituals, banjo plucking, and the square dance; of the way movies, plays, and musical comedies turn the serious business of war into operetta fare (for example, M-G-M's *Mata Hari*, Romberg's *The Desert Song*); of military costumes, uniforms, and protocol. And, finally, it is a specific parody of American history and its wars—Paul Revere, the Spirit of '76, the Civil War, World War I. But beneath the parody is the reduction of the solemn events of American history to total nonsense.

At the end of the film (and war), after Freedonia achieves a miraculous —and inane—victory, Mrs. Teasdale (Margaret Dumont) bursts into a stirring soprano chorus of "Hail, Freedonia." The Marx Brothers pelt her with fruit. The business of all the mature Marx Brothers Paramounts is this throwing of fruit at respectable, sanctified social institutions. Although the brothers threw the fruit, they were dependent on their writers for picking both the kinds of fruit and the targets at which they would be thrown.

This dependence became clear after they left Paramount. The first of their M-G-M films, *A Night at the Opera* (1935), retained the social assumptions of the earlier films (for the opera is a center of social snobbery, a pure luxury that collects money from the rich to provide "entertainment" for the rich). It also gave the Marx Brothers the only accomplished social satirists to write for them after they left Paramount, George S. Kaufman and Morrie Ryskind. But after this film, the Marx Brothers films got steadily worse. And even *A Night at the Opera* shows signs of the collapse.

First, the M-G-M films lost Zeppo, who got tired of saying "Yes." Zeppo was a parody of the romantic juvenile—too schleppy, too nasal, and too wooden to be taken seriously. Instead, M-G-M gave us real romantic juveniles (such as Allan Jones, Kenny Baker, and Tony Martin) and ingenues (such as Kitty Carlisle and Maureen O'Sullivan). In addition to the parodic plot, the M-G-M films offered a lengthy romantic plot that was to be taken seriously (or at least to be taken). Second, M-G-M emasculated Harpo, turning him into a cute, childlike imp who honks rather than a lecherous, asocial man of nature who grabs and unmasks. M-G-M kept the angelic pixy and deleted the brash vulgarity and blatant sexuality. He became a child-man rather than a natural man. Harpo had always been more at home with children than with adults in the Paramounts—with his pet frog and at the Punch-and-Judy show in *Monkey*

Business, with the horse and dogs of *Horsefeathers.* He even sleeps with a horse in *Duck Soup.* At M-G-M his relationship to animals became a conventional one (what could be a more standardized relationship than horse and jockey in *A Day at the Races?*) rather than a bizarre and irrational kinship between natural man and other creatures. The result was the relegation of Harpo from the equal rank he shared with Chico and Groucho in the Paramounts to third place.

Then M-G-M gradually began deleting the social centers of the films and building them around neutral locations—a Florida sanitarium and race track (still vaguely related to the world of the rich) in *A Day at the Races* (1937), a circus in *At the Circus* (1939), the wild West in *Go West* (1940), and a department store in *The Big Store* (1941). To buttress the films' weakening satire, M-G-M added more and longer production numbers. The lavish production number of *A Night at the Opera,* "Co Si Co Sa," in which alleged Italian immigrants, elegantly costumed in "quaint" Tyrolean outfits, sing and dance, mushroomed into Tony Martin's singing the bombastic "Tenement Symphony" in *The Big Store,* backed by a sea of cherubic children's Caucasian faces allegedly representing New York's melting pot. The all-white perfection of *The Big Store*'s chorus was perhaps a variation on the equally ludicrous all-black one of "All God's Chillun Got Rhythm" in *A Day at the Races.*

M-G-M also sought motivation for the obligatory piano and harp solos.* The Paramount films either did the numbers without apology or motivation (Groucho even invites the audience to go out for a smoke during the piano solo in *Horsefeathers*), or omitted them altogether (*Duck Soup*). The only reason for Harpo's playing the harp is that he is—at least partly —an angel. But M-G-M tried to make these intrusions logical—and fancy (for example, the elaborate mirror effects during Harpo's solo in *The Big Store*). The proportion of this non-comic drivel steadily increased in the M-G-M films, climbing close to half the film's screen time. Although one might apply the aesthetic of the vaudeville or variety show to the M-G-M films—some boring musical numbers alternating with delightful comic talk and business—no successful variety show could contain so many dead spots.

M-G-M then built each of the plots of the films up to a frantic, acrobatic chase, capitalizing on the virtuosity of doubles and the cameraman rather than on the comedy of the Marxes themselves. The climaxes of the Paramount films—the absurdly long fistfight while Groucho serves as ringside announcer in *Monkey Business,* the daffy football game that also parodies *Ben-Hur* in *Horsefeathers,* the zany war parody in *Duck Soup*— are perfect Marx Brothers endings because they don't really end anything.

---

* Motivation was a key concept for Thalberg and M-G-M. They reasoned that women did not like zany, unmotivated comedies—and that women were the key to box-office success. See Joe Adamson, *Groucho, Harpo, Chico, and Sometimes Zeppo.*

They are deliberately sloppy contrivances to finish a film that has no logical finish and that was not really going anywhere anyway. The chaotic incongruity of the Paramount endings was in perfect harmony with the lunatic comedy of the Marxes. Once M-G-M decided that Marx Brothers comedy needed logic and motivation, what could be more logical than to end this process with the predictable tricks of a chase?

Ironically, one can see the M-G-M additions to the Marx Brothers' films as more "cinematic" than the talk and business of Groucho, Chico, and Harpo—whose routines were descendants of the stage. But who would prefer the "cinematic" "Co Si Co Sa" to the brilliant "party of the first part" dialogue routine of *A Night at the Opera,* or the more "cinematic" "All God's Chillun Got Rhythm" to the "Tootsie Fruitsie Ice Cream" routine of *A Day at the Races?* The Paramount films produced much better comic cinema by sticking with the qualities of the clowns rather than interjecting the "cinematic" splash of music, costumes, dance, chases, and decor.

For the brilliance of the Marx Brothers' comedy had much more to do with their essential comic spirit than their use of cinema. More than any other comedians of the sound era, the Marx Brothers were descendants of the most ancient ribald comedy, the violent bawdiness built around Priapus and his mammoth tool. Priapus could use his huge instrument in two ways: he could stick it into someone, or he could smash someone over the head with it. Rape and destruction. The Marx Brothers were thoroughly destructive; they broke as many fancy objects and fancy people (who had inhumanly turned themselves into objects) as possible. And for the more attractive objects, there were Groucho's leers and Harpo's gropes. The interrelation of sexuality and iconoclasm in the Marx Brothers' Paramount films is a constant—and constantly unspoken—source of all the effects that follow.

And so is the unity of the Priapian clowns and their vicariously participating producer, writers, and directors. The men who wrote the scripts and controlled the camera enjoyed the same gleeful, violent destructiveness as the clowns in front of the camera. The Marxes' Paramount writers and producer not only enjoyed ripping polite social institutions and assumptions to shreds; they also enjoyed destroying the very conventions of their craft and the aesthetics of their employers, creating films with deliberately irrelevant plot twists, incongruous sight gags, inconclusive conclusions, red herrings, faceless and forgettable supporting players (as in Sennett films, all people but the Marxes are reduced to inanimate things), human behavior that is absurdly contrived, incredible, and functionless. And the two skillful directors of the three best films simply allowed the camera to capture the rowdy and rebellious fun. Artfulness would have betrayed the joyous contempt for art of both the writers and the brothers. But this cinematic artlessness had to be competently artless, for the first two Paramounts (*Cocoanuts,* 1929; *Animal Crackers,* 1930) were so leadenly

stagey, clumsily paced, and cinematically incompetent that the artlessness
was merely unintentional sloppiness rather than a vicious and intentional
assault on the cinema's pretensions to art.

At M-G-M the Marx Brothers were smoothed and polished and "artisti-
cized" and "cinematicized," and, essentially, emasculated. Priapus lost
more and more of his tool—both on camera and behind it. The brothers
were no longer bawdy, no longer vulgar, no longer nasty, no longer the
foes of propriety, and, eventually, no longer funny. The fault was perhaps
not entirely M-G-M's.* The Marx Brothers' career at Paramount ended in
1933, the same year that iconoclasm, vulgarity, and anti-sentimentality suffered the effects of the Breen Code and the American yearning for a nicer,
better world. The M-G-M films were the Marx Brothers' attempt to enter
the world of gentility at least halfway. The result was something less than
half-good.

W. C. Fields also had two film careers, one of them at Paramount. But
for Fields, his later, post-Paramount career was freer and more consistent
with the spirit of the man himself. Only after Paramount dumped him
could Fields begin expanding his Priapian tool. At Paramount, Fields, like
the Marx Brothers, performed in comedies written by others, but he rarely
enjoyed the same quality and care of writing and production. Fields
starred in Paramount shorts and an occasional feature, but he was primarily a featured player at Paramount, dropping into dozens of other stars'
films to do a memorable bit that was usually better than the lamentable
rest of the picture.

In his films, Fields is a far more domesticated misanthrope than the
Marx Brothers. The brothers have no legal, social, or moral responsibilities
whatever; they are more like animals—as the animal titles of the Paramount films indicate—than people. But Fields frequently finds himself
with a wife, a daughter, or both, who depend on him for support. Confined by this domestic prison, Fields never keeps his opinion of his captors
a secret: first, he comments about them under his breath; second, he escapes to the masculine freedom of the local tavern; and third, he resorts to
direct assault. Where the Marx Brothers films comment on the grand
social institutions, the Fields films usually confine themselves to the family, where Fields himself is confined.

Like Groucho, whatever it was, Fields was against it. *The Fatal Glass
of Beer* (1933) burlesques sentimentality and Victorian morality. *The
Pharmacist* (1933), *It's a Gift* (1934), and *The Man on the Flying Trapeze* (1934) comically attack such elements of family life as the prim,
moralistic wife; the nagging mother-in-law; the sponging loafer of a
brother-in-law; the saccharine young love of the eldest daughter; and the

---

* The Marx Brothers were just as misused in R.K.O.'s dreadful *Room Service* (1938).
Talk about being at the mercy of a script!

cutesy, tomboyish pranks of the youngest daughter. In *The Pharmacist*, Fields straps his martini shaker to his little girl's pogo stick (the only sensible use for the floor-shaking toy); she cutely responds by eating the family's pet parrot. *The Pharmacist* and *It's a Gift* burlesque small-town Americana. In both films, Fields owns a little store that gets reduced to rubble. In *The Pharmacist*, he comments on the timidity of prissy women when shopping for certain "delicate" items in drugstores. Two old prunes insist on speaking solely to Fields' wife—just to ask for the ladies' room. In *It's a Gift*, he uses the most sacrosanct of figures, a helpless, blind old man, as the comic villain who destroys his general store. In *The Old-Fashioned Way* (1934), he boots Baby Leroy, who also causes him trouble in *It's a Gift*, in the seat of his Little Lord Fauntleroy velvet pants.

In the Paramounts, Fields plays characters who are dishonest, incompetent, or both. He is a crooked gambler in *Tillie and Gus* (1933) and *Mississippi* (1935), a crooked actor-manager in *The Old-Fashioned Way* and *Poppy* (1936). Fields' crook-conniver pictures are inevitably costume pictures, his florid clothing perfectly matching his florid rhetoric and mannerisms—and both the clothing and the rhetoric are equally effective camouflage for his essential selfishness and dishonesty. These costume roles that revolve around the theater are especially appropriate, for both the costumes and the situations are descendants of the Belasco theater and the Belasco era, where and when Fields first began trooping from town to town and stage to stage. And in that Victorian era of respectability and propriety, the actor was as unrespectable and unsavory a character as the gambler.

In most of Fields' other Paramounts, he plays a bungling and domesticated citizen in modern dress—a drunken sheriff in *Six of a Kind* (1934) who can't tell whether his pool cues are straight or bent; an incompetent merchant and husband in *It's a Gift*; in *The Man on the Flying Trapeze*, an inconsistent office worker whose amazing filing system defies anyone to master it since it also defies alphabetical order, and who prefers drinking "apple jack" in his cellar with burglars to sleeping with his own wife. In these domestic films, Fields' conventional clothing is a compromise with his florid actor-gambler self, just as the domestic role itself is a compromise (and a comically uncomfortable one) with his loner, antisocial self.

The remaining Fields Paramounts transport him to some never-never land where he plays bizarre roles—the crazy inventor of *International House* (1932); the denizen of Lewis Carroll's looking glass (*Alice in Wonderland*, 1933) and of Dickens' London (in M-G-M's *David Copperfield*, 1935)—the latter two guises closely related to his costume roles in 1890s America. And for pure fantasy, Fields plays the head of the government of Klopstokia in *Million Dollar Legs* (1932). Only in a mythical land where might makes right could Fields head a government—not because Fields is credible as a strong man (hangovers don't help lifting weights), but only because it would take a total inversion of American social values to put a Fields at the top of the social ladder.

But *Million Dollar Legs*, as funny as the film often is, clearly reveals Fields' problem at Paramount. It is an iconoclastic, parodic Paramount film, in the same spirit as *Duck Soup* (and with the same Mankiewicz spirit presiding over it), that is only peripherally a Fields film. The Marx Brothers swim at the center of their *Duck Soup*, but Fields only does calisthenics on the outskirts of Klopstokia. The film is far more interested in parody than in Fields: parody of government and the New Deal ("What this country needs is money"); of Marlene Dietrich and Greta Garbo films (its title evokes the Dietrich trademark; the spy, Mata Machree—Mata Hari plus Mother Machree—sings a Dietrich song in a key light and is known as "the woman no man can resist"); of Lubitsch pictures (the Klopstokian love song uses the melody of the title song of Lubitsch's *One Hour with You* of the same year, but its lyrics go, "Woof bloogle jig, woof bloogle jig jig"). *Million Dollar Legs* is really a Sennett picture (Sennett was on the Paramount lot at the time), complete with Sennett parodies of other films and stars, Sennett undercranking (to show the speedy antics of former Sennett clowns Andy Clyde and Ben Turpin), a Sennett director (Eddie Cline), and Sennett's use of footage of an actual event (the 1932 Olympic games in Los Angeles).

Only when he went from the major studio, Paramount, to the minor one, Universal, in 1939 did Fields acquire his freedom. Universal gave him almost complete independence to do what he wanted, just so it didn't cost very much. But money was never one of Fields' cinematic prerequisites. Within the informality and cheapness of the minor studio, Fields wrote his own scripts (under such pseudonyms as Otis Cribblecobbis and Mahatma Kane Jeeves) that crucially relied on informality and cheapness for their effects.

The Bank Dick (1940) is the culmination of Fields' studies of small-town, proper, moralistic Americana. As Egbert Sousé, Fields, like the character's own last name, is the town drunk masquerading as something respectable. Fields suffers the tortures of nasty mother-in-law; thin, acerbic wife; sweet adolescent daughter; and little brat daughter (who lovingly hurls such missiles as catsup bottles and rocks at Daddy's head). Rather than spend his time with this lovable group, the "dick" prefers the comforts of his favorite saloon, appropriately called "The Black Pussy." (That subtle obscenity could only have slipped past the censors because they didn't understand it.) By the end of the film, Sousé's luck has reaped the family incredible riches. They all move into a huge, posh house, the family transformed by money from WASP meanness into classy gentility. This transformation from orneriness to gentility is as bogus as their transformation from middle-class penury to gracious wealth. If the beginning of the film burlesques the propriety of the Protestant ethic, its ending burlesques the American Dream of happiness through wealth.

In addition, the film burlesques the notion of getting rich through human exertion. Sousé expends almost no effort at all. He merely bumps into his pot of gold. And this gold comes from several sources; he hits not one jackpot, but three! He gets a $10,000 movie contract and a $5,000 reward for capturing a bank robber, and is half-owner of the fabulously wealthy Beefsteak Mines, previously presumed worthless. The American success ethic has been reduced to the absurd. And, finally, Fields reduces movie plots and conventions to the absurd as well, for almost all the twists in the plot are red herrings, all the success falls upon Sousé for no coherent or credible reasons, and the film's structure wanders aimlessly from episode to episode, tied together at the end by an obligatory and irrelevant chase.

But Fields' film of the next year, *Never Give a Sucker an Even Break,* is an even stronger satire of Hollywood production values and a very clear indication that Fields saw the interrelationship of pretentious American social values and Hollywood movie values. *Never Give a Sucker an Even Break* may be the worst movie ever made—a judgment that Fields would probably take as a supreme compliment, since it was intended to be the worst movie ever made. According to legend, Fields wrote the script for this film on the back of an envelope while sitting on the toilet. Whether the story is true or not, it gives an accurate idea of the film's spirit.

Never Give a Sucker is a film about making films. Or rather, part of it is. Other parts are about nothing at all, for Fields has refused to make this film about any single, coherent thing. That would be too logical. Fields indicates his opinion of movie glamor in the film's first sequence, as he stands at the entrance of the Universal studios in front of a large poster of himself in *The Bank Dick.* Although many people stroll past both the poster and the star, no one recognizes him. Such is movie fame. From this starting point, the film runs off several irrelevancies—a confrontation between Fields and a nasty, buxom waitress in a greasy-spoon café; the cavorting of Butch and Buddy, two nasty Hollywood kiddies; the saccharine soprano singing of Gloria Jean, who indulges in her operatic trills and tra-la-las while extras in various costumes (for example, two Nazi Storm Troopers) "make crosses" in the background.*

After this miscellany, the film finally settles down to what appears to be its plot. Fields presents a story idea to the studio head, Franklin Pangborn. (Fields consistently uses Pangborn as Sturges did—the supreme example of prissy, snoopy, nasty propriety.) Although the pushy cleaning lady disrupts the story conference in Pangborn's office—another comment

* To "make a cross" is extra jargon for irrelevantly and randomly crossing back and forth in the background of a shot to give the impression of movement and depth.

on who really has the power and control in the movie business, or might as well have—the conference finally gets down to business. And what business!—an absurd film within a film set in an exotic, schmaltzy land named Russia (but Klopstokia or Freedonia would have done just as well), where Fields falls out of an airplane, chasing after an errant bottle of booze.

He falls miraculously into the ivory-tower mountain lair of Mrs. Hemaglobin, played in the typical Marx Brothers manner by Margaret Dumont. Fields toys with Hemaglobin's nubile, pretty, virginal, and naïve daughter (another Hollywood cliché) but decides in favor of the rich, ugly old mother. Meanwhile, the characters traipse around in absurd, "quaint" costumes and drink exotic native brew (for example, spiked goat's milk). When the action lags, Fields throws in Gloria Jean to sing a bit of operetta nonsense with the Russians, who, like all foreigners in Hollywood operettas, have nothing to do but sit around and sing.

As if this film pastiche weren't absurd enough, Fields ends the film with further irrelevancy. Pangborn fires Fields for conceiving such a rotten script. And then, for no reason at all, the film ends with a climactic, hairraising chase, rather similar to the one that ends *The Bank Dick*. When in doubt, throw in a chase—a good Hollywood maxim. When the chase eventually comes to an end, *Never Give a Sucker*, like the Sennett films, simply stops. (Both Fields and his director, Eddie Cline, had worked for Sennett.) The film never resolves any of its issues, but then it hasn't defined any to be resolved. In his contempt for film logic, in the deliberately sloppy, non sequitur construction, Fields ironically synthesized his view of life and his control of cinematic form. The form (or formlessness) of the film says what he believes, and what he believes creates that form.

It was especially appropriate for Fields to team up with his female counterpart in impropriety and unconventionality, Mae West, for *My Little Chickadee* (1940). Although the film might disappoint many who expect an apotheosis of comic fireworks from Fields' bouncing off Mae West—and vice versa—Fields' deliberate decision to use Mae in other ways than for ten reels of verbal sparring reveals his consciousness of his (and her) moral system as well as his attitude toward cinematic form. First, Fields purposely did not do the expected. He did not fill a whole film with his comments about Mae's body and her comments about his, because that would have been too predictable. Second, in making this parody of Western movies, Fields realized that a Mae West was an ally, not an opponent, in a world where good men convert open chaos to law and order and good women sit at home darning socks and cooking soup until the good man returns to the ranch.

The real antagonist of *My Little Chickadee* is Margaret Hamilton, fresh from playing the Wicked Witch in *The Wizard of Oz*. In *My Little Chickadee* she plays a much wickeder, witchier woman. For Margaret Hamilton embodies the very moralistic ideals that persecute sensualists like Mae West and con men like Fields. He can convert her with his florid rhetoric, one of the tools of his trade—the fancy, proper-sounding, multisyllabic words that for this lady of surfaces define the man of breeding and respectability. But Mae can only placate Hamilton's kind by getting married—for in Hamilton's mind, marriage is the ultimate panacea for sexual transgression. Mae simply uses the marriage as camouflage for her still-rampant sexual appetite, just as Fields uses the words to mask his selfishness.

The film's attitude toward marriage is at its center—just as marriage is at the center of respectable, bourgeois society. Fields knows that his marriage to Mae is a legal hoax. But she couldn't care less whether they are married or not. She never allows the marriage of pure convenience to interfere with her clandestine meetings with Black Bart. And marriage never gets in the way of Fields' crooked games of poker. (Remember John Bunny's *A Cure for Pokeritis?*) So Fields and Mae become allies in the film, married on the surface but going their own ways in private regardless of their theoretical, moral, and legal obligations. Marriage is not for the likes of either of them. Both are loners; both are antisocial (if the society includes more than one other). She continues her affair to "unmask" Black Bart. ("I like to see what I'm kissin'.") He continues playing poker. ("Is this a game of chance?" "Not the way I play it.") And the two show their complete spiritual unity by staying as far away from each other as possible.

Jacques Tati

As opposed to the Marx Brothers and W. C. Fields, who casually and unreflectingly drifted into their comic styles and their relationships to the film medium, Jacques Tati's comedy was the result of self-conscious study. Tati's study included not only the specific devices and styles of the great silent comedians, but also the theoretical means of integrating physical comedy with the fact of synchronized sound. Although Tati claims he owes his largest debt to Keaton,[1] his films reveal large doses of Chaplin as well. The Tati concoction might be analyzed into the Chaplin theme (the unfettered man of nature as opposed to the sterility, regularity, and routine of modern society), the Keaton use of the body (the single unit against a dwarfing environment), the corresponding Keaton use of the camera (reliance on the far shot), and the Chaplin principle of using sound in *City Lights* and *Modern Times* (musical motifs and contrapuntal noises rather than talk). In addition, Tati developed his own slow, quiet rhythm, his delicate sense of whimsy, his visual sense of angle and line, and his unmistakable hint of nostalgia for something valuable that is disappearing from the earth—just as the world of his teachers had disappeared.

The foes in all five Tati feature films are modernity, inhuman efficiency, deadening routine. In his first feature, *Jour de Fête* (1949), a rural post-man decides that his bicycle delivery route needs American efficiency. In the process of trying to turn himself into a speedy machine, François (Tati) merely turns himself into a menace. At the end of the film, François renounces his quest and joins a group of farmers raking hay: "If the Americans want speed, let them have it." Americanisms and Americaniza-tion play large roles in three of Tati's other four features. The modern factory, the dependence on the automobile, the automated house, the modern furniture and gadgets in *Mon Oncle* (1958) all show signs of the spread of American culture and American machines. The American tour-ists, the bureaucratic office building, the industrial exposition, and the pre-fabricated nightclub in *Playtime* (1967) also imply that the world is now run for the convenience of Americans, according to the assumptions of Americans, so as to make the most money from Americans.

Tati's most brutal portrait of American assumptions is *Traffic* (1971), in which the public-relations director for an automobile company is a cal-lous, obtuse American woman who assumes that the world functions for her convenience. In the course of the film, this lady has such relations with the public as racing illegally through foreign customs, ordering the Dutch police around, and causing a massive automobile collision. She accomplishes nothing from all this rushing and pushing except to change into as many different coordinated outfits as possible. Her insensitive re-duction of people to things keeps the automobile from ever arriving at the exposition—the goal of all her racing and shoving.

The routinization of *Mr. Hulot's Holiday* (1953) is much subtler—perhaps one of the reasons this film is Tati's best. The spirit of America and Americanism is not much present in this film. Britain and the British tourist play a much larger role. The bitter irony of *Mr. Hulot's Holiday* is that its people, British and French alike, spend 50 weeks a year working at their stifling, routine jobs so they can come to a tacky seaside hotel and continue the stifling, boring routine—eating on schedule, relaxing on schedule, sleeping and waking on schedule. For most of them the "holi-day" is merely a change of location, not of feelings, attitudes, or human responses. The Hôtel de la Plage is a kind of morgue.

Once Tati adopted his Mr. Hulot character—the name obviously echoes Chaplin's nickname in France, Charlot—he defined his attitude as both film actor and filmmaker toward the deadening sterility and mechaniza-tion he saw in the world about him. Where François tries to convert him-self into a machine without success, Mr. Hulot hardly seems aware that he is surrounded by a world of machines and mechanical people. Tati the director is aware of the machines and comments on their enveloping om-nipresence, but Hulot the character simply goes about his business (an-other Keaton similarity). In his business, his manners, his style of living, moving, responding, Hulot contrasts with the inhuman mechanisms without even realizing it.

In *Mr. Hulot's Holiday*, he is the unconventional tourist with the funny walk, the silly pirate costume for the *bal masqué*, the coughing old car, the strange (but overpowering) style of playing tennis, the noisy record player, the dirty shoes, and many other clumsy unconventionalities. He is unaware that he is unconventional, but the other tourists are terribly aware of (and terribly interested in) Hulot's unconventionality—as the film's running gag powerfully reveals. (The hotel windows suddenly fill with light each time Hulot does something disruptive.) Similarly, in *Playtime* Hulot merely wants to get a job or go to a nightclub, and in *Traffic* he merely wants to set up the automotive camper at an international automobile show.

Tati's most explicit contrast of Hulot's naturalness and the modern world's artificiality is *Mon Oncle*, but again Hulot is unaware of the points that the director is making. Hulot lives in the ramshackle old quarter of the town rather than in a modern suburb. He rides a bicycle instead of driving a car. He lives in an area of the city that is old, dirty, irregular in its architecture and street planning, full of dogs, garbage, children—and life. The modern section of the city is geometrically regular, antiseptically clean, dominated by machines that open cans and garage doors and windows, that cook meals at the touch of a button, and that service still other machines.

Significantly, the man who lives in that horrible modern house also owns a factory that manufactures plastics; his world is truly plastic. Hulot works at that same factory very incompetently. When he supervises the plastic piping, it comes out in bizarrely contorted shapes and colors. (The pipe is grotesquely beautiful rather than functional.) Hulot's young nephew prefers his uncle to his father because his uncle is alive and fun whereas his father is a dead machine.

Given this Tati conception, it follows that Hulot is much more passive and much less reflective than Buster or Charlie. Hulot doesn't try to make anything happen. He doesn't try to win anything, get anything, or stop anything. He simply exists as a sounding board for the rest of the activities in the film. Everything bounces off Hulot, but he doesn't bounce back or react in any way. The only bouncing he does is in his springy walk; he is seemingly not properly anchored to the earth. His pipe sticks from his mouth at an oblique angle, his raincoat is too short, his umbrella dangles limply at his side. He is too tall and gawky. He is somehow "off"—without knowing it. Hulot is far more passive and unresponsive than Keaton, the supposed model of stony imperviousness. He is so much himself, the natural man, that he doesn't even notice that the world has and wants nothing to do with him.

From such a premise, it follows that Tati as director must compensate for the intentional inactivity of Hulot; he must manipulate the comic detail and texture of the inhuman world surrounding Hulot so as to give the man's naturalness its significance. As a comic film director Tati's three great assets are his control of sound, his imaginative sight gags, and his brilliant composition—all inseparable. No director of sound comedies was more aware of the comic possibilities of sound and the comic integration of sound and picture. In Tati's first feature, as François gargles, Tati adds the noise of airplane propellers to the sound track. The idea is not only a funny surprise, but is also crucially related to the film's idea—the gap between men (gargling) and machines. Such comic ideas with sound continue throughout the films.

In *Mr. Hulot's Holiday*, Tati uses the screaming noises of train stations, the incomprehensible babble of train announcements over a nasal loudspeaker, the dull twang of the hotel's swinging dining-room door every time it opens, the forlorn putt-putt-putt of Hulot's little car (which parallels the forlorn tinkling bell on François' bicycle in the earlier film). In *Mon Oncle*, there is the cacophonous whir and drilling of machines, the gargling sounds of the water-spouting mechanical fish in the modern garden, and the dull, abrasive buzz of the garden gate every time someone pushes the electric button that opens it. (The buzzing gate parallels the twanging door in *Holiday*.) In *Playtime*, there is the sucking sound of the plastic and foam-rubber sofa; in *Traffic*, the syrupy, mechanical female voice over the public-address system at the automobile exhibition.

Tati's sense of sound also leads him to alternate noise and silence and to use musical motifs (another Chaplin device) that underscore the films' thematic contrasts. In *Mr. Hulot's Holiday*, Tati shatters the deadening silence of the resort with Hulot's deafening jazz music. The contrast parallels the contrast of the resort's dead routine with Hulot's exuberant vitality. In *Mon Oncle*, Tati uses jazz in a different way. Jazz and rhythmic percussion accompany the frenetic life in the modern suburb, particularly the nerve-jangling use of the automobile. (Tati uses jazz and percussion similarly in *Traffic*.) The musical *leitmotif* in the old quarter of *Mon Oncle* is a melodic, nostalgic *chanson*, of the type that a Piaf or a Patachou used to sing. Perhaps the most obvious sign of Tati's extraordinary control of sound is that only two of his films (*Jour de Fête* and *Mon Oncle*) use English subtitles, and *Mon Oncle* doesn't even need them (and uses very few). Tati did not make talkies.

Tati's eye is as imaginative as his ear. Extraordinary far shots dominate the films: the little bicycle weaving down winding roads in *Jour de Fête*; the train platforms in *Mr. Hulot's Holiday* as the tourists scamper from one to the other, trying to respond to the garbled announcements over the loudspeaker; the geometric cubicles in *Playtime*, which visually turn business offices into cages and people into rats in Skinner boxes; the cavernously empty exhibition hall in *Traffic*, with its invisible dividing wires that mysteriously trip the little ant-people who try to walk across it. In *Mon Oncle*, Tati also uses color to underline the film's contrast of nature and mechanization. For scenes in the modern suburb, Tati uses bland, neutral, lifeless colors—white, gray, beige—whereas the old quarter glows with warm, striking colors—brown, pink, green, orange.

But ultimately Tati's greatest talent is the power of his comic conception, not his mechanical and technical skills. *Mr. Hulot's Holiday* contains such brilliant comic ideas as a paint can that the tide pushes perfectly under Hulot's paint brush (without his knowing it) so he can paint his kayak; later that kayak snaps shut and appears to swallow Hulot, like the beak of some gigantic bird. When Hulot's car develops a flat, he pulls into a cemetery to change tires; the spare tire gets so covered with leaves that it is mistaken for a funeral wreath. Like Chaplin, Tati was a master of transposition, of turning one kind of object into another. In *Mon Oncle*, for another example, he turns a house into a huge face and its windows into two eyeballs, simply by making the owner and his wife look out of the round window frames. In *Traffic*, Tati conceives a visual-aural symphony of windshield wipers, a rhythmic series of cuts, punctuated by the sounds of wipers, as people drive their automobiles during a rainstorm. The personalities of the wipers (their speed, rhythm, sound, shape, direction) perfectly match the types of people driving the cars. This is yet another parallel between people and things—and a wonderfully clever one.

The quiet, subtle irony of *Traffic* is that Hulot works as an advertising artist for a company that manufactures automotive campers—machines that take people out into the world of nature without leaving the world of machines. The camper is full of marvelous gadgets. The horn detaches and becomes an electric shaver; the bumper becomes a barbecue grill; the pull of a cord inflates the back seat into a bed, where the campers can lie down and watch television in the woods. And, significantly, the TV program they watch is of the landing of Apollo 12 on the moon. Tati subtly emphasizes the artificiality of needing a machine to enjoy nature: the display booth for the camper at the international automobile exposition is a cardboard forest complete with tape-recorded sounds of chirping birds.

But Tati knows that this spread of industrialization is unstoppable. Significantly, the settings for *Mr. Hulot's Holiday*, *Playtime*, and *Traffic* are international. All nations share the same assumptions. Hulot's naïve spontaneity is a universal anachronism. This implication gives the Tati films their sense of regret and loss. At the end of *Mon Oncle*, Hulot's old quarter is being renovated. The dogs—those symbols of nature in the film—have no comfortable place to urinate. Even the sea and the forest, those last regions of uncorrupted nature—as *Mr. Hulot's Holiday* and *Traffic* show—have been corrupted by the routine and the machine.

But Tati makes his caustic points with great subtlety and delicate irony.

Like Hulot, the films flow by—with a spring, a lilt, a bounce. Tati neither proclaims nor exclaims; he simply presents his comic arguments and lets us draw our own conclusions. This restrained understatement often makes the second and third viewings of a Tati film seem richer and fuller than the first. The fertility of Tati's comic ideas, controlled by the flowing pace, turns the potentially predictable and obvious contrast of man and machine, nature and artifice, into something unique, surprising, tender, funny, and personal.

From the vantage point of 1978, Tati's most remarkable comic conception appears to be the film that seemed least funny, most enigmatic, and most disappointing when it first appeared. *Playtime* is Jacques Tati's least known and least commercially successful film; not distributed in America until 1973, six years after it was made, it met with a reception that was both cool and brief. The film is perhaps Tati's most ambitious conception, his most spectacular visual accomplishment, and his most subtle integration of physical comedy and cinema technique. Tati's other comedies tread a narrow path between two major comic traditions—the clown tradition (to which M. Hulot obviously belongs) and the ironic tradition (to which the paradoxical and complex structures, symbols, and situations of the films obviously belong). *Playtime* plays with this balance between the two by embracing the ironic tradition altogether, reducing the clown Hulot almost literally to a background figure. Much of the discomfort and disappointment caused by the film might well be traced to the frustration of waiting for Hulot to perform some act of clownish virtuosity or for Tati to execute some dazzling transposition of one kind of object into another—which he for once adamantly refuses to do.* Just as in Chaplin's *A Woman of Paris* or Woody Allen's *Interiors*, in *Playtime* the dominant clown removes his powerful presence—except that Tati removes Hulot as the focus of the film's action without removing him from the frame altogether.

In *Playtime*, Hulot's first entrance indicates his different function. He enters the frame from the right, far in the background of a very deep focus shot; he drops his umbrella (with a slight clatter) in the same long shot, picks it up (still the same deep shot), and walks back out of the frame to the right. Tati makes no cut to Hulot's facial or bodily actions or reactions to allow us to observe them more closely or centrally. His business seems merely a parenthetic footnote to a very long shot (in both time and space), in which everything seems merely a parenthetic footnote and nothing any more (or less) important than anything else. Many seeing *Playtime* for the first time miss this first entrance by Hulot completely. This is simply not the way that the central clown makes his entrance in the typical clown film

---

* Tati casually "throws away" some of the delightful transpositions late in the film—transposing a restaurant serving-window into a Napoleonic hat or a marble pillar into a map of Paris. He refuses to dwell on this kind of magical joke for more than a second or two, however. Part of the film's flavor is that everything seems "thrown away."

(think of Charlie confronting the automobile on the road in *The Tramp*, or strolling through the garbage in *The Kid*, or sleeping on the statue in *City Lights*). The clown comedy inevitably focuses attention on the central figure from the first moment he enters the frame. *Playtime* does not.

Tati's diminution of the clown's star status can also be seen in the fact that the film is packed with Hulot surrogates, lookalikes who wear the identical Hulot hat, pipe, raincoat, and umbrella and walk the bouncy Hulot walk. These surrogates either play pivotal roles in scenes or simply walk around as extras in the background of various shots, just as Hulot himself often does. Clown comedies carefully avoid using other figures who resemble the central clown, emphasizing his uniquely strange funniness. (Who else in a Fields, or Laurel and Hardy, or Marx Brothers, or Keaton, or Chaplin, or Woody Allen movie resembles the clown star?)

Why does Tati deliberately undercut the unique force and presence of the Hulot figure in *Playtime?* The reason is that *Playtime* is a comedy about the ordinary and everyday, not the bizarre and strange, a comedy of the mundane, not of the special. Whereas the unique clown figure inevitably converts the comic world itself into the strange and bizarre, the fact that there are so many Hulots implies how commonplace and ordinary the Hulot type and manner are. *Playtime* is a comedy about *look*ing at the everyday world (an intriguing subject for a film, at which all we do is look). More specifically, *Playtime* is about the potential magic and beauty that can still be found in the everyday, banal, and sterile modern world simply by looking at it.

The film begins with the premise that our times are indeed modern, that all the world looks alike, and that we have no choice but to live with skyscrapers, buses, airplanes, and automobiles. The Old Quarter of *Mon Oncle*, a charming anachronism in that earlier film, is gone altogether in this one. One can lament its passing, or one can satirize the ugliness and sterility of the new world that has replaced it. Tati had done both in earlier films and would return to these familiar themes in *Traffic*. Instead, *Playtime* asks if any possibility remains for magic, for beauty, for mystery in the world as it is now. Its answer is yes—if we take the time and the trouble to *look* for them. And looking for them, in this film, means looking at them —looking at the frame and the world within it and doing the work for ourselves, without the comments or cues of a dominantly central clown. Hence M. Hulot becomes merely one small object in this film's world and one more figure in its inevitably full and vast (originally 70 mm vast!) frame.

The film begins in the clouds, which appear under the opening credits. We do not know it at the time (this film uses what we do not know at the time as its dominant comedic and narrative device), but we sit in the position of the American tourists aboard the plane that is about to deposit them in Paris. Like those tourists, we members of the audience are being led from the skies in this first shot, from some never-never region of romantic expectation down to earth and its visual realities. If there is to be any beauty or romance in Paris (or anywhere else in the world, since all places in the world look like this one, according to the film's travel posters), it will have to be a beauty on earth, not in the skies.

The film's second image is of a modern skyscraper (we do not know at the time that it is the Orly Airport building), a geometric configuration of steel and glass, sharp angles, a perfect and gleaming rectangularity. The building proclaims itself as both now and new; at first glance it is unmistakably hard, cold, rigid, and sterile. But upon looking longer at the building, we see that its glass windows are alive with reflections of the very clouds we saw in the film's first image. The reflected clouds glow with the luminescent purple-rose color of dawn, underscored by the voices of a choir on the soundtrack that bring the film's romantic, musical theme to a crescendo. The building is simultaneously sterile and beautiful, hard and soft, still and moving, dead and alive.

Are the reflections of the clouds on the windows real, or are they merely superimposed in the laboratory, one of the magical tricks of cinema? The film repeatedly raises this question in its constantly recurring shots of various reflections on glass. The Eiffel Tower and Arc de Triomphe both appear briefly as fleeting reflections on glass doors—their only appearance in this film set in Paris (except as a painted mural in a café and a design on a silk handkerchief). Perhaps the film's most memorable reflection occurs in the final sequence, when the busload of tourists, reflected in a pane of glass that is opened and closed while being cleaned, appears to ride through the skies on a roller coaster (again recalling the opening image of flight and clouds).

Playtime's glass reflections are part of the film's consistent treatment of this essential component of modern life. Glass may be soulless, characterless, hard, and cold. But one can see magical things by looking on it, at it, or through it. Glass is a means, a medium, for seeing something else before, behind, or beyond itself. The movies themselves capture images through lenses made of glass. The camera lens is a window, and the shape of the cinema frame parallels the rectangular dimensions of the windows with which this film is so filled. The cinema makes magic with glass, enabling the audience of *Playtime* to see magic on glass. Hence, it does not matter if this film's magical reflections on windows are real reflections or trick processes of cinema (indeed, although they look natural, they are certainly tricks). They are pieces of visual magic in either event. Life and art, the world and the world filmed, fuse.

The film's first extended sequence takes place at the Paris airport. However, the filmmaker has again refused to let us know we are looking at an airport (by suppressing the obvious aid of the appropriately named "establishing shot"). We see no airplane in the clouds, nor do we see any sign on the modern building proclaiming its function. (Think of how many movies set in Paris begin with a stock shot of the Eiffel Tower!) Tati's comic game in the film's first major sequence is to deceive us into believing that we are looking at a hospital, not an airport. He feeds us such apparently reliable clues as two bouncily walking nuns (again, we do not know if there is one nun or two, if both exist or if one is really a reflection on glass), two people talking in hushed tones in some sort of waiting area, a military man carrying a gift-wrapped box, the sounds of bottles being wheeled and babies crying, the look of white uniforms and wheelchairs. Only after this shot (which lasts at least three minutes), when Tati cuts to a reverse angle, do we discover that things are the reverse of our expectations: the uniforms are those of stewardesses, not nurses, the woman apparently wheeling a wheelchair is in fact wheeling her suitcase, the man with the bottles is merely the lavatory attendant, and so forth. What we had inferred from the previous shot has been expanded or altered by additional information in the new shot (this is, after all, what adding one shot to another is in theory supposed to produce in cinema).

Tati spins this elaborate airport-hospital joke not merely by withholding essential information but by deliberately manipulating our expectations as an audience watching the opening sequence of a movie (yet another sense in which this film is as much a comic inquiry into filming the world as it is into the world it films). At the beginning of a film, knowing little about what will follow, an audience is eager to find out where it is and what is important, so it can play the mental game that allows the narrative to proceed. The filmmaker throws out clues, and the audience gobbles them up. But in this film, Tati cunningly throws out clues that he knows we will swallow; just as we begin to feel the satisfaction of knowing what we are looking at, Tati makes us spit those clues out and start over again. As a piece of comic exposition, the opening sequence is a warning that we must continue to look carefully at the remainder of the film or we will surely miss the unique comic meal that Tati has cooked up for us.

But even while Tati induces us to swallow the false clues, he warns us that our ordinary method of making inferences from movies will not do for this film. He feeds us our misinformation by shooting and editing the opening sequence in a very unusual and atypical way. The openings of movies inevitably focus down to a point of central concern for the film that is to follow. Their compositional and editing strategies pick out the significant from the peripheral, the foreground from the background, the stars from the extras. They quickly inform us about what part of the world the film will ask us to see. But *Playtime* asks us to see the world itself. It is therefore appropriate that the "star" of such a film make his entrance as an extra. Everyone in this movie turns out to be no more (and no less) important than anyone else. Everyone is an extra—because our visual world, the world as a visual phenomenon, is peopled by extras, not by stars.

The shots in the hospital-airport refuse to focus on anything, to pick out anyone or anything for us in the entire visual world. They are vast shots (well over one hundred feet deep), lengthily held (three minutes or more), with a contrapuntal balance of emphasis between deep and close. The eye of the viewer must explore the frame, doing the visual and conceptual work of picking and selecting the points of interest in each image.* Of course, the further joke of our mistaking the airport for a hospital is that it is not a total mistake. In the first sequence, the American tourists are "born" into the world of Paris and we, the viewers, are "born" into the visual and stylistic world of this film.

As we continue to watch this world-film, Tati progressively rewards us for the labor he has forced upon us. The film's colors, muted and neutrally grayish in the opening airport sequence, insistently threaten to invade the image, eventually erupting into spectacular primary brightness for the final carnival sequence. The hard, harsh lines, dominated almost exclusively by verticals and horizontals at perfect right angles in the airport sequence, collapse into geometric chaos in the nightclub sequence. The customers begin to enjoy themselves only when the restaurant's harsh right angles dissolve in disarray as the newly pasted together place becomes literally unglued. (Significantly, at the point of architectural dissolution, the film's music shifts from the frenetic cacophony of percussive jazz to the lilt of a French *chanson*—parallel to the musical motifs of *Mon Oncle*.) By the end of the film, the dominant shape is not the line but the circle, and even the tangle of a Paris traffic jam has been playfully transposed into a carnival carousel of circular color (again underscored by playful carnival music).

The film also sustains its circular visual motif structurally (a clear Chaplin echo), for the busload of tourists must return on the same bus, traveling the same expressway, to the same modern airport building where it was "born." But the bus returns at night, when the harsh lines of the city's architecture have been obliterated by darkness, transformed into a fairytale world of starlike illuminated windows, jewellike street lamps, and sparkling red automobile taillights, an apparent galaxy of glowing, floating light and color. Although the viewer and the tourists have come full circle, the journey has produced not geographical progress but the mental and visual revelation that the world, however geometric and sterile it may appear, is still full of play. Tati's film is a playtime because he plays with the audience's expectations about film (and film comedy), plays with the rigidly angular look of modern life, and plays with the spontaneously improvisatory ways that people themselves play to maintain their humanity in the midst of that life.

The radicalnesss of this visual-comic conception may well explain why it alienated or disappointed many who expected another clown comedy fea-

---

* *Playtime's* visual and editing style conforms as closely as any film's ever has to André Bazin's theoretical ideal. The viewer has been granted the visual freedom to gather the meaning and significance of every image for himself.

turing the pranks and pratfalls of M. Hulot. Although *Playtime* has begun to attract an academic following, it remains perhaps the most radical comic conception to have been attempted specifically for cinema as a visual medium, its humor and intelligence still many years ahead of the average filmgoer's ability to understand and appreciate.

The Problem of Jerry Lewis

The primary critical problem of Jerry Lewis is whether he should be taken seriously at all. Where American critics and audiences see him as the banal equal of, say, Abbott and Costello, European critics and audiences see him as at least the equal of Jacques Tati and the rival in comic imagination of Chaplin, Keaton, Langdon, and Lloyd. For the European critic, Lewis' comic strength is the comically accurate depiction of the American mentality—its brash, vulgar overzealousness. They see Americans' intellectual distaste for Lewis as a symptom of our discomfort at seeing such a nasty reflection of ourselves in Lewis' comic mirror. Favorable Lewis criticism is invariably psychological and sociological:

> Jerry Lewis exercises a strange and really disquieting fascination over the patrons of the cinema's darkened halls. . . . [H]e is the incarnation of all the average man's repressions (eroticism, sadism, masochism, hysteria, homosexuality, destructive violence). . . . This monster named Jerry fascinates us by the double game of attraction-repulsion. . . . Jerry Lewis is a pathological case. . . . [L]et us say no more than that Lewis seems to us to represent the lowest degree of physical, moral, and intellectual abasement to which a comic actor can descend.[2]

Such interesting psychoanalytic observations may be true but are not demonstrable, and are therefore irrefutable. However, since many serious people do indeed take Jerry Lewis seriously, he cannot be casually dismissed.

Jerry Lewis' primary failure is that he never discovered who he was. The great American clowns (and Tati as well, modeling Hulot in their image) defined themselves as particular kinds of human beings. From that definition stemmed every element in the great clown's world—his comic personality, his facial expressions, his costumes, his stunts, his sight gags, his handling of cinematic devices, and his view of human and social relationships. Jerry Lewis simply does shtick. He contrives gags—many of them good ones. But the gags do not flow from any human or personal center.

Although the characters he plays are consistently schlepps (with names like Melvin and Stanley), Lewis merely impersonates them; he does not define himself as one. While the Lewis character demonstrates how stupid he is, Lewis the creator and director insists on demonstrating how smart, imaginative, and clever he is—particularly in his self-consciously arty cam-

era angles and editing tricks. Where there is harmony in the distance between Chaplin the creater-director and Charlie the performer, Keaton and
Rollo-Johnny-Alfred-Willie, Tati and Hulot, Lewis unknowingly battles
with Stanley in an ironic war of mutual contradiction.

Of all the classic silent comedians, Lewis is closest to Harold Lloyd. Like
Lloyd's, Lewis' characterization is a deliberate contrivance imposed from
outside the essential personality. Like Lloyd, Lewis concentrates on gags
and gag sequences, not whole stories or the development of a unified comic
investigation. Like Lloyd, Lewis seems to say over and over again, look at
me, I'm funny; look at that, that's funny. Like Lloyd, Lewis regularly cuts
the clowning to give the character (and the audience) a little uplifting
moral lecture torn out of Polonius' hornbook.

But Lloyd gets away with his dishonesty more successfully. First, his
gag sequences are longer, fuller, funnier, and more carefully developed.
Second, he calls attention to his funniness rather quietly rather than screaming this assertion. Third, his moral homilies are unobtrusive literary clichés,
not self-righteous, heart- and gut-felt sermons.* Lloyd is more fortunate
with these homilies than Lewis, because in the silents the banality merely
flashes on a title card; it need not be uttered sincerely by a talking character. Fourth, Lloyd was more successful at controlling the editing rhythms
of individual sequences and whole films. Lewis' editing is often tricky
without producing cohesion. Fifth, Lloyd could manage a whole plot from
beginning to end.

Jerry Lewis might well have made brilliant two-reelers. He might even
have made brilliant features if he had first had the opportunity to make
two-reelers. He would necessarily have recognized (as Keaton did) that to
extend a film from 20 minutes to 90, the creator must do more than add
gags. The first 20 minutes of a Lewis film are often funny and interesting.
The comic premise of the film, the visual tricks and surprises, and the ex-
pository introduction of the central comic character and problem are often
so dazzling that the viewer wonders why Jerry Lewis has been so maligned.
By the end of the film he knows. Lewis is a master at exposition, at beginning, but he is incompetent at complicating and developing.

The Bellboy (1960), which is the first film Lewis directed himself, begins
with an interesting premise—a non-plot film about funny incidents in an
American hotel. It is a Sennett riffing film. But after the first few incidents,
we simply get more and more of the same kinds of gags. The Nutty Professor (1963) also begins with a great comic idea. A crazy, sexless scientist
discovers a drug that converts him into a suave, greasy, smooth stereotype
of sexuality and romance. But once the Jekyll-Hyde premise has been
comically stated, nothing develops to further the tension and schizophrenia.
(Dr. Jekyll and Mr. Hyde was a short novel; and the existence of the one

---

* Andrew Sarris' discussion of Lewis in The American Cinema (pp. 239–44) makes
the same point and is one of the most valuable essays in the book.

personality began to overwhelm that of the other). Lewis' plot degenerates into a series of wandering (and predictable) incidents. Many European critics see *The Nutty Professor* psychoanalytically, a comic study of the sexual schizophrenia in the American psyche: the sexless, Puritan surface that masks the lecherous, bestial urges beneath, and the impossibility of synthesizing the two. Unfortunately, Lewis' comic style, business, gags, and plot seem to have little to do with such a psychological theme. Lewis merely milks his double character for sexual gags. In psychoanalyzing *The Nutty Professor*, Europeans tend to psychoanalyze Americans (a rather clichéd and unflattering view of Americans, stemming from the European prejudice that we are a nation of vulgar, unreflecting, and romantic fools), instead of analyzing Jerry Lewis' comic technique and form.

The Patsy's (1964) brilliant premise is the problem of turning a clumsy bellboy into a great comedian. But rather than concentrating on the question of what comedy is and what makes a great comedian, the film wanders through superficial problems (buying the bellboy clothing and haircuts) and egomaniacal digressions (Lewis' desire to show he can do ballet, Chaplin mime, and pathos). *The Big Mouth* (1967) begins with a funny parody of a James Bond spy story and degenerates into incomprehensible (and ultimately unresolved) plot twists.

Lewis' failure to manage a plot is one not of mechanics but of insight, courage, and vision. *The Bellboy* is set in Miami's Fontainebleau Hotel, one of the monuments to American vulgarity in the city that vulgarity built. Lewis does not build a single gag on the assumption that the Fontainebleau may be vulgar, may be a waste of money on a very big, bad thing, may be inhuman in its ornate tastelessness. He does not imply that a single one of its customers might be spending money that could be more sensibly and richly spent. (There is the same reverence for the Hilton Hotel and Sea World in *The Big Mouth*.) The Fontainebleau is simply a place (with no moral, social, or financial implications) where funny things happen to bellboys, customers, and furniture.

What Lewis lacks is a point of view about that place. And point of view is precisely what produced Chaplin, Keaton, Tati, and the other great clowns. Whereas the Hôtel de la Plage actually becomes a character in *Mr. Hulot's Holiday*, the Hotel Fontainebleau is merely a backdrop in *The Bellboy*. By running off miscellaneous gags against such a vague backdrop, Lewis is doing exactly what Sennett did—but stretching the method to fill up a feature film. If Lewis' film does indeed mirror the vulgarity of the hotel, its patrons, and its employees (especially Lewis himself), it does so unconsciously and unintentionally. If it is a work of art that successfully depicts vulgarity, so is a picture postcard of the hotel itself.

The Patsy, on the other hand, seemingly cannot avoid a conscious discussion of values and the criteria for human success. After the death of a famous comedian, the members of his staff (writers, press agent, business manager, and so on) decide to stay together. They want to see if they can create a new comic star, turn a nobody into a comic somebody. And Stanley, of course, turns out to be the nobody. It would seem that Lewis could not avoid such questions as what makes a man funny, what is funny, and how can a man with a grain of raw talent refine that into a comic art. But Lewis does avoid these questions, and instead raises only one: How does a man become a comic star? Further, in answering that "how," Lewis stays with pure externals—buying him snappy clothes, teaching him to sing and dance, getting him guest appearances on television. At the end of the film, for no reason discernible from the movie, Stanley Belt becomes a big star.

Rather, there is one reason that Lewis tries to put over on us. Ina Balin, Stanley's press agent, tells him before his first press conference: "Be yourself. Honest and sincere." Stanley demonstrates his subsequent sincerity by laughing at Hedda Hopper's ridiculous hat—an umbrella. Hedda then compliments Stanley for his sincerity (the typical Lewis worship of the institutions of Hollywood culture). So Stanley Belt is a good comedian because he is sincere. But is he funny?

That Lewis should be so devoted to sincerity, the primary moral characteristic of all the schlepps he plays, is ironic, since there is something insincere and calculating about this sermonizing. Not content to be only a Mack Sennett who spins clever gags, laughs at pretentiousness and sanctimoniousness, and refuses to take anything in life seriously, Lewis wants to be Frank Capra, the sentimental, optimistic moralist, as well. Because he likes to think of himself as nice and warm (the Capra quality), Lewis refuses to be impolite (the Sennett specialty). And because he refuses to be impolite, he avoids saying anything about human and social relationships, for how can a meaningful relationship be defined without also defining its opposite? Great comedy is always impolite. Chaplin, Tati, Keaton, Langdon, Sennett, Fields, the Marx Brothers, Lubitsch, Renoir treat certain kinds of people very nastily. The Jerry Lewis films prove conclusively that great film comedy is not a matter of sight gags, pratfalls, funny faces, easy sentimentality, fancy camera angles, clever sound effects, or tricky cutting. The soul of comedy is the brain.

From Parody to Psychocomedy:
Woody Allen and Others

What knockabout physical farce was to American comic films of the 1910s, parody—particularly parody of other films—is to American comic films of the 1970s. And just as knockabout physical farce was the comic soil out of which America's most distinctive film clown of the first era, Charles Chaplin, grew, so has parody produced Woody Allen, America's most interesting new film comedian in forty years. What distinguished Chaplin from his able but less interesting competitors was precisely his ability to add character, thematic richness, emotional poignancy, and structural complexity to mere roughhouse. Similarly, what distinguishes Woody Allen is his ability to add character, thematic richness, a psychoanalytic examination of the modern temper, and a sociological analysis of our modern times to mere parody.

Parody is certainly not new to American films, its roots firmly planted in the comic-film past. Mack Sennett made parodies of Griffith melodramas while he was still working for Griffith at Biograph in 1911 and 1912. The decade of the 1920s was American film comedy's previous Golden Age of parody; the fast, funny, two-reel pastiches of Sennett and Hal Roach parodied the popular film hits of the day, while Ben Turpin and Will Rogers parodied its famous stars, such as Erich von Stroheim, Tom Mix, and Will S. Hart. Of the four major film comedians of the 1920s—Chaplin, Lloyd, Keaton, and Langdon—Buster Keaton had the strongest taste for parody, basing whole films on the plots and situations of other, serious, movies—the western, the Civil War romance, the backwoods feud, the Sherlock Holmes thriller, and so forth. *The Three Ages* was a deliberate parody of *Intolerance*, *The Playhouse* a deliberate parody of the egomania of Thomas Ince, and *The Frozen North* an equally deliberate parody of William S. Hart.

One clear difference between the parody of the 1970s and that of the 1920s is that the earlier parody travestied contemporary film hits and styles while today's travesties the films and styles of Hollywood Past.* In order to be funny, parody obviously requires a general audience familiarity with its sources, so that the comic variations that are being rung (and wrung) upon it can be understood, appreciated, and therefore enjoyed. One implication, then, of this difference between 1920s parody and today's is that contemporary films of fifty years ago possessed a general cultural power that films today lack.

Another implication is that today's audiences are conscious, in a way that earlier audiences were not, of film as an art form with a history. The self-consciousness of today's comic directors, who base their films on the classic works of the American film tradition, must be matched by the audience's consciousness of the same works and the same tradition. If the knockabout physical farce of the 1900s and 1910s was a social mirror of a rough-and-tumble, antipretentious, working-class audience, the intellectual parody of the 1970s is a social mirror of an audience that (rightly or wrongly) views itself as knowledgeable, aware, intellectual, and "hip."

* The one exception to this rule is *The Big Bus* (1976), a deliberate parody of contemporary disaster films.

A second major difference between the film parodies of the 1970s and those of the 1920s is that most of the earlier comedies were short films while all of today's are full-length feature films themselves. To extend a parody beyond the fifteen-minute limit causes severe problems for both comic artists and audience. By definition, a parody is not a new, original, interesting narrative in its own right, but an echo of a previous one. How long can one prolong an echo before it seems empty, boring, trivial, trite, silly, self-indulgent, and superficial? That question becomes the central problem to confront every maker of full-length parodic works, and his ability to answer it successfully determines the artistic and comic success of the result.

There are four ways that comic-film parodists have gone about their business of sustaining a full-length work.

The first is that a comic film can begin as a parody of some other plot or situation, but as it progresses it gradually absorbs the viewer in its own narrative, its own situations and characters, as if it were an original and exciting narrative in its own right. This method has a distinguished literary heritage—particularly in the comic novels of Henry Fielding. Although *Joseph Andrews* began as a deliberate parody of the sentimental excesses and moral purities of Samuel Richardson's *Pamela*, one can feel Fielding's creations seizing control of the author's imagination as he goes along, leaving the spirit of parody far behind by the time author and reader are midway into the work.

The most successful film manipulator of this comic method is Buster Keaton, who begins with a parodic premise and then works on us so successfully with his magnificently supple body, his awesome visual compositions, and his driving narrative rhythms that we hope as earnestly for his success and participate as vicariously in his experiences as if we were watching the real melodrama on which his parody is based. Precisely this ability allowed Keaton to expand from the two-reel form to the comic feature, and precisely this quality explains how a parody of a melodrama, like *The General*, and a genuine melodrama with wit and irony, like Hitchcock's *The 39 Steps*, can produce such similar responses. To begin by proclaiming the worthlessness and silliness of a narrative situation, announcing that it is not a "real" fiction but merely a copy of some other fiction, and then to entangle us emotionally in that narrative as it goes along is to perform a comic magic and mystery that few, other than a Keaton, could bring off.* Significantly, not one of the major parodists of the 1970s risks the attempt. Perhaps the only American film comedy since those of Keaton to succeed entirely at being simultaneously parodic and narratively exciting was Kubrick's *Dr. Strangelove;* though we consistently laugh at the film's burlesque of the military mentality, by its conclusion we are as emotionally entangled in its essential narrative questions (Will the Leper Colony suc-

* *The Black Bird* (1975) attempted to be both a parody of *The Maltese Falcon* and an engaging narrative in its own right—with questionable success at either.

ceed in dropping that bomb? And do we wish it to succeed or not?) as if it were *Seven Days in May.*

The second way of extending a parody beyond the fifteen-minute limit might be termed the method of multiplicity. Among the literary works to manipulate this method is Tom Stoppard's brilliantly clever *Travesties,* a play which weaves together extended parodies of Joyce's *Ulysses,* Wilde's *The Importance of Being Earnest,* the writing of Marx and Lenin, Dadaist poetry, and dozens of other literary milestones. Among recent comic films, the two written by Neil Simon and directed by Robert Moore, *Murder by Death* (1976) and *The Cheap Detective* (1978), also attempt to overcome the thinness of parodying a single work or genre by multiplying the subjects of parody. *Murder by Death* begins by parodying the situation of Agatha Christie's *Ten Little Indians* (and René Clair's *And Then There Were None,* 1945), into which it introduces parodies of six famous film detectives—the gruff, Humphrey Bogartish Sam Spade, the chic and ever-drinking Nick and Nora Charles, the epigrammatic Charlie Chan, the effete Hercule Poirot, and the cunning, ratiocinative old Miss Marple. The film seeks its laughs by gathering all six of these supersleuths into a single film (where they could never otherwise coexist), by parodying each of their individual styles, mannerisms, and personae, by engaging them in a contest of out-deducing and outsleuthing one another, and by building a plot that per-petually twists and resolves and reresolves unmercifully, each new deduction producing a solution and revelation that negates the one preceding it.

The Cheap Detective, on the other hand, attempts to multiply its in-terest by taking all the films of Humphrey Bogart (with a few non-Bogart detectives thrown in for good measure) as its parodic targets. The film squeezes its laughs from the audience recognition that we are exploring a universe composed of Bogart and Bogart-like movies: *Casablanca, The Maltese Falcon, The Big Sleep, Murder, My Sweet,* and *To Have and Have Not.* We wander among the different regions of a country that could be called Bogart, its narrative map linked by events, situations, and char-acters that, like the detectives of *Murder by Death,* could never otherwise coexist in the same film. The comic pleasure of such a film (for those who find it funny) is a highly intellectual and cognitive one, somewhat akin to the delight of a trivia game or nostalgia quiz—the pleasure of remem-bering and recognizing forgotten details while, at the same time, finding them in a new and surprising context. The response of those who take no pleasure from the film resembles that of those who are irritated by such games or quizzes: what is the profit or pleasure of working so hard to recall bits of data with no intrinsic interest or value except as pieces of esoteric junk? Although cramming a film full of different parodic morsels may be an attempt to escape the potential banality of parody, its danger is that it may accomplish precisely the opposite result—of confirming how thin, how fragile, and how banal a purely parodic work with no intrinsic content can be.

Mel Brooks's *High Anxiety* (1977) similarly explores a country called "Hitchcock," as we recognize snatches of *Spellbound, The Birds, Vertigo, Psycho, The Wrong Man,* and so forth. But the Brooks films seem generally richer and cleverer than the Simon-Moore comedies because their usual method is not that of multiplicity but what might be termed the method of anomalous surprise. This third parodic method usually sticks close to a single subject, but then surprisingly injects some character, situation, or event into the parodic narrative that makes absolutely no sense in that context, producing a devastating and delightful violation of audience expectations. In *High Anxiety,* for example, the "closet," sadomasochistic love scene between Dr. Montague (Harvey Korman) and Nurse Diesel (Cloris Leachman) has no specific or explicit analogue in any Hitchcock film (although it is a sly and brazen burlesque of the closeted sexual aberrations in any number of late Hitchcock films).

The method of filling a parody with anomalous surprises also has a long and distinguished literary heritage. One of its early prime examples is the Beaumont and Fletcher play *The Knight of the Burning Pestle* (1607), which parodies both *Don Quixote* specifically and the tradition of knight errantry in general by putting the knight (really a grocer's clerk) through a series of increasingly anomalous and unconnected adventures. In so far as Joyce's *Ulysses* is a parody of *The Odyssey,* it also adopts the method of anomalous surprise, disrupting the familiar epic material with the novelty of its verbal and stylistic pyrotechnics.

Many of the most effective and enduring film parodies have also introduced the anomalous surprise as a means of sustaining and propelling the parodic experience. In *Tillie's Punctured Romance* (1914), the first feature-length film comedy ever made in America, Mack Sennett sustained his parody of "country gal gets swindled by city slicker" by introducing such anomalies as fat harridan Marie Dressler in the role of the helpless country gal and runty Charlie Chaplin as the city slicker. He also introduces narrative situations (for example, a drunken dance by Tillie, looking like a dazed and crazed elephant, or a climactic chase by the incompetent Keystone Kops) which would destroy the serious version of the melodrama. The Marx Brothers parodies (particularly *Horsefeathers* and *Duck Soup*) also interjected the anomalous surprise (for example, Groucho's chorus line of professors in the former and the operetta pastiche of military pageantry in the latter). And W. C. Fields's *Never Give a Sucker an Even Break* succeeds at being a parody of moviemaking in general and of itself in particular by constructing itself as a purely illogical maze of perpetual anomalies. That these American comedies delighted and dazzled the more serious Surrealists and Dadaists of an earlier generation can be partially explained by their shared taste for the non sequitur.

The Mel Brooks parodies—*Blazing Saddles* (1974), *Young Frankenstein* (1974), *Silent Movie* (1976), and *High Anxiety*—also succeed with audiences because of their stunning violations of a familiar formula. In *Blazing Saddles*, as the cowboy rides across the vast visual vistas of the American West, so appropriate to the Western genre which is Brooks's parodic subject in this film, he trots past the Count Basie Orchestra, which has no business in either the desert or a Western. As the black prisoners on the chain gang work on the railroad (another inevitable Western motif), they sing the obligatory song to lift their spirits. Except their song is not of the expected "Go Down Moses" sort but Cole Porter's "I Get a Kick Out of You," perhaps the quintessence of white urbanity, and it is the gang of white prisoners who sings the Negro spiritual. Of course, Brooks's decision to build his parody of the Western around a black sheriff introduces a social and generic anomaly into the film's very premise. And when that same cowboy, at the apparent end of the narrative, rides off not into the sunset but onto the set of another movie—a Busby Berkeleyish, kaleidoscopic production number—Brooks delivers the final shock to our expectations. The original parodic premise of the film itself disintegrates, and we are no longer watching a parody of a specific movie genre, as we believed, but of moviemaking itself.

Musical numbers in the Mel Brooks films consistently produce the most delightful anomalies—just as they did in the Marx Brothers parodies. *Young Frankenstein* sticks fairly closely to parodying the familiar monster series from Universal—the deliberate use of black-and-white rather than color, the young doctor's refusal to acknowledge his destiny (and the pronunciation of his name), the humpbacked assistant (with the wandering hump), the unearthing of the cadaver, the substitution of the bad brain for the good one, the bubbling liquids and sizzling electrical apparatus in the laboratory, the monster with a child by a well, the monster with the blind man who befriends him, and so forth. But when *Young Frankenstein* reaches its musical numbers it takes a leap into wild illogic that justifies and excuses the more predictable moments of the parody.

The first of these is the top-hat-white-tie-and-cane duet between Dr. Frankenstein (Gene Wilder) and "The Creature" (Peter Boyle), Irving Berlin's "Puttin' on the Ritz." The number is a delightful non sequitur for a number of reasons. First, Brooks has injected a parodic motif from another species of movie into his Frankenstein movie, where it does not belong. The beast as performing artiste is a familiar motif of ape-creature films (both *King Kong* and *Mighty Joe Young* use it), as is the creature's running amok as a result of some fiery short-circuiting (either figurative or literal) during the performance. The duet's second irony is the allusion to Fred Astaire, who sang "Puttin' on the Ritz" in *Blue Skies* (1946) and a similar Irving Berlin song, "Top Hat, White Tie, and Tails," in the black-and-white *Top Hat* (1935). The anomaly of seeing the hulking monster as a suave, sleek Astaire (he is actually dancing the Ginger Rogers partner to Wilder's Astaire) takes this Frankenstein parody into some other, almost surreal dimension (as the Busby Berkeley number does in *Blazing Saddles*). The second musical moment that transcends the Frankenstein parody is a very brief one; Elizabeth (Madeline Kahn) sings the opening phrase of Victor Herbert's "Ah, Sweet Mystery of Life" when she discovers it as a result of experiencing the monster's huge "shvantzenstücker."

Similarly, *High Anxiety* transcends its Hitchcock parody when, for no reason of plot or character, the distinguished psychiatrist croons the film's title tune, à la Tony Bennett or Frank Sinatra, in the bar of San Francisco's Hyatt Hotel. Although the song may be a sly allusion to Doris Day's "Que Sera Sera" in Hitchcock's 1956 version of *The Man Who Knew Too Much*, it seems more a comment on Hollywood's general willingness to abandon the logic of plot and character if the star is one that the audience expects to sing (except we most certainly do not expect Mel Brooks to sing, either as Dr. Thorndyke or in any other guise!)

But in all these imaginative leaps that transcend the predictable level of pure parody (as the Simon-Moore movies do not), Brooks's allegiance is strictly to the stunt, the leap, the gag itself. Brooks, like Neil Simon (and Carl Reiner), served his apprenticeship as a gag writer for Sid Caesar's "Show of Shows" television program; for him, all comedy is purely diverting—in both senses of the word. It amuses us, and it diverts our eye from seeing beneath it.* In comparison, consider the moment near the end of Woody Allen's *Annie Hall* (1977), in which two young actors, clearly resembling Annie and Alvie Singer (although both of them are more conventionally pretty and less facially interesting than the originals), reenact in a rehearsal hall the farewell scene that we just witnessed between Annie and Alvie at the outdoor health-food restaurant. The comedian, Alvie, has taken the events and feelings of his personal inner life and objectified them by converting them into art, scripted lines that can be performed competently and professionally (although with some obvious decrease in the spiritual voltage) by hired strangers for an audience of strangers. This scene may be a metaphor for Allen's entire career, an attempt to channel his personal feelings and concerns into the form of comic works of art.

Woody's Allen's comedies are perhaps unique in demonstrating the fourth method of extending a parodic conception into a full-length work: by letting life into it. There are traces of the methods both of multiplicity and anomalous surprise in the Allen parodies—particularly the early films. *Take the Money and Run* (1968) combines parodies of *Bonnie and Clyde* (the bank robber and his moll), *In Cold Blood* (the psychological case history of a criminal mentality), *Cool Hand Luke* (working on the chain gang), *Modern*

---

* Stanley Donen's *Movie Movie* (1978), though no less committed to the surface than Brooks's films, is probably the film that Mel Brooks would want to make if he only could. Donen combines two methods of extending a parody to a full-length work—multiplicity and anomaly—with a genuine affection for the works he is parodying (Brooks seems to find the originals as silly as his parodies) and an ability to handle the camera and compose in film space that Mel Brooks never had (and never will).

Times (life in prison for an oddball), the *cinéma vérité* documentary (the "candid" interviews with Vergil's parents), newsreels, even travelogues ("Trout Fishing in Canada"). *Bananas* (1971) combines parodies of political-revolution and "banana republic" movies with pastiches of such diverse works as *Potemkin*, *Wild Strawberries*, and ABC television's "Wide World of Sports." But unlike Mel Brooks, who has moved in a circle from one subject of parody to the next in his career, Woody Allen has followed a straight line from the purely parodic toward the personal, psychological, and emotional, so that his two most recent films, *Annie Hall* and *Interiors* (1978), reveal few traces of the parodic at all.*

Woody Allen's relationship to the American film-clown tradition is more French than American, more like Jacques Tati's than that of the earlier American clowns. Like Tati, Allen is conscious of the aims and accomplishments of that rich tradition. Hence, his comedies are, like Tati's, very conscious of themselves as conceptions for the film medium. Like Tati's, they straddle the line between the anarchic clown tradition (which is primarily an American one) and the ironic tradition (which is primarily French).† The Allen comic persona seems almost a deliberate synthesis of the four major American clowns of the 1920s. Both Chaplin's Tramp and the Allen persona are loners and oddballs, somehow out of step with the ordinary race of social mortals, yet somehow superior as a result of their distance from that race. If the tramp displays a greater human sensitivity, Allen's persona displays a greater perceptivity, intellectual awareness, and psychological astuteness. Like Langdon, the Woody persona is a kind of child-man, an innocent cast adrift in a harsh, mean, adult world, which he is incapable of either combatting or comprehending. Like Keaton, Woody Allen has a taste for the absurd, for the bizarre gag, for parody, and for achieving the impossible. Also like Keaton, Allen plays a series of characters with different names and costumes—Vergil Starkwell (*Take the Money*), Fielding Melish (*Bananas*), Miles Monroe (*Sleeper*), Boris (*Love and Death*), Alvie Singer (*Annie Hall*)—who are all essentially the same. And like Harold Lloyd, the Woody Allen figure is inevitably a "glass character," his glasses being as important to his comic personality as they were to Lloyd's.

Although there are other spiritual links that seem strong (to Groucho's mouth, Harpo's synthesis of angel and satyr, Sennett's sense of speed), the link to Lloyd is stronger than may first appear. Like Harold, the Woody persona is very much the embodiment of the expectations and values of the age in which he lives. He is very much a reflection of the audience's

---

* *Interiors*, however, may be seen in part as combining parodies of Bergman's *Cries and Whispers* and American soap opera.

† Woody Allen's cinema consciousness can be likened to that of another French director, François Truffaut. Both Allen and Truffaut, being high-school dropouts, received their essential education in the movie house. In contrast, Chaplin, who never even reached high school to drop out of, received his essential education on the streets and on the stage. That is as revealing a contrast of the two comic generations as any.

tastes, opinions, aspirations, fears, sensibilities, and attitudes. Even the glasses of these two "glass characters" reveal the cultural differences between them. Lloyd's glasses increase the impression of his innocence and his energetic incompetence, Allen's of his intellectuality, his defensiveness, and his physical insignificance. If the cultural portrait that Allen paints of his era is a much stranger one than that of the optimistic, energetic Lloyd, it is because Allen's age is a much stranger one.

First of all, the Woody Allen figure is scrawny, unheroic, physically unimpressive and unappealing to a greater degree than any of the earlier film comedians except Harry Langdon. His physical slightness (another clear link to his comic ancestors) is matched, however, by a spiritual slightness that makes him quite unlike his ancestors. The Allen persona's psychological and emotional difficulties come almost entirely from within himself. He is the one who feels frightened, insecure, unsure of himself, suspicious of his own competence, aware of his physical inadequacies. Whereas Chaplin, Lloyd, and Keaton had tough insides that helped them in the fight against a world trying to make them feel small, the Allen persona cannot help agreeing that he is an insignificant nebbish and schlepp. The Allen character is a kind of emotional and psychological stutterer, a figure who cannot assert without wondering about the value of assertion, and whether he has the right to make an assertion, and if the assertion strikes others as foolish, and if there is anything to assert in the first place. It is not simply that the Allen character is unheroic or antiheroic (antiheroism has been an essential characteristic of all the major film comedians). Allen is such a spectacular combination of post-Freudian complexes and insecurities that the very notion of heroism and its opposite has no place in his world at all. Although the comic world is always full of pain for the central clown, in no one else's comedies is the pain so much the product of self-mortification.

This self-mortification, self-doubt, and self-consciousness inevitably lead Allen back to his parents, the typical point of Freudian departure. In *Take the Money and Run*, Allen's first film, Vergil's mother and father, disguised by fake glasses and plastic noses, unfeelingly reveal their hostile distance from their no-account son, in a parody of both documentary films and psychological-sociological probes for the childhood roots of adult criminality. The fake glasses and noses serve as the distancing devices that convert potential pathos into howling comedy. *Sleeper* reveals a much more spectacular piece of comic psychodrama when Miles passes out a playlet to be enacted by his friends at a dinner table. The scene depicts the grief, distress, and discomfort of that fateful Passover seder when Allen informed his parents that he was separating from his wife. The whining rage, the pushy insistence, the domineering pressure of his parents' responses reveal quite clearly the roots from which such a timid, insecure, unassertive man could spring. Yet Allen's brilliant comic distancing device in this scene is to assign the roles of the two parents to two supergoyim, Diane Keaton and John Beck. The two physically beautiful, young, non-Jewish actors read the part of the old, unbeautiful, Jewish parents, reproducing the Jewish accents and the phonetically correct pronunciations of the Yiddish words so diligently that they hopelessly and hilariously fail to capture the nuances of Jewish vocal inflections. As with the farewell scene played by the two young actors in *Annie Hall*, Allen here produces comedy from psychodrama by putting the painful words in the mouths of two anomalous faces.

A similar scene of psychodrama occurs at a dinner table in *Annie Hall* (the dinner table obviously provides Allen with the most painful memories of the most terrible family scenes).* Allen executes a lengthy comparison between the tasteful, airy, gracious (but also cold and dead) way that the gentile Halls dine in Minnesota and the cackling, nagging, noisy way that the Jewish Singers eat in Coney Island. Allen's brilliant use of the cinematic trick of split screen, which juxtaposes the two families within the same frame, accomplishes the comic distancing effect in this otherwise painful comparison. The self-conscious Alvie feels himself so much a freak at the Halls' table that he visually projects himself as a Hassidic Jew (complete with full beard, long sideburns, and black yarmulke), a concrete visual image which complexly projects Alvie's point of view of how the Halls must see him from their point of view (another gag based on self-mortification). Allen's ultimate examination of parental (particularly maternal) pressure and dominance is his most recent, primarily noncomic film, *Interiors*, in which the three daughters are psychologically incapable of ridding themselves of their mother's influence, unconsciously living with the same values and the same tastes in furniture, lamps, objets d'art, wall textures, clothing, and colors as their mother and as one another.

If maternal dominance is Allen's initial Freudian concern, sexual insecurity is the second. Obviously, Woody Allen's face and body conform to no romantic ideal of masculine sexual beauty (another link to the major film clowns of the 1920s). But while Chaplin in *City Lights* (his most specific examination of the tramp's yearning for sexual love) compensated for the tramp's apparently inadequate material and physical gifts with the immaterial warmth of his heart and soul, the Woody Allen persona seems to succeed sexually not in spite of his sexual defects but because of them. There is no glowing soul to compensate for Allen's puny body, freckly face, and frizzy hair. The most he seems to offer is his complicated, neurotic, and vital brain—his very complexes and insecurities themselves. The one thing that the Allen character can perhaps offer a woman is the promise that being with him will be different, interesting, surprising, fun. As the delightful battle with the lobsters in *Annie Hall* reveals, life with Woody will never be ordinary, routine, safe, or dull.

Like the earlier film clowns, the Allen persona uses various ploys to ob-

* In *Interiors*, Arthur informs Eve that he is leaving her in front of the entire family at the dinner table.

tain the lady's favor. While Chaplin and Lloyd smiled, Langdon stared, and Keaton posed, Allen, being a gifted verbal comic in a now partly verbal medium, talks (frequently employing exaggerations or outright lies). In his first wooing scene (with Janet Margolin in *Take the Money*), Allen tries to impress his new acquaintance by telling her that he is a concert musician (his futile attempts to scrape pleasing sounds out of his cello are one of the film's running gags). Allen's examination of the verbal fabrication that underlies sexual courtship culminates in the first extended conversation between Alvie Singer and Annie Hall, in which he uses the familiar cinema device of subtitling in a very unfamiliar and revealing way. The printed letters do not translate the words of a foreign speaker but reveal the real feelings of the characters beneath the words they are saying aloud to one another. The device translates the communicative gap between Alvie's lustful thoughts and his glibly pretentious, pseudointellectual talk, a brilliant revelation of his attempt to manipulate the accepted social strategies for spinning one's sexual web.

Another sexual joke that consistently dominates the Allen films is the patent absurdity that the scrawny, schleppy Woody is a superb sexual athlete. Allen supplies a metaphor for this absurdity in the final scene of *Bananas*, in which the wedding-night action between Fielding and Nancy is presented as a special event on ABC television's "Wide World of Sports," complete with Howard Cosell's postgame interviews and commentary. This vision of the puny Allen figure as a virile Superstud is obviously a piece of comic wish fulfillment, revealing both the Allen figure's genuine drives and desires and his self-conscious realization of their absurdity. The difference between the wish fulfillment in the Allen films and a parallel wish fulfillment in such Chaplin films as *Sunnyside* and *The Circus* is that Chaplin never allows the wish to fulfill itself so concretely or so spectacularly as Allen does, consistently reminding us (usually by bursting the bubble of the wish when Charlie wakes from a dream) of the impossibility of the tramp's attaining his desires.

Despite Allen's fantasies of sexual prowess (including an entire film, *Everything You Always Wanted to Know about Sex but Were Afraid to Ask*, 1972, devoted to sexual jokes), the later Allen films also explore the limits of sexual gratification. In *Annie Hall*, a superimposed ghost of Annie rises from the bed and her lovemaking with Alvie (another brilliant use of a cinema trick, evoking both Chaplin's *The Circus* and Keaton's *Sherlock Jr.*) to watch herself distantly and coldly in action. The device brilliantly captures the gap between love and lovemaking, between Annie and Alvie, between body and soul, between action and aspiration—like the use of the subtitles in the same film. It is also a sign of Allen's temperament, sensitivity, and insecurity that he is incapable of ignoring another human being's point of view.

Indeed, the handling of point of view in this shot is so complex that it is not certain whether Annie genuinely feels herself distant from Alvie or whether the self-conscious Alvie fears that she feels distant from him—or both. Although the shot appears to be an objective one—from the point of view of an omniscient director-observer, watching the two characters in bed and the separate, superimposed ghost—that director happens to be Allen himself, who is very much like Alvie Singer, the man in bed with Annie. There is a complex ambiguity as to whether the shot is truly objective (in effect, reliably conveying Annie's attitudes) or whether it captures Alvie-Allen's subjective projection (like the shot of Alvie as a Hassidic Jew at the Halls' dinner table). Precisely this mastery of the complexity of point of view, which keeps the Woody Allen figure as a photographic object in the frame but lets the thoughts and attitudes of that object's mind control the meaning and information of the shot, is one of the essential discoveries that have allowed Allen's comedy to transcend pure parody.

The repeated references to *Annie Hall's* cunning manipulation of uniquely cinematic devices imply that Allen's ten-year film career has also demonstrated a growing mastery of other cinema tools. Like Chaplin, Lloyd, and Keaton, Woody Allen was able to serve an apprenticeship that allowed him to discover the most effective way to put his persona, his gags, and his ideas on film (he was also fortunate in that, like those earlier clowns, even his apprenticeship films were accomplished and popular enough to allow him to make more of them). *Take the Money and Run* depends on voiceover narration for most of its gags and continuity, a kind of nightclub verbal track with accompanying pictures. But with *Love and Death* (aided by the lushly visual cinematography of Ghislain Cloquet, Robert Bresson's cinematographer) Allen's visual imagery could successfully parody both the Imperial Splendor of Tolstoy's Russia and the visual symbolism of Ingmar Bergman. *Interiors* (photographed, like *Annie Hall*, by Gordon Willis) is so careful in its handling of composition, indoor lighting (an essential metaphor in the film—as its title implies), color, shapes, textures, and visual metaphors that it makes most of its most subtle (and subtly funny) points without any dialogue at all. If *Love and Death*, *Annie Hall*, and *Interiors* are Allen's three best films, it is partly because they are visually his three richest films, aided by the contributions of the most distinguished cinematographers with whom Allen has collaborated.

Another lesson of Allen's apprenticeship, as of Chaplin's, was the gradual discovery of his persona. From the untalented, un-Jewish, unmusical Vergil Starkwell in *Take the Money and Run*, Allen has evolved a comic character who is very close to himself. Alvie Singer in *Annie Hall* is a Jewish, New York, offbeat, hip, neurotic comedian, just as Allen is. He has difficulties managing a complicated love affair with a gentile woman played by the gentile Diane Keaton, one of the many actresses in Allen's movies who have also played a role in his offscreen life. Alvie's opinions, attitudes, and concerns are almost identical to Allen's own. Allen's films reveal his increasing awareness that the way to develop their most interesting and complicated comic persona was simply to explore himself. Even the three sisters in *Interiors* can be seen as psychoanalytic fragments of Allen's own personality—the genuinely gifted artist in fear of drying up, the person with nothing to say who yearns to say something significant, and the slick, popular entertainer whose success is merely cheap.

Along with Allen's increasing understanding of his own comic persona has come the gradual elimination of physical, slapstick gags, which in the early Allen films were almost obligatory homages to the silent clowns. These attempts at physical comedy usually produced the most embarrassing moments of each film—Vergil's clumsy fit of giggling when he is tickled during a prison inspection in *Take the Money*, the merest beginning of a battle with a door knob that comes off in Fielding Melish's hand (*Bananas*—Chaplin would have built a five-minute physical symphony from such an opening theme; Allen simply states the theme and stops), the flying and climbing stunts in *Sleeper* requiring the use of doubles. One of the reasons that the physical comedy always seemed forced is obviously that Allen is not very good at it. His brain, his mouth, and, more recently, his eye are his comic tools, not his body. A second reason is that such physicality contradicts the Allen persona as one of the least physical and physically able human beings (hence the irony of his inevitable sexual exploits).

The result of Woody Allen's artistic evolution is the creation of a comic figure who is a mass of internal contradictions which Allen sees both in himself and in society as a whole. He is an urban dweller with a sentimental longing for the country (the lush outdoor imagery of *Love and Death*, the Minnesota landscapes in *Annie Hall*, the beach in *Interiors*) and yet realizes the bizarre instability of the people who live there (Annie has a maniacally suicidal brother; the beach is a place both of childhood play and adult suicide). He is the ethnic product of immigrant stock who envies the exquisite, classical tastes of the native American WASPs (Annie, Annie's mother, or Eve in *Interiors*) and yet sees the coldness and lack of vitality of that life. He sees both the noisy vulgarity of Jewish family life and its human energy at the same time. (Many were puzzled by Pearl in *Interiors*, the most "Jewish" of the film's characters, wondering if Allen intended her as a comic burlesque of vulgarity or a sympathetic figure of vitality. In typical Allen fashion, she must be seen not as an either-or but as a both-and—simultaneously comic and sympathetic, vulgar and vital.) Allen is an Easterner who sees both the attractiveness of California (its climate, its physicality, its spaciousness) and its ugliness (its faddishness, its lack of cultural character: "the only cultural advantage is you can make a right turn on a red light"). He has a yearning for the serious (Alvie's devotion to *The Sorrow and the Pity*, the very decision to make *Interiors*) and a loathing for pretentiousness (the devastating confrontation between Marshall Mc-Luhan and the pseudointellectual who bastardizes McLuhan's ideas—another attempt to spin a sexual web of words—in *Annie Hall*). He is obsessed by death (his three most recent films) and still can joke about it (in *Love and Death* he returns from the grave to inform us that Death is even more terrible than a particularly terrible chicken-salad sandwich).

Woody Allen has arrived at that stage in his career when he has mastered both his cinematic craft and his subject (himself, and the many others of us who share his self-doubts, his internal contradictions, his commitments and lack of commitments). As with Chaplin, each film Allen has made has arguably been his best to that point in his career (unlike Mel Brooks, whose *Blazing Saddles* and *Young Frankenstein* are probably superior to his later works), and, like Chaplin's, every Allen film is simultaneously a unique creation and unmistakably linked to his work as a whole. He has reached the point when, also like Chaplin, he may not only be the best American comic filmmaker of his age but, arguably, the best American filmmaker of his age period.

CHAPTER 18

The Ironic Tradition

———

THE third major tradition of sound comedy descends from the films of Lubitsch, Clair, and Renoir—comedies of complex structural conception rather than of personality or dialogue. In these films, parallel lines of action comment on each other; consistent thematic motifs run through the films, creating a system of symbols (both verbal and visual) that speak to one another; complex character foils and balances reveal different choices and styles of living. Many of these comedies are the works of directors who specialized in films that were not comedies. They used the comic form to make ironic comments on human values, usually contrasting the dead assumptions of a sterile society with a more personal kind of human response. In this contrast, the ironic tradition, which is essentially a European one, is closely related to the iconoclasm of the American clowns and the anti-pretentiousness of the American dialogue tradition. The films mentioned in this chapter in no way form an exhaustive list but are merely examples of the strength and length of this ironic tradition.

Zéro de Conduite

Jean Vigo's *Zéro de Conduite* (1933) is a vigorous, breezy contrast of the freedom of youth and the bondage of age, the joy of spontaneity and the crime of authority. The central institution is a boy's school, devoted to the cause of turning unfettered boys into useful slaves of the adult society's assumptions. When the boys are free of their teachers, they do surprising things—play with balls, feathers, trumpets, cigars; turn a balloon into a woman's breasts (though young boys, according to the official society, are not supposed to think about women's breasts).

But the boys suffer under the captivity of their teachers. Huguet, the one sympathetic, spontaneous teacher on the staff, is a new member of that staff. Among the regular teachers is "the Creep," who, with grotesque comic villainy, sneaks around corners and windowsills to steal the kids' candy; "Fishface," who supervises their behavior in the dormitory and whose two favorite words are "Silence" and "No"; and the anatomy professor, a fat, sweaty homosexual whose favorite classroom companion is a skeleton. The most grotesque member of the staff is its highest-ranking member, the principal—a three-foot dwarf with a nasal twang and a tiny, pointed beard. His brain is as small as his body. His delight in his own authority is merely a reaction to his essential smallness.

The most remarkable device of this film about spontaneity and freshness is that it uses a deliberately spontaneous, incongruous style to depict its theme. The film's comic style and iconoclastic content are identical and inseparable. Like Tati's later *Mon Oncle*, the film is a child's-eye view of the world. Huguet at times wears a Buster Keaton porkpie hat; at others he ambles about like Charlot with a derby and cane. There is Émile Cohl* in the line-drawing that comes alive on Huguet's desk, and Eisenstein's *October* in the cartoon that converts "the Creep" into Napoleon. There is Sennett undercranking to burlesque the walk of a priest, and perhaps Vigo's midget principal echoes Chaplin's use of an authoritative midget in several of the First Nationals. Vigo summons the comic spirits of the past because both their spontaneous film styles and the spontaneity of their era can serve as striking examples of human surprise and flexibility.

Vigo endows all his scenes with the same spirit of incongruity and surprise. The film begins with the sounds of children shouting and singing— free and unfettered—under the titles. Then the film plunges into its first image—a thick smoke. The children are entering an inferno; the freeness of the summer ends when they enter the train that takes them back to hell-prison-school. In the train, Vigo continues elliptically in a variety of styles—a mimed sequence using only music, no talk; the kids' astonished, fanciful belief that one of the passengers is dead (he is Huguet and is, ironically, entering the world of the dead); the kids delighting in a last pleasure, smoking cigars (which kids are not supposed to do) in a car marked "*Non-fumeurs.*"

Once they arrive at the school, Vigo continues with equally grotesque comic surprises—games with visual images and the sound track—without comment, explanation, or preparation. The sexton who turns the bare, sterile dormitory's lights on and off is, ironically, blind. The raucous sounds

* French cartoonist, in the first decade of the century, whose animated line drawings bordered on the surreal.

of children playing in the dormitory cease instantaneously, turning to deathly silence, as soon as one of the teachers walks in. When the children arise in the morning, Vigo adds a drum roll to the sound track, the familiar sound that accompanies a prisoner's final walk to the guillotine. When the midget principal gives a lecture on sex to a sensitive student, Vigo cuts instantly to a shocking close-up of the man's face in an extreme down-shot, accompanied by an animal yowl on the sound track. Vigo leaps at will from objective depiction to subjectivity. As the dignitaries assemble on the platform for speeches to the parents on Alumni Day, Vigo incongruously uses wooden dummies rather than human extras to impersonate several of these dignitaries. Ironically, the living men on that platform are no more alive than the wooden ones.

The result of this comic conflict between the young and the old, the quick and the dead is a comic revolution. The boys tie Fishface to his bed and then indulge in a riotous pillow fight, a chance to release the feelings that have been dammed up throughout the film. The pillows burst open (a kind of fertile fruit), the feathers fly all over the room, and Vigo shifts his camera into slow motion. The feathers drift down on the boys, falling gently around their smiling faces like flakes of snow, as they continue to leap and tumble—their violent play suddenly converted to an elegant dance of life; their barren, cold dormitory suddenly converted to a place of texture, life, and warmth. The impression of falling snow converts the indoors to the outdoors, the artificial to the natural. And Vigo adds a wry comic touch when the blind sexton, unaware of this activity, walks through this vital blizzard to turn off the dormitory light. He continues operating on schedule regardless of the circumstances.

The revolution continues outdoors on Alumni Day. The boys pelt the dignitaries with rocks, knocking off their top hats, dirtying their fancy uniforms, forcing them to take cover. The wooden dummies, unable to move, merely topple over like ducks in a shooting gallery. The kids lower the flag of France and raise the skull and crossbones. They sing their raucous, exuberant song of unity, replacing the mechanical, formal march that the school band has so dutifully practiced. In his handling of comic surprise and non sequitur, Vigo the filmmaker also raises his own skull and crossbones, sings his own exuberant song. The comic irrationality and incongruity of a Sennett serves the serious function of creating a contrast between life as it is and as it should be.

Bizarre, Bizarre

Bizarre, Bizarre (1938), directed by Marcel Carné and written by Jacques Prévert, is an incredibly rich comic concoction of irony piled upon irony, illusion upon illusion, mistake upon mistake. It is a farcical murder mystery about a crime that has not been committed, by a murderer who does not exist, of a woman and man who are not dead. Beneath the drollery of this *Drôle de drame* (its French title) there is plenty of sordidness and unpleasantness—as one would expect from Carné and Prévert. In addition to building their comedy around death, the creators also note the hypocrisies of moralistic clergymen, the inefficiencies of public servants, the bloodthirstiness of the masses, and the banality of conventional lives that are so devoid of genuine drama that they must invent some or indulge vicariously in the drama of others. It is a farce of human fallibility, selfishness, and blindness.

The players in this black farce include a botanist who is really a murder-mystery novelist, a murderer who is really a poet, a moralistic clergyman who is a lecher, a milkman who really writes the stories that the botanist pretends to write (though the botanist pretends *not* to write them), an ace reporter who is drunk, asleep, or absent whenever a big story breaks, a bourgeois wife who is really a figure of romance, and a stern, moralistic aunt who leaves all her money to the vile author of mystery stories rather than to her own moralistic family. No one is what he seems; nothing is as it appears.

Mr. Molyneux (Michel Simon) seems to be a retiring, bumbling botanist; he secretly publishes spicy mystery stories under the *nom de plume* of Felix Chapel. Chapel's stories become the rage of Victorian London, but also stimulate the rage of moralistic preachers. When Molyneux' wife seems to disappear, the erroneous conclusion that he has murdered her leaks to the newspapers and occupies the attention of Scotland Yard. The scandalous murder case so intrigues the public that Felix Chapel seems the man to write its story and expose the villainous criminal, Molyneux (who happens to be Chapel himself). So Molyneux returns to his own house in the guise of Chapel (Molyneux is also worried about the health of his mimosas), only to be threatened with genuine murder by a mass murderer who wants to kill Chapel. Therefore, Chapel-Molyneux lies to the murderer, saying that he is really Molyneux (which he is) and that he poisoned both the real Chapel and Mrs. Molyneux, but has assumed the name Chapel.

William Kramps (Jean-Louis Barrault) is a mass murderer who kills butchers ("the butcher of butchers"); he hates those who kill. But Kramps is really a romantic poet who loves flowers (like Molyneux—and also like Chaplin's Verdoux, and Avril of Carné-Prévert's *Les Enfants du Paradis*). When Molyneux and Margaret, his allegedly dead wife, take refuge in Chinatown to dodge the police and scandal, they move into a room next door to Kramps. And Kramps, seeing Margaret, falls instantly in love, wooing her with his romantic poetry and christening her "Daisy," after the flower (a parallel with Garance of *Les Enfants*). To show his love, Kramps sends his thugs to roll drunks, stealing their boutonnieres rather than their wallets (also Chaplinesque) so he can give "Daisy" a bouquet.

When Kramps meets Molyneux masquerading as Chapel, he becomes fast friends with the man who is really "Daisy's" husband. In the final unraveling, Kramps makes the ultimate sacrifice for his friend, taking the blame for the murder of Chapel-Molyneux, one murder he did not commit (and that was never committed). Kramps takes his poetic farewell of "Daisy" and departs with the police, not without his parting sally: "I always escape."

The Vicar of Bedford is a stern moralist who inveighs from his pulpit against the wickedness of murder stories. He, however, enjoys the sins of the flesh—as his autographed program from the music hall, his pursuit of Eva, the maid, and his own enormous family (some 12 children) reveal. Noting the mysteries in the Molyneux household—particularly Mrs. Molyneux's absence at dinner (she is really in the kitchen cooking, but suffers too much bourgeois embarrassment to admit that her cook has left her)—the Vicar of Bedford phones Scotland Yard to inform them of her disappearance. He returns to the Molyneux house to do his own detective work, wearing a Scottish kilt and sunglasses—only to be mistaken by a drunk reporter as the evil murderer, Molyneux himself. Molyneux (then assumed to be Chapel) locks the Vicar (then assumed to be Molyneux) in a room and telephones Scotland Yard that the murderer Molyneux has been caught (an ironic reversal of the Vicar's earlier phone call). Only the revelation that the Vicar is not Molyneux keeps the angry mob from lynching him as the murderer.

Binding the farcical mistakes and confusing twists of a purposely hyper-complicated plot is the contrast between appearances and realities, surfaces and essences. The characters consistently make erroneous inferences from the human facts they can see. When Inspector Bray, the detective from Scotland Yard, sees all the milk bottles in the Molyneux kitchen, he idiotically concludes, "Where there's an antidote, there must be poison." In reality, there are so many milk bottles because the maid is in love with the milkman. If people misinterpret what they see, it is because they see poorly—either because they believe experience conforms to their opinions of experience or because they intend to thrust their view of experience on the world. But in the comic reality of this film, the gap between a botanist and a mystery writer, a murderer and a poet, a preacher and a lecher is much narrower than it is in moral, literary, and psychological clichés. In the opening sequence of the film, Scotland Yard detectives masquerade as little old ladies at a religious revival meeting. Disguising the reality is as simple as putting on a dress.

To keep this contrast between the apparent and the real a comic one (Pirandello turned it into tragedy), the creators employ a variety of delightful and playful comic devices. The film begins and ends with "Ta Ra

Ra Boom-di-ay." No matter how sordid and perverse its action gets, it never deserts the flavor of this tune. The film's stylistic devices are pure burlesque. Carné-Prévert play games with the sound track (a blast of trumpets and a roll of drums after both telephone calls to Scotland Yard; a tinkling piano to undercut the seriousness of Margaret's despair at losing her servants). They use the camera parodically (extreme up-angle shots to burlesque the Vicar's sermon; tense compositions, meaningfully slow traveling shots, nervously significant close-ups—all the cinematic clichés of mystery thrillers—to burlesque both the story and the characters). And they use comically ironic details—stealing boutonnieres; the contrast between the Vicar's opening sermon ("In this crowded temple . . .") and the empty hall; Mrs. Molyneux's bourgeois desire to straighten pictures; the Vicar's belief that he must exorcize a devil when he sees Margaret Molyneux alive (his interpretation of the data).

Although Carné-Prévert burlesque the mobs of people who gather outside the Molyneux house (a vendor sets up a stall, "Murder House Beer Stand"), there is also contempt for these thrill-seekers, who serve as the film's chorus. The chorus wants somebody's head. When they can no longer get Molyneux's, they shift their demand to the captured Kramps. The mob is guilty of the same crime as everyone else in the film—making the appearance suit their fancies. Despite the burlesque, for Carné-Prévert such a selfish, blind view of experience is a vicious (and, unfortunately, inevitable) human crime. The mob that wants Kramps' head seems far more murderous than the murderer himself. For Carné and Prévert, even in a farce life is the real murderer.

La Ronde

Max Ophuls' *La Ronde* (1950) also contrasts appearances and realities. But whereas Carné-Prévert see error as a defect in human vision, Ophuls (and Arthur Schnitzler, author of the play on which the movie is based) sees error as the result of human self-contradiction. What people say and what they feel, what they think they feel and what they really feel are at war in *La Ronde*. Whereas *Bizarre, Bizarre* is a black farce of life and death, *La Ronde* is an ironic clash of sex and manners. In *Bizarre, Bizarre* the characters see poorly because life is more complex than their vision of it. In *La Ronde* they see quite well; they simply lie—to others and to themselves—about what they see. If all social and moral definitions in the abstract are the comic targets of *Bizarre, Bizarre*, the specific social and moral definitions of human sexuality are the targets of *La Ronde*.

Ophuls' *La Ronde* is less bitter than Schnitzler's. He omits the implication of syphilis in the play. He adds two specific scenes of melancholy, when the Little Miss stands up the Husband, and the Poet, in turn, stands up the Little Miss. Ophuls makes the theme of time more explicit—especially in the two added scenes and with the clock in the scene between Husband and Young Wife. Ophuls cuts the last three scenes of the play to the structural bone—for these lengthy, talky scenes, though marvelous for their psychological game-playing, are better suited to the stage than to the screen. What Ophuls adds to the film—the narrator, who does not exist in the play, the Strauss waltz, the clever visual symbols, and the richly ornate costume and décor—transforms a talky play into a completely cinematic film that preserves the spirit of the play without retaining the spatial restrictions of the stage.

La Ronde may be Ophuls' best film. It avoids the wooden posing of Martine Carol as Lola Montès and sustains the delicate irony of the first part of Madame de . . . through a whole film, rather than building to (or lapsing into) the operatic romanticism of the last part of that film. A key question about Madame de . . . is whether the brutally convincing comic irony of its early sections leads very credibly to the grand passion of its late ones. Can a world as decorative, as ornate, as whipped-cream-covered as Ophuls' ever fail to comment on the essential hollowness of its inhabitants?* La Ronde never raises these questions because Ophuls never abandons comic irony (which he seems to handle better than romantic passion) and because the overdecorativeness of his world never does anything but comment comically on its inhabitants.

La Ronde is a comic film of directorial comment, like Boudu or Trouble in Paradise, in which the director's hand is delightfully obvious. La Ronde's circular structure—A sleeps with B, B with C, C with D, and so on until we return to A again—is a comment in itself. Ophuls does not keep his comments a secret. He invents a narrator to comment for him. The narrator (Anton Walbrook) serves several functions: he is our guide around the sexual circle, he makes general philosophical observations, he plays bit roles in several seduction scenes. But he is essentially Ophuls' alter ego. Further, he adds cinematic flow and unity to a stage work that lacks that kind of unity, that depends entirely on its structural pattern and the concreteness of the unchanging proscenium arch for its unity. The narrator gives the film a center around which to pivot.

He is also a concrete admission that the film is artifice and metaphor rather than natural reality. Artifice serves several vital functions in the film. First, it convincingly sets the action everywhere, somewhere, and nowhere. The narrator emerges from a fog at the film's beginning and strolls past film cameras and microphones, theater stages and footlights, painted backdrops. "Where are we?" he asks. "On a stage, in a studio. Oh, we are in Vienna." The apparent differences between stage,

---

* The same conflict between decor and melodrama seems to flaw Ophuls' Letter from an Unknown Woman, despite its other beauties.

studio, and Vienna collapse. The film takes place in an imaginative space, not literal space. As the narrator later walks with the Maid, he tells her, "We are taking a walk through time." When he leaves her, he continues walking through the symphony orchestra that plays the film's musical theme, picks up a clapboard, and begins the next scene with the drop of the clapstick. The effect of this blending of artifice and nature, life and cinema, this total freedom in the collapsing of space and time emphasize the action as imaginative metaphor of human conduct and consciousness rather than as literal story. It also adds cohesion to a work that was originally ten disparate vignettes.

Ophuls' second use of artifice is to develop comic symbols and other clever cinematic devices that comment on the characters and also contribute to the film's comic spirit. The film is full of comic Freudian symbols (many of them suggested by Schnitzler's play)—pipes, swords, a balloon (which disappears after the Maid has surrendered), a cork that won't come out of a wine bottle (later the Young Gentleman has similar troubles with his sexual performance), a candle. (Ophuls resembles Lubitsch in this comic use of Freud.)

Ophuls also uses comic symbols for the sexual culmination of each scene, the part that Schnitzler coyly and purposely omitted. The narrator blows a trumpet; Ophuls tracks in to a statue of a satyr with a winking eye and broken horn; the narrator's carousel breaks down and he must repair it (when the Young Gentleman can't get his cork to function); Ophuls cuts to the narrator with a pair of editing scissors, snipping a particularly sensual scene out of the film. These intrusive comic touches purposely detach us further from the illusion of the film, pushing us to a comic distance from which to think about the action. The detached and disinterested narrator becomes the audience's alter ego as well as the director's. He is both chorus and conductor.

The third function of Ophuls' elaborate artifice is to reveal and communicate the characters' feelings and values. There is a deliberate counterpoint in the film's personal emotion (lust-love) and impersonal decor. The film is an examination of love in a whipped-cream world. The elaborate mirrors, trellises, staircases, banisters, drapes, and candelabra are concrete embodiments of the material and social values of that world of artificiality, distance, and detachment. So the problem of human beings in this world of gilt and curlicue is to cut through the elaborate externals (which they love as much as the director does) so they can feel something with one another. Their sexual desire is the undeniably sincere reality beneath the veneer of architectural elegance.

Perhaps Ophuls sees sexual contact as the one kind of human reality that cuts through this social whipped cream. Or perhaps he sees that the calcifications of society have unfortunately shrunk human sincerity to brief moments of animal desire. Or perhaps he sees that the elaborate

sexual games are of the same material as the walls, drapes, and mirrors—
undeniably deadening but undeniable fun. Or perhaps Ophuls makes all
three harmonizing suggestions.

Ophuls uses the decor (and the camera's relationship to it) not just
for general implications about social restrictions, but as a specific means
of defining a character's responses and desires. In *La Ronde*, Ophuls'
tracking shot not only adds visual energy and movement; it perfectly
mirrors the strategy of the character at the time, for the tracking camera
follows the pursuer chasing the pursued, shifting its direction when the
roles shift (as they inevitably do in these scenes).

As an example of the interrelation of decor, composition, and cutting
as a means of producing emotional awareness, the scene between the Husband and Wife is remarkable. Ophuls shoots the scene from several angles
—a distant shot of the two grotesquely shaped, symmetrical beds, emphasizing the gulf between them (and the people in them); a shot through
the clock in the foreground, its stand looking like two legs and its pendu-
lum like a pulsating phallus (the clock fills the gap between the beds); a
shot with the Wife lying in the foreground, listening, her eyes open, as
her husband sits up and talks in the rearground; the mirror image of this
shot (and this scene, more than any other in the film, gives the impression
of being shot in a room full of mirrors from the vantage point of each of
the mirrors); the close-ups of both faces. Ophuls' camera strategy for the
scene is a perfect circle—beginning far, coming close, returning to far
again. And each shift in the circle, each of Ophuls' cuts is tied to a beat
when the characters' responses or interests change.

La Ronde is an ironic look at the contrast between sexual expression
and the way that expression gets decorated. Ophuls' irony is sometimes
derisive, sometimes mellow and sad, sometimes warm and gentle. Despite
the social shams—the codes of morality and propriety, the dishonesty, the
selfishness, the callousness—the sexual dance goes on. At the end of their
scene, the Wife and Husband join hands across the gulf between their
beds. If for Schnitzler the circle was a dead end, for Ophuls it is a process
of continuity. The dominant symbol he added to the film—the turning
carousel—indicates woodenness, mechanical repetition, childish pastime,
and going nowhere, but it also indicates a kind of fun, a lightness, a continuity, a physical object that revolves just as the earth does. The music
for the film, the Oscar Strauss waltz, is warm, rich, and sentimental; it
comments on the action but provides it with a lilt as well. The circle and
the waltz (a musical circle)—despite their repetitiousness and stasis—
imply a comic view of life's motion, if not progress; continuity, if not
purpose.

Tight Little Island

Where *La Ronde* comically examines reality by disguising itself as pure contrivance, Alexander Mackendrick's *Tight Little Island* (*Whisky Galore*, 1948) comically examines reality by disguising itself as absolute reality. This story of the Hebrides Islands looks more like Flaherty's *Man of Aran* than a studio comedy. The luminous, marbled shots of the sea and sky, of the earth and rock, of the stone cottages and wood-paneled rooms, the observant and detailed shots of the Scottish islanders' faces, mannerisms, and gestures all give the film the rich, convincing texture of documentary reality rather than cinema fiction. This texture became a dominant method of the Ealing Comedies, of which Mackendrick's is a prime example. These British films defined comedy as beginning with complex, credible human beings within a social milieu that is also as believable as possible. With this human context as a base, the clever writers build a bizarre structure of almost incredible events that manipulate ironies, comic mistakes, and comic twists.

Tight Little Island combines a comic structural conception with the detailed reality of these people, their society, and their natural surroundings. In this tight little plot (in which *everything* counts), the central contrast is between personal happiness (symbolized by the whisky) and the outside forces of law and government (symbolized by the World War, which seeks to deprive the island of its whisky). Every major incident in the plot is a comic war, couched in the terms of war, between the World War and whisky.

On the little Hebrides isle of Thodday (pronounced "toddy," like the drink), the whisky supply runs dry as a result of wartime scarcity. In a thick fog, a freighter runs aground; its cargo—50,000 cases of whisky. The residents of Thodday plan to seize the precious cargo for themselves. But comic obstacles block their intentions. First, the freighter has run aground on Sunday, the Sabbath, and the men of this religious society can expend no labor on the Sabbath (another general restriction imposed on individuals). They helplessly watch the freighter from the shore, praying (quite literally, for it is the Lord's day) that it does not sink before they can remove its precious cargo.

Second, and an even greater comic obstacle, the military leader of the island's "home guard," Captain Waggett, decides that the freighter's cargo must be protected against possible theft. This man, an Englishman rather than a native islander, is a parody of the military mentality. He believes that the cargo should go down with the ship, because he believes in rules even when it is inhuman nonsense to apply them. Waggett has insisted on drilling the locals in all the procedures of military defense (which they perform sloppily and unenthusiastically) in the absurd event that the

Nazis should invade the little island. (Why would the Nazis want it? And if they did, how could this handful of peaceful folk stop them?) In the same spirit, Waggett orders the "home guard," the very locals who want that whisky, to "protect" the cargo from sabotage and theft so it can sink to the bottom of the sea.

Waggett assigns his sergeant, another man with experience in the outside world, to watch the freighter. But the sergeant, accepting the values of the island and falling in love with one of its inhabitants, really does not want to "protect" the cargo—especially since he needs whisky to celebrate his upcoming wedding (one of the local customs). How can the locals steal the whisky without causing the sergeant an internal conflict between his duty and his desire? They decide to stage a guerrilla raid on the ship, using the military tactics that Waggett and the sergeant have taught them, tying up the sergeant so he cannot be blamed for the theft. This military campaign is a sparkling success (and photographed with the documentarist's insistence on illuminating an entire process), and the liquid happiness flows again all over the island, bringing joy, peace, and health to everyone. The engagement party takes place; a sick old man miraculously recovers by filling his formerly unbeneficial hot-water bottle with whisky; a frightened young man, previously tied to his mother's apron strings, gets drunk and tells his moralistic mother to untie him; and even the mother takes a drink and melts into an almost-human being.

But Captain Waggett declares his own private war against the whisky, and the locals must devise a series of clever hiding places for their stockpile (another use of military strategy) to protect it. Waggett decides on a military subterfuge. He reports the theft to the customs officials on the mainland. (The tax men are, of course, very interested in the smuggling of whisky on which no taxes have been paid.) Waggett and the tax men plan a military sneak attack, coming across in a boat under the cover of night while the locals are all drunkenly celebrating. But a native spots the boat and sounds the alarm (a parody of Paul Revere). The "home guard" goes into action again, deciding to treat the invading British customs agents as if they were invading Nazis.

Although the locals do not perform their maneuvers with much more competence than earlier, they do show more spirit. Eventually that spirit —and luck—pays off; they succeed in protecting their arsenal. Ironically, the only man whom the customs agents detect with the contraband whisky is Captain Waggett himself, for the box of military cartridges he carries is one of the locals' hiding places for the liquor (yet another comic juxtaposition of war and whisky). Waggett receives a dose of classic comic justice, and the film's action concludes, as most classical comedies do, with laughter, a wedding, and a dance.

But Mackendrick adds an epilogue. The supply of free whisky runs out, the price goes up on the commercial supply after the war (another attack of government on the "home"), and no one can afford to buy the whisky that is now in abundant supply. Mackendrick sums up his comedy with a purposely bogus piece of moralizing:

They all lived unhappily ever after. Except for Peggy and her sergeant. They weren't whisky drinkers. And if that isn't a moral story, what is it?

The irony of the question is that the genuine morality of the film has nothing to do with such a platitude. The film's real moral position is that one cannot talk about morality without knowing what genuine, personal, human morality is. Further, one cannot fight wars and create "home guards" to repulse the invader unless one knows what is really worth guarding, who the invader is, and what is the meaning of home.

As a comic conception, *Tight Little Island* demonstrates the mixture of credibility and improbability, nature and artifice essential to a well-made comedy. The film is anchored to reality by its people (performances by such gifted actors as Joan Greenwood and Gordon Jackson add weight to that anchor), its settings, and its cultural milieu (the interrelation of people and setting). With such an anchor the film can introduce a bizarrely farcical comic antagonist (Waggett) and a self-conscious structural pattern in which every event in the plot is couched in the terms of military strategy.

The Alec Guinness films of the same era and studio fulfill precisely the same pattern, for Guinness (unlike later British comic stars such as Terry-Thomas and Peter Sellers) was not a comedian but an actor (and not exclusively a comic actor either). The human fullness of Guinness as dowdy bank employee (*The Lavender Hill Mob*, 1951), eccentric inventor (*The Man in the White Suit*, 1952), suave officer (*The Captain's Paradise*, 1953), and bohemian artist (*The Horse's Mouth*, 1958) and the detailed texture of his milieu (bank, factory, naval life, artist's world) were the bases of outrageous and uproarious farcical constructions. These British "little comedies" demonstrate the principle that in sound comedy people act like people; the director and writers build the context that make these people funny.

Smiles of a Summer Night

Ingmar Bergman's *Smiles of a Summer Night* (1955) is a comedy of love and manners, very much in the style of Jean Renoir. There are interlocking pairs of lovers—of different ages, temperaments, social classes, and moral principles. The film is a very mellow farce, a potential French bedroom romp of the Feydeau style, warmed and softened into a series of bedroom mistakes that help the foolish mortals unscramble their own mistaken loves and lives. This is a comedy of smiling, not of raucous laughter. It is a comedy of summer—a midsummer night's dreamlike reality—of a gentle, warm sun, of trees, moonlight, and haystacks. The felicity of nature in the film helps all of the characters discover their natural selves and their own felicity. If the film's spirit is a mellow Feydeau, its structure is a mellow, less fanciful retelling of A *Midsummer Night's Dream*.[1]

At the beginning of the film, the lovers are grouped in three unsatisfactory pairs. (1) Fredrik Egerman, a lawyer of about fifty, has a young wife of twenty-one. Although they have been married two years, they have never slept together. For Fredrik, Anne is an ideal of young purity; he sees her as a series of beautiful pictures (conveyed in Bergman's effective use of the photographs Egerman has just taken of her, underscored with a languid tracking shot and lyrical, wistful music). For Anne, Fredrik is the kind of mature, solid, paternal figure that a young, frightened girl can trust. (2) Henrik Egerman, Fredrik's idealistic, philosophical son, who is Anne's own age, flirts with Petra, the buxom blonde maid. The two feel they ought to want each other for the reasons that young masters want buxom maids and vice versa. But although Henrik ought to want her, he can't. He apologizes, "The first time is always a farce." He secretly nurses a love for Anne, an ideal figure of his own pure dreams; and Petra nurses an interest in Henrik's father, who seems mature, solid, and paternal. (3) Desirée Arnfeldt is a great star of the stage who has professed to be twenty-nine for the past three years. (Anne Egerman says, "She's fifty if she's a day.") Desirée is Fredrik's former mistress, and she happens to have a young son named Fredrik. Her present lover is Count Malcolm, a man who lives his life as if it were the theater. He is a stickler for points of honor, and especially for points of vanity. Bergman comically deflates this soldier into toy soldier by accompanying Malcolm's walk with rhythmic, march-time drumming on the sound track. Malcolm contradicts himself constantly—he is not sure whether he should be more upset about his mistress' or his wife's deceiving him. And he believes that all life's contradictions and quarrels can be settled with pistols, as they are on the stage.

Add to the three couples Charlotte Malcolm (the Count's scheming, vicious wife, who also enjoys theatrics), Frid (another servant), and Desirée's mother (a lady with such an interesting past that she was given a beautiful manor house *not* to write her memoirs), and the sexual ingredients are ready for mixing.

In that mixture, Bergman's primary contrast is between the love of youth and the love of age. The film contains four generations: (1) Desirée's mother; (2) Desirée and Fredrik; (3) Anne and Henrik; (4) young Fredrik. For the youngest and oldest, love can exist only in the future or in memories of the past. But the others are absurdly paired. Fredrik belongs with Desirée (especially since, as the film implies, the boy Fredrik is their child), and Anne belongs with Henrik (especially since both of these idealists must suffer through the "farce" of the first time). The problem for all of these lovers is knowing which farce is theirs.

The second contrast of the film is between life and the theater, or rather the melodramatic passion of real love and the theatrical conventions of farce. In the first jealous confrontation between Egerman and the Count over Desirée, Egerman, the loser, walks out without his trousers. At the romantic dinner party in the manor house, where all the couples are present, Bergman underscores the discoveries of desire and infidelity with farcically crashing chords and comically shocking close-ups. The film resolves its complicated human tangle in two major scenes that follow this romantic-mystical-farcical dinner party, both of which begin as melodrama and end as farce.

In the first, young Henrik, seeing the ridiculous results of his idealistic speech at the dinner, considers suicide. He ties his belt around his neck, climbs onto a ledge, tightens the noose, jumps off the ledge, and breaks the pole holding the belt. His suicide is merely a slapstick gag. Further, in his clumsiness he accidentally triggers the little button that sets a whole non-infernal machine in operation. Miraculously (except that we know the explanation for the miracle), the wall separating Henrik's and Anne's bedrooms opens, and Anne's bed slides into Henrik's room, depositing her sleeping body beside him. Bergman accompanies the operation of this music-box bed with the tinkling waltz of a music box, climaxing with a few blasts of Cupid's trumpet. Suicidal melodrama has dissolved into bedroom farce. The *deus ex machina* (this time a goddess is in the machine) that negates Henrik's clumsiness appears with a theatrical flourish that would be worthy of Feydeau. Henrik luckily recovers from his amazement in time to take advantage of the situation.

The film's final scene of unraveling, the ultimate confrontation between Egerman and the Count, also begins tensely and ends with a trick. Count Malcolm challenges Egerman to a game of Russian roulette to settle their rivalry, finally and honorably. So the two men, showing the most polite form, chat amiably, drink a shot of cognac, spin the barrel, hold the pistol against the temple, pull the trigger. Click. No bullet. Bergman repeats the pattern five times (wonderfully building suspense), for all three of the Count's turns, the first two of Fredrik's. On Fredrik's final turn, Bergman cuts away from Egerman to outside the room just before Fredrik pulls the trigger. Bang. The two women—Desirée and Charlotte—assume that the game is over. We assume that Egerman has lost. The Count appears at the door looking very grim. Suddenly he laughs. The bullet was a blank. ("A nobleman doesn't duel with a scribe.")

Bergman has played a deliberate trick on us (Bergman likes tricks, as *The Magician* clearly shows), raising our emotions very theatrically and then popping the tension with an unexpected comic reversal. In the film,

Bergman, like the summer night, smiles at and on us, defining nature as a comic force that slowly, sometimes sadly, but inevitably takes its beneficent course. All the human pairs sort out properly, according to their natures: Egerman and Desirée; Charlotte and the Count ("I'll be faithful—in my fashion"); Anne and Henrik ("A toast to youth," say Malcolm and Egerman as they drink before using the pistol); Petra and Frid, the servants who "haven't the gift of being young lovers." Although there is a hint of sadness in Egerman's loss of Anne, the film ends with shots of the morning, of windmills, of the fields bathed in fresh light.

Doctor Strangelove

Whereas *Smiles of a Summer Night* is a farce of light, Stanley Kubrick's *Doctor Strangelove: or How I Learned to Stop Worrying and Love the Bomb* (1963) is a very dark one. Where Bergman ends man's battle with nature in harmony, Kubrick and Terry Southern, the scriptwriter, show man battling so successfully with nature that he destroys both nature and himself. The film is full of audacious sight gags, plot twists, and dialogue. It comically startles us at its beginning with two war planes in coitus (one is "refueling" the other) accompanied by the syrupy tune, "Try a Little Tenderness." (The planes are trying a little.) From that starting point it continues with its dominant ironic device—the synthesis of two opposites, sex and death, fertility and sterility. It uses the synthesis to develop its primary comic and serious material, a devastating satiric portrait of the military mind.

General Buck Turgidson (George C. Scott) is the tough, virile lecher who treats tactical military problems in the same rough way he treats problems with his mistress. His primary tool is deceit, which he uses to cover his basic brutality and callousness. He lies to his mistress (he tells her he loves her) just as he lies to the President about his fears for the world's safety. But he reveals the vicious animal beneath the pious surface when asked if the single American plane with its atomic bombs can possibly make it through the Soviet defense systems. Rather than voicing his fear of the consequences, Turgidson erupts into roaring praise for the American pilots, building to the joyous climax that those "sons of bitches" can "make it." Only after the words leap out does he realize that he has supported the wrong side of the question and that "making it" this time means "unmaking it"—the final "it" being the earth.

General Jack Ripper (Sterling Hayden) is the psychotic military leader, obsessed with his own power, using that power to eliminate whoever he feels needs eliminating. His natural opponents are the Commies, who he thinks are subtly poisoning America from within by fluoridating the water.

This tainted water saps our "purity of essence," weakening us so that we become easy prey to the inevitable Russian attack. Ripper developed this mad theory when he became sexually impotent, reasoning that the cause of his own sapped bodily fluids must be this very fluoridated water (yet another confusion of sex and death). The ultimate result of Ripper's sexual failure is the orgasmic destruction of the earth in hypnotic mushroom clouds.

Two types of the flunkey military mind are brilliantly portrayed by Keenan Wynn and Slim Pickens. Wynn is Bat Guano, the dour sergeant who leads the troops that finally overrun Jack Ripper's base. (Ripper shoots himself; he is Hitler to the end.) A British military attaché (the first of Peter Sellers' three impersonations in the film), an outside figure of reason, knows the secret recall code and wants to telephone Washington to tell the President how to stop the war planes. Because the military phones are out of order, he has to use a pay phone. But he hasn't enough change. When Colonel Mandrake (Sellers) asks Wynn to get it by shooting the coin box of the Coca-Cola machine, Wynn is skeptical. He suspects that all these atrocities are the doings of "deviated preeverts" (he is ironically right) and Mandrake must also be a "preevert" if he wants to molest that sacred dispenser of American nectar, the Coca-Cola machine. Eventually Wynn relents but tells Sellers with complete seriousness, "You'll have to answer to the Coca-Cola company."

Slim Pickens, the pilot of the only bomber to get through the Russian defenses (its name, ironically, is the *Leper Colony*), becomes so devoted to his task of dropping the bomb that he too forgets the consequences of that action. When the *Leper Colony* is damaged, he feverishly works to repair the bomb door. When the bomb won't fall, Pickens climbs astride it to pry it loose. He eventually succeeds, riding the bomb down to its detonation, whooping like a cowboy on a bronco at a rodeo (or a man astride an immense phallus). Although Pickens realizes the solemnity of dropping the atomic bomb (he delivers a patriotic pep talk and solemn prayer before releasing it), he doesn't consider the horrifying results. He takes the destruction of the earth about as seriously as winning a football game.

The feeling of game in the film is strong. The President (Sellers' second role) Merkin Muffley, is more referee than captain. The President is a liberal, rational, patient, uncommitted man—hence, he is totally befuddled by the committed insanity around him. The important meeting in the War Room becomes a school debate. The most successful and maniacal of all the game players is Doctor Strangelove himself (Sellers again), the former Nazi scientist who now works for us. Sellers' three roles in the film—Mandrake, Muffley, Strangelove—are purposefully calculated to reveal the varying mixtures of reason, insanity, and efficiency in the human animal. Although Strangelove masquerades as the man of reason, he is really devoted to the manias of Hitler (that is, Ripper). And it is this maniac, not the reasonable Mandrake or Muffley, who really has the power.

Beneath Strangelove's pieties, the crippled man loves slaughter. He can't disguise his savoring of the word "slaughter"; he can't restrain his gnarled right arm from rising into a *"Sieg heil,"* which it does involuntarily; he can't mask his delight in his plan to create a small, fascistic colony of survivors after the atomic holocaust; and he can't disguise his admiration for the concept of a doomsday machine that will blow up the entire earth automatically if a single atomic weapon goes off inside Russia. In terms of the film's argument, as soon as one employs scientists to devise doomsday machines and plans for survival after atomic holocaust, the game is horrifyingly over.

Kubrick's tone in the film is a kind of combination of *The Great Dictator*'s political farce and *Monsieur Verdoux*'s murderous grimness, seasoned with the grotesque black and back-shadowed photography of Orson Welles. But Kubrick's most successful technique is keeping the disparate gags together in a unified, driving plot. *Doctor Strangelove* is Terry Southern's best screenplay because he has a Stanley Kubrick to control his digressive reveling in the perverse. The wildly farcical sequences could easily break the film into funny pieces that add up to an unsatisfying whole (like Kubrick's *Lolita*), but the plot assimilates the gags with its narrative drive.

Strangelove is another of those comedies in which suspense is important. We care about whether the plane gets through or not. The suspense— will the plane drop that bomb?—keeps the film together and our interest from sagging. Kubrick's editing rhythms, his increase of pace and tension in the late stages of the film, the perfect timing of the cross-cuts between the War Room and the plane, the rhythmic humming and drumming of "When Johnny Comes Marching Home" on the sound track, the spare but exciting use of camera trickery (the zoom shots on the instrument panel as the plane prepares for attack) make *Doctor Strangelove* progress inevitably and hypnotically toward its orgasmic climax, as the bombs explode before our eyes in graceful slow motion. Ironically, the film handles suspense so that we are not sure whether to pull for the plane to make it or not. (The people in the plane are the most sympathetic in the film.) We become sucked into the same process as everyone in the film, emotionally, almost sexually, hoping for the destruction of the earth against the wisdom of our judgment and reason. The final cataclysm is beautiful and horrifying, sensual and sickening, funny and appalling at the same time.

Kubrick also keeps the film together with his consistent point of view toward the horrors he comically describes. If these maniacs have brought the earth to its doom, it is because both the maniacs and the perfectly sane confuse the greater good with the lesser, ends with means, important consequences with trivial ones. The film, like the filmmaker and audience, becomes fascinated, hypnotized, delighted by the *process* of a mechanism, the *process* of destroying the world. That process can only be halted by wrenching ourselves out of the fascination and examining the process from a distance.

A Coca-Cola machine, sexual prowess, an argument with a mistress, photographing secret maps, repairing a broken bomb door, reading a manual of instructions, finding a dime for the telephone—all these trivialities become more significant than the destruction of the earth and everyone on it. That mistake in priorities, Kubrick farcically notes, will surely lead us to horror. Once we write manuals for dropping the atomic bomb, broken down into step-by-step procedures that can be read rationally, dispassionately, clinically, then the bomb will surely fall. Kubrick's film is a warning to unfreeze us, to (in Bergson's terms) replace the mechanical with flexible life. For Kubrick's farce depicts a mechanical society in which everyone is frozen—perhaps to death.

The Case for Comedy

NOTHING to be done." The opening line of Beckett's *Waiting for Godot*, which is also its ultimate statement, might be applied to comedy as well. From the beginning, comedy has been bent on destruction—of objects, egos, social assumptions, society's leaders, and the goals of society itself. Aristophanes was a perfectionist of destruction. Similarly, the greatest comic artists in film—Sennett, Chaplin, Keaton, Lubitsch, Renoir, the Marx Brothers, Fields, Tati, Sturges—are pure destroyers. They wreck the idol that society and men have built to, for, and of themselves, and they fail to build anything in its place.

Although Chaplin suggests self-sacrifice as a human moral course, his films note that such sacrifice is a rare exception to the general human rule, just as his tramp figure is merely a metaphoric aspiration toward a perfect human being who does not and cannot exist. Renoir recognizes the positive claims of both art and nature; he merely has difficulty reconciling and synthesizing their equally legitimate and mutually exclusive claims. The cynics—such as Sturges, Wilder, and Lubitsch—falsely and incredibly betray their cynicism to make things work out hopefully and positively. And the clowns—Keaton, the Marxes, Fields, Tati—destroy social expectations, conventions, and assumptions in the very assertions of their being. If all men asserted themselves in such a way, there would be no society at all.

Such comic films raise questions that have no answers, pose dilemmas whose horns cannot be avoided, state social and human problems that have no solutions. In short, they expose human folly and present no cure, for folly is an incurable human disease for which there is "nothing to be done."

Tragedy is built around one kind of implacable inevitability: men die. Comedy is built around another equally implacable inevitability: men are fools. It might seem that some of the older comic artists were not so implacable about human folly and not so purely destructive. But take a closer look. True, Shakespeare's comedies always end with unanimity and marriage. But the solution of the specific human difficulties has in no way erased the general human foolishness. Many of the comedies cannot end without a deliberate contrivance imposed on the characters from without (the love juice in *Midsummer Night's Dream*, certainly no less miraculous a contrivance than Bergman's mechanical bed; the miraculous conversions of all the evil-doers in *As You Like It*, certainly no less miraculous than that conversion in Chaplin's *Easy Street*; the forced wedding in *Much Ado About Nothing*, certainly no less forced than the one in Clair's *Italian Straw Hat*; and so forth). Shakespeare implies that only such miraculous contrivances can reverse the effects of folly, for if you leave man to his own devices, he will continue to blunder from mess to mess, as he does in life—that is the difference between art and life for Shakespeare (and for Chaplin). The endings of Shakespeare's comedies often feel uncomfortable (how could she marry the man after all that?) precisely because he has imposed a positive conclusion without rebuilding the moral statures of the characters he has destroyed.

Shakespeare's most perceptive analyses of comedy belong to Puck and Jaques, two characters who function primarily as commentators in their respective plays. Puck, from his detached, non-mortal position, can observe, "What fools these mortals be." And Jaques in *As You Like It*, whose function has puzzled critics (and students at exam time), is a mortal personification of the spirit of comedy itself—a detached observer who views all men (including himself) in all "seven ages" as members of the same foolish species.

Ben Jonson appears more constructive. His comedies chastise the foolish, but they also give examples of balanced, virtuous behavior. However, there is a tension in Jonson also, for though he morally applauds his Lovewits and Celias and Peregrines, he has written them the most boring, bland, and forgettable parts in the plays. Only Jonson's fools live. As a song from *Volpone* states, "Fools they are the only nation." Jonson may not approve of a Sir Epicure Mammon morally and intellectually, but he dearly loves his creation and positively wallows in Mammon's exotic imagery and sensual references. As a comic artist Jonson invests all his spirit in his Mammons and Volpones and Moscas. Only as a "good citizen" does he realize that he had better show some other way for human beings to comport themselves.

This yearning to be a "good citizen," to temper the violently destructive spirit of comedy with the hope for progress and human improvement, is understandable. It takes a tough, hard mind to face the conclusion that there is "nothing to be done" and not turn away from the sight. Unfortunately, tempering the destructive spirit of comedy also seems to tamper with it and castrate it. When English playwrights of the early eighteenth century turned away from the bawdy, amoral comedy of the Restoration, they created a genre called "sentimental comedy," which had more to do with sentiment than comedy. The result is that whereas such purely destructive, licentious Restoration comedies as *The Country Wife, Love for Love, The Way of the World,* and *The Beaux' Stratagem* still hold the stage (in England anyway, where the stage still exists to be held), a sentimental comedy such as Richard Steele's *The Conscious Lovers* is familiar only to graduate students in English literature.

The partial failures of comic artistry noted in these pages (Lloyd, Langdon, the final speech of *The Great Dictator,* Clair, Capra, McCarey, Lewis) are primarily failures to look the destructive spirit of comedy unflinchingly in the eye. The lesser comic artist (including most of the comic craftsmen not discussed in this book) hedges his comic bets and contradictorily tries to glue together the idol he has smashed.

Comedy is truly the foe of progress and the social order. It laughs at the illusions that such terms imply. Comedy does not deny that men can build a better rocket ship or effect a more equitable distribution of goods and chattels. It merely denies that men can be any better—or, rather, it denies that they can be anything but men, anything but foolish mortals. What, then, is the good of this purely destructive, negative thing?

First, there is something uniquely human about being able to see that all of the social and moral constructs that make life possible are merely illusions. Man is apparently the only animal who is conscious of his own non-existence (the starting point of tragedy). He is also apparently the only animal aware of his own imperfections and failures, of the gap between existence as it is and as it ought to be. This self-consciousness is the starting point of comedy.

One of the comic themes that recurs throughout this book—so often, perhaps, that it becomes bothersome—is the shredding of illusions and the contrast between surface and essence. Sennett and Hal Roach shred the illusion of human dignity; Chaplin, the illusions of social respectability and human justice; Keaton, the illusions of the capabilities of certain human types; Lubitsch, the illusions of social forms that try to conceal the underlying lust and lies; the Marx Brothers and W. C. Fields, the illusion of social propriety; Renoir, the illusion that a human being can ever find perfect and unalloyed happiness. And so forth.

Such illusions are, of course, the oxygen that both men and society require to survive. They produce such indispensable ideas as Progress, Justice, Wisdom, Law, Virtue, and Happiness. But the comic artist reminds us that such abstractions are merely the unattainable inventions of fallible beings and are therefore less concrete, tangible, and real than a pie in the kisser. In the twentieth century, comedy serves a purpose that might ironically be described as both Christian and religious. For the lesson of comedy (a lesson that no longer comes very forcefully from the pulpit) is that "all is vanity," that the temporal is temporary, and that mortal perfection is a contradiction in terms. All social theories for human improvement, all attempts at social or technological progress, the unshakable faith in reason, science, and social justice of our own century (and the two preceding it), are built on the assumption that human life is perfectible, tends toward perfection as a limit. Comedy's assumption is the opposite: there is change, but not progress. Human and social life does not move unswervingly in one direction, in a line, but in a circle. Perhaps that is why so many of the greatest film comedies (especially those of Chaplin, Renoir, and Lubitsch) are circular.

Most comic-film artists, of course, are unaware of such implications. The most intellectual and self-conscious comic masters (especially Chaplin, Renoir, and Lubitsch—once again) perhaps perceive the destructiveness of their paradoxes and realize the consequences of not being able to assert without questioning the assertion. Other film comics are quite seriously interested in nothing but laughs. Keaton thought of himself as a pure gag man; the Marx Brothers denied that there is a single social intention in any of their films. (Even Renoir adds to *The Rules of the Game* the disclaimer that the film is merely entertainment, not social criticism.) But the very subjects that such "pure" funnymen find laughable imply a rebellious, destructive, and comically contemptuous attitude toward social conventions. One cannot laugh at such institutions as government, the law courts, and the family without implying that such pillars of our society are potentially laughable. Perhaps a politician or judge would find *Duck Soup* amusing (he might just find it dumb or silly, and the sillier he found it, the less he would think about its implications), but a politician or judge could never create a *Duck Soup*, because such a creation would disparage his entire life's work.

But disparagement (conscious or not) is the life's work of the comic. And that disparagement diverts our attention from the illusory means by which we live to the incomprehensibility of the end for which we live, reminding us that we are all human, and mortal, and fallible; that existence is irrational; and that we have merely invented the reasons that keep us going. In its underlying emphasis on the meaning (or lack of meaning) of existence itself, the goals of comedy and tragedy merge. No wonder then that "tragi-comedy" or "serious comedy" or "existential comedy" has become the dominant twentieth-century mode—especially in a century which no longer believes in Eternal Justice and Fate and the other metaphysical explanations for human suffering in classical tragedy. The twentieth century examines tragic questions in the comic form—using comic probabilities, comic destructiveness, comic characters, and comic structures.

One of the values of a purely destructive form such as comedy, then, is simply its assertion that it is human, that we are human, and that to reveal the paradoxes, ironies, and ambiguities of existence is the act of being human. A second value is perhaps more specific and pragmatic. In shaking us out of our assumptions, comedy reminds us not to inflict pain on those who do not share those assumptions. The comic films are full of pain. The simple comic pain of *L'Arroseur arrosée*, in which a gardener receives a face full of water, becomes much more complicated in later films. There is Charlie's pain at being rejected by respectable society and by the girl who accepts the values of respectable society; Buster's pain at being considered weak and incompetent; Mrs. Erlynne's pain (*Lady Windermere's Fan*) at being considered morally shady; Boudu's pain in his new clothes and shoes; Sugar Cane's pain at being the victim of sexual clichés; and so forth. Although comedy may doubt that human beings are capable of heeding its comic warning, it does warn us not to take our assumptions so seriously that we misjudge or mistreat those who appear different. Beneath the surface, we are all members of the same race.

Notes

Introduction

1. In *Comedy* (Garden City, N.Y., 1956), pp. 193–255.
2. Olson, *The Theory of Comedy* (Bloomington, Ind., and London, 1968). I will refer to this essay often. I am extremely indebted to Professor Olson, both for influencing my insights and methods and for providing a system of ideas against which I can react and measure my own.

Chapter 2

1. Raymond Durgnat, *The Crazy Mirror* (New York, 1970), pp. 94–5.
2. *Ibid.*, p. 95.

Chapter 4

1. Charles Ford, *Max Linder* (Paris, 1966), p. 18.
2. Lewis Jacobs, *The Rise of the American Film* (New York, 1939), pp. 128–29.

Chapter 5

1. Statistics cited are from Kalton C. Lahue and Terry Brewer, *Kops and Custard* (Norman, Oklahoma, 1967).
2. See Sennett's autobiography, *King of Comedy* (Garden City, N.Y., 1954).
3. From Lahue and Brewer, *op. cit.*, pp. 16 ff.
4. Sennett, *op. cit.*, p. 77.
5. Lahue and Brewer explain Sennett's "stretcher" by showing he confused one of his 1912 Biograph comedies, *The Would-Be Shriner*, which he directed in California in the winter of 1911–12, with his first Keystone (*Kops and Custard*, p. 28).
6. Sennett, *op. cit.*, p. 29.

7. Durgnat, *op. cit.*, pp. 69, 71.

8. A fuller discussion of many of the films whose titles I only mention here can be found in *A Short History of the Movies* (New York, 1971), pp. 99–107.

Chapter 6

1. For a good example of a critic's accusing Chaplin of such "flaws," see Donald W. McCaffrey, *Four Great Comedians* (New York and London, 1968), pp. 24–50.

2. For these statistics I am dependent on Theodore Huff's biography, *Charlie Chaplin* (New York, 1964).

3. I discuss many of the specific Keystones and Mutuals in *A Short History of the Movies*, pp. 107–19.

Chapter 9

1. J. P. Lebel makes the same point in his perceptive study *Buster Keaton* (London and New York, 1967).

2. Keaton, *My Wonderful World of Slapstick* (London, 1967), p. 130.

3. Lebel, *op. cit.*, pp. 86 *ff.*

4. Keaton, *op. cit.*, p. 176.

Chapter 10

1. Lloyd, *An American Comedy* (New York, 1971), pp. 167 *ff.* The autobiography was originally published in 1928.

2. See McCaffrey, *op. cit.*, pp. 134–5.

3. McCaffrey's opinion. See p. 73 of *Four Great Comedians*.

4. Lloyd, *op. cit.*, p. 86.

Chapter 11

1. Agee, "Comedy's Greatest Era," in *Agee on Film* (Boston, n.d.), p. 8.

2. Capra, *The Name Above the Title* (New York, 1971), pp. 57–80.

Chapter 12

1. Capra, *op. cit.*, p. 40.

2. Keaton, *op. cit.*, p. 176.

Chapter 14

1. In Herman G. Weinberg, *The Lubitsch Touch* (New York, 1967), p. 258.

2. *Ibid.*, p. 49.

Chapter 15

1. See the interviews with Renoir in Bernard Chardère, *Jean Renoir* (Paris, 1962), pp. 8, 16.

2. *Ibid.*

3. For this point I am indebted to Leo Braudy's fine study *Jean Renoir: The World of His Films* (Garden City, N.Y., 1972).

4. Leo Braudy notes (*ibid.*, p. 194) that the house where Renoir was born appears distantly in the background of *French Cancan*.

Chapter 16

1. See Capra, *op. cit.*, pp. 69–72.

2. *Ibid.*, p. 297.

3. *Ibid.*, p. 294 *ff.*

4. See Joe Adamson's discussion of the evolution of *Duck Soup* in *Groucho, Harpo, Chico, and Sometimes Zeppo* (New York, 1973).

Chapter 17

1. Armand J. Cauliez, *Jacques Tati* (Paris, 1968), p. 13.

2. The opinions of Bernard Davidson and J. P. Coursodon, quoted in Durgnat, *op. cit.*, p. 47. Rather strange praise.

Chapter 18

1. For specific parallels between Bergman's film and Shakespeare's play, see Stanley Cavell, *The World Viewed* (New York, 1971), p. 50.

Selective Bibliography

Adamson, Joe. *Groucho, Harpo, Chico, and Sometimes Zeppo*. New York: Simon and Schuster, 1973.

Agee, James. "Comedy's Greatest Era," in *Agee on Film: Reviews and Comments*. Boston: Beacon Press, n.d. Pp. 1–21.

Bazin, André. *Jean Renoir*, edited and with an introduction by François Truffaut, translated by W. W. Halsey, II, and William H. Simon. New York: Simon and Schuster, 1973.

————. *What Is Cinema?* Berkeley and Los Angeles: University of California Press, 1967.

Bergson, Henri. "Laughter," in *Comedy*, ed. Wylie Sypher. Garden City, N.Y.: Doubleday Anchor, 1956. Pp. 61–190.

Blesh, Rudi. *Keaton*. New York: Macmillan, 1966.

Braudy, Leo. *Jean Renoir: The World of His Films*. Garden City, N.Y.: Doubleday, 1972.

Brownlow, Kevin. *The Parade's Gone By*. New York: Knopf, 1968.

Capra, Frank. *The Name Above the Title*. New York: Macmillan, 1971.

Cauliez, Armand J. *Jacques Tati*. Paris: Éditions Seghers, 1968.

Cavell, Stanley. *The World Viewed*. New York: Viking, 1971.

Chaplin, Charles. *My Autobiography*. New York: Simon and Schuster, 1964.

Chardère, Bernard. *Jean Renoir*. Lyon: Premier Plan, 1962.

Clair, René. *Reflections on the Cinema*. London: William Kimber, 1953.

Domarchi, Jean. *George Cukor*. Paris: Éditions Seghers, 1965.

Durgnat, Raymond. *The Crazy Mirror: Hollywood Comedy and the American Image*. New York: Horizon Press, 1970.

Everson, William K. *The Films of Laurel and Hardy*. New York: Citadel, 1967.

————. *The Films of Hal Roach*. New York: Museum of Modern Art, 1971.

Eyles, Allen. *The Marx Brothers: Their World of Comedy*. New York: A. S. Barnes, 1966.

Ford, Charles. *Max Linder*. Paris: Éditions Seghers, 1966.

Fowler, Gene. *Father Goose: The Story of Mack Sennett*. New York: Covici, Friede Publishers, 1934.

Huff, Theodore. *Charlie Chaplin*. New York: Pyramid Books, 1964.

Keaton, Buster. *My Wonderful World of Slapstick*. London: Allen and Unwin, 1967.

Kerr, Walter. *The Silent Clowns*. New York: Knopf, 1975.

Lahue, Kalton C. *The World of Laughter: The Motion Picture Comedy Short, 1910–1930*. Norman, Okla.: University of Oklahoma Press, 1966.

———— and Terry Brewer. *Kops and Custard: The Legend of Keystone Films*. Norman, Okla.: University of Oklahoma Press, 1967.

Lebel, J. P. *Buster Keaton*. Translated by P. D. Stovin. New York: A. S. Barnes, 1967.

Leprohon, Pierre. *Jean Renoir:* New York, Crown, 1971.

Lloyd, Harold. *An American Comedy*. New York: Benjamin Blom, 1971.

Madsen, Axel. *Billy Wilder*. Bloomington, Ind. and London: Indiana University Press, 1969.

Maland, Charles J. *American Visions: The Films of Chaplin, Ford, Capra, and Welles*. New York: Arno Press, 1977.

Maltin, Leonard. *Movie Comedy Teams*. New York: New American Library, 1970.

Marx, Harpo. *Harpo Speaks*. London: Gollancz, 1961.

Mast, Gerald. *A Short History of the Movies*. New York: Bobbs-Merrill, 1976.

McCabe, John. *Charlie Chaplin*. Garden City, N.Y.: Doubleday, 1978.

McCaffrey, Donald W. *Focus on Chaplin*. Englewood Cliffs, N.J.: Prentice-Hall, 1971.

————. *Four Great Comedians: Chaplin, Lloyd, Keaton, Langdon*. New York: A. S. Barnes, 1968.

————, ed. *Focus on Chaplin*. Englewood Cliffs, N.J.: Prentice-Hall, 1971.

Moews, Daniel. *Keaton: The Silent Films Close Up*. Berkeley and Los Angeles: University of California Press, 1977.

Nathan, David. *The Laughtermakers: A Quest for Comedy*. London: Peter Owen, 1971.

Olson, Elder. *The Theory of Comedy*. Bloomington, Ind. and London: Indiana University Press, 1968.

Payne, Robert. *The Great God Pan*. New York: Hermitage House, 1952.

Quigley, Isabel. *Charlie Chaplin: Early Comedies*. New York and London: Dutton/Vista, 1968.

Ramsaye, Terry. *A Million and One Nights*. New York: Simon and Schuster, 1964.

Robinson, David. *Buster Keaton*. Bloomington, Ind. and London: Indiana University Press, 1969.

Sarris, Andrew. *The American Cinema: Directors and Directions 1929–1968*. New York: Dutton, 1968.

Sennett, Mack. *King of Comedy*. Garden City, N.Y.: Doubleday, 1954.

Sypher, Wylie. "The Meanings of Comedy," in *Comedy*, ed. Sypher. Garden City, N.Y.: Doubleday Anchor, 1956. Pp. 193–255.

Taylor, Robert Lewis. *W. C. Fields: His Follies and Fortunes*. Garden City, N.Y.: Doubleday, 1949.

Turconi, David. *Mack Sennett*. Paris: Éditions Seghers, 1966.

Tyler, Parker. *Chaplin: Last of the Clowns*. New York: Horizon Press, 1972.

Wead, George. *Buster Keaton and the Dynamics of Visual Wit*. New York: Arno Press, 1976.

Weinberg, Herman G. *The Lubitsch Touch*. New York: Dutton, 1968.

Wood, Robin. *Howard Hawks*. Garden City, N.Y.: Doubleday, 1968.

Appendix A

DISTRIBUTORS OF COMIC FILMS
KEY TO ABBREVIATIONS LISTED IN INDEX

CCM
C.C.M. Films Inc. (Audio-Brandon)
34 MacQuesten Parkway South
Mount Vernon, New York   10550
(914) 664–5051

or

1619 North Cherokee
Los Angeles, California   90028
(213) 463–0357

or

Branch offices in Oakland, California, Dallas, Brookfield, Illinois, Tucson, and Canton, Ohio

COL
See SWA. Films now distributed by Swank.

CON
Contemporary Films—most Contemporary Films now distributed by:
Corinth Films
410 East 62nd Street
New York, New York   10021
(212) 421–4770

EMG
Em Gee Film Library
16024 Ventura Boulevard
Encino, California   91436
(213) 981–5506

FI
Films Incorporated
440 Park Avenue South
New York, New York   10016
(212) 889–7910

or

5625 Hollywood Boulevard
Los Angeles, California   90028
(213) 466–5481

or

Branch offices in Atlanta and Wilmette, Illinois

JAN
Janus Films
745 Fifth Avenue
New York, New York   10022
(212) PL 3–7100

MMA
Museum of Modern Art
11 West 53rd Street
New York, New York   10019
(212) 956–4205

MOG
Mogull's
235 West 46th Street
New York, New York   10036
(212) 757–1414

NYF
New Yorker Films
250 West 57th Street
New York, New York   10019
(212) 265–1690

SWA
Swank Motion Pictures
201 South Jefferson
St. Louis, Missouri   63166
(314) 534–6300

or

393 Front Street
Hempstead, New York   11550
(516) 538–6500

or

1200 Roosevelt Road
Glen Ellyn, Illinois   60137
(312) 629–9004

or

Branch offices in Boston, Washington,
D.C., Houston, and Los Angeles

TWY
Twyman Films
329 Salem Avenue
Dayton, Ohio   45401
(513) 222–4014

or

2321 West Olive Avenue
Burbank, California   91505
(213) 843–8052

or

175 Fulton Avenue, #306
Hempstead, New York   11550
(516) 481–4050

UA
United Artists Sixteen
729 7th Avenue
New York, New York   10019

UNI
Universal Sixteen
445 Park Avenue
New York, New York
(212) 759–7500

or

8901 Beverly Boulevard
Los Angeles, California   90048
(213) 550–7461

or

Branch offices in Atlanta, Chicago, and
Dallas

WAL
Walter Reade Sixteen
666 Fifth Avenue
New York, New York   10019
(212) 246–1000

WAR
Warner Brothers 16
4000 Warner Boulevard
Burbank, California   91503
(213) 843–6000

WIL
Willoughby-Peerless
110 West 32nd Street
New York, New York   10001
(212) 564–1600

Appendix B

——

Stills of the following films from the Museum of Modern Art Film Stills Archive:

L'Arroseur arrosée; Lizzies of the Field; Bunny Attempts Suicide; Barney Oldfield's Race for Life; Three Foolish Weeks; Caught in the Kitchen; Making a Living; Kid Auto Races at Venice; Mabel's Married Life; The Tramp; The Immigrant; The Kid; Sunnyside; Modern Times; The Great Dictator; Limelight; The Love Nest; The General; Luke and the Mermaids; Grandma's Boy; Safety Last; The Strong Man; Three's a Crowd; His Majesty, the American; Brats; The Marriage Circle; The Italian Straw Hat; À Nous la liberté; The Golden Coach; Horse Feathers; It's a Gift; Mr. Hulot's Holiday; I Was a Male War Bride; Easy Living; Mad Wednesday; Zéro de Conduite; Doctor Strangelove.

Stills of *Uncle Josh at the Moving Picture Show* and *The Cook in Trouble* from the Kemp R. Niver paperprint collection of the Library of Congress.

Index

Selected distributors of 16 mm prints appear in parentheses following film titles. For a key to the abbreviations, see Appendix A.

A Nous la liberté (CON), 7, 14, 23,
    110–11, 203, 225–26, 227–28,
    229, 231, 235, 241
Abbott, Bud, and Lou Costello, 5,
    89, 196n, 200, 280, 281, 303
Academy Award ("Oscar"), 63, 257
Adam's Rib (FI), 5, 278
Adjustable Bed, The, 33
Adventurer, The (CCM, EMG), 67,
    78, 79, 81, 82, 113
After the Ball, 46
Agee, James, 63, 166, 270
Alchemist, The, 9, 16
Alice in Wonderland (UNI), 289
All on Account of the Milk, 46
All Lit Up, 186
All Wet (EMG), 188
Allen, Phyllis, 51, 55
Allen, Woody, 5, 8, 34, 36, 166,
    200, 204, 205, 279, 298, 299, 307,
    312–19
"Ambrose and Walrus," 54
American Mutoscope and Biograph
    Company, 33, 35, 43–44, 45–47,
    49, 70
And Then There Were None
    (EMG), 229
Angel, 211, 223, 224

Animal Crackers (SWA), 287
Anna Boleyn, 209, 210
Annie Hall (UA), 312, 313, 315,
    316–17, 318, 319
Apartment, The (UA), 8, 272, 273,
    274, 275, 278
Arbuckle, Roscoe C. ("Fatty"), 24,
    38, 44, 49, 50, 51n, 52, 54, 68,
    70, 73, 82, 85, 126, 133n, 167,
    195, 204
Aristophanes, 3, 5, 6, 21, 338
Aristotle and Aristotelian theory, 5,
    8, 12, 115, 151, 153, 154
Arkin, Alan, and Jules Feiffer, 279
Arnold, Edward, 168, 264
Arroseur arrosée, L' (EMG,
    MMA), 31–32, 43, 47, 51, 342
Arsenic and Old Lace (UA), 265
Art and life, 122, 133, 243–48, 251,
    252, 288, 291, 327, 333, 338
Arthur, Jean, 203, 204, 260, 264,
    266, 273, 276n
Astaire, Fred, 311
As You Like It, 4, 6, 17, 63, 68, 339
At the Circus (FI), 200, 286
Awful Truth, The (CCM), 5, 254,
    257, 278
Axelrod, George, 279

Back Stage (EMG), 151
Backstage, 24
Bacon Grabbers (CCM, EMG),
    185, 191
Bald Soprano, The, 5
Ball, Lucille, 281
Ball of Fire, 255n
Bananas (UA), 5, 10, 200, 201, 313,
    316, 318
Bank, The (CCM, EMG, MMA),
    75, 91
Bank Dick, The (UNI), 42, 290,
    291, 292
Barney Oldfield's Race for Life
    (CCM, EMG), 5, 47, 54, 57
Barrault, Jean-Louis, 305
Barrymore, John, 251
Barrymore, Lionel, 265n
Battle of the Century, The
    (EMG), 184–85, 193
Battling Butler (CCM), 128, 134,
    135, 136, 137, 141
Bazin, André, 66, 202, 203, 302n
Beaumont, Francis, and John
    Fletcher, 310
Be Your Age (EMG), 189
Beach Club, The, 56
Beauhunks (EMG), 191
Beaumarchais, Pierre, 233
Beauties of the Night (CON), 228,
    231
Beauty and the Devil (CON), 228
Beckett, Samuel, ix, x, 16, 107, 193n
Behind the Screen (CCM, EMG),
    78, 81
Bellamy, Ralph, 257
Bellboy, The (CCM), 304, 305
Below Zero (CCM, EMG), 185,
    191
Bergman, Ingmar, 25, 239n, 313, 317,
    331–33, 334, 339
Bergson, Henri, 4, 9, 21, 50, 52, 131,
    154, 170, 184, 337
Berkeley, Busby, 311, 312
Berlin, Irving, 311
Bête Humaine, La (CCM), 248
Bevan, Billy, 45, 56, 184, 186
Big Bus, The (FI), 307n

Big Business (CCM, EMG,
    MMA), 185, 191, 193
Big Idea, The, 186
Big Mouth, The (CCM), 120n, 305
Big Sleep, The (UA), 14
Big Store, The (FI), 200, 286
Biograph. See American Mutoscope
    and Biograph Company
Birth of a Nation, The (CCM,
    EMG, MMA), 5, 67, 117
Bitter Tea of General Yen, The,
    259
Bizarre, Bizarre (CCM), 7, 204,
    322–29
Blazing Saddles (SWA), 310, 311,
    312, 319
Bloom, Claire, 122
Blore, Eric, 271
Boat, The (CCM), 137
Bogart, Humphrey, 273, 276n, 309
Bogdanovich, Peter, 254–56
Bombshell (FI), 145, 252
Born Yesterday (CCM), 278
Boudu sauvé des eaux (CON), 7,
    14, 15, 204, 234, 235, 236, 237–
    42, 243, 244, 326, 342
Boyle, Peter, 311
Brackett, Charles, 272
Brats (CCM, EMG), 191, 193
Brave Hunter, The, 47
Brecht, Bertolt, ix, x, 15, 16, 21, 83,
    84, 93n, 106, 108, 115n, 137
Brennan, Walter, 262
Bringing Up Baby (FI), 5, 14, 26,
    204, 253–56
Broken China (EMG), 195
Brooks, Mel, 310–12, 313, 319
Brown, Joe E., 277
Browning, Tod, 182
Buchanan, Jack, 221
Bullitt (WAR), 256
Bumping into Broadway (EMG),
    156
Bunny, John, 34, 40–42, 46, 281,
    293
Burke, Billie, 223n
Burns, George, and Gracie Allen,
    280–81

Butcher Boy, The, 195
By the Sea (EMG), 74n

Cameraman, The, 126, 131, 134,
   141, 143, 195
Campbell, Eric, 81–82, 83
Camus, Albert, 21, 235
Candide, 240, 245
Capra, Frank, 16, 22, 25, 117, 168–
   74, 176, 190, 193, 199, 219, 229,
   250, 251, 259–65, 272, 274, 278,
   306, 340
Captain's Paradise, The (TWY),
   331
Carabiniers, Les (CCM), 34
Caretaker, The, 14
Carmen (1916) (CCM, EMG), 40,
   76–77, 78n, 80, 116, 214
Carmen (1918), 209, 210
Carnal Knowledge (CCM), 209, 279
Carné, Marcel, 7, 199, 239n, 243,
   322–25
Carol, Martine, 243, 326
Catch-22 (FI), 16, 279
Caucasian Chalk Circle, The, 93n
Caught in a Cabaret (EMG), 70,
   73
Caught in the Rain (EMG), 71, 73
Champion, The (CCM, EMG),
   73, 108, 128
Chaplin, Charles, x, 3, 4, 7, 9, 10n,
   11, 15, 15n, 18, 21n, 22, 23, 24,
   25, 26, 34, 36, 37, 38, 40, 40n, 42,
   44, 48n, 49, 51, 53, 55, 61–124,
   125, 126, 127, 128, 129, 130, 131,
   132, 135, 136, 137, 138, 143, 144,
   146, 149, 150, 151, 152, 153, 155,
   156, 158, 164, 165, 166, 167, 168,
   169, 170, 172, 173, 175, 176, 177,
   178, 179, 180, 182, 185, 186, 189,
   190, 195, 199, 201, 202, 203, 204,
   206, 208, 209, 210, 214, 218, 219,
   225, 226, 227, 228, 229, 230, 232,
   233, 235, 236, 239n, 242, 246,
   247, 248, 258, 262, 273, 281, 283,
   293, 294, 295, 296, 297, 298, 299,
   302, 303, 304, 305, 306, 307, 310,
   313, 314, 315, 316, 317, 318, 319,
   321, 323, 324, 338, 339, 340, 341,
   342
  Biographic background, 62, 64,
    76, 93n, 102, 124
  Cinematic technique, 23, 65–68,
    72, 74, 78, 88, 94, 98, 100, 110,
    119
  Contrast of rich and poor, 70, 75,
    80, 85, 89, 93, 106
  Critical misconceptions, 64–68
  Definitions of law, 74, 75, 93,
    107, 109, 113, 120, 122, 124
  Dreams, sleep and reality, 75, 83,
    88, 90, 91, 94, 101, 102, 110,
    113, 114, 116, 123
  Drunkenness, 24, 69, 85, 86, 106
  Evolution of character, 68, 69,
    71–73, 78, 87, 102, 115
  Evolution of costume, 68, 73
  Implication technique, 83, 91, 97,
    101, 102, 107, 116
  Irony, 72, 76, 77, 81, 82, 83, 90,
    94, 102, 106, 110, 111, 114, 117,
    121
  "Legitimacy," 87, 92, 93, 94, 100,
    106, 108
  Pathos, 76, 77, 80, 82, 90, 100,
    101, 107, 108, 113, 123
  Prostitution, 89, 101, 120
  Road life and "home," 74, 78, 91,
    102, 109, 110, 111, 113
  Social implications, 70, 72, 75,
    81, 82, 87, 105, 110, 120, 121
  Society and nature, 78, 87, 89, 92,
    95, 98, 110, 112, 114
  Sound track, 105, 106, 107, 108,
    114, 115, 116, 117, 120, 121,
    146
  Structural pattern, 64, 65, 74, 78,
    81, 82, 102, 115
  Surface and essence, 71, 77, 83,
    87, 90, 91, 92, 95, 99, 101, 106,
    110, 116, 118
  Survival, 72, 75, 87, 100, 101, 112,
    121
  Symbolism and metaphor, 72, 76,
    82, 86, 90, 92, 93, 94, 96, 99, 101,
    102, 106, 110

Chaplin, Charles (*cont.*)
  Use of objects, 68, 69, 75, 78, 90,
    93, 107, 108, 111
  Vicarious experiencing of success,
    70, 90, 101
  "Vulgar," unpleasant details, 79,
    83, 86, 112, 172
Chaplin, Sydney, 122
Chase, Charley, 184, 185, 187–90
Chaser, The (CCM), 166, 167, 168,
  176–78
Cheap Detective, The, 309
Cherrill, Virginia, 108
Chevalier, Maurice, 11, 222, 223,
  229, 230, 283
Children of Paradise (FI), 8, 243,
  323
Christie, Al, 143, 146, 165, 193–96
Christmas in July (UNI), 267, 268,
  270
Circus, The (RBC), 65, 89, 102–04,
  106, 107, 115, 229, 316
Circus Today (EMG), 57
Citizen Kane (FI, JAN), 117, 118,
  236
City Lights (FI), 3, 11, 24, 64, 66,
  67, 70, 74, 80, 85, 88, 105–10,
  111, 113, 114, 119, 121, 122,
  128, 177, 203, 229, 293, 299, 315,
  316
City Slicker, The (EMG), 155, 156
Clair, René, 7, 25, 36, 110–11, 203,
  206–07, 218, 222*n*, 224–31, 232–
  41 *passim*, 247–48, 270, 320,
  339, 340
  Cinematic devices, 227, 230
  Cops and crooks, 228
  Fantasy, 225, 231
  Friendship, 225, 226
  Money, 226
  Property, 227
  Social criticism, 224, 226, 229
  Sound track, 225, 230
Clever Dummy, The (EMG,
  MMA), 56
Cline, Eddie, 290, 292
Clockwork Orange, A (SWA), 7
Clubman and the Tramp, The, 46

Cluny Brown (FI), 224
Clyde, Andy, 52, 290
Cocoanuts, The (UNI), 283, 287
Cody, Lew, 216
Cohen Collects a Debt, 48
Cohl, Émile, 303
Colbert, Claudette, 259, 266
Collars and Cuffs (EMG), 190
College (CCM), 14, 125, 126, 128,
  134, 135, 136, 138, 141, 142,
  160
Columbia Pictures Corp., 143, 193,
  259
Comedy, definitions of, 3–13, 14–15,
  20–21
Comedy and the mechanical, 4, 21,
  35, 50, 51, 57, 79, 89, 111, 112,
  130, 131, 133, 135, 140, 186,
  194, 294, 337
Comedy and society, 307, 313–14,
  318
Comic character, 10, 32, 35–36, 38,
  41, 43, 50–51, 56, 61, 71, 73, 87,
  102, 103, 115, 129, 132, 135, 150,
  152, 167, 178, 183, 184, 186, 188,
  191, 194, 201, 203, 213, 221,
  250, 255–56, 264, 267, 271, 274,
  280, 294, 303, 314–16
Comic chase, 43, 47, 52, 55, 57, 61,
  135, 136, 141*n*, 194, 195, 228,
  253, 255, 256, 286, 291, 292
Comic cinematic devices, 11–13, 23,
  26–27, 35, 36, 51–52, 65–67,
  106, 114, 119, 120, 130–32, 157,
  158, 159, 177, 182, 184, 192,
  207, 208, 212, 213, 215, 216,
  220, 221, 223, 230, 232, 239,
  255, 256, 258, 266–67, 274–
  75, 287, 292, 293, 296–303, 304,
  316, 323, 324–25, 327–28,
  333, 336
Comic detachment, 15–19, 26, 50,
  121, 232, 258, 314–15, 327
Comic dialogue, 10, 116, 121, 201,
  222, 232, 239, 249, 257, 263,
  265–66, 278, 279, 282–83, 293
Comic iconoclasm, 21, 77, 82, 106,
  222, 241, 249, 252, 269, 271,

Comic iconoclasm (*cont.*)
278, 281–82, 287–88, 290, 319,
320, 321, 338–42
Comic non sequitur (illogic, surrealism), 43, 49, 56, 57, 183, 185,
200, 291, 292, 310–12, 322
Comic objects, 32, 51, 61, 68–70, 75,
78–79, 90, 93, 116, 130, 139,
170, 193, 199, 207, 209, 210,
212, 215, 216, 225, 227, 255,
274–75, 297
Comic pain, 51, 72, 74, 94, 101, 106,
170, 171, 173, 174, 189, 191,
217, 218, 258, 314–15, 342
Comic probabilities, 14–19, 26, 50,
141*n*, 160*n*, 256, 264, 331
Comic reflexivity, 300–303
Comic self-consciousness, 10–11, 36,
86, 201, 224, 248, 256, 265, 293,
304, 307, 313, 331, 340
Comic structure, 3–9, 25, 38, 39, 52–
53, 64–65, 81, 100, 102, 112,
115, 135, 140–42, 153–54, 159,
168, 172–73, 184, 185, 200, 201,
211, 232, 233, 236, 239–47, 249,
257–58, 273, 274, 280, 281, 287,
291, 304, 308–12, 320, 326, 329–
30, 332–34, 336
Comic subjects, 10
Comic themes, 53–54, 70–71, 82, 86,
89, 91, 92, 96, 101, 106, 109,
123–24, 130, 131, 136, 168–69,
173, 181, 192–93, 211, 216, 225,
226–28, 234, 242–43, 246–48,
254, 259–63, 271, 272, 273, 274,
288, 294, 320, 331, 333, 340–42
Comic theory. *See* Comedy, definitions of
Comic "worthlessness," 9, 11, 14,
16, 18, 308–9
Comrades (MMA), 46
Congreve, William, 7
Conklin, Chester, 44, 51, 54, 55,
56*n*, 70, 111, 186
Conley, Lige, 195
Conlin, Jimmy, 271
Conquest of the Pole (CCM,
EMG, MMA), 34

Convict 13 (CCM), 135, 140, 144
Coogan, Jackie, 87, 92–95, 110, 113
Cook in Trouble, The, 35
Cooper, Gary, 203, 255*n*, 261–62,
264, 276*n*
Cops (CCM, EMG), 134, 137,
140–41
Costello, Lou. *See* Abbott, Bud, and
Lou Costello
Count, The (CCM, EMG), 70, 78
Countess from Hong Kong, A
(UNI), 63, 258
Country Cupid, A, 46
Country Wife, The, 7, 340
Coward, Noël, 222
Crawford, Joan, 168
Crazy Ray, The (EMG, MMA),
226–27, 228
Crime of M. Lange, The (CCM),
234
Cukor, George, 64, 278–79
Cummings, Robert, 160*n*
Cure, The (CCM, EMG), 78, 79,
81, 151
Cure for Pokeritis, A (EMG), 41,
293
Cursed by His Beauty (EMG), 186
Curtis, Tony, 275, 276–78

Dalio, Marcel, 236
Damsel in Distress, A (FI), 281
Danger Girl, The (EMG), 55
Daniels, Bebe, 156
D'Arrast, Harry, 279
David Copperfield (FI), 289
Davis, Joan, 281
Davis, Mildred, 156, 157, 158
Day, Marceline, 143
Day in the Country, A (CON),
234, 235, 237
Day at the Races, A (FI), 286, 287
Daydreams (CCM), 137
Day's Pleasure, A (RBC), 87
Débuts d'un Patineur, Les
(MMA), 37
Delmar, Viña, 254
Demarest, William, 268, 271

De Mille, Cecil B., 67, 77, 97n, 210, 217, 265

Depression, 219, 223, 259, 263, 271

Design for Living (UNI), 222

Destiny (CCM, EMG), 210

Deux Timides, Les (CON), 231

Diamond, I.A.L., 199, 272

Dietrich, Marlene, 273, 290

Dinner at Eight (FI), 145, 223n, 278, 284

Doctor Strangelove: or How I Learned to Stop Worrying and Love the Bomb (COL), 3, 6, 9, 10, 11, 16, 25, 116, 204, 308–9, 334–37

Dog's Life, A (FI), 77, 87, 88–89, 92, 113, 189, 229

Domesticity, assault against, 41, 70, 109, 240, 288, 293

Donen, Stanley, 312n

Donlevy, Brian, 268

Double Indemnity (UNI), 273n, 275

Dough and Dynamite (CCM, EMG), 68, 70, 74

Down to Earth (CCM), 180

Dressler, Marie, 55, 310

Duck Soup (UNI), 38, 183, 200, 278, 281, 284–85, 286, 290, 310, 341

Dumont, Margaret, 42, 283, 285, 292

Dunne, Irene, 203, 254

Durante, Jimmy, 144

Durfee, Minta, 55, 68

Durgnat, Raymond, 18, 53, 56n

Ealing Studios, 311

Easy Go (*Free and Easy*) (FI), 144, 146

Easy Living (UNI), 204, 266, 267, 268, 270, 271

Easy Street (CCM, EMG), 23, 67, 77, 79, 81, 82–83, 87, 88, 89, 90 94, 111, 113, 117, 121, 173, 182, 229, 339

Edison, Thomas, 31, 32, 35, 43, 68

Educational comedies, 45, 143, 165, 193–96

Edwards, Harry, 169

Edwards, Snitz, 141

8½ (CCM), 247

Eisenstein, Sergei M., 88, 110, 114, 221, 321

Electric House, The (CCM), 125

Elena et les Hommes (CON), 241

Elsom, Isobel, 118

Emerson, John, 180–83

Enchanted Well, The, 35

Entr'acte (MMA), 227–28

Erotikon, 240

Erwin, Stu, 184

Essanay (S. and A.) Company, 7, 18, 38, 40, 53, 62, 68, 72–78, 150

Étaix, Pierre, 146, 171, 201, 204, 205

Everything You Always Wanted to Know about Sex (but Were Afraid to Ask) (UA), 316

Examination Day at School, 46

Fairbanks, Douglas, 39, 56, 137, 180–83, 185

Fast and Furious (EMG), 195

Fatal Glass of Beer, The (CCM, EMG), 288

Feet of Mud (EMG), 169–70

Fellini, Federico, 239n, 247

Feydeau, Georges, 6, 233, 255, 331–32, 333

Fielding, Henry, 5, 308

Fields, W. C., x, 25, 34, 40, 42, 45, 145, 200, 204, 205, 218, 280, 281, 288–93, 299, 310, 319, 338, 340

Finch, Flora, 41

Finishing Touch, The (CCM, EMG), 191

Finlayson, James, 184, 192

Fireman, The (CCM, EMG), 71, 78, 79, 81, 151

Fireman Save My Child (EMG), 151

First National Distributors' Circuit, 44, 63, 67, 86–96, 100, 101, 102, 321

Flaherty, Robert, 329
Fleming, Victor, 180–83, 252
Floorwalker, The (CCM, EMG), 71, 78, 79, 81, 195
Fluttering Hearts, 189
Forbidden Fruit, 210–11
Forbidden Paradise, 209, 213–14, 215
Ford, John, 4, 208, 209, 269
Foreign Affair, A (UNI), 272–73, 275, 278
Fourteenth of July, The, 226, 228
"Foxy Grandpa," 33, 34
Francis, Kay, 218
"Francis, the Talking Mule," 196n
Fred Ott's Sneeze, 31, 32
Frederick, Pauline, 216
French Cancan (CCM), 237, 247
Freshman, The, 8, 152, 153, 154–55, 158, 159, 161–63
Freud, Sigmund, 215n, 314, 327
Friganza, Trixie, 144
Front Page, The, 256, 257
Frozen North, The (CCM), 101, 125, 135, 307
Fun in a Chinese Laundry (MMA), 32, 35, 43
Furs, The, 46

Gabin, Jean, 236, 247
Gable, Clark, 260
Gabourie, Fred, 132
Garage, The (EMG), 133n
Garbo, Greta, 223, 290
Garvin, Anita, 184
Gates of Paris, 226, 228
General, The (CCM), 8, 9, 12, 23, 67, 127, 128, 131, 134, 135, 136, 137, 138, 141n, 142, 144, 160, 201, 256, 308
Gentlemen of Nerve (EMG), 69
Gentlemen Prefer Blondes (FI), 258
Get Out and Get Under, 158, 188
Getting Acquainted (EMG, MMA), 69, 73
Gilbert, Billy, 192
Gish, Lillian, 55, 135

Gleason, Jackie, 40
Gleason, James, 260
Godard, Jean-Luc, 15n, 34
Goddard, Paulette, 86, 110
Going My Way (UNI), 278
Gold Ghost, The (EMG), 195
Gold Rush, The (CCM, JAN, EMG), 11, 14, 65, 66, 83, 93, 100–02, 107, 108, 111, 113, 130, 151, 175, 177, 201, 206, 229, 273
Golden Coach, The, 7, 234, 235, 236, 237–38, 243–47
Gone with the Wind, 180, 253n
Go West (1925) (CCM), 130, 134, 135, 136, 138, 141
Go West (1940) (FI), 200, 286
Good Woman of Setzuan, The, 84
Graduate, The (CCM), 5, 209, 279
Grand Illusion (JAN), 235, 236
Grandma's Boy, 153, 154, 160–61, 163
Grant, Cary, 203, 251, 253–59, 264, 277
Grapes of Wrath, The (FI), 269
Great Dictator, The (FI), 7, 25, 26, 66, 67, 76, 80, 83, 88, 115–17, 120, 336, 340
Great McGinty, The (UNI), 266, 267, 268–69
Great Race, The (CCM, SWA), 201
Greenwood, Joan, 331
Grégor, Nora, 236
Greig, Robert, 271
Griffith, David Wark, 5, 35, 36, 44, 45–46, 47, 48, 52, 55, 67, 68, 70, 102, 117, 135, 181, 208, 216, 265, 307
Guinness, Alec, 331

Hail the Conquering Hero (UNI), 8, 270
Hale, Georgia, 100–02, 175
Hamilton, Margaret, 292–93
Hard Day's Night, A (UA), 8
Hardy, Oliver. *See* Laurel, Stan, and Oliver Hardy

Harlow, Jean, 252, 283
Hart, William S., 56, 101, 135, 307
Haunted House, The (CCM,
  EMG), 131, 195
Hawks, Howard, 25, 199, 208, 250–
  59, 263, 264, 265, 266, 271, 272,
  274, 276, 279
Hayden, Sterling, 334
He Did and He Didn't (EMG), 56
Hecht, Ben, 199, 249, 252, 253, 256,
  271
Heller, Joseph, ix, 16, 21
Help! (UA), 8
Help! Help!, 47
Henderson, Del, 44
Hepburn, Audrey, 273
Hepburn, Katharine, 203, 204, 253–
  56
*Herr Puntilla and His Knight,
  Matti*, 106
High Anxiety, 310, 312
High Sign, The (CCM), 131
High and Dizzy (MMA), 38, 154,
  157, 158
His Bitter Pill (MMA), 54
His Favorite Pastime (EMG), 68,
  69–70
His Girl Friday (CCM), 256–57
His Majesty the American, 180, 183
His New Job (EMG), 73, 76
His Picture in the Papers (EMG),
  181
His Trysting Places (CCM, EMG),
  70, 73
His Wife's Mother, 46
Hitchcock, Alfred, 13, 160n, 208,
  210n, 308, 310, 312
Holden, William, 273
Hollywood Production Code, 222,
  259, 268
Hollywood studio system and
  values, 249, 250, 252n, 268, 270,
  271, 272, 276, 277, 287, 291–92,
  306
Hooks and Jabs, 195
Hope, Bob, 200, 280, 281
Hopkins, Miriam, 222
Hopper, Hedda, 306

Horsefeathers (UNI), 162, 200,
  281, 283, 284, 286, 310
Horse's Mouth, The (JAN), 331
Horton, Edward Everett, 218, 219,
  220, 222
Houdini, Harry, 126, 128
Hurlock, Madeleine, 57

I Do, 158
I Married a Witch (CON), 229
I Was a Male War Bride (FI), 251,
  257–59, 276
Ibsen, Henrik, 16
Ideas through comedy, 14–19, 22,
  64, 72, 76, 81, 82, 86, 97, 110–
  11, 116, 133, 136, 139–40, 152,
  181, 208, 213, 219, 221, 229, 236,
  250, 259, 265, 270, 278, 285,
  292, 297, 304, 318–19, 322,
  327–28, 334
Idle Class, The (RBC), 70, 76, 87,
  115
Immigrant, The (CCM, EMG),
  67, 74, 78, 80, 81, 102, 108, 116,
  173, 228
Importance of Being Earnest, The,
  14, 309
In Again, Out Again, 181
In the Park (EMG), 73
Ince, Thomas, 45, 48, 135, 307
Insley, Charles, 75
Interiors (UA), 298, 313, 315, 317,
  318
International House (UNI), 289
Intolerance (CCM, EMG, MMA),
  ix, 5, 117, 135, 140, 209, 307
Ionesco, Eugene, ix, 3, 5, 6, 15, 16,
  21
Irma La Douce, 273
It Happened One Night (COL), 5,
  259, 260, 265
It Happened Tomorrow, 229
Italian Straw Hat, The (CON), 23,
  225, 227, 228, 229, 339
It's a Gift (1923) (EMG), 133, 186
It's a Gift (1934) (UNI), 42, 288,
  289

It's a Mad, Mad, Mad, Mad World
(UA), 24, 200–01
It's a Wonderful Life (EMG), 260,
261, 264, 265n

Jack, or The Submission, 5
Jackson, Gordon, 331
James, Henry, 267
Jean, Gloria, 291, 292
Jests, 31–34, 35, 38, 41, 43, 45, 50,
61, 70, 271
Jitney Elopement, The (CCM,
EMG), 73, 74
John Bunny Dips into Society
(EMG), 41
Johnstone, Will B., 284
Jolson, Al, 144
Jonson, Ben, 14, 15, 16, 20, 21, 339
Joseph Andrews, 5, 308
Jour de Fête, 294, 296
Joyce, James, ix, x, 309, 310
Jules and Jim (JAN), 225n
Just Nuts, 150, 155

Kafka, Franz, ix, 16
Kahn, Madeline, 255, 312
Kalmar, Bert, and Harry Ruby, 200,
284
Kanin, Garson, and Ruth Gordon,
249
Karno Pantomime Troupe, 24, 62,
69, 76, 190
Kaufman, George S., and Morrie
Ryskind, 200, 284
Kaye, Danny, 26, 200, 280
Kazan, Elia, 239n
Keaton, Buster, 4, 5, 7, 8, 9, 12, 23,
24, 26, 48n, 61–62, 64, 67, 101,
102, 123–24, 125–46, 149, 150,
151, 152, 153, 154, 155, 156,
158n, 159, 160n, 164, 165, 166,
167, 168, 169, 170, 171, 172,
176, 177, 178, 179, 180, 181,
182, 186, 194, 195, 196, 199,
201, 202, 203, 204, 208, 218,
230, 234, 281, 293, 294, 295,
299, 303, 304, 305, 306, 307,
308, 313, 314, 316, 321, 338,
340, 341, 342
    Assertion of human will, 139
    Biographical background, 125–26,
    142–43
    Body, 126, 128, 129, 131, 142, 143,
    145, 146
    Character, 129, 134–35, 142
    Cinematic technique, 130–33,
    142, 146
    Collapse of career, 143–46
    "Elmer," 143–44, 146
    Face, 127, 129, 142, 143, 144, 145
    Failure and fatalism, 137–39
    Immensity of objects and uni-
    verse, 130
    Keaton "imperative," 135
    Machines, 125, 130, 131, 133, 140
    Melodrama, 135, 141n, 308
    Nature, 129, 130, 132, 133, 144
    Parody, 135, 138, 141, 142, 307–8
    Sense and nonsense, 132, 134
    Sound track, 145–46
    Sports, 125, 126, 141
    Strategy, 127, 128, 131, 134, 142
    Structures, 129, 130, 133, 140–42
    Stunts, 131, 132, 133, 140, 145
    Surface and essence, 136–37
    Symmetry, 135, 141, 142
    Women, 138–39
Keaton, Diane, 314, 317
Keaton, Eleanor, 139n
Keaton, Joe, 125
Kelly, Gene, 180
Kennedy, Edgar, 44, 184, 192, 271,
278
Kennedy, Merna, 103–04
Kessel, Adam, and Charles Bauman,
48, 62n
Keystone Kops, 50, 51, 53, 54, 228
Keystone Pictures, 7, 24, 43, 45, 47–
54, 55, 56, 61, 62, 68–72, 73,
100, 150, 151, 155, 185, 187,
188
Kid, The (RBC), 67, 77, 80, 81, 87,
88, 92–95, 97, 98, 102, 107, 109,
110, 113
Kid Auto Races at Venice (EMG),
49, 68, 69

Kid Brother, The, 8, 153, 154, 158, 163
Kid Speed (EMG), 194
King Lear, 8, 10n
King in New York, A (RBC), 63
Kiss Me Again, 225
Knight of the Burning Pestle, The, 310
Knockout, The (CCM, EMG, MMA), 52, 73
Korman, Harvey, 310
Kramer, Stanley, 24, 239n
Kubrick, Stanley, 25, 208, 239n, 308, 334–37
Kuhn, Edward, 32

La Cava, Gregory, 279
Lady for a Day, 259, 261
Lady Eve, The (UNI), 267, 268, 270
Lady Windermere's Fan (EMG), 216, 218, 342
Lamont, Charles, 196
Lang, Fritz, 110
Langdon, Harry, 7, 45, 102, 128, 133, 149, 165–78, 179, 182, 191, 192, 195, 196, 200, 201, 202, 203, 259, 303, 306, 307, 313, 314, 316, 340
  Biographical background, 165
  Childishness, 166–67, 169, 175, 176
  Face and body, 166
  Gag situations, 169, 170, 171–72, 176–77
  Mentality, 166
  Pathos, 165–66, 175
  Physical gestures, 167
  Sexuality, 167, 171, 176, 177
  Thematic implications, 168–70, 173
  Use of the cinema, 177–78
La Rocque, Rod, 213
La Ronde (JAN), 14, 325–28
Last Laugh, The (CCM, EMG, MMA), ix, 182
Last Millionaire, The (CON), 231
Laughton, Charles, 264

Laurel, Stan, and Oliver Hardy, x, 6, 18, 34, 136, 152, 178, 184, 185, 190–93, 226, 299
Lavender Hill Mob, The (JAN), 8, 331
Leachman, Cloris, 310
Lederer, Charles, 199, 249, 256, 257
Lehar, Franz, 207, 218
Lehrman, Henry ("Pathé"), 44, 49
Leisen, Mitchell, 266
Lemmon, Jack, 273, 276–78
Lesson, The, 6
Lester, Richard, 8, 36
Letter from an Unknown Woman (CCM), 326n
Lewis, Jerry, 26, 34, 120n, 200, 204, 205, 303–6, 340
Limelight (FI), 10n, 24, 67, 68, 76, 80, 86, 109, 115, 120, 121–24, 143, 246, 247, 248
Linder, Max, 36–40, 48n, 68
Literary parallels, ix, 3–9, 18, 21, 234, 308, 309, 310, 338–41
Little Murders, 279
Lizzies of the Field (EMG), 57
Lloyd, Harold, 7, 37, 128, 137, 149–64, 165, 166, 168, 169, 170, 172, 177, 178, 179, 180, 182, 183, 184, 185, 186, 187, 188, 190, 199, 201, 203, 234, 303, 304, 313–14, 316, 317
  American dream, 152, 163
  Biographical background, 150, 164
  Cinematic control, 156, 158, 159, 161
  Gag construction, 152, 159–64
  Glass character, 151, 313
  "High rise" films, 157, 160n, 163
  "Lonesome Luke," 150
  Physical control, 150, 155, 156, 157
  Plot construction, 153–55, 159
  Push and energy, 160–61, 162–63
  Social naïveté, 154–55, 163–64
  Social success, 156
  "Willie Work," 155
Lola Montès (CCM), 243, 326

Lolita (FI), 336
Lombard, Carole, 251, 253
Lonely Villa, The (EMG, MMA), 47
Lonesome Luke on Tin Can Alley, 150–51
Long Pants (CCM), 166, 167, 168, 173–74, 178
Loos, Anita, 180–83
Lorenz, Pare, 269
Lost Horizon (CCM), 224, 259, 261, 265
Lost Weekend, The (UNI), 275
Love, Speed, and Thrills (EMG), 57
Love in the Afternoon, 272
Love and Death (UA), 313, 317, 318, 319
Love for Love, 7, 340
Love Parade, The (UNI), 211, 212, 213, 214, 220, 230
Lubitsch, Ernst, 8, 11, 12, 25, 36, 97, 98, 145, 190, 199, 206–24, 225, 226, 230, 238, 239, 250, 251, 257, 259, 267–68, 271, 272, 274, 278, 290, 306, 320, 327, 338, 340
  Anti-romanticism, 209, 210, 214, 216, 217, 218, 220
  Cinematic devices, 207, 208–09, 212, 213, 215, 216, 220, 223
  German career, 209
  Intellect, 208, 221
  Love and sex, 209, 211, 213, 217, 220, 221, 222
  Marital tensions, 211, 214, 217
  Objects, 207, 209, 210, 212, 215, 216
  Parody, 213–15, 221–22
  Surface and essence, 218, 219, 221
  Symbolism, 213, 215, 216, 218
  Vocation and desire, 211
Luck o' the Foolish, The, 169
Luke and the Bangtails, 150
Lumière, Louis and Auguste, 31–33, 35, 38
Lynn, Diana, 268

"Ma and Pa Kettle," 196*n*

"Mabel and Fatty," 54, 56
Mabel's Dramatic Career (MMA), 34
Mabel's Married Life (EMG), 69
MacArthur, Charles, 252, 256
MacBeth, 8, 9
MacDonald, Jeannette, 221
Mace, Fred, 44
Mack, Marian, 138
Mackendrick, Alexander, 329–31
MacLaine, Shirley, 273
MacMurray, Fred, 273
Mad Wednesday (EMG), 163, 270
Madame de . . . (CON), 326
Madame Du Barry (MMA), 209, 210
Magician, The (JAN), 333
Magnani, Anna, 236, 243–47
Magnificent Men in Their Flying Machines, Those (FI), 201
Making a Living (EMG, MMA), 68, 69
Malle, Louis, 8
Maltese Falcon, The (UA), 8, 308*n*, 309
Man of Aran (CON), 329
Man on the Flying Trapeze, The (UNI), 288, 289
Man and Superman, 5, 251
Man in the White Suit, The (JAN), 331
Mankiewicz, Herman J., 249, 284, 290
Mann, Hank, 44, 55
Man's a Man, A, 137
Marivaux, Pierre, 233
Marriage Circle, The (MMA), 5, 9, 211–13, 214, 216–17, 218
Marshall, Herbert, 10, 218, 224
Martin, Dean, and Jerry Lewis, 89
Martin, Tony, 285, 286
Marx Brothers, 18, 25, 34, 38*n*, 40, 143, 145, 162, 200, 204, 205, 218, 280, 281–88, 290, 292, 293, 299, 306, 310, 311, 338, 340, 341
Marx, Chico, 282–83

Marx, Groucho, 42, 144, 282, 283, 310, 313
Marx, Harpo, x, 278, 283, 284, 285–86, 313
Marx, Karl, 64, 117, 207, 219, 224, 230, 233, 309
Marx, Zeppo, 282, 285
Masquerader, The (EMG, MMA), 73
Max Plays at Drama (EMG), 38
Max and the Quinquina (EMG), 37–38
Mayer, Louis B., 142, 144, 145*n*, 223
McCarey, Leo, 184, 190, 191, 254, 257, 264, 278, 284, 322
McLeod, Norman Z., 284
Meet John Doe (EMG), 10, 168, 260, 261, 265
Méliès, Georges, 33, 34–35, 38*n*, 43, 52, 94, 229
Menjou, Adolphe, 97, 212, 213
Merry Widow, The (1925) (FI), 8, 12
Merry Widow, The (1934) (FI), 8, 11, 12, 211, 213, 214, 222–23
Metropolis (CCM, EMG, MMA), 110
M-G-M (Metro-Goldwyn-Mayer), 125, 142, 143, 223, 271, 285–88, 289
Mickey (EMG, MMA), 50, 55
Midsummer Night's Dream, A, 4, 6, 63, 332, 339
Million, Le (EMG), 203, 222*n*, 226, 227, 228, 230, 231, 241
Million Dollar Legs (UNI), 183, 289–90
Minnelli, Vincente, 279
Miracle of Morgan's Creek, The (FI), 268, 270
Mississippi (UNI), 289
Mr. Deeds Goes to Town (CCM), 16–17, 22, 168–69, 259, 260, 263–64, 265
Mr. Hulot's Holiday, 23, 26, 295, 296, 297, 305
Mr. Jones Has a Card Party, 46
Mr. Smith Goes to Washington

(CCM), 8, 22, 168, 169, 219, 260, 263–64, 265
Mitchell, Thomas, 260
Mix, Tom, 185, 307
Modern Times (RBC), 7, 9, 15, 23, 37, 65, 66, 67, 69, 77, 79, 80, 83, 86, 95, 102, 110–14, 117, 121, 201, 203, 226, 229, 230, 293, 312–13
Molière, 233
Mollycoddle, The (CCM, MMA), 8, 180, 182
Mon Oncle, 294, 295, 296, 297, 299, 302, 321
Monkey Business (UNI), 200, 281, 283, 285, 286
Monroe, Marilyn, 275, 276*n*, 277–78
Monsieur Verdoux (FI), 6, 10, 22, 63, 65, 66, 67, 70, 76, 77, 83, 98, 102, 107, 115, 117–21, 151*n*, 219, 323, 336
Monte Carlo (UNI), 214, 221–22, 230
Montgomery, Robert, 144
Moore, Robert, 309, 310, 312
Morgan, Frank, 252
Morrison, Ernie, 186
Motion Picture Academy of Arts and Sciences. *See* Academy Award
Movie Movie, 312*n*
Movie Night (EMG), 184, 188
Much Ado About Nothing, 4, 6, 9, 233, 251, 339
Muddy Romance, A (EMG), 49
Multilevel plot structure, 6–7, 113–14, 233, 243–45, 320, 331
Murder by Death (SWA), 309
Music Box, The (CCM, EMG), 18, 185, 191, 192, 193
Music hall tradition, 24, 38*n*, 40*n*, 62, 76, 125, 150, 280, 286, 287
Mutual Film Corporation, 40, 62, 65, 67, 78–84, 85, 150
My Darling Clementine (FI), 8
My Little Chickadee (UNI), 292–93

Mystery of the Leaping Fish, The (MMA), 180, 182

Nature in opposition to society, 21, 41–42, 96, 113–14, 217, 225–27, 234–36, 238, 239–42, 244–45, 293, 295, 297, 322
Navigator, The (CCM), 8, 128, 131, 134, 141
Negri, Pola, 209, 210, 213
Neighbors (CCM), 133n
Never Give a Sucker an Even Break (UNI), 183, 291, 310
Never Weaken (EMG), 152, 154, 157, 158, 159
"New" Comedy, x, 3, 14–15, 168, 211–12, 250
New Janitor, The (EMG), 68, 70–71, 75
New Tenant, The, 6
Nichols, Dudley, 249, 253
Nichols, Mike, 279
Nietzsche, Friedrich Wilhelm, ix, 64
Night at the Opera, A (FI), 200, 285, 286, 287
Night in the Show, A (CCM, EMG), 24, 76
Night Out, A (EMG), 24, 38, 73, 76, 85
Nights of Cabiria (CCM), 7
Ninotchka (FI), 211, 219, 223–34
Noise from the Deep, A, 51n
Normand, Mabel, 44, 47, 48, 49, 50, 51n, 55, 56, 62n, 69
North by Northwest (FI), 8
Nothing Sacred (MOG), 252–53
Nudnick of the North, 101
Nutty Professor, The (FI), 304–5

O'Brien, Pat, 275
October (CCM, MMA), 321
O'Donnell, Specs, 184
"Old" comedy, 5, 14, 15, 287
Old Fashioned Way, The (UNI), 289
Olson, Elder, ix, x, 9, 15

One A.M. (CCM, EMG), 24, 67, 69, 78, 79, 81, 82, 130, 177
One Hour with You (UNI), 213, 290
One, Two, Three (UA), 272
O'Neal, Ryan, 255–56
One Week (CCM), 138–39
Only Angels Have Wings, 255n
Ophuls, Max, 25, 218, 243, 325–28
Othello, 8, 63
Our Gang, 185
Our Hospitality (CCM), 5, 128, 134, 136, 141–42, 153, 159n, 167

Pair of Tights, A (EMG), 184
Palace at the Arabian Nights, The (MMA), 34
Paleface, The (CCM), 130–31, 134
Pallette, Eugene, 267
Palm Beach Story, The (UNI), 14, 266, 267, 271–72
Pamela, 308
Pangborn, Franklin, 271, 291, 292
Paramount Pictures Corporation, 44, 45, 145, 223, 278, 281, 282, 285, 286, 287, 288, 289
Pardon Us (EMG), 191
Parody, 5, 38, 39, 47, 53, 54, 56, 73, 76–7, 90, 119, 135–7, 138, 140, 141n, 163, 180–3, 185, 200, 209, 213, 214, 220, 221–22, 252, 257, 268, 270, 275, 277, 281, 282, 283, 285, 290, 306–13, 325
Passion of Joan of Arc, The (CCM), ix
Passionate Plumber, The (FI), 144
Pat and Mike (FI), 289
Pathé Film Company, 43, 45, 156
Patsy, The (FI), 300, 305–6
Pawnshop, The (CCM, EMG), 67, 71, 78, 79, 80, 81, 100
Pay Day, 87
"Peppering" structure, 52, 55
Perelman, S. J., 200, 284
Pharmacist, The (CCM, EMG), 42, 288, 289

Philadelphia Story, The (FI), 278

Physical business and motion, 11,
     27, 32, 34, 35, 38, 46–47, 49–50,
     56, 57, 58, 61, 71–72, 99–100,
     103, 107, 109, 112, 116, 123,
     126, 129, 132, 146, 150, 156,
     157, 162, 166, 171, 172, 173,
     174, 179, 181, 185, 188, 194,
     199, 200, 201, 202, 212, 214,
     225, 263, 284, 293

Picaresque structure, 7, 65, 113

Pickens, Slim, 317

Pickford, Mary, 55, 210

Picking Peaches (EMG), 170, 195

Picnic on the Grass (CON), 234,
     235, 238

Pilgrim, The (FI), 22, 64, 65, 77, 87,
     88, 94, 95, 97, 102, 110, 113,
     121, 130, 201, 229

Pipe the Whiskers, 151

Pirandello, Luigi, 244, 306

Pitts, ZaSu, 264

Platinum Blonde (COL), 259

Plautus, 4

Playhouse, The (CCM, EMG), 24,
     132, 135, 140, 144, 307

Play it Again, Sam (FI), 201, 279

Playtime (TWY), 294, 296, 297,
     298–303

Police (CCM, EMG), 77, 83

Pollard, Snub, 122, 133, 185–6, 282

Poppy (UNI), 289

Porter, Edwin S., 33

Potemkin (CCM, MMA), ix, 221,
     313

Pretension, attack against, 34, 37,
     42, 46, 53, 105, 107, 183, 192,
     218, 220, 224, 228, 240, 250,
     253, 271, 281, 284, 287, 291,
     306, 320

Prévert, Jacques, 199, 232, 243, 322–
     25

Property Man, The (EMG), 24,
     71–72, 151

Pudovkin, V. I., 98, 114, 207

Purviance, Edna, 72–102

Quiet Man, The (FI), 4n

Radio, influence of, 280–81

Raft, George, 275

Raphaelson, Samson, 199

Rastus and the Game Cock, 53

Rat's Knuckles (EMG), 189

Raye, Martha, 66–67, 107, 118, 119

Reaching for the Moon (MMA),
     180, 181, 183

Red Dust (FI), 180

Reductio ad absurdum, 5–6, 115

Reid, Wallace, 149, 180

Renoir, Jean, 6, 15, 199, 218, 229,
     232–48, 306, 320, 321, 339, 340,
     341
  Art and life, 242–48
  Cinematic control, 234–35, 237,
     239, 242, 246
  Classical traditions, 233
  Detachment and irony, 232, 239–
     40, 244
  Inevitability, 233
  Influences, 232–33
  Intellectual ambivalence, 242–43,
     247, 248
  Nature and society, 234–35, 238,
     239–43, 244
  Sound track, 237–38
  Structure, 232, 236, 239–47

Rhinoceros, 14

Richardson, Samuel, 5, 171, 308

"Riffing" structure, 7, 39, 52, 70,
     201, 304

Rink, The (CCM, EMG), 37, 67,
     70, 78, 79, 86

Rio Bravo (WAR), 8

Ripley, Arthur, 169

Riskin, Robert, 199, 249, 259

R.K.O. Radio Pictures, 288n

Roach, Hal, 151–52, 155, 183–93,
     278, 307

Roberts, "Big Joe," 141

Rogers, Will, 185, 307

Romances, 5, 8, 14

Romanticism, assault against, 136,
     208, 209, 214, 216, 217, 218–19,
     223, 252, 287, 293

Room Service (CCM), 288n

Rosita, 210

Rounders, The (EMG, MMA), 24, 38, 68, 70, 85
Ruggles, Charles, 218, 219, 256, 264
Ruggles of Red Gap (UNI), 264, 278
Rules of the Game, The (JAN), 6, 7, 14, 23, 26, 201, 233, 234, 235, 236, 237, 238–39, 242–43, 245, 248, 331
Russell, Rosalind, 256

Saboteur (UNI), 160n
Sabrina (FI), 272, 273, 274, 275, 278
Safety Last, 153, 159–60
St. John, Al, 55
Saturday Afternoon (CCM, EMG), 166, 168
Scarecrow, The (CCM), 133
Schenk, Joseph, 145
Schenk, Nicholas, 145n
Schnitzler, Arthur, 215n, 218, 222, 325–28
Schoolmaster's Surprise, The, 33, 43
Scott, George C., 204, 334
Sea Squawk, The (CCM), 167, 169
Sebastian, Dorothy, 138
Sellers, Peter, 331, 335
Selznick, David O., 253
Semon, Larry, 194
Sennett, Mack, 5, 7, 14, 18, 24, 34, 36, 42, 43–58, 62, 64, 68–69, 70, 71, 72, 73, 74n, 75, 76, 82, 103, 111, 126, 129, 131, 136n, 141n, 150, 151–52, 155, 165, 169, 170, 179, 180, 183, 184, 185, 186, 187, 188, 193, 194, 195, 201, 202, 228, 255, 256, 281, 290, 292, 304, 305, 306, 307, 310, 313, 321, 322, 339, 340
Settled at the Seaside (EMG), 188
Seven Chances (CCM), 5, 134, 135, 142
Seven Days in May (FI), 309
Seven Years Bad Luck (EMG), 38
Shakespeare, William, 4, 5, 6, 10, 14, 15, 17, 62, 63, 121–22, 136, 233, 251, 339

Shanghaied (EMG), 76
Shaw, George Bernard, ix, 5, 15, 21, 63
Sheekman, Arthur, 200
She Meets with Wife's Approval, 33, 41
Sheridan, Ann, 251, 257–8
Sherlock Jr. (CCM), 26, 125, 132–33, 136, 137, 142, 195, 316
Shoulder Arms (FI), 65, 87, 88, 89–90, 115, 173
Shut Up, 33, 34
Silence est d'or, Le, 229
Silent comedy, theory of, 23–26, 146, 201–05
Silent Movie (FI), 310
Simon, Michael, 204, 236, 241–42, 323
Simon, Neil, 279, 309, 312
Singin' in the Rain (FI), 11, 180
Six of a Kind (UNI), 278, 281, 289
Skelton, Red, 26, 200, 280, 281
Sleeper (UA), 313, 314–15, 318
Sleuth, The (EMG), 136
Slipping Wives (EMG), 190
Smiles of a Summer Night (JAN), 23, 331–34
Smith, C. Aubrey, 218
So This Is Paris (EMG), 11, 211, 213, 214–15, 217, 218, 220
Soldier Man (CCM, EMG), 167, 178
Some Like It Hot (UA), 272, 273, 275–78, 342
Sons of the Desert (EMG), 190, 191
Sound comedy, theory of, 23, 24–25, 145–46, 199–205, 239n, 296–97
Sous les Toits de Paris (CON), 225, 226, 228, 230
Southern, Terry, 316, 318
Spaak, Charles, 199, 232
Speedy, 153
Spellbound (CCM), 5, 310
Spite Marriage, 128, 134, 135, 138, 139, 141n, 142, 171
Sprezzatura, 26–27, 50, 251, 253, 254, 256, 304

Spring Fever (EMG), 155
Stagecoach (MOG), 5, 14
Stalag 17 (FI), 272, 273, 275
Stanwyck, Barbara, 10, 260, 262, 263
Steamboat Bill, Jr. (CCM), 128, 134, 135, 142
Stenographer Wanted (MMA), 41
Sterling, Ford, 44, 48, 49, 50, 68
Stevens, George, 184, 191, 279
Stewart, James, 264
Stoppard, Tom, 309
Storm Over Asia (CCM, MMA), 207
Strauss, Oscar, 325, 328
Strauss, Johann, 240, 242
Streisand, Barbra, 255–56
Strike (CCM, MMA), 88, 110, 182
Strong Man, The (CCM), 7, 166, 167, 168, 171–73, 174, 177
Stunt Man, The (EMG), 194
Sturges, Preston, 8, 10, 16, 22, 145, 163, 249, 263, 265–71, 272, 278, 279, 291, 339
Suitor, The, 171
Sullivan's Travels (UNI), 8, 10, 16, 266, 267, 268, 269, 271
Summerville, Slim, 44, 51
Sunnyside, 77, 83, 87, 88, 89, 90–92, 94, 102, 103, 110, 111, 113, 117, 130, 195, 229, 316
Sunset Boulevard (FI), 273, 275
Super-Hooper-Dyne Lizzies (EMG), 9, 57
Surf Girl, The (MMA), 54, 57
Surface and depths, 88, 91, 94, 110, 116, 127, 137, 151–52, 218, 254, 255, 264, 265, 312, 323, 324–25, 327, 340–41
Swain, Mack, 51, 54, 55, 68, 71, 82, 100
Swanson, Gloria, 55, 195, 276n

Take the Money and Run (FI), 5, 200, 312, 313, 314, 316, 317, 318
Talmadge, Natalie, 135, 143
Tango Tangles (EMG), 49, 69, 107
Tars and Stripes, 195

Tashlin, Frank, 200
Tati, Jacques, 7, 25, 26, 114, 146, 201, 203, 204, 205, 293–303, 304, 305, 306, 313, 321, 339
Taurog, Norman, 195
Teddy at the Throttle (CCM, EMG, MMA), 5, 47, 54
Television, influence of, 280–81
Tempest, The, 68, 121–22
Terence, 3, 4
Thalberg, Irving, 144–45, 286n
39 Steps, The, 5, 12–15, 308
Thomas, Terry, 331
Three Ages, The (CCM), 5, 134, 135–36, 137, 141, 142, 307
Three Must-Get-Theres, The, 38, 39–40
Three Women, 216, 217
Threepenny Opera, The, 83, 84
Three's a Crowd (CCM), 9, 133, 175–76, 177
Tight Little Island (JAN), 329–31
Tillie and Gus (UNI), 289
Tillie's Punctured Romance (CCM, EMG), 54–56, 68, 310
To Be or Not To Be (WIL), 214, 224
Todd, Thelma, 283–84
Tomboy Bessie, 47
Toni (CON), 236–37
Totheroh, Rollie, 199
Tracy, Spencer, 203
Traffic (SWA), 294, 296–97, 299
Tramp, The (CCM, EMG, MMA), 73–75, 76, 77, 78, 80, 82, 95, 102, 110, 112, 113, 248, 299
Tramp, Tramp, Tramp (CCM), 7, 167, 168, 170–71
Travesties, 309
Triangle Film Corporation, 54
Trick films, 35
Trip to the Moon, A (CCM, EMG, MMA), 33, 34, 35
Troilus and Cressida, 5, 136
Trouble in Paradise (UNI), 5, 10, 11, 23, 211, 214, 218–19, 222, 224, 251, 325
Truffaut, François, 225n, 239n, 313n

Turpin, Ben, 24, 45, 51*n*, 56, 73, 76, 85, 101, 180, 184, 185, 282, 290, 307
Twelfth Night, 3, 4
Twentieth Century (CCM), 251–52, 253, 256, 257
Twentieth-century literary tradition, ix–x, 16, 21, 341
Twenty Minutes of Love (EMG), 70, 73
Two Tars (CCM, EMG, MMA), 191, 193

Ulysses, 309, 310
"Uncle Josh," 33–34
Unfaithfully Yours (WAL), 266–67, 268
United Artist's Corporation, 25, 38–47
Universal Pictures, 281, 311

Vagabond, The (CCM, EMG), 78, 80–81, 94, 107, 122
Valentino, Rudolph, 56, 185, 214, 216
Vallee, Rudy, 266
Vaudeville. *See* Music-hall tradition
Vernon, Bobby, 195
Versatile Villain, A (EMG), 188
Vigo, Jean, 320–22
Vitagraph Company, 40–41
Vivaldi, Antonio, 237–38, 244, 247
Volpone, 21, 339
Voltaire, 233, 240, 242
Von Stroheim, Erich, 8, 12, 56, 90, 185, 190, 208, 222, 233, 236, 307

Walbrook, Anton, 326
Waltz Me Around (EMG), 186
Wandering Willie, 57
Washday Troubles (MMA), 32–33, 43

Water Nymph, The (EMG), 48, 49, 50
Way Down East (CCM, EMG, MMA), 5, 46, 135
Welles, Orson, 117–18, 208, 336
Wellman, William, 253
West, Mae, 25, 200, 280, 292–93
What! No Beer? (FI), 144
What's Up, Doc? (SWA), 254–56, 259
Why Change Your Wife?, 97*n*, 210
Wild Duck, The, 16
Wild and Woolly (CCM, EMG, MMA), 180, 182–83
Wilde, Hagar, 253
Wilde, Oscar, 218, 309
Wilder, Billy, 8, 199, 272–78, 279, 339
Wilder, Gene, 311
Willis, Gordon, 317
Wizard of Oz, The (FI), 180, 292
Woman, A (CCM, EMG, MMA), 75, 167
Woman of Paris, A, 25, 66, 81, 96–100, 107, 108, 206, 210, 298, 334
Work (CCM, EMG), 18, 74–75
World War II, 259, 265, 269, 271
Wringing Good Joke, A (MMA), 32
Wrong Again (CCM, EMG), 185
Wynn, Keenan, 204, 335

Yokel, The, 187
You Can't Take It With You (CCM), 168, 260, 264
Young Frankenstein (FI), 310, 311–12, 319
You're Darn Tootin' (CCM, EMG), 184, 185, 191, 193

Zazie dans le metro (NYF), 8, 100
Zecca, Ferdinand, 43, 229
Zéro de Conduite (CCM), 320–22
Zukor, Adolph, 45